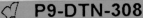

Practice*Planners*

Arthur E. Jongsma, Jr., Series Editor

Helping therapists help their clients

Treatment Planners cover all the necessary elements for developing formal treatment plans, including detailed problem definitions, long-term goals, short-term objectives, therapeutic interventions, and DSM™ diagnoses.

The **Complete Treatment and Homework Planners** series of books combines our bestselling *Treatment Planners* and *Homework Planners* into one easy-to-use, all-in-one resource for mental health professionals treating clients suffering from the most commonly diagnosed disorders.

Over 800,000 Practice*Planners*® sold

WILEY

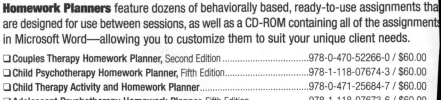

The Child Psychotherapy Treatment Planner,
Fifth Edition

Practice*Planners*® Series

Treatment Planners
The Complete Adult Psychotherapy Treatment Planner, Fifth Edition
The Child Psychotherapy Treatment Planner, Fifth Edition
The Adolescent Psychotherapy Treatment Planner, Fifth Edition
The Addiction Treatment Planner, Fifth Edition
The Continuum of Care Treatment Planner
The Couples Psychotherapy Treatment Planner, Second Edition
The Employee Assistance Treatment Planner
The Pastoral Counseling Treatment Planner
The Older Adult Psychotherapy Treatment Planner, Second Edition
The Behavioral Medicine Treatment Planner
The Group Therapy Treatment Planner
The Gay and Lesbian Psychotherapy Treatment Planner
The Family Therapy Treatment Planner, Second Edition
The Severe and Persistent Mental Illness Treatment Planner, Second Edition
The Mental Retardation and Developmental Disability Treatment Planner
The Social Work and Human Services Treatment Planner
The Crisis Counseling and Traumatic Events Treatment Planner, Second Edition
The Personality Disorders Treatment Planner
The Rehabilitation Psychology Treatment Planner
The Special Education Treatment Planner
The Juvenile Justice and Residential Care Treatment Planner
The School Counseling and School Social Work Treatment Planner, Second Edition
The Sexual Abuse Victim and Sexual Offender Treatment Planner
The Probation and Parole Treatment Planner
The Psychopharmacology Treatment Planner
The Speech-Language Pathology Treatment Planner
The Suicide and Homicide Treatment Planner
The College Student Counseling Treatment Planner
The Parenting Skills Treatment Planner
The Early Childhood Intervention Treatment Planner
The Co-Occurring Disorders Treatment Planner
The Complete Women's Psychotherapy Treatment Planner
The Veterans and Active Duty Military Psychotherapy Treatment Planner

Progress Notes Planners
The Child Psychotherapy Progress Notes Planner, Fifth Edition
The Adolescent Psychotherapy Progress Notes Planner, Fifth Edition
The Adult Psychotherapy Progress Notes Planner, Fifth Edition
The Addiction Progress Notes Planner, Fifth Edition
The Severe and Persistent Mental Illness Progress Notes Planner, Second Edition
The Couples Psychotherapy Progress Notes Planner, Second Edition
The Family Therapy Progress Notes Planner, Second Edition
The Veterans and Active Duty Military Psychotherapy Progress Notes Planner

Homework Planners
Couples Therapy Homework Planner, Second Edition
Family Therapy Homework Planner, Second Edition
Grief Counseling Homework Planner
Group Therapy Homework Planner
Divorce Counseling Homework Planner
School Counseling and School Social Work Homework Planner, Second Edition
Child Therapy Activity and Homework Planner
Addiction Treatment Homework Planner, Fifth Edition
Adolescent Psychotherapy Homework Planner, Fifth Edition
Adult Psychotherapy Homework Planner, Fifth Edition
Child Psychotherapy Homework Planner, Fifth Edition
Parenting Skills Homework Planner
Veterans and Active Duty Military Psychotherapy Homework Planner

Client Education Handout Planners
Adult Client Education Handout Planner
Child and Adolescent Client Education Handout Planner
Couples and Family Client Education Handout Planner

Complete Planners
The Complete Depression Treatment and Homework Planner
The Complete Anxiety Treatment and Homework Planner

PracticePlanners®

Arthur E. Jongsma, Jr., Series Editor

The Child Psychotherapy Treatment Planner, Fifth Edition

Arthur E. Jongsma, Jr.

L. Mark Peterson

William P. McInnis

Timothy J. Bruce

WILEY

Library of Congress Cataloging-in-Publication Data:

Jongsma, Arthur E., Jr., 1943–
  The adolescent psychotherapy treatment planner / Arthur E. Jongsma, Jr., L. Mark Peterson, William P. McInnis, Timothy J. Bruce.—Fifth edition.
      pages cm
  Includes bibliographical references and index.
  ISBN 978-1-118-06785-7 (pbk. : alk. paper)
  ISBN 978-1-118-41590-0 (ebk.)
  ISBN 978-1-118-41888-8 (ebk.)
  1. Child psychotherapy. 2. Adolescent psychotherapy. I. Peterson, L. Mark. II. McInnis, William P. III. Bruce, Timothy J. IV. Title.
  RJ504.J664 2014
  618.92'8914—dc23

                            2013030812

Printed in the United States of America
10 9 8 7 6 5 4

To my daughters and sons-in law, Kendra and Erwin van Elst and
Michelle and David DeGraaf, who give themselves creatively and
sacrificially to the task of parenting my grandchildren: Tyler, Kaleigh,
Justin, and Carter.
—A.E.J.

To Zach and Jim, who have expanded and enriched my life.
—L.M.P.

To my three children, Breanne, Kelsey, and Andrew,
for the love and joy they bring into my life.
—W.P.M.

To Lori, Logan, and Madeline, for everything.
—T.J.B.

CONTENTS

PRACTICE*PLANNERS*® SERIES PREFACE

Accountability is an important dimension of the practice of psychotherapy. Treatment programs, public agencies, clinics, and practitioners must justify and document their treatment plans to outside review entities in order to be reimbursed for services. The books in the Practice*Planners*® series are designed to help practitioners fulfill these documentation requirements efficiently and professionally.

The Practice*Planners*® series includes a wide array of treatment planning books including not only the original *Complete Adult Psychotherapy Treatment Planner*, *Child Psychotherapy Treatment Planner*, and *Adolescent Psychotherapy Treatment Planner*, all now in their fifth editions, but also *Treatment Planners* targeted to specialty areas of practice, including:

- Addictions
- Co-occurring disorders
- Behavioral medicine
- College students
- Couples therapy
- Crisis counseling
- Early childhood education
- Employee assistance
- Family therapy
- Gays and lesbians
- Group therapy
- Juvenile justice and residential care
- Mental retardation and developmental disability
- Neuropsychology
- Older adults
- Parenting skills
- Pastoral counseling
- Personality disorders
- Probation and parole
- Psychopharmacology
- Rehabilitation psychology
- School counseling and school social work
- Severe and persistent mental illness
- Sexual abuse victims and offenders

- Social work and human services
- Special education
- Speech-Language pathology
- Suicide and homicide risk assessment
- Veterans and active military duty
- Women's issues

In addition, there are three branches of companion books that can be used in conjunction with the *Treatment Planners*, or on their own:

- *Progress Notes Planners* provide a menu of progress statements that elaborate on the client's symptom presentation and the provider's therapeutic intervention. Each *Progress Notes Planner* statement is directly integrated with the behavioral definitions and therapeutic interventions from its companion *Treatment Planner*.

- *Homework Planners* include homework assignments designed around each presenting problem (such as anxiety, depression, substance use, anger control problems, eating disorders, or panic disorders) that is the focus of a chapter in its corresponding *Treatment Planner*.

- *Client Education Handout Planners* provide brochures and handouts to help educate and inform clients on presenting problems and mental health issues, as well as life skills techniques. The handouts are included on CD-ROMs for easy printing from your computer and are ideal for use in waiting rooms, at presentations, as newsletters, or as information for clients struggling with mental illness issues. The topics covered by these handouts correspond to the presenting problems in the *Treatment Planners*.

The series also includes adjunctive books, such as *The Psychotherapy Documentation Primer* and *The Clinical Documentation Sourcebook*, which contain forms and resources to aid the clinician in mental health practice management.

The goal of our series is to provide practitioners with the resources they need in order to provide high-quality care in the era of accountability. To put it simply: We seek to help you spend more time on patients, and less time on paperwork.

ARTHUR E. JONGSMA, JR.
Grand Rapids, Michigan

ACKNOWLEDGMENTS

Since 2005, we have turned to research evidence to inform the treatment Objectives and Interventions in our latest editions of the *Psychotherapy Treatment Planner* books. While much of the content of our *Planners* was "best practice" and also from the mainstream of sound psychological procedure, we have benefited significantly from a thorough review that looked through the lens of evidence-based practice. The later editions of the *Planners* now stand as content not just based on "best practice" but based on reliable research results. Although several of my coauthors have contributed to this recertification of our content, Timothy J. Bruce has been the main guiding force behind this effort. I am very proud of the highly professional content provided by so many coauthors who are leaders in their respective subspecialties in the field of psychology such as addiction, family therapy, couples therapy, personality disorder treatment, group treatment, women's issues, military personnel treatment, older adult treatment, and many others. Added to this expertise over the past seven years has been the contribution of Dr. Tim Bruce who has used his depth of knowledge regarding evidence-supported treatment to shape and inform the content of the last two editions, *Adult, Adolescent, Child,* and *Addiction Psychotherapy Treatment Planners.* I welcome Tim aboard as an author for these books and consider it an honor to have him as a friend, colleague, and coauthor.

I must also add my acknowledgment of the supportive professionalism of the Wiley staff, especially that of my editor, Marquita Flemming. Wiley has been a trusted partner in this series for almost 20 years now and I am fortunate to be published by such a highly respected company. Thank you to all my friends at Wiley!

And then there is our manuscript manager, Sue Rhoda, who knows just what to do to make a document presentable, right up to the standards required by a publisher. Thank you, Sue.

Finally, I tip my hat to my coauthors, Mark Peterson and Bill McInnis, who launched this *Child Psychotherapy Treatment Planner* with their original content contributions many years ago and have supported all the efforts to keep it fresh and evidence-based.

AEJ

I am fortunate to have been invited some seven years ago by Dr. Art Jongsma to work with him on his well-known and highly regarded *Psychotherapy Treatment Planner* series and to now be welcomed as one of his coauthors on this *Planner* along with Mark Peterson and Bill McInnis. As readers know, Art's treatment planners are highly regarded as works of enormous value to practicing clinicians as well as terrific educational tools for "students" of our profession. That Art's brainchild would have this type of value to our field is no surprise when you work with him. He is the consummate psychologist, with enormous breadth and depth of experience, a profound intellect, and a Rogerian capacity for empathy and understanding—all of which he would modestly deny. When you work with Art, you not only get to know him, you get to know his family, colleagues, and friends. In doing so, you get to know his values. If you are like me, you have relationships that you prize because they are with people whom you know to be, simply stated, good. Well, to use an expression I grew up with, "Art is good people." And it is my honor to have him as a friend, colleague, and coauthor. Thank you, Art!

I also would like to thank Marquita Flemming and the staff at Wiley for their immeasurable support, guidance, and professionalism. It is just my opinion, but I think Marquita should publish her own book on author relations.

I would also like to extend a big thank-you to our manuscript manager, Sue Rhoda, for her exacting work and (needed) patience. In fact, I am sure Sue will take it in stride when we ask to do one more edit of this acknowledgment section after it has been "finalized."

Lastly, I would like to thank my wife, Lori, and our children, Logan and Madeline, for all they do. They're good people, too.

TJB

The Child Psychotherapy Treatment Planner,
Fifth Edition

INTRODUCTION

ABOUT PRACTICE*PLANNERS*® TREATMENT PLANNERS

Pressure from third-party payors, accrediting agencies, and other outside parties has increased the need for clinicians to quickly produce effective, high-quality treatment plans. *Treatment Planners* provide all the elements necessary to quickly and easily develop formal treatment plans that satisfy the needs of most third-party payers and state and federal review agencies.

Each *Treatment Planner:*

- Saves you hours of time-consuming paperwork.
- Offers the freedom to develop customized treatment plans.
- Includes over 1,000 clear statements describing the behavioral manifestations of each relational problem, and includes long-term goals, short-term objectives, and clinically tested treatment options.
- Has an easy-to-use reference format that helps locate treatment plan components by behavioral problem.

As with the rest of the books in the Practice*Planners*® series, our aim is to clarify, simplify, and accelerate the treatment planning process so you spend less time on paperwork and more time with your clients.

ABOUT THIS FIFTH EDITION *CHILD PSYCHOTHERAPY TREATMENT PLANNER*

This fifth edition of the *Child Psychotherapy Treatment Planner* has been improved in many ways:

- Updated with new and revised evidence-based Objectives and Interventions
- Revised, expanded, and updated the Professional Reference Appendix B

- Many more suggested homework assignments from the companion book, *The Child Psychotherapy Homework Planner*, have been integrated into the Interventions
- Extensively expanded and updated self-help book list in the Bibliotherapy Appendix A
- New Recovery Model Appendix E listing Goals, Objectives, and Interventions allowing the integration of a recovery model orientation into treatment plans
- Addition of a chapter on Overweight/Obesity
- Renamed several chapters: Anger Management is now Anger Control Problems, Autism/Pervasive Developmental Disorder is now Autism Spectrum Disorder, Mental Retardation is now Intellectual Developmental Disorder, and Social Phobia/Shyness is now Social Anxiety
- Integrated *DSM-5*/ICD-10 diagnostic labels and codes into the Diagnostic Suggestions section of each chapter
- Added Appendix C with a listing of other professional references for cited books and articles not referenced in Appendix B
- Added Appendix F for listing an index of sources for assessment tests and interview forms cited in the chapter interventions

Evidence-based practice (EBP) is steadily becoming the standard of care in mental healthcare as it has in medical healthcare. Professional organizations such as the American Psychological Association, National Association of Social Workers, and the American Psychiatric Association, as well as consumer organizations such as the National Alliance for the Mentally Ill (NAMI), have endorsed the use of EBP. In some practice settings, EBP is becoming mandated. It is clear that the call for evidence and accountability is being increasingly sounded. So, what is EBP and how is its use facilitated by this *Planner*?

Borrowing from the Institute of Medicine's definition (Institute of Medicine, 2001), the American Psychological Association (APA) has defined EBP as "the integration of the best available research with clinical expertise in the context of patient characteristics, culture, and preferences" (APA Presidential Task Force on Evidence-Based Practice, 2006). Consistent with this definition, we have identified those psychological treatments with the best available supporting evidence, added Objectives and Interventions consistent with them in the pertinent chapters, and identified these with this symbol: ▽. As most practitioners know, research has shown that although these treatment methods have demonstrated efficacy (e.g., Nathan & Gorman, 2007), the individual psychologist (e.g., Wampold, 2001), the treatment relationship (e.g., Norcross, 2002), and the patient (e.g., Bohart & Tallman, 1999) are also vital contributors to the success of psychotherapy. As noted by the APA, "Comprehensive evidence-based practice will consider all of these determinants and their optimal combinations" (APA, 2006, p. 275). For more information and instruction on constructing evidence-based psychotherapy treatment plans, see our DVD-based training series entitled *Evidence-Based Psychotherapy Treatment Planning* (Jongsma & Bruce, 2010–2012).

The sources listed in the Professional Reference Appendix B and used to identify the evidence-based treatments integrated into this *Planner* are many. They include supportive studies from the psychotherapy outcome literature, current expert individual, group, and organizational reviews, as well as evidence-based practice guideline recommendations. Examples of specific sources used include the Cochrane Collaboration reviews, the work of the Society of Clinical Psychology (Division 12 of the American Psychological Association), and the Society of Clinical Child and Adolescent Psychology (Division 53 of the American Psychological Association) identifying research-supported psychological treatments, evidence-based treatment reviews such as those in Nathan and Gorman's *A Guide to Treatments That Work* (2007) and Weisz and Kazdin's *Evidence-Based Psychotherapies for Children and Adolescents* (2010), as well as evidence-based practice guidelines from professional organizations such as the American Psychiatric Association, the American Academy of Child & Adolescent Psychiatry, the National Institute for Health and Clinical Excellence in Great Britain, The National Institute on Drug Abuse (NIDA), the Substance Abuse and Mental Health Services Administration (SAMHSA), and the Agency for Healthcare Research and Quality (AHRQ), to name a few.

Although each of these sources uses its own criteria for judging levels of empirical support for any given treatment, we favored those that use more rigorous criteria typically requiring demonstration of efficacy through randomized controlled trials or clinical replication series, good experimental design, and independent replication. Our approach was to evaluate these various sources and include those treatments supported by the highest level of evidence and for which there was consensus in conclusions/ recommendations. For any chapter in which EBP is identified, references to the sources used are listed in the Professional References Appendix B, and can be consulted by those interested for further information regarding criteria and conclusions. In addition to these references, this appendix also includes references to Clinical Resources. Clinical Resources are books, manuals, and other resources for clinicians that describe the details of the application, or "how to" of the treatment approaches described in a chapter.

There is debate regarding evidence-based practice among mental health professionals who are not always in agreement regarding the best treatment or how to weigh the factors that contribute to good outcomes. Some practitioners are skeptical about changing their practice on the basis of research evidence, and their reluctance is fueled by the methodological challenges and problems inherent in psychotherapy research. Our intent in this book is to accommodate these differences by providing a range of treatment plan options, some supported by the evidence-based value of "best available research," others reflecting common clinical practices of experienced clinicians, and still others representing emerging approaches so the user can construct what they believe to be the best plan for their particular client.

Each of the chapters in this edition has also been reviewed with the goal of integrating homework exercise options into the Interventions. Many (but not all) of the client homework exercise suggestions were taken from and can be found in the *Child Psychotherapy Homework Planner* (Jongsma, Peterson, & McInnis, 2014). You will find many more homework assignments suggested for your consideration as part of the Intervention process in this fifth edition of the *Child Psychotherapy Treatment Planner* than in previous editions.

The Bibliotherapy Suggestions Appendix A of this *Planner* has been significantly expanded and updated from previous editions. It includes many recently published offerings as well as more recent editions of books cited in our earlier editions. All of the self-help books and client workbooks cited in the chapter Interventions are listed in this Appendix. There are also many additional books listed that are supportive of the treatment approaches described in the respective chapters. Each chapter has a list of self-help books consistent with it listed in this Appendix.

Appendix C lists additional clinical resources for professionals that are not listed in the evidence-based resources of Appendix B and are cited in the chapters listed in Appendix C. Therapeutic games, workbooks, toolkits, DVDs, and audiotapes that are cited in chapters are referenced in Appendix D. A new Appendix F provides an alphabetical index of sources for assessment instruments and clinical interview forms cited in interventions. We hope that this index makes it easier for readers to find these resources if they are added to the treatment plan.

In its final report entitled *Achieving the Promise: Transforming Mental Health Care in America,* The President's New Freedom Commission on Mental Health called for recovery to be the "common, recognized outcome of mental health services" (New Freedom Commission on Mental Health, 2003). To define recovery, the Substance Abuse and Mental Health Services Administration (SAMHSA) within the U.S. Department of Health and Human Services and the Interagency Committee on Disability Research in partnership with six other Federal agencies convened the National Consensus Conference on Mental Health Recovery and Mental Health Systems Transformation (SAMHSA, 2004). Over 110 expert panelists participated including mental health consumers, family members, providers, advocates, researchers, academicians, managed care representatives, accreditation bodies, state and local public officials, and others. From these deliberations, the following consensus statement was derived:

"Mental health recovery is a journey of healing and transformation for a person with a mental health problem to be able to live a meaningful life in a community of his or her choice while striving to achieve maximum human potential. Recovery is a multifaceted concept based on the following 10 fundamental elements and guiding principles:

1. Self-direction
2. Individualized and person-centered
3. Empowerment
4. Holistic
5. Nonlinear
6. Strengths-based
7. Peer support
8. Respect
9. Responsibility
10. Hope

These principles are defined in Appendix E. We have also created a set of Goal, Objective, and Intervention statements that reflect these 10 principles. The clinician who desires to insert into the client treatment plan specific statements reflecting a Recovery Model orientation may choose from this list.

In addition to this list, we believe that many of the Goal, Objective, and Intervention statements found in the chapters reflect a recovery orientation. For example, our assessment interventions are meant to identify how the problem affects this unique client and the strengths that the client brings to the treatment. Additionally, an intervention statement such as, "Develop with the client a list of positive affirmations about himself/herself, and ask that it be read three times daily" from the Low Self-Esteem chapter is evidence that recovery model content permeates items listed throughout our chapters. However, if the clinician desires a more focused set of statements directly related to each principle guiding the recovery model, they can be found in Appendix E.

The topic of our children (and adults, too) becoming seriously overweight or obese is getting increasing media and professional attention in recent years. Because obesity predisposes individuals to an increased risk of several diseases and medical conditions, it is included in the International Classification of Diseases (or ICD) as a general medical condition. It does not appear in the *DSM* because it is not consistently associated with a psychological or behavioral syndrome. It is, however, a highly prevalent medical issue, influenced by psychological and behavioral factors, and has proven to be responsive to psychological treatment. Therefore, we have added a chapter on Overweight/Obesity to provide evidence-based guidance in developing a treatment plan for this problem. We hope you find this addition helpful.

We have made a title change for the chapter previously entitled Mental Retardation. Even though the term "mental retardation" was selected about 50 years ago to replace what was seen as overly general terminology (e.g., mental deficiency) or pejorative labels (e.g., idiocy), in recent years the term mental retardation has been seen similarly. Instead, we replaced the title Mental Retardation with the title Intellectual Developmental Disorder to improve specificity and bring our title in line with the latest classification system terminology.

With the publication of the *DSM-5* (American Psychiatric Association, 2013) we have updated the Diagnostic Suggestions listed at the end of each chapter. The *DSM-IV-TR* (American Psychiatric Association, 2000) was used in previous editions of this *Planner*. Although many of the diagnostic labels and codes remain the same, several have changed with the publication of the *DSM-5* and are reflected in this *Planner*.

Lastly, some clinicians have asked that the Objective statements in this *Planner* be written such that the client's attainment of the Objective can be measured. We have written our Objectives in behavioral terms and many are measurable as written. For example, this Objective from the Anxiety chapter is one that is measurable as written because either it is done or it is not: "Participate in live, or imaginal then live, exposure exercises in which worries and fears are gradually faced." But at times the statements are too broad to be considered measurable. Consider, for example, this Objective from the Anxiety chapter: "Identify, challenge, and replace biased, fearful self-talk with positive, realistic, and empowering self-talk." To make it quantifiable a clinician might modify it to read, "Give two examples of identifying, challenging, and replacing biased, fearful self-talk with positive, realistic, and empowering self-talk." Clearly, the use of two examples is arbitrary, but it does allow for a quantifiable measurement of the attainment of the Objective. Or consider this example prescribing an increase in potentially rewarding activities: "Identify and engage in pleasant activities on a daily basis." To make it more measurable, the clinician might simply add a desired target number of pleasant activities; thus: "Identify and report engagement in two pleasant activities on a daily basis." The exact target number that the client is to attain is subjective and should be selected by the individual clinician in consultation with the client. Once the exact target number is determined, then our content can be very easily modified to fit the specific treatment situation. For more information on psychotherapy treatment plan writing, see Jongsma (2005).

We hope you find these improvements to this fifth edition of the *Child Psychotherapy Treatment Planner* useful to your treatment planning needs.

HOW TO USE THIS TREATMENT PLANNER

Use this *Treatment Planner* to write treatment plans according to the following progression of six steps:

1. **Problem Selection.** Although the client may discuss a variety of issues during the assessment, the clinician must determine the most significant

problems on which to focus the treatment process. Usually a primary problem will surface, and secondary problems may also be evident. Some other problems may have to be set aside as not urgent enough to require treatment at this time. An effective treatment plan can deal with only a few selected problems or treatment will lose its direction. Choose the problem within this *Planner* that most accurately represents your client's presenting issues.

2. **Problem Definition.** Each client presents with unique nuances as to how a problem behaviorally reveals itself in his or her life. Therefore, each problem that is selected for treatment focus requires a specific definition about how it is evidenced in the particular client. The symptom pattern should be associated with diagnostic criteria and codes such as those found in the *DSM-5* or the International Classification of Diseases. This *Planner* offers such behaviorally specific definition statements to choose from or to serve as a model for your own personally crafted statements.

3. **Goal Development.** The next step in developing your treatment plan is to set broad goals for the resolution of the target problem. These statements need not be crafted in measurable terms but can be global, long-term goals that indicate a desired positive outcome to the treatment procedures. This *Planner* provides several possible goal statements for each problem, but one statement is all that is required in a treatment plan.

4. **Objective Construction.** In contrast to long-term goals, objectives must be stated in behaviorally measurable language so that it is clear to review agencies, health maintenance organizations, and managed care organizations when the client has achieved the established objectives. The objectives presented in this *Planner* are designed to meet this demand for accountability. Numerous alternatives are presented to allow construction of a variety of treatment plan possibilities for the same presenting problem.

5. **Intervention Creation.** Interventions are the actions of the clinician designed to help the client complete the objectives. There should be at least one intervention for every objective. If the client does not accomplish the objective after the initial intervention, new interventions should be added to the plan. Interventions should be selected on the basis of the client's needs and the treatment provider's full therapeutic repertoire. This *Planner* contains interventions from a broad range of therapeutic approaches, and we encourage the provider to write other interventions reflecting his or her own training and experience.

   Some suggested interventions listed in the *Planner* refer to specific books that can be assigned to the client for adjunctive bibliotherapy. Appendix A contains a full bibliographic reference list of these materials. For further information about self-help books, mental health professionals may wish to consult the *Authoritative Guide to Self-Help Resources in Mental Health, Revised Edition* (Norcross et al., 2003).

6. **Diagnosis Determination.** The determination of an appropriate diagnosis is based on an evaluation of the client's complete clinical presentation. The clinician must compare the behavioral, cognitive, emotional, and interpersonal symptoms that the client presents with the criteria for diagnosis of a mental illness condition as described in *DSM-5*. Despite arguments made against diagnosing clients in this manner, diagnosis is a reality that exists in the world of mental health care, and it is a necessity for third-party reimbursement. It is the clinician's thorough knowledge of *DSM-5* criteria and a complete understanding of the client assessment data that contribute to the most reliable, valid diagnosis.

Congratulations! After completing these six steps, you should have a comprehensive and individualized treatment plan ready for immediate implementation and presentation to the client. A sample treatment plan for Anxiety is provided at the end of this introduction.

A FINAL NOTE ON TAILORING THE TREATMENT PLAN TO THE CLIENT

One important aspect of effective treatment planning is that each plan should be tailored to the individual client's problems and needs. Treatment plans should not be mass produced, even if clients have similar problems. The individual's strengths and weaknesses, unique stressors, social network, family circumstances, and symptom patterns must be considered in developing a treatment strategy. Drawing upon our own years of clinical experience and the best available research, we have put together a variety of treatment choices. These statements can be combined in thousands of permutations to develop detailed treatment plans. Relying on their own good judgment, clinicians can easily select the statements that are appropriate for the individuals whom they are treating. In addition, we encourage readers to add their own definitions, goals, objectives, and interventions to the existing samples. As with all of the books in the *Treatment Planners* series, it is our hope that this book will help promote effective, creative treatment planning—a process that will ultimately benefit the client, clinician, and mental health community.

REFERENCES

American Psychiatric Association. (2000). *Diagnostic and statistical manual of mental disorders* (4th ed., text rev.). Washington, DC: Author.
American Psychiatric Association. (2013). *Diagnostic and statistical manual of mental disorders* (5th ed.). Arlington, VA: American Psychiatric Publishing.

American Psychological Association Presidential Task Force on Evidence-Based Practice. (2006). Evidence-based practice in psychology. *American Psychologist, 61*(4), 271–285.

Bohart, A., & Tallman, K. (1999). *How clients make therapy work: The process of active self-healing.* Washington, DC: American Psychological Association.

Institute of Medicine. (2001). *Crossing the quality chasm: A new health system for the 21st century.* Washington, DC: National Academies Press. Available at http://www.iom.edu/Reports.aspx?sort=alpha&page=15

Jongsma, A. E. (2005). Psychotherapy treatment plan writing. In G. P. Koocher, J. C. Norcross, and S. S. Hill (Eds.), *Psychologists' desk reference* (2nd ed., pp. 232–236). New York, NY: Oxford University Press.

Jongsma, A. E., & Bruce, T. J. (2010–2012). *Evidence-based psychotherapy treatment planning* [DVD-based series]. Hoboken, NJ: Wiley. Available at www.Wiley.com/go/ebtdvds

Jongsma, A. E., Peterson, L. M., & McInnis, W. P. (2014). *Child psychotherapy homework planner.* Hoboken, NJ: Wiley.

Nathan, P. E., & Gorman, J. M. (Eds.). (2007). *A guide to treatments that work* (3rd ed.). New York, NY: Oxford University Press.

New Freedom Commission on Mental Health. (2003). *Achieving the promise: Transforming mental health care in America* (Final report. DHHS Publication No. SMA-03-3832). Rockville, MD: Author. Available at http://www.mentalhealthcommission.gov

Norcross, J. C. (Ed.). (2002). *Psychotherapy relationships that work: Therapist contributions and responsiveness to patient needs.* New York, NY: Oxford University Press.

Norcross, J. C., Santrock, J. W., Campbell, L. F., Smith, T. P., Sommer, R., & Zuckerman, E. L. (2003). *Authoritative guide to self-help resources in mental health, revised edition.* New York, NY: Guilford Press.

Substance Abuse and Mental Health Services Administration's (SAMHSA) National Mental Health Information Center: Center for Mental Health Services (2004). *National consensus statement on mental health recovery.* Washington, DC: Author. Available at http://mentalhealth.samhsa.gov/publications/allpubs/sma05-4129/

Wampold, B. E. (2001). *The great psychotherapy debate: Models, methods, and findings.* Mahwah, NJ: Erlbaum.

Weisz, J., & Kazdin, K. (Eds.). (2010). *Evidence-based psychotherapies for children and adolescents.* New York, NY: Guilford Press.

SAMPLE TREATMENT PLAN

ANXIETY

BEHAVIORAL DEFINITIONS

Excessive anxiety, worry, or fear that markedly exceeds the normal level for
the client's stage of development.
High level of motor tension, such as restlessness, tiredness, shakiness, or muscle
tension.
Autonomic hyperactivity (e.g., rapid heartbeat, shortness of breath, dizziness,
dry mouth, nausea, diarrhea).

GOAL

Reduce overall frequency, intensity, and duration of the anxiety so that daily
functioning is not impaired.

SHORT-TERM OBJECTIVES

1. Describe current and past
experiences with specific fears,
prominent worries, and anxiety
symptoms including their impact
on functioning and attempts to
resolve it. (1, 2)

THERAPEUTIC INTERVENTIONS

1. Actively build the level of trust
with the client or client and
parents through consistent eye
contact, active listening,
unconditional positive regard,
and warm acceptance to help
increase his/her ability to identify
and express concerns.

2. Assess the focus, excessiveness,
and uncontrollability of the
client's fears and worries and the
type, frequency, intensity, and
duration of his/her anxiety
symptoms (see *The Anxiety
Disorders Interview Schedule for
Children—Parent Version* or
Child Version; assign "Finding
and Losing Your Anxiety" in the
Child Psychotherapy Homework

2. Verbalize an understanding of how thoughts, physical feelings, and behavioral actions contribute to anxiety and its treatment.

Planner by Jongsma, Peterson, and McInnis).

1. As part of an individual cognitive behavioral approach, educate the client about the interrelated physiological, cognitive, emotional, and behavioral components of anxiety, including how fears and worries typically involve excessive concern about unrealistic threats, various bodily expressions of tension, overarousal, and hypervigilance, and avoidance of what is threatening, which interact to maintain problematic anxiety (e.g., see the *Coping C.A.T. Series* at workbookpublishing.com; *Helping Your Anxious Child* by Rapee et al.).

2. Assign the client and/or parents to read psychoeducational sections of books or treatment manuals to emphasize key therapy concepts (e.g., *The Coping C.A.T. Workbook* by Kendall and Hedtke (for ages 7–13); *Helping Your Anxious Child* by Rapee et al.).

3. Learn and implement calming skills to reduce overall anxiety and manage anxiety symptoms.

1. Teach the client calming skills (e.g., progressive muscle relaxation, guided imagery, slow diaphragmatic breathing) and how to discriminate better between relaxation and tension; teach the client how to apply these skills to his/her daily life.

2. Assign the client homework each session in which he/she practices calming daily (or assign "Deep Breathing Exercise" in the *Child Psychotherapy Homework Planner* by Jongsma, Peterson, and McInnis); review and

reinforce success while providing corrective feedback toward improvement.

4. Identify, challenge, and replace fearful self-talk with positive, realistic, and empowering self-talk.

1. Explore the client's schema and self-talk that mediate his/her fear response; challenge the biases; assist him/her in replacing the distorted messages with reality-based alternatives and positive self-talk that will increase his/her self-confidence in coping with irrational fears or worries. ▽

2. Assign the client a homework exercise in which he/she identifies fearful self-talk and creates reality-based alternatives (or assign "Tools for Anxiety" in the *Adolescent Psychotherapy Homework Planner* by Jongsma, Peterson, and McInnis); review and reinforce success, providing corrective feedback toward improvement.

3. Assign parents to read and discuss with the client cognitive restructuring of fears or worries in relevant books or treatment manuals (e.g., *Coping C.A.T. Series* at workbookpublishing .com; *Helping Your Anxious Child* by Rapee et al.).

5. Learn and implement a stimulus control strategy to limit the association between various environmental settings and worry, delaying the worry until a designated "worry time."

1. Explain how using "worry time" limits the association between worrying and environmental stimuli; agree upon setting a worry time and place with the client and implement.

2. Teach the client to recognize and postpone worry to the agreed-upon worry time and place using skills such as thought-stopping, relaxation, and redirecting attention (or

assign "Worry Time" in the *Child Psychotherapy Homework Planner* by Jongsma, Peterson, and McInnis to assist skill development); encourage use in daily life, reviewing and reinforcing success while providing corrective feedback toward improvement.

DIAGNOSIS

Axis I: 300.02   (F41.1)   Generalized Anxiety Disorder

ACADEMIC UNDERACHIEVEMENT

BEHAVIORAL DEFINITIONS

1. History of overall academic performance that is below the expected level according to measured intelligence or performance on standardized achievement tests.
2. Repeated failure to complete school or homework assignments and/or current assignments on time.
3. Poor organizational or study skills that contribute to academic underachievement.
4. Frequent tendency to procrastinate or postpone doing school or homework assignments in favor of playing or engaging in recreational and leisure activities.
5. Family history of members having academic problems, failures, or disinterest.
6. Feelings of depression, insecurity, and low self-esteem that interfere with learning and academic progress.
7. Recurrent pattern of engaging in acting out, disruptive, and negative attention-seeking behaviors when encountering difficulty or frustration in learning.
8. Heightened anxiety that interferes with performance during tests or examinations.
9. Excessive or unrealistic pressure placed by parents to the degree that it negatively affects academic performance.
10. Decline in academic performance that occurs in response to environmental factors or stress (e.g., parents' divorce, death of a loved one, relocation move).

—. _____
   _____
—. _____
   _____

—. _____

_____

LONG-TERM GOALS

1. Demonstrate consistent interest, initiative, and motivation in academics, and bring performance up to the expected level of intellectual or academic functioning.
2. Complete school and homework assignments on a regular and consistent basis.
3. Achieve and maintain a healthy balance between accomplishing academic goals and meeting social, emotional, and self-esteem needs.
4. Eliminate the pattern of engaging in acting out, disruptive, or negative attention-seeking behaviors when confronted with difficulty or frustration in learning.
5. Significantly reduce the level of anxiety related to taking tests.
6. Parents establish realistic expectations of the client's learning abilities and implement effective intervention strategies at home to help the client keep up with schoolwork and achieve academic goals.
7. Resolve family conflicts and environmental stressors to allow for improved academic performance.

—. _____

_____

—. _____

_____

—. _____

_____

SHORT-TERM OBJECTIVES

1. Complete a psychoeducational evaluation. (1)

THERAPEUTIC INTERVENTIONS

1. Arrange for psychoeducational testing to evaluate the presence of a learning disability, and determine whether the client is eligible to receive special education services; provide feedback to the client, his/her family, and school officials regarding the psychoeducational evaluation.

2. Complete psychological testing. (2)

2. Arrange for psychological testing to assess whether possible Attention-Deficit/Hyperactivity Disorder (ADHD) or emotional factors are interfering with the client's academic performance; provide feedback to the client, his/her family, and school officials regarding the psychological evaluation.

3. The client and parents provide psychosocial history information. (3)

3. Gather psychosocial history information from the client and parents that includes key developmental milestones and a family history of educational achievements and failures.

4. Provide behavioral, emotional, and attitudinal information toward an assessment of specifiers relevant to a *DSM* diagnosis, the efficacy of treatment, and the nature of the therapy relationship. (4, 5, 6, 7, 8)

4. Assess the client's level of insight (syntonic versus dystonic) toward the "presenting problems" (e.g., demonstrates good insight into the problematic nature of the "described behavior," agrees with others' concern, and is motivated to work on change; demonstrates ambivalence regarding the "problem described" and is reluctant to address the issue as a concern; or demonstrates resistance regarding acknowledgment of the "problem described," is not concerned, and has no motivation to change).

5. Assess the client for evidence of research-based correlated disorders (e.g., oppositional defiant behavior with ADHD, depression secondary to an anxiety disorder) including vulnerability to suicide, if appropriate (e.g., increased suicide risk when comorbid depression is evident).

6. Assess for any issues of age, gender, or culture that could help explain the client's currently defined "problem behavior" and factors that could offer a better understanding of the client's behavior.

7. Assess for the severity of the level of impairment to the client's functioning to determine appropriate level of care (e.g., the behavior noted creates mild, moderate, severe, or very severe impairment in social, relational, vocational, or occupational endeavors); continuously assess this severity of impairment as well as the efficacy of treatment (e.g., the client no longer demonstrates severe impairment but the presenting problem now is causing mild or moderate impairment).

8. Assess the client's home, school, and community for pathogenic care (e.g., persistent disregard for the child's emotional needs or physical needs, repeated changes in primary caregivers, limited opportunities for stable attachments, persistent harsh punishment or other grossly inept parenting).

5. Cooperate with a hearing, vision, or medical examination. (9)

9. Refer the client for a hearing, vision, or medical examination to rule out possible hearing, visual, or health problems that are interfering with school performance.

6. Comply with the recommendations made by the multi-disciplinary evaluation team at school regarding educational interventions. (10, 11)

10. Attend an Individualized Educational Planning Committee (IEPC) meeting with the parents, teachers, and school officials to determine the client's

7. Parents and teachers implement educational strategies that maximize the client's learning strengths and compensate for learning weaknesses. (12)

8. Participate in outside tutoring to increase knowledge and skills in the area of academic weakness. (13, 14)

9. Implement effective study skills to increase the frequency of completion of school assignments and improve academic performance. (15, 16)

eligibility for special education services, design education interventions, and establish educational goals.

11. Based on the IEPC goals and recommendations, arrange for the client to be moved to an appropriate classroom setting to maximize his/her learning.

12. Consult with the client, parents, and school officials about designing effective learning programs for intervention strategies that build on his/her strengths and compensate for weaknesses.

13. Recommend that the parents seek outside tutoring after school to boost the client's skills in the area of his/her academic weakness (e.g., reading, mathematics, written expression).

14. Refer the client to a private learning center for extra tutoring in the areas of academic weakness and assistance in improving study and test-taking skills.

15. Teach the client more effective study skills (e.g., remove distractions, study in quiet places, develop outlines, highlight important details, schedule breaks).

16. Consult with the teachers and parents about using a study buddy or peer tutor to assist the client in the area of academic weakness and improve study skills.

10. Implement effective test-taking strategies to decrease anxiety and improve test performance. (17, 18)

17. Teach the client more effective test-taking strategies (e.g., study over an extended period of time, review material regularly, read directions twice, recheck work).

18. Train the client in relaxation techniques or guided imagery to reduce his/her anxiety before or during the taking of tests.

11. Parents maintain regular (i.e., daily to weekly) communication with the teachers. (19)

19. Encourage the parents to maintain regular (i.e., daily or weekly) communication with the teachers to help the client remain organized and keep up with school assignments.

12. Use self-monitoring checklists, planners, or calendars to remain organized and help complete school assignments. (20, 21, 22)

20. Encourage the client to use self-monitoring checklists to increase completion of school assignments and improve academic performance (suggest *How to Do Homework Without Throwing Up* by Romain).

21. Direct the client to use planners or calendars to record school or homework assignments and plan ahead for long-term projects.

22. Monitor the client's completion of school and homework assignments on a regular, consistent basis (or use the "Establish a Homework Routine" program in the *Child Psychotherapy Homework Planner* by Jongsma, Peterson, and McInnis).

13. Establish a regular routine that allows time to engage in play, to spend quality time with the family, and to complete homework assignments. (23)

23. Assist the client and his/her parents in developing a routine daily schedule at home that allows the client to achieve a healthy balance of completing school/homework assignments, engaging in independent play,

and spending quality time with family and peers.

14. Parents and teachers increase the frequency of praise and positive reinforcement of the client's school performance. (24, 25)

24. Encourage the parents and teachers to give frequent praise and positive reinforcement for the client's effort and accomplishment on academic tasks (recommend *How to Help Your Child with Homework* by Schumm).

25. Identify a variety of positive reinforcers or rewards to maintain the client's interest and motivation to complete school assignments.

15. Identify and resolve all emotional blocks or learning inhibitions that are within the client and/or the family system. (26, 27)

26. Teach the client positive coping mechanisms (e.g., relaxation techniques, positive self-talk, cognitive restructuring) to use when encountering anxiety, frustration, or difficulty with schoolwork.

27. Conduct family sessions that probe the client's family system to identify any emotional blocks or inhibitions to learning; assist the family in resolving identified family conflicts.

16. Parents increase the time spent being involved with the client's homework. (28, 29)

28. Encourage the parents to demonstrate and/or maintain regular interest and involvement in the client's homework (e.g., parents reading aloud to or alongside the client, using flashcards to improve math skills, rechecking spelling words).

29. Assist the parents and teachers in the development of systematic rewards for progress and accomplishment (e.g., charts with stars for goal attainment, praise for each success, some material reward for achievement).

17. Parents decrease the frequency and intensity of arguments with the client over issues related to school performance and homework. (30, 31)

30. Conduct family therapy sessions to assess whether the parents have developed unrealistic expectations or are placing excessive pressure on the client to perform; confront and challenge the parents about placing excessive pressure on the client.

31. Encourage the parents to set firm, consistent limits and use natural, logical consequences for the client's noncompliance or refusal to do homework; instruct the parents to avoid unhealthy power struggles or lengthy arguments over homework each night.

18. Parents verbally recognize that their pattern of over-protectiveness interferes with the client's academic growth and responsibility. (32)

32. Observe parent–child interactions to assess whether the parents' overprotectiveness or infantilization of the client contributes to his/her academic underachievement; assist the parents in developing realistic expectations of his/her learning potential.

19. Increase the frequency of on-task behavior at school, increasing the completion of school assignments without expressing frustration and the desire to give up. (33, 34)

33. Consult with school officials about ways to improve the client's on-task behaviors (e.g., keep him/her close to the teacher; keep him/her close to positive peer role models; call on him/her often; provide frequent feedback to him/her; structure the material into a series of small steps).

34. Assign the client to read material designed to improve his/her organization and study skills (e.g., *13 Steps to Better Grades* by Silverman); process the information gained from the reading.

20. Increase the frequency of positive statements about school experiences and confidence in the ability to succeed academically. (35, 36, 37)

21. Decrease the frequency and severity of acting out behaviors when encountering frustrations with school assignments. (38, 39, 40, 41)

35. Reinforce the client's successful school experiences and positive statements about school.

36. Confront the client's self-disparaging remarks and expressed desire to give up on school assignments.

37. Assign the client the task of making one positive self-statement daily about school and his/her ability and have him/her record it in a journal (or assign "Positive Self-Statements" in the *Child Psychotherapy Homework Planner* by Jongsma, Peterson, and McInnis).

38. Help the client to identify which rewards would increase his/her motivation to improve academic performance; implement these suggestions into the academic program.

39. Conduct individual play therapy sessions to help the client work through and resolve painful emotions, core conflicts, or stressors that impede academic performance.

40. Help the client to realize the connection between negative or painful emotions and decrease in academic performance.

41. Teach the client positive coping and self-control strategies (e.g., cognitive restructuring; positive self-talk; "stop, look, listen, and think") to inhibit the impulse to act out or engage in negative attention-seeking behaviors when encountering frustrations with schoolwork.

22. Identify and verbalize how specific, responsible actions lead to improvements in academic performance. (42, 43)

23. Develop a list of resource people within the school setting to whom the client can turn for support, assistance, or instruction for learning problems. (44)

24. Increase the time spent doing independent reading. (45)

25. Express feelings about school through artwork and mutual storytelling. (46, 47, 48)

42. Explore periods of time when the client completed schoolwork regularly and/or achieved academic success; identify and encourage him/her to use similar strategies to improve his/her current academic performance.

43. Examine coping strategies that the client has used to solve other problems; encourage him/her to use similar coping strategies to overcome problems associated with learning.

44. Identify a list of individuals within the school to whom the client can turn for support, assistance, or instruction when he/she encounters difficulty or frustration with learning.

45. Encourage the parents to use a reward system to reinforce the client for engaging in independent reading (or use the "Reading Adventure" program in the *Child Psychotherapy Homework Planner* by Jongsma, Peterson, and McInnis).

46. Use mutual storytelling techniques whereby the therapist and client alternate telling stories through the use of puppets, dolls, or stuffed animals. The therapist first models appropriate ways to manage frustration related to learning problems; then the client follows by creating a story with similar characters or themes.

47. Have the client create a variety of drawings on a posterboard or large sheet of paper that reflect how his/her personal and family life would be different if he/she

completed homework regularly; process the content of these drawings.

48. Instruct the client to draw a picture of a school building; then have him/her create a story that tells what it is like to be a student at that school to assess possible stressors that may interfere with learning and academic progress.

___ · _____   ___ · _____
_____   _____
___ · _____   ___ · _____
_____   _____
___ · _____   ___ · _____
_____   _____

DIAGNOSTIC SUGGESTIONS

Using DSM-IV/ICD-9-CM:

Axis I:		
	315.00	Reading Disorder
	315.1	Mathematics Disorder
	315.2	Disorder of Written Expression
	V62.3	Academic Problem
	314.01	Attention-Deficit/Hyperactivity Disorder, Combined Type
	314.00	Attention-Deficit/Hyperactivity Disorder, Predominantly Inattentive Type
	300.4	Dysthymic Disorder
	313.81	Oppositional Defiant Disorder
	312.9	Disruptive Behavior Disorder NOS
	_____	_____
	_____	_____
Axis II:	317	Mild Mental Retardation
	V62.89	Borderline Intellectual Functioning
	V71.09	No Diagnosis
	_____	_____
	_____	_____

Using DSM-5/ICD-9-CM/ICD-10-CM:

ICD-9-CM	ICD-10-CM	*DSM*-5 Disorder, Condition, or Problem
315.00	F81.0	Specific Learning Disorder With Impairment in Reading
315.1	F81.2	Specific Learning Disorder With Impairment in Mathematics
315.2	F81.2	Specific Learning Disorder With Impairment in Written Expression
V62.3	Z55.9	Academic or Educational Problem
314.01	F90.2	Attention-Deficit/Hyperactivity Disorder, Combined Presentation
314.00	F90.0	Attention-Deficit/Hyperactivity Disorder, Predominantly Inattentive Presentation
314.01	F90.1	Attention-Deficit/Hyperactivity Disorder, Predominately Hyperactive /Impulsive Presentation
300.4	F34.1	Persistent Depressive Disorder
313.81	F91.3	Oppositional Defiant Disorder
312.9	F91.9	Unspecified Disruptive, Impulse Control, and Conduct Disorder
312.89	F91.8	Other Specified Disruptive, Impulse Control, and Conduct Disorder
317	F70	Intellectual Disability, Mild
V62.89	R41.83	Borderline Intellectual Functioning

Note: The ICD-9-CM codes are to be used for coding purposes in the United States through September 30, 2014. ICD-10-CM codes are to be used starting October 1, 2014. Some ICD-9-CM codes are associated with more than one ICD-10-CM and *DSM-5* disorder, condition, or problem. In addition, some ICD-9-CM disorders have been discontinued resulting in multiple ICD-9-CM codes being replaced by one ICD-10-CM code. Some discontinued ICD-9-CM codes are not listed in this table. See *Diagnostic and Statistical Manual of Mental Disorders* (2013) for details.

ADOPTION

BEHAVIORAL DEFINITIONS

1. Adopted into the present family since infancy.
2. Adopted into the present family after the age of 2.
3. Adopted as an older special-needs child or as a set of siblings into the family.
4. Relates to significant others in a withdrawn, rejecting way, avoiding eye contact and keeping self at a distance from them.
5. Exhibits a pattern of hoarding or gorging food.
6. Displays numerous aggressive behaviors that are out of proportion for the presenting situations and seems to reflect a need to vent pent-up frustration.
7. Lies and steals often when it is not necessary to do so.
8. Displays an indiscriminate pattern of showing open affection to casual friends and strangers.
9. Parents experience excessive, unnecessary frustration with the adopted child's development and level of achievement.
10. Parents are anxious and fearful of the adopted child's questioning of his/her background (e.g., "Where did I come from?" "Who do I look like?").

—. _____
_____

—. _____
_____

—. _____
_____

LONG-TERM GOALS

1. Termination of self-defeating, acting-out behaviors and acceptance of self as loved and lovable within an adopted family.
2. Resolution of the key adoption issues of loss, abandonment, and rejection.
3. The establishment and maintenance of healthy family connections.
4. Removal of all barriers to enable the establishment of a healthy bond between parents and child(ren).
5. Develop a nurturing relationship with parents.
6. Build and maintain a healthy adoptive family.

—. _____
   _____
—. _____
   _____
—. _____
   _____

SHORT-TERM OBJECTIVES

1. Family members and the client develop a trusting relationship with the therapist that will allow for open expression of thoughts and feelings. (1)

2. Cooperate with and complete all assessments and evaluations. (2, 3)

THERAPEUTIC INTERVENTIONS

1. Actively build the level of trust with the client and his/her family members by using consistent eye contact, active listening, unconditional positive regard, and empathic responses to help promote the open expressions of their thoughts and feelings about the adoption.

2. Conduct or refer the parents and child(ren) for a psychosocial assessment to evaluate the parents' strength of marriage, parenting style, stress management/coping strengths, resolution of infertility issues, and to assess the child's developmental level, attachment capacity, behavioral issues, temperament, and strengths.

3. Provide behavioral, emotional, and attitudinal information toward an assessment of specifiers relevant to a *DSM* diagnosis, the efficacy of treatment, and the nature of the therapy relationship. (4, 5, 6, 7, 8)

3. Conduct or arrange for a psychological evaluation to determine the client's level of behavioral functioning, cognitive style, and intelligence.

4. Assess the client's level of insight (syntonic versus dystonic) toward the "presenting problems" (e.g., demonstrates good insight into the problematic nature of the "described behavior," agrees with others' concern, and is motivated to work on change; demonstrates ambivalence regarding the "problem described" and is reluctant to address the issue as a concern; or demonstrates resistance regarding acknowledgment of the "problem described," is not concerned, and has no motivation to change).

5. Assess the client for evidence of research-based correlated disorders (e.g., oppositional defiant behavior with ADHD, depression secondary to an anxiety disorder) including vulnerability to suicide, if appropriate (e.g., increased suicide risk when comorbid depression is evident).

6. Assess for any issues of age, gender, or culture that could help explain the client's currently defined "problem behavior" and factors that could offer a better understanding of the client's behavior.

7. Assess for the severity of the level of impairment to the client's functioning to determine appropriate level of care

(e.g., the behavior noted creates mild, moderate, severe, or very severe impairment in social, relational, vocational, or occupational endeavors); continuously assess this severity of impairment as well as the efficacy of treatment (e.g., the client no longer demonstrates severe impairment but the presenting problem now is causing mild or moderate impairment).

8. Assess the client's home, school, and community for pathogenic care (e.g., persistent disregard for the child's emotional needs or physical needs, repeated changes in primary caregivers, limited opportunities for stable attachments, persistent harsh punishment or other grossly inept parenting).

4. Comply with all recommendations of the evaluations or assessments. (9)

9. Summarize assessment data and present the findings and recommendations to the family; encourage and monitor the family's follow-through on all the recommendations.

5. Parents acknowledge unresolved grief associated with their infertility. (10)

10. Assess the parents' unresolved grief around the issue of their infertility; refer them for further conjoint or individual treatment, if necessary.

6. Family members attend family therapy sessions and report on their perception of the adjustment process. (11)

11. Establish a wellness plan whereby the family goes at 3-month intervals for a checkup with the therapist to evaluate how the assimilation and attachment process is proceeding. If all is well, checkups can be annual after the first year.

7. Parents commit to improving communication and affection expression within the marriage relationship. (12)

12. Refer the parents to a skills-based marital program such as "PREP" (see *Fighting for Your Marriage* by Markman, Stanley, and Blumberg) to strengthen their marital relationship by improving responsibility acceptance, communication, and conflict resolution.

8. Attend and actively take part in play therapy sessions to reduce acting-out behaviors connected to unresolved rage, loss, and fear of abandonment. (13, 14, 15, 16)

13. Conduct filial therapy (i.e., parents' involvement in play therapy sessions), in which the client takes the lead in expressing anger and the parents respond empathically to the client's feelings (e.g., hurt, fear, sadness, helplessness) beneath the anger.

14. Employ psychoanalytic play therapy (e.g., explore and gain understanding of the etiology of unconscious conflicts, fixations, or arrests; interpret resistance, transference, or core anxieties) to help the client work through and resolve issues contributing to acting-out behaviors.

15. Conduct individual play therapy sessions to provide the opportunity for expression of feelings surrounding past loss, neglect, and/or abandonment.

16. Employ the ACT model (see *Play Therapy: The Art of the Relationship* by Landreth) in play therapy sessions to *acknowledge* feelings, *communicate* limits, and *target* acceptable alternatives to acting out or aggressive behaviors.

9. Verbalize the connection between anger and/or withdrawal and the underlying feelings of fear, abandonment, and rejection. (17)

10. Identify feelings that are held inside and rarely expressed. (18, 19, 20)

11. Identify and release feelings in socially acceptable, nondestructive ways. (21, 22, 23)

17. Assist the client in making connections between underlying painful emotions of loss, rejection, rage, abandonment, and acting-out and/or aggressive behaviors.

18. Use puppets, dolls, or stuffed toys to tell a story to the client about others who have experienced loss, rejection, or abandonment to show how they have resolved these issues; then ask the client to create a similar story using puppets, dolls, or stuffed toys.

19. Ask the client to draw an outline of himself/herself on a sheet of paper, and then instruct him/her to fill the inside with pictures and objects that reflect what he/she has on the inside that fuels the acting out behaviors.

20. Use expressive art materials (e.g., Play-Doh, clay, fingerpaint) to create pictures and sculptures that aid the client in expressing and resolving his/her feelings of rage, rejection, and loss.

21. Read with the client, or have the parents read to him/her, *A Volcano in My Tummy: Helping Children to Handle Anger: A Resource Book for Parents, Caregivers, and Teachers* by Whitehouse and Pudney or *Don't Rant and Rave on Wednesday!* by Moser to help him/her to recognize his/her anger and to present ways to handle angry feelings.

22. Play with the client, or have the parents play with him/her, The Talking, Feeling, Doing Game

by Gardner or The Anger Control Game by Berg to assist him/her in identifying and expressing feelings and thoughts.

23. Use a feelings chart, felts, or cards to increase the client's ability to identify, understand, and express thoughts and feelings about being adopted.

12. Express feelings directly related to being an adopted child. (24, 25)

24. Ask the child to share his/her thoughts about being adopted (or assign "Questions and Concerns about Being Adopted" in the *Child Psychotherapy Homework Planner* by Jongsma, Peterson, and McInnis).

25. Assign the client to read books on adoption to help him/her clarify issues and not feel alone (e.g., *How It Feels to Be Adopted* by Krementz or *Adoption Is for Always* by Girard); process the reading material in subsequent sessions.

13. Parents verbalize an increased ability to understand and handle acting-out behaviors. (26, 27, 28)

26. Affirm often with the parents the health of their family while they are working with the disturbed client to avoid triangulation and undermining of parental authority by him/her.

27. Refer the parents and/or the client to an adoption support group.

28. Work with the parents in conjoint sessions to frame the client's acting out behaviors as opportunities to reparent the client; then strategize with them to come up with specific ways to intervene in the problem behaviors.

14. Parents affirm the client's identity as based in self, bioparents, and adoptive family. (29, 30, 31)

29. Ask the parents to read material to increase their knowledge and understanding of adoption (e.g., *Helping Children Cope with Separation and Loss* by Jarrett; *Adoption Wisdom* by Russell; *The Whole Life Adoption Book* by Schooler and Atwood; *Making Sense of Adoption* by Medina; *Why Didn't She Keep Me?: Answers to the Question Every Adopted Child Asks* by Burlingham-Brown).

30. Refer the parents to reliable Internet sites that provide information and support to adoptive parents (e.g., adoption.com; adoption.about.com; olderchildadoptions.com; adoptionsites.com).

31. Educate the parents on the importance of affirming the client's entire identity (i.e., self, bioparents, adoptive parents), and show them specific ways to reaffirm him/her (e.g., verbally identify talents, such as art or music, that are similar to those of the biological parents; recognize positive tasks that the client does that are similar to those of the adoptive mom or dad).

15. Express and preserve own history and its contribution to identity. (32)

32. Assign the parents to help the client create a *life book* that chronicles his/her life to this point in order to give him/her a visual perspective and knowledge of his/her own history and identity (or assign the "Create a Memory Album" exercise in the *Child Psychotherapy Homework*

16. Verbalize needs and wishes. (33)

17. Verbalize a feeling of increased confidence and self-acceptance. (31, 32, 34)

Planner by Jongsma, Peterson, and McInnis).

33. Assist the client in clarifying and expressing his/her needs and desires (or assign the exercise "Three Wishes Game" or "Some Things I Would Like You to Know About Me" from the *Child Psychotherapy Homework Planner* by Jongsma, Peterson, and McInnis).

31. Educate the parents on the importance of affirming the client's entire identity (i.e., self, bioparents, adoptive parents), and show them specific ways to reaffirm him/her (e.g., verbally identify talents, such as art or music, that are similar to those of the biological parents; recognize positive tasks that the client does that are similar to those of the adoptive mom or dad).

32. Assign the parents to help the client create a *life book* that chronicles his/her life to this point in order to give him/her a visual perspective and knowledge of his/her own history and identity (or assign the "Create a Memory Album" exercise in the *Child Psychotherapy Homework Planner* by Jongsma, Peterson, and McInnis).

34. Assign a self-esteem building exercise to help the client develop self-knowledge, acceptance, and confidence (see *SEALS & Plus* by Korb-Khara, Azok, and Leutenberg).

18. Parents verbalize reasonable expectations for the client's behavior given his/her developmental stage and the process of adjustment to adoption. (35)

35. Process the parents' expectations for the client's behavior and adjustment; confront and modify unrealistic expectations and foster realistic expectations considering his/her developmental stage and adjustment to the adoption process.

19. Parent spends one-on-one time with the client in active play. (36, 37)

36. Use a *Theraplay* (Booth and Jernberg) attachment-based approach, in which the therapist takes charge by planning and structuring each session. The therapist uses his/her power to entice the client into the relationship and to keep the focus of therapy on the relationship, not on intrapsychic conflicts. Also, parents are actively involved and are trained to be co-therapists.

37. Assign each parent to spend time in daily one-on-one active play with the client.

20. Parents increase the frequency of expressing affection verbally and physically toward the client. (38)

38. Encourage the parents to provide large, genuine, daily doses of positive verbal reinforcement and physical affection; monitor and encourage them to continue this behavior and to reinforce positive attachment signs when they appear.

21. Parents speak only positively regarding the client's bioparents. (39)

39. Encourage the parents to refrain from negative references about the bioparents and to speak in positive terms about them; ask the parents to list some positive aspects of the bioparents.

22. Parents feel free to ask questions regarding the details of adoption adjustment. (40)

40. Conduct sessions with the parents to give them opportunities to raise adoption-specific issues of

concern to them (e.g., how to handle an open adoption, how much to share with the client about his/her bioparents) in order to give them direction and support.

23. Parents verbalize reasonable discipline and nurturance guidelines. (41, 42, 43)

41. Provide the parents with education about keeping discipline related to the offense reasonable and always respectful to reduce resentment and rebellion (recommend *The Kazdin Method for Parenting the Defiant Child* by Kazdin; *Parenting the Strong-Willed Child* by Forehand and Long).

42. Ask the parents to read *The Seven Habits of Highly Effective Families: Building a Beautiful Family Culture in a Turbulent World* by Covey for suggestions on how to increase their family's health and connections.

43. Have the parents spend individual, one-on-one time with the children who were part of the family prior to the adoption.

24. Family members express an acceptance of and trust in each other. (44, 45)

44. Refer the family to an initiatives weekend (e.g., high- and low-ropes course, tasks, and various group-oriented physical problem-solving activities) to increase trust, cooperation, and connections with each other.

45. In a family session, construct a genogram that includes all family members, showing how everyone is connected in order to demonstrate the client's origins and what he/she has become a part of.

— . ———————————————   — . ———————————————
———————————————   ———————————————
— . ———————————————   — . ———————————————
———————————————   ———————————————
— . ———————————————   — . ———————————————
———————————————   ———————————————

DIAGNOSTIC SUGGESTIONS

Using DSM-IV/ICD-9-CM:

Axis I:	309.0	Adjustment Disorder With Depressed Mood
	309.4	Adjustment Disorder With Mixed Disturbance of Emotions and Conduct
	300.4	Dysthymic Disorder
	314.01	Attention-Deficit/Hyperactivity Disorder, Combined Type
	309.81	Posttraumatic Stress Disorder
	313.89	Reactive Attachment Disorder of Infancy or Early Childhood
	———	———————————————————
	———	———————————————————
Axis II:	V71.09	No Diagnosis
	———	———————————————————
	———	———————————————————

Using DSM-5/ICD-9-CM/ICD-10-CM:

ICD-9-CM	ICD-10-CM	*DSM-5* Disorder, Condition, or Problem
309.0	F43.21	Adjustment Disorder, With Depressed Mood
309.4	F43.25	Adjustment Disorder, With Mixed Disturbance of Emotions and Conduct
300.4	F34.1	Persistent Depressive Disorder
314.01	F90.2	Attention-Deficit/Hyperactivity Disorder, Combined Presentation
309.81	F43.10	Posttraumatic Stress Disorder
313.89	F94.1	Reactive Attachment Disorder

Note: The ICD-9-CM codes are to be used for coding purposes in the United States through September 30, 2014. ICD-10-CM codes are to be used starting October 1, 2014. Some ICD-9-CM codes are associated with more than one ICD-10-CM and *DSM-5* disorder, condition, or problem. In addition, some ICD-9-CM disorders have been discontinued resulting in multiple ICD-9-CM codes being replaced by one ICD-10-CM code. Some discontinued ICD-9-CM codes are not listed in this table. See *Diagnostic and Statistical Manual of Mental Disorders* (2013) for details.

ANGER CONTROL PROBLEMS

BEHAVIORAL DEFINITIONS

1. Shows a pattern of episodic excessive anger in response to specific situations or situational themes.
2. Shows cognitive biases associated with anger (e.g., demanding expectations of others, overly generalized labeling of the targets of anger, anger in response to perceived "slights").
3. Describes experiencing direct or indirect evidence of physiological arousal related to anger.
4. Displays body language suggesting anger, including tense muscles (e.g., clenched fist or jaw), glaring looks, or refusal to make eye contact.
5. Demonstrates an angry overreaction to perceived disapproval, rejection, or criticism.
6. Rationalizes and blames others for aggressive and abusive behavior.
7. Repeated angry outbursts that are out of proportion to the precipitating event.
8. Excessive yelling, swearing, crying, or use of verbally abusive language when efforts to meet desires are frustrated or limits are placed on behavior.
9. Frequent fighting, intimidation of others, and acts of cruelty or violence toward people or animals.
10. Verbal threats of harm to parents, adult authority figures, siblings, or peers.
11. Persistent pattern of destroying property or throwing objects when angry.
12. Consistent failure to accept responsibility for anger control problems accompanied by repeated pattern of blaming others for anger control problems.
13. Repeated history of engaging in passive-aggressive behaviors (e.g., forgetting, pretending not to listen, dawdling, procrastinating) to frustrate or annoy others.
14. Strained interpersonal relationships with peers due to aggressiveness and anger control problems.

15. Underlying feelings of depression, anxiety, or insecurity that contribute to angry outbursts and aggressive behaviors.

__. _____
_____
__. _____
_____
__. _____
_____

LONG-TERM GOALS

1. Learn and implement anger management skills that reduce irritability, anger, and aggressive behavior.
2. Significantly reduce the frequency and intensity of temper outbursts.
3. Interact consistently with adults and peers in a mutually respectful manner.
4. Markedly reduce frequency of passive-aggressive behaviors by expressing anger and frustration through controlled, respectful, and direct verbalizations.
5. Parents establish and maintain appropriate parent-child boundaries, setting firm, consistent limits when the client reacts in a verbally or physically aggressive or passive-aggressive manner.
6. Parents learn and implement consistent, effective, parenting practices.

__. _____
_____
__. _____
_____
__. _____
_____

SHORT-TERM OBJECTIVES

1. Identify situations, thoughts, and feelings that trigger angry feelings, problem behaviors, and the targets of those actions. (1, 2)

THERAPEUTIC INTERVENTIONS

1. Actively build the level of trust with the client through consistent eye contact, active listening, unconditional positive regard, and warm acceptance to

help increase his/her ability to identify and express feelings.

2. Thoroughly assess the various stimuli (e.g., situations, people, thoughts) that have triggered the client's anger and the thoughts, feelings, and actions that have characterized his/her anger responses.

2. Parents identify major concerns regarding the child's angry behavior and the associated parenting approaches that have been tried. (3)

3. Assess how the parents have attempted to respond to the child's anger and the triggers and reinforcements that may be contributing to its expression.

3. Parents describe any conflicts that result from the different approaches to parenting that each partner has. (4)

4. Assess the parents' approach and consistency in addressing their child's anger control problem and any conflicts between them resulting from parenting practices.

4. Cooperate with a medical evaluation to assess possible contributions of a general medical condition and substance use to anger control problems. (5)

5. Refer the client to a physician for a complete medical evaluation to rule out medical conditions (e.g., brain damage, tumor, elevated testosterone levels) and substance-related condition (e.g., stimulant use) to anger control problems.

5. Complete psychological testing. (6)

6. Conduct or arrange for psychological testing to supplement assessment of the anger control problem, including possible clinical syndromes and comorbid conditions (e.g., anxiety, depression, Attention-Deficit/Hyperactivity Disorder); follow up accordingly with client and parents regarding treatment options.

6. Provide behavioral, emotional, and attitudinal information toward an assessment of specifiers relevant to a *DSM*

7. Assess the client's level of insight (syntonic versus dystonic) toward the "presenting problems" (e.g., demonstrates

diagnosis, the efficacy of treatment, and the nature of the therapy relationship. (7, 8, 9, 10, 11)

good insight into the problematic nature of the "described behavior," agrees with others' concern, and is motivated to work on change; demonstrates ambivalence regarding the "problem described" and is reluctant to address the issue as a concern; or demonstrates resistance regarding acknowledgment of the "problem described," is not concerned, and has no motivation to change).

8. Assess the client for evidence of research-based correlated disorders (e.g., oppositional defiant behavior with ADHD, depression secondary to an anxiety disorder) including vulnerability to suicide, if appropriate (e.g., increased suicide risk when comorbid depression is evident).

9. Assess for any issues of age, gender, or culture that could help explain the client's currently defined "problem behavior" and factors that could offer a better understanding of the client's behavior.

10. Assess for the severity of the level of impairment to the client's functioning to determine appropriate level of care (e.g., the behavior noted creates mild, moderate, severe, or very severe impairment in social, relational, vocational, or occupational endeavors); continuously assess this severity of impairment as well as the efficacy of treatment (e.g., the client no longer demonstrates severe impairment

but the presenting problem now is causing mild or moderate impairment).

11. Assess the client's home, school, and community for pathogenic care (e.g., persistent disregard for the child's emotional needs or physical needs, repeated changes in primary caregivers, limited opportunities for stable attachments, persistent harsh punishment or other grossly inept parenting).

7. Cooperate with a physician evaluation for possible treatment with psychotropic medications and take medications consistently, if prescribed. (12, 13)

12. Assess the client for the need for psychotropic medication to assist in anger and behavioral control, referring him/her, if indicated, to a physician for an evaluation for a medication prescription.

13. Monitor the client's prescription compliance, effectiveness, and side effects; provide feedback to the prescribing physician.

8. Increase the number of statements that reflect an acceptance of responsibility for the consequences of angry and/or aggressive behavior. (14, 15, 16)

14. Use a motivational interviewing approach involving active listening, clarifying questions, and the examination of consequences toward the client's acceptance of responsibility and willingness to change anger control problems.

15. Therapeutically confront statements in which the client lies and/or blames others for his/her misbehaviors and fails to accept responsibility for his/her actions toward the client's acceptance of responsibility and willingness to change anger control problems.

16. Explore and process the factors that contribute to the client's pattern of blaming others (e.g., harsh punishment experiences,

9. Parents verbalize a willingness to learn and implement consistent parenting practices. (17)

▽ 10. Parents verbalize an understanding of Parent Management Training, its rationale, and techniques. (18, 19)

▽ 11. Parents implement Parent Management Training skills to recognize and manage problem behavior of the client. (20, 21, 22)

family pattern of blaming others) toward the client's acceptance of responsibility and willingness to change anger control problems.

17. Explore parents' willingness to learn and implement new parenting techniques designed to manage their child's anger control problem and to increase positive, prosocial behavior while decreasing undesirable behavior; confirm their commitment.

18. Teach parents a Parent Management Training approach conveying how parent and child behavioral interactions can encourage or discourage positive or negative behavior and that changing key elements of those interactions (e.g., prompting and reinforcing positive behaviors) can be used to promote positive change (e.g., see *Parenting the Strong-Willed Child* by Forehand and Long; *Living With Children* by Patterson). ▽

19. Ask the parents to read parent training books or manuals (e.g., *Parenting the Strong-Willed Child* by Forehand and Long). ▽

20. Teach the parents how to specifically define and identify problem behaviors, identify their reactions to the behavior, determine whether the reaction encourages or discourages the behavior, and generate alternatives to the problem behavior. ▽

21. Teach parents how to implement key parenting practices

consistently, including establishing realistic age-appropriate rules for acceptable and unacceptable behavior, prompting of positive behavior in the environment, use of positive reinforcement to encourage behavior (e.g., praise), use of clear and direct instruction, time-out, and other loss-of-privilege practices for problem behavior.▽

22. Assign the parents home exercises in which they implement and record results of implementation exercises (or assign "Clear Rules, Positive Reinforcement, Appropriate Consequences" in the *Adolescent Psychotherapy Homework Planner* by Jongsma, Peterson, and McInnis); review in session, providing corrective feedback toward improved, appropriate, and consistent use of skills.▽

▽ 12. Older children agree to learn alternative ways to think about and manage frustration, anger, and aggressive behavior. (23, 24)

23. Assist the client in identifying the positive consequences of managing frustration and anger (e.g., respect from others and self, cooperation from others, improved physical health); ask the client to agree to learn new ways to conceptualize and manage anger and misbehavior (or assign "Anger Control" from the *Child Psychotherapy Homework Planner* by Jongsma, Peterson, and McInnis).

24. Using an Anger Control Training (ACT) approach (Williams and Barlow) assist the client in reconceptualizing frustration and anger as involving different domains of

response (cognitive, physiological, affective, and behavioral) that go through predictable sequences (e.g., demanding expectations not being met leading to increased arousal and anger leading to acting out), and that can be managed by intervening within the domains. ▽

▽ 13. Learn and implement calming strategies as part of a new way to manage reactions to frustration. (25)

25. Teach the client calming techniques (e.g., muscle relaxation, paced breathing, calming imagery) as part of a tailored strategy for responding appropriately to angry thoughts and feelings when they occur. ▽

▽ 14. Identify, challenge, and replace self-talk that leads to frustration, anger, and aggressive actions with self-talk that facilitates more constructive reactions. (26)

26. Explore the client's self-talk that mediates his/her frustration and anger (e.g., demanding expectations reflected in should, must, or have to statements); identify and challenge biases, assisting him/her in generating appraisals and self-talk that corrects for the biases and facilitates a more flexible and temperate response to frustration. ▽

▽ 15. Learn and implement thought-stopping to manage intrusive, unwanted thoughts that trigger anger and angry actions. (27)

27. Teach the client the "thought-stopping" technique as part of his/her new anger management skill set and assign implementation on a daily basis between sessions; review implementation, reinforcing success and providing corrective feedback toward improvement (or assign the parents to assist the child in working through "Making Use of the Thought-Stopping Technique" in the *Adult Psychotherapy Homework Planner* by Jongsma). ▽

▽ 16. Verbalize feelings of frustration, disagreement, and anger in a controlled, assertive way. (28)

▽ 17. Implement problem-solving and/or conflict resolution skills to manage personal and interpersonal problems constructively. (29)

▽ 18. Practice using new calming, communication, conflict resolution, and thinking skills. (30, 31)

▽ 19. Practice using new anger management skills in between-session homework exercises. (32)

28. Use behavioral techniques such as instruction, videotaped or live modeling, and/or role-playing to teach the client direct, honest, and respectful assertive communication skills; if indicated, refer him/her to an assertiveness training group for further instruction. ▽

29. Teach the client conflict resolution skills (e.g., empathy, active listening, "I messages," respectful communication, assertiveness without aggression, compromise); use modeling, role-playing, and behavior rehearsal to work through several current conflicts. ▽

30. Assist the client in consolidating his/her new anger management skill set that combines any of the somatic, cognitive, communication, problem-solving, and/or conflict resolution skills relevant to his/her needs. ▽

31. Use any of several techniques (e.g., relaxation, imagery, behavioral rehearsal, modeling, role-playing, feedback of videotaped practice) in increasingly challenging situations to help the client consolidate the use of his/her new anger management skills. ▽

32. Assign the client homework exercises to help him/her practice newly learned calming, assertion, conflict resolution, or cognitive restructuring skills as needed; review and refine toward the goal of consolidation. ▽

▽ 20. Decrease the number, intensity, and duration of angry outbursts, while increasing the use of new skills for managing anger. (33)

33. Monitor the client's reports of angry outbursts toward the goal of decreasing their frequency, intensity, and duration through the client's use of new anger management skills (or assign "Anger Control" or "Child Anger Checklist" in the *Child Psychotherapy Homework Planner* by Jongsma, Peterson, and McInnis); review progress, reinforcing success and providing corrective feedback toward improvement. ▽

▽ 21. Identify social supports that will help facilitate the implementation of new skills. (34)

34. Encourage the client to discuss and/or use his/her new anger management skills with trusted peers, family, or otherwise significant others who are likely to support his/her change. ▽

▽ 22. Parents and client participate in play sessions in which they use their new approaches to interacting. (35)

35. Conduct Parent-Child Interaction Therapy (see *Parent-Child Interaction Therapy* by McNeil and Hembree-Kigin) in which child-directed and parent-directed sessions focus on teaching appropriate child behavior and parental behavioral management skills (e.g., clear commands, consistent consequences, positive reinforcement). ▽

▽ 23. Parents and client enroll in a formal behavior management program to improve parenting knowledge and skills. (36)

36. Facilitate the parents' enrollment in an evidence-based parent skills training program such as *Helping the Noncompliant Child* (McMahon and Forehand), the enhanced version of the *Positive Parenting Program* (*Triple P*) (Sanders), or *The Incredible Years* program (Webster-Stratton). ▽

▽ 24. Increase compliance with rules at home and school. (37)

37. Design a reward system and/or contingency contract for the client and meet with parents and school officials to reinforce identified positive behaviors at home and school and deter angry, impulsive, or otherwise maladaptive behaviors (or use the "Record of Reinforced Behavior" in the *Parenting Skills Homework Planner* by Sarah Knapp). ▽

25. Parents verbalize appropriate boundaries for discipline to prevent further occurrences of abuse and to ensure the safety of the client and his/her siblings. (38, 39)

38. Explore the client's family background for a history of neglect and physical or sexual abuse that may contribute to his/her behavioral problems; confront the client's parents to cease physically abusive or overly punitive methods of discipline.

39. Implement the steps necessary to protect the client or siblings from further abuse (e.g., report abuse to the appropriate agencies; remove the client or perpetrator from the home).

26. Increase the frequency of civil, respectful interactions with parents/adults. (40)

40. Establish with the client the basics of treating others respectfully. Teach the principle of reciprocity, asking him/her to agree to treat everyone in a respectful manner for a 1-week period to see if others will reciprocate by treating him/her with more respect.

27. Demonstrate the ability to play by the rules in a cooperative fashion. (41)

41. Use puppets, dolls, or stuffed animals to create a story that models appropriate ways to manage anger and resolve conflict; ask the client to create a story with similar characters or themes; play games (e.g., checkers) toward the same goals.

28. Increase the frequency of responsible and positive social behaviors. (42, 43)

42. Direct the client to engage in three altruistic or benevolent acts (e.g., read to a developmentally disabled student, mow grandmother's lawn) before the next session to increase his/her empathy and sensitivity to the needs of others.

43. Place the client in charge of tasks at home (e.g., preparing and cooking a special dish for a family get-together, building shelves in the garage, changing oil in the car) to demonstrate confidence in his/her ability to act responsibly.

29. Identify and verbally express feelings associated with past neglect, abuse, separation, or abandonment. (44)

44. Encourage and support the client in expressing feelings associated with neglect, abuse, separation, or abandonment and help process (e.g., assign the task of writing a letter to an absent parent); use the empty-chair technique (or assign "The Lesson of Salmon Rock . . . Fighting Leads to Loneliness" in the *Child Psychotherapy Homework Planner* by Jongsma, Peterson, and McInnis).

30. Parents participate in marital therapy. (45)

45. Assess the marital dyad for possible substance abuse, conflict, or triangulation that shifts the focus from marriage issues to the client's acting-out behaviors; refer for appropriate treatment, if needed.

▽ 31. Participate in family therapy to explore and change family dynamics that contribute to the emergence of anger control problems. (46, 47, 48)

46. Conduct Functional Family Therapy (Sexton) or Brief Strategic Family Therapy to assess and intervene within the family system toward reducing its contributions to the client's anger control problems. ▽

47. Assess the family dynamics by employing the family-sculpting technique, in which the client defines the roles and behaviors of each family member in a scene of his/her choosing.

48. Give a directive to uninvolved or disengaged parent(s) to spend more time with the client in leisure, school, or work activities; review progress, reinforcing success and providing supportive, corrective feedback toward consistent use.

__ . _____   __ . _____

_____   _____

__ . _____   __ . _____

_____   _____

__ . _____   __ . _____

_____   _____

DIAGNOSTIC SUGGESTIONS

Using DSM-IV/ICD-9-CM:

Axis I:	312.81	Conduct Disorder, Childhood-Onset Type
	312.89	Conduct Disorder, Unspecified Onset
	313.81	Oppositional Defiant Disorder
	312.9	Disruptive Behavior Disorder NOS
	314.01	Attention-Deficit/Hyperactivity Disorder, Predominantly Hyperactive-Impulsive Type
	314.9	Attention-Deficit/Hyperactivity Disorder NOS
	312.34	Intermittent Explosive Disorder
	V71.02	Child Antisocial Behavior
	V61.20	Parent-Child Relational Problem
	_____	_____
	_____	_____

Axis II: V71.09   No Diagnosis

         _____   _____

         _____   _____

Using DSM-5/ICD-9-CM/ICD-10-CM:

ICD-9-CM	ICD-10-CM	_DSM_-5 Disorder, Condition, or Problem
312.81	F91.1	Conduct Disorder, Childhood-Onset Type
312.89	F91.9	Conduct Disorder, Unspecified Onset
313.81	F91.3	Oppositional Defiant Disorder
312.9	F91.9	Unspecified Disruptive, Impulse Control, and Conduct Disorder
312.89	F91.8	Other Specified Disruptive, Impulse Control, and Conduct Disorder
314.01	F90.1	Attention-Deficit/Hyperactivity Disorder, Predominately Hyperactive/Impulsive Presentation
314.01	F90.9	Unspecified Attention-Deficit/ Hyperactivity Disorder
314.01	F90.8	Other Specified Attention-Deficit/ Hyperactivity Disorder
312.34	F63.81	Intermittent Explosive Disorder
V71.02	Z72.810	Child or Adolescent Antisocial Behavior
V61.20	Z62.820	Parent-Child Relational Problem

Note: The ICD-9-CM codes are to be used for coding purposes in the United States through September 30, 2014. ICD-10-CM codes are to be used starting October 1, 2014. Some ICD-9-CM codes are associated with more than one ICD-10-CM and _DSM-5_ disorder, condition, or problem. In addition, some ICD-9-CM disorders have been discontinued resulting in multiple ICD-9-CM codes being replaced by one ICD-10-CM code. Some discontinued ICD-9-CM codes are not listed in this table. See _Diagnostic and Statistical Manual of Mental Disorders_ (2013) for details.

▽ Indicates that the Objective/Intervention is consistent with those found in evidence-based treatments.

ANXIETY

BEHAVIORAL DEFINITIONS

1. Excessive anxiety, worry, or fear that markedly exceeds the normal level for the client's stage of development.
2. High level of motor tension, such as restlessness, tiredness, shakiness, or muscle tension.
3. Autonomic hyperactivity (e.g., rapid heartbeat, shortness of breath, dizziness, dry mouth, nausea, diarrhea).
4. Hypervigilance, such as feeling constantly on edge, concentration difficulties, trouble falling or staying asleep, and a general state of irritability.
5. A specific fear that has become generalized to cover a wide area and has reached the point where it significantly interferes with the client's and the family's daily life.
6. Excessive anxiety or worry due to parent's threat of abandonment, overuse of guilt, denial of autonomy and status, friction between parents, or interference with physical activity.

—. _____
   _____
—. _____
   _____
—. _____
   _____

LONG-TERM GOALS

1. Reduce overall frequency, intensity, and duration of the anxiety so that daily functioning is not impaired.
2. Stabilize anxiety level while increasing ability to function on a daily basis.

3. Resolve the core conflict that is the source of anxiety.
4. Enhance ability to effectively cope with the full variety of life's anxieties.
5. Parents effectively manage child's anxious thoughts, feelings, and behaviors.
6. Family members function effectively without undue anxiety.

__. _____
   _____
__. _____
   _____
__. _____
   _____

SHORT-TERM OBJECTIVES

THERAPEUTIC INTERVENTIONS

1. Describe current and past experiences with specific fears, prominent worries, and anxiety symptoms including their impact on functioning and attempts to resolve it. (1, 2)

1. Actively build the level of trust with the client or client and parents through consistent eye contact, active listening, unconditional positive regard, and warm acceptance to help increase his/her ability to identify and express concerns.

2. Assess the focus, excessiveness, and uncontrollability of the client's fears and worries and the type, frequency, intensity, and duration of his/her anxiety symptoms (see *The Anxiety Disorders Interview Schedule for Children—Parent Version* or *Child Version*; assign "Finding and Losing Your Anxiety" in the *Child Psychotherapy Homework Planner* by Jongsma, Peterson, and McInnis).

2. Complete questionnaires designed to assess fear, worry, and anxiety symptoms. (3)

3. Administer a patient and/or parent-report measure to help assess the nature and degree of the client's fears, worries, and

anxiety symptoms (e.g., *Revised Children's Manifest Anxiety Scale*; *Fear Survey Schedule for Children–Revised*); repeat administration as desired to assess therapeutic progress.

3. Provide behavioral, emotional, and attitudinal information toward an assessment of specifiers relevant to a *DSM* diagnosis, the efficacy of treatment, and the nature of the therapy relationship. (4, 5, 6, 7, 8)

4. Assess the client's level of insight (syntonic versus dystonic) toward the "presenting problems" (e.g., demonstrates good insight into the problematic nature of the "described behavior," agrees with others' concern, and is motivated to work on change; demonstrates ambivalence regarding the "problem described" and is reluctant to address the issue as a concern; or demonstrates resistance regarding acknowledgment of the "problem described," is not concerned, and has no motivation to change).

5. Assess the client for evidence of research-based correlated disorders (e.g., oppositional defiant behavior with ADHD, depression secondary to an anxiety disorder) including vulnerability to suicide, if appropriate (e.g., increased suicide risk when comorbid depression is evident).

6. Assess for any issues of age, gender, or culture that could help explain the client's currently defined "problem behavior" and factors that could offer a better understanding of the client's behavior.

7. Assess for the severity of the level of impairment to the client's functioning to determine appropriate level of care (e.g., the behavior noted creates mild, moderate, severe, or very severe impairment in social, relational, vocational, or occupational endeavors); continuously assess this severity of impairment as well as the efficacy of treatment (e.g., the client no longer demonstrates severe impairment but the presenting problem now is causing mild or moderate impairment).

8. Assess the client's home, school, and community for pathogenic care (e.g., persistent disregard for the child's emotional needs or physical needs, repeated changes in primary caregivers, limited opportunities for stable attachments, persistent harsh punishment or other grossly inept parenting).

▽ 4. Cooperate with an evaluation by a physician for anti-anxiety medication. (9, 10)

9. Refer the client to a physician for a psychotropic medication consultation. ▽

10. Monitor the client's psychotropic medication compliance, side effects, and effectiveness; confer regularly with the physician. ▽

▽ 5. Verbalize an understanding of how thoughts, physical feelings, and behavioral actions contribute to anxiety and its treatment. (11, 12, 13)

11. As part of an individual cognitive behavioral approach, educate the client about the interrelated physiological, cognitive, emotional, and behavioral components of anxiety, including how fears and worries typically involve excessive concern about

unrealistic threats, various bodily expressions of tension, overarousal, hypervigilance, and avoidance of what is threatening, which interact to maintain problematic anxiety (e.g., see the *Coping C.A.T. Series* at workbookpublishing.com; *Helping Your Anxious Child* by Rapee et al.). ▽

12. Discuss how treatment targets the interrelated components of anxiety to help the client identify and manage thoughts, overarousal, and effectively overcome unnecessary avoidance. ▽

13. Assign the client and/or parents to read psychoeducational sections of books or treatment manuals to emphasize key therapy concepts (e.g., the *Coping C.A.T. Workbook* by Kendall and Hedtke (for ages 7–13); *Helping Your Anxious Child* by Rapee et al.). ▽

▽ 6. Learn and implement calming skills to reduce overall anxiety and manage anxiety symptoms. (14, 15, 16, 17)

14. Teach the client calming skills (e.g., progressive muscle relaxation, guided imagery, slow diaphragmatic breathing) and how to discriminate better between relaxation and tension; teach the client how to apply these skills to his/her daily life. ▽

15. Assign the client homework each session in which he/she practices calming daily (or assign "Deep Breathing Exercise" in the *Child Psychotherapy Homework Planner* by Jongsma, Peterson, and McInnis); review and reinforce success while providing corrective feedback toward improvement. ▽

16. Assign the client and/or parents to read and discuss progressive muscle relaxation and other calming strategies in relevant books or treatment manuals (e.g., *New Directions in Progressive Relaxation Training* by Bernstein, Borkovec, and Hazlett-Stevens; *The Relaxation and Stress Reduction Workbook for Kids* by Shapiro and Sprague; the *Coping C.A.T. Series* at workbookpublishing.com). ▽

17. Use biofeedback techniques to facilitate the client's success at learning calming skills. ▽

7. Verbalize an understanding of the role that fearful thinking plays in creating fears, excessive worry, and persistent anxiety symptoms. (18, 19, 20)

18. Discuss examples demonstrating that unrealistic fear or worry typically overestimates the probability of threats and underestimates the client's ability to manage realistic demands. ▽

19. Assist the client in challenging his/her fear or worry by examining the actual probability of the negative expectation occurring, the real consequences of it occurring, his/her ability to manage the likely outcome, the worst possible outcome, and his/her ability to accept it. ▽

20. Help the client gain insight into the notion that fear and worry involve a form of avoidance of the problem, that this creates anxious arousal, and precludes resolution. ▽

8. Identify, challenge, and replace fearful self-talk with positive, realistic, and empowering self-talk. (21, 22, 23, 24) ▽

21. Explore the client's schema and self-talk that mediate his/her fear response; challenge the biases; assist him/her in replacing the distorted messages with reality-based alternatives and positive

self-talk that will increase his/her self-confidence in coping with irrational fears or worries. ▽

22. Assign the client a homework exercise in which he/she identifies fearful self-talk and creates reality-based alternatives (or assign "Tools for Anxiety" in the *Adolescent Psychotherapy Homework Planner* by Jongsma, Peterson, and McInnis); review and reinforce success, providing corrective feedback toward improvement. ▽

23. Teach the client to implement a "thought-stopping" technique (thinking of a STOP sign and then a pleasant scene) for fears or worries that have been addressed but persist (or assign "Making Use of the Thought-Stopping Technique" in the *Adult Psychotherapy Homework Planner* by Jongsma); monitor and encourage the client's use of the technique in daily life between sessions. ▽

24. Assign parents to read and discuss with the client cognitive restructuring of fears or worries in relevant books or treatment manuals (e.g., the *Coping C.A.T. Series* at workbookpublishing .com; *Helping Your Anxious Child* by Rapee et al.). ▽

▽ 9. Learn and implement a stimulus control strategy to limit the association between various environmental settings and worry, delaying the worry until a designated "worry time." (25, 26)

25. Explain how using "worry time" limits the association between worrying and environmental stimuli; agree upon setting a worry time and place with the client and implement. ▽

26. Teach the client to recognize and postpone worry to the agreed

upon worry time and place, using skills such as thought-stopping, relaxation, and redirecting attention (or assign "Worry Time" in the *Child Psychotherapy Homework Planner* by Jongsma, Peterson, and McInnis to assist skill development); encourage use in daily life, reviewing and reinforcing success while providing corrective feedback toward improvement. ▽

▽ 10. Participate in live, or imaginal then live, exposure exercises in which worries and fears are gradually faced. (27, 28, 29, 30)

27. Direct and assist the client in constructing a hierarchy around two to three spheres of worry for use in exposure (e.g., fears of school failure, worries about relationship problems). ▽

28. Select initial exposures that have a high likelihood of being a successful experience for the client; develop a coping plan for managing the negative affect engendered by exposure; mentally rehearse the procedure. ▽

29. Ask the client to vividly imagine conducting the exposure, or conduct it live until anxiety associated with it weakens and a sense of safety and/or confidence strengthens; process the experience. ▽

30. Assign the client a homework exercise in which he/she does gradual exposure to identified fears and records responses (see *Phobic and Anxiety Disorders in Children and Adolescents* by Ollendick and March); review, reinforce success, and provide corrective feedback toward improvement (or assign

"Gradually Facing a Phobic Fear" in the *Adolescent Psychotherapy Homework Planner* by Jongsma, Peterson, and McInnis). ▽

▽ 11. Learn and implement new strategies for realistically addressing fears or worries. (31, 32)

31. Ask the client to develop a list of key conflicts that trigger fear or worry; process how skills learned in therapy can be applied to help manage/resolve problems (e.g., relaxation, problem-solving, assertiveness, acceptance, cognitive restructuring). ▽

32. Assign the client a homework exercise in which he/she works on solving a current problem using skills learned in therapy (see the *Coping C.A.T. Series* at workbookpublishing.com; *Helping Your Anxious Child* by Rapee et al.; or "An Anxious Story" from the *Child Psychotherapy Homework Planner* by Jongsma, Peterson, and McInnis); review, repeat, reinforce success, and provide corrective feedback toward effective use of skills. ▽

▽ 12. Increase participation in daily social and academic activities. (33)

33. Encourage the client to increase daily social and academic activities and other potentially rewarding experiences to strengthen his/her new nonavoidant approach and build self-confidence. ▽

▽ 13. Parents verbalize an understanding of the client's treatment plan and a willingness to participate in it with the client. (34)

34. If acceptable to the client and if possible, involve the client's parents in the treatment, having them participate in selective activities.

▽ 14. Participate in a cognitive behavioral group treatment for anxiety to learn about anxiety,

35. Conduct cognitive behavioral group therapy (e.g., *Cognitive Behavioral Therapy for Anxious*

develop skills for managing it, and use the skills effectively in everyday life. (35)

Children: Therapist Manual for Group Treatment by Flannery-Schroeder and Kendall) in which participant youth are taught the cognitive, behavioral, and emotional components of anxiety; learn and implement skills for coping with anxiety; and then practice their new skills in several anxiety-provoking situations toward consistent, effective use. ▽

▽ 15. Participate in group cognitive behavioral therapy with parents to learn about anxiety, develop skills for managing it, and use the skills effectively in everyday life, while parents learn and implement constructive ways to respond to the client's fear and avoidance. (36, 37, 38)

36. Conduct cognitive behavioral group therapy with parents and clients (e.g., *Cognitive Behavioral Therapy for Anxious Children: Therapist Manual for Group Treatment* by Flannery-Schroeder and Kendall) in which the clients are taught the cognitive, behavioral, and emotional components of anxiety; learn and implement skills for coping with anxiety; and then practice their new skills in several anxiety-provoking situations toward consistent, effective use. ▽

37. Teach parents constructive skills for managing their child's anxious behavior, including how to prompt and reward courageous behavior, empathetically ignore excessive complaining and other avoidant behaviors, manage their own anxieties, and model the behavior being taught in session (recommend *Helping Your Anxious Child* by Rapee et al.). ▽

38. Teach family members anxiety management, problem-solving, and communication skills to

▽ 16. Learn and implement relapse-prevention strategies for managing possible future fears or worries. (39, 40, 41, 42)

reduce family conflict and assist the client's progress through therapy. ▽

39. Discuss with the client the distinction between a lapse and relapse, associating a lapse with an initial and reversible return of a fear, worry, anxiety symptom, or urges to avoid and relapse with the decision to return to a fearful and avoidant manner of dealing with the fear or worry. ▽

40. Identify and rehearse with the client the management of future situations or circumstances in which lapses could occur. ▽

41. Instruct the client to routinely use his/her newly learned skills in relaxation, cognitive restructuring, exposure, and problem-solving exposures as needed to address emergent fears or worries, building them into his/her life as much as possible. ▽

42. Develop a "coping card" or other reminder on which coping strategies and other important information (e.g., "Breathe deeply and relax," "Challenge unrealistic worries," "Use problem-solving") are recorded for the client's/parent's later use. ▽

▽ 17. Participate in family therapy in which all family members learn about anxiety, develop skills for managing it, and use the skills effectively in everyday life. (43)

43. Conduct cognitive behavioral family therapy in which the client learns anxiety management skills and parents learn skills for managing the child's anxious behavior and facilitate the client's progress (see *Cognitive-Behavioral Family Therapy for Anxious Children* by Howard

et al.; the *FRIENDS Program for Children* series by Barrett, Lowry-Webster, and Turner; *Helping Your Anxious Child* by Rapee et al.). ▽

18. Verbalize an increased understanding of anxious feelings and their causes. (44, 45, 46)

44. Use child-centered play therapy approaches (e.g., provide unconditional positive regard; reflect feelings in a nonjudgmental manner; display trust in child's capacity to work through issues) to increase the client's ability to cope with anxious feelings.

45. Assign the client the task of drawing two or three situations that generally bring on anxious feelings.

46. Conduct psychoanalytical play therapy sessions (e.g., explore and gain an understanding of the etiology of unconscious conflicts, fixations, or arrests; interpret resistance or core anxieties) to help the client work through to resolutions of the issues that are the source of his/her anxiety.

19. Identify areas of conflict that underlie the anxiety. (47, 48)

47. Use puppets, felts, or a sand tray to enact situations that provoke anxiety in the client. Involve him/her in creating such scenarios, and model positive cognitive responses to the situations that bring on anxiety.

48. Play the therapeutic game, My Home and Places (Flood) with the client to help identify and talk about divorce, peers, alcohol abuse, or other situations that make him/her anxious.

20. Identify and use specific coping strategies for anxiety reduction. (49, 50, 51, 52)

49. Use a Narrative Approach (White) in which the client writes out the story of his/her anxiety

or fear and then acts out the story with the therapist to externalize the issues. Work with the client to reach a resolution or develop an effective way to cope with the anxiety or fear (see "An Anxious Story" from the *Child Psychotherapy Homework Planner* by Jongsma, Peterson, and McInnis).

50. Conduct sessions with a focus on anxiety-producing situations in which techniques of storytelling, drawing pictures, and viewing photographs are used to assist the client in talking about and reducing the level of anxiety or fear.

51. Use a Mutual Storytelling Technique (Gardner) in which the client tells a story about a central character who becomes anxious. The therapist then interprets the story for its underlying meaning and retells the client's story while weaving in healthier adaptations to fear or anxiety and resolution of conflicts.

52. Prescribe a Prediction Task (de Shazer) for anxiety management. (The client predicts the night before whether the anxiety will bother him/her the next day. The therapist directs the client to be a good detective and bring back key elements that contributed to it being a "good day" so the therapist then can reinforce or construct a solution to increasing the frequency of "good days.")

— · _____   — · _____
   _____   _____
— · _____   — · _____
   _____   _____
— · _____   — · _____
   _____   _____

DIAGNOSTIC SUGGESTIONS

Using DSM-IV/ICD-9-CM:

Axis I: 300.02   Generalized Anxiety Disorder
                 300.00   Anxiety Disorder NOS
                 314.01   Attention-Deficit/Hyperactivity Disorder,
                             Combined Type

                 _____   _____
                 _____   _____

Axis II: V71.09   No Diagnosis

                 _____   _____
                 _____   _____

Using DSM-5/ICD-9-CM/ICD-10-CM:

ICD-9-CM	ICD-10-CM	*DSM*-5 Disorder, Condition, or Problem
300.02	F41.1	Generalized Anxiety Disorder
300.09	F41.8	Other Specified Anxiety Disorder
300.00	F41.9	Unspecified Anxiety Disorder
314.01	F90.2	Attention-Deficit/Hyperactivity Disorder, Combined Presentation
309.24	F43.22	Adjustment Disorder, With Anxiety

Note: The ICD-9-CM codes are to be used for coding purposes in the United States through September 30, 2014. ICD-10-CM codes are to be used starting October 1, 2014. Some ICD-9-CM codes are associated with more than one ICD-10-CM and *DSM-5* disorder, condition, or problem. In addition, some ICD-9-CM disorders have been discontinued resulting in multiple ICD-9-CM codes being replaced by one ICD-10-CM code. Some discontinued ICD-9-CM codes are not listed in this table. See *Diagnostic and Statistical Manual of Mental Disorders* (American Psychiatric Association, 2013) for details.

▽ Indicates that the Objective/Intervention is consistent with those found in evidence-based treatments.

REACTIVE ATTACHMENT/DISINHIBITED SOCIAL ENGAGEMENT DISORDER

BEHAVIORAL DEFINITIONS

1. Brought into family through adoption after coming from an abusive, neglectful, biological family.
2. Rarely seeks or responds to comfort when distressed
3. Minimal social and emotional responsiveness to others.
4. Limited positive affect.
5. Unexplained episodes of irritability, sadness, or fearfulness even during nonthreatening interactions with adult caregivers.
6. Lacks usual reticence in approaching unfamiliar adults.
7. Overly familiar verbal or physical behavior (e.g., affection).
8. Often does not touch base with adult caregiver after wandering away in an unfamiliar environment.
9. Will easily accompany an unknown adult with little or no hesitation.
10. Raised in a setting that severely limited opportunities to form selective attachments.
11. Has experienced persistent disregard for his/her emotional and/or physical needs.
12. Has been subjected to frequent changes in primary caregiver.

__. _____

_____

__. _____

_____

__. _____

_____

LONG-TERM GOALS

1. Establishment and maintenance of a bond with primary caregivers.
2. Resolution of all barriers to forming healthy connections with others.
3. Capable of forming warm physical and emotional bonds with the parents.
4. Has a desire for and initiates connections with others.
5. Keeps appropriate distance from strangers.
6. Tolerates reasonable absence from presence of parent or primary caregiver without panic.

—. _____
    _____
—. _____
    _____
—. _____
    _____

SHORT-TERM OBJECTIVES	THERAPEUTIC INTERVENTIONS
1. Openly express thoughts and feelings. (1, 2, 3)	1. Actively build the level of trust with the client through consistent eye contact, active listening, unconditional positive regard, and empathic responses to help promote the open expressions of his/her thoughts and feelings.
	2. Conduct a celebrity-style interview with the client to elicit information (e.g., school likes/dislikes, favorite food, music, best birthday, hopes, wishes, dreams, "If I had a million dollars") in order to build a relationship and help him/her learn more about himself/herself.
	3. Conduct all sessions in a consistent and predictable manner so that all is clear for the client and he/she can start to

2. Cooperate with and complete all assessments and testing. (4, 5)

3. Provide behavioral, emotional, and attitudinal information toward an assessment of specifiers relevant to a *DSM* diagnosis, the efficacy of treatment, and the nature of the therapy relationship. (6, 7, 8, 9, 10)

take a risk and trust the therapist.

4. Conduct a psychosocial evaluation to assess the strength of the parents' marriage, parenting style, stress management/coping strengths, resolutions of the infertility issue, and to assess the client's developmental level, attachment capacity, behavior issues, temperament, and strengths.

5. Conduct or arrange for psychological evaluation to determine level of behavioral functioning, cognitive style, and intelligence.

6. Assess the client's level of insight (syntonic versus dystonic) toward the "presenting problems" (e.g., demonstrates good insight into the problematic nature of the "described behavior," agrees with others' concern, and is motivated to work on change; demonstrates ambivalence regarding the "problem described" and is reluctant to address the issue as a concern; or demonstrates resistance regarding acknowledgment of the "problem described," is not concerned, and has no motivation to change).

7. Assess the client for evidence of research-based correlated disorders (e.g., oppositional defiant behavior with ADHD, depression secondary to an anxiety disorder) including vulnerability to suicide, if appropriate (e.g., increased

suicide risk when comorbid depression is evident).

8. Assess for any issues of age, gender, or culture that could help explain the client's currently defined "problem behavior" and factors that could offer a better understanding of the client's behavior.

9. Assess for the severity of the level of impairment to the client's functioning to determine appropriate level of care (e.g., the behavior noted creates mild, moderate, severe, or very severe impairment in social, relational, vocational, or occupational endeavors); continuously assess this severity of impairment as well as the efficacy of treatment (e.g., the client no longer demonstrates severe impairment but the presenting problem now is causing mild or moderate impairment).

10. Assess the client's home, school, and community for pathogenic care (e.g., persistent disregard for the child's emotional needs or physical needs, repeated changes in primary caregivers, limited opportunities for stable attachments, persistent harsh punishment or other grossly inept parenting).

4. Comply with all recommendations of assessments and evaluations. (11)

11. Summarize assessment data and present findings and recommendations to the family; monitor and encourage their follow through on all the recommendations on each evaluation and assessment.

5. Parents commit to improving the communication and affection within the marriage relationship. (12)

12. Refer the parents to a skills-based marital program such as "PREP" (e.g., *Fighting for Your Marriage* by Markman, Stanley, and Blumberg) to strengthen their marital relationship by improving personal responsibility, communication, and conflict resolution.

6. Parents acknowledge unresolved grief associated with infertility. (13)

13. Assess the parents' unresolved grief around the issue of their infertility; refer them for further conjoint or individual treatment if necessary.

7. Parent(s) make a verbal commitment to take an active role in the client's treatment and in developing skills to work with the client and his/her issues. (14, 15, 16)

14. Elicit from the parents a firm commitment to be an active part of the client's treatment by participating in sessions and being co-therapists in the home.

15. Work with the parents in conjoint sessions to frame the client's acting-out behaviors as opportunities to reparent the client. Then strategize with them to come up with specific ways to intervene in the problem behaviors.

16. Train and empower the parents as co-therapists (e.g., being patient, showing unconditional positive regard, setting limits firmly but without hostility, verbalizing love and expectations clearly, seeking to understand messages of pain and fear beneath the acting-out behavior) in the process of developing the client's capacity to form healthy bonds/connections.

8. Parents verbalize an understanding of the dynamics of attachment and trauma. (17)

17. Provide education to the parents on the nature of attachment and the overall effect of trauma on children and families (or assign

"Attachment Survey" from the *Child Psychotherapy Homework Planner* by Jongsma, Peterson, and McInnis).

9. Parents verbalize reasonable expectations regarding progress. (18, 19)

18. Process with the parents the issue of expectations for the client's behavior and adjustment; confront and modify unrealistic expectations regarding their child's emotional attachment progress and foster more realistic expectations considering the client's history.

19. Explore with the parents the reality that attachment in a relationship takes a long time and many experiences where trust is rewarded (recommend *Understanding Attachment: Parenting, Child Care, and Emotional Development* by Mercer).

10. Attend and actively take part in play therapy sessions. (20, 21, 22)

20. Use the Theraplay (Booth and Jernberg) attachment-based approach, in which the therapist takes charge by planning and structuring each session. The therapist uses his/her power to entice the client into a relationship and to keep the focus of therapy on the relationship, not on intrapsychic conflicts. Also, the parents are actively involved and are trained to be co-therapists.

21. Employ the ACT Model (Landreth) in play therapy sessions to acknowledge feelings, communicate limits, and target acceptable alternatives to acting-out or aggressive behaviors.

22. Conduct filial therapy (i.e., parent involvement in play therapy sessions), whereby the

client takes the lead in expressing anger and the parent responds empathically to the client's feelings (e.g., hurt, fear, sadness, helplessness) beneath the anger.

11. Parents acknowledge their frustrations regarding living with a detached child and state their commitment to keep trying. (23, 24)

23. Suggest to the parents that they read books to increase their understanding and give encouragement in continuing to work with their child (e.g., *The Difficult Child* by Turecki; *The Challenging Child* by Greenspan; *When Love Is Not Enough: A Guide to Parenting Children with RAD* by Thomas).

24. Empathize with the parents' frustrations regarding living with a detached child; allow them to share their pain and disappointment while reinforcing their commitment to keep trying.

12. Share fears attached to new relationships. (25)

25. Encourage the client to share his/her fears in order to gain self-acceptance (or assign the exercise "Dixie Overcomes Her Fears" or "Building Relationships" from the *Child Psychotherapy Homework Planner* by Jongsma, Peterson, and McInnis).

13. Identify specific positive talents, traits, and accomplishments about self. (26)

26. Assign a self-esteem building exercise from *SEALS+PLUS* (Korb-Khalsa, Azok, and Leutenberg) to help develop self-knowledge, acceptance, and confidence.

14. Verbalize memories of the past that have shaped current identity and emotional reactions. (27)

27. Assign the parents to help the client create a *life book* that chronicles his/her life to this point in order to give a visual perspective and knowledge of his/her history and identity (or assign the exercise "Create a Memory Album" in the *Child*

Psychotherapy Homework Planner by Jongsma, Peterson, and McInnis).

15. Parents acknowledge the client's history and affirm him/her as an individual. (28)

28. Educate the parents on the importance of affirming the client's entire identity (i.e., self, bioparents, adoptive parents), and show them specific ways to reaffirm him/her.

16. Parents spend one-on-one time with the client in active play. (29)

29. Assign the parents to each spend specific time in daily, one-on-one active play with the client.

17. Parents gradually increase the frequency of expressing affection verbally and physically toward the client. (30)

30. Encourage the parents to provide large, genuine, daily doses of positive verbal reinforcement and physical affection. Monitor and encourage the parents to continue this behavior and to identify positive attachment signs when they appear.

18. Report an increased ability to trust, giving examples of trust. (31, 32)

31. Have the client attend an initiative or adventure-based summer camp to build his/her self-esteem, trust in self and others, conflict resolution skills, and relationship skills.

32. Conduct a family session in which the parents, client, and therapist take part in a trust walk. (One person is blindfolded and led around by a guide through a number of tasks. Then roles are reversed and the process is repeated.) The object is to increase the client's awareness of his/her trust issues and to expand his/her sense of trust. Process and repeat at intervals over the course of treatment as a way to measure the client's progress in building trust.

19. Recognize and express angry feelings without becoming emotionally out of control. (33, 34)

33. Train the client in meditation and focused breathing as self-calming techniques to use when tension, anger, or frustration is building (recommend *The Relaxation and Stress Reduction Workbook for Kids* by Shapiro and Sprague).

34. Read and process with the client *Don't Rant and Rave on Wednesdays!* by Moser to assist him/her in finding ways to handle angry feelings in a controlled, effective way.

20. Parents demonstrate firm boundaries on the client's expressions of anger. (23, 35, 36)

23. Suggest to the parents that they read books to increase their understanding and give encouragement in continuing to work with their child (e.g., *The Difficult Child* by Turecki; *The Challenging Child* by Greenspan; *The Kazdin Method for Parenting the Defiant Child* by Kazdin).

35. Help the parents design preventive safety measures (i.e., supervision and environmental controls) if the client's behavior becomes dangerous or frightening.

36. Direct the parents to give constant feedback, structure, and repeated emphasis of expectations to the client in order to reassure him/her that they are firmly in control and that they will not allow his/her intense feelings to get out of hand.

21. Family engages in social/recreational activities together. (37)

37. Encourage the parents to engage the client and family in many "cohesive shared experiences" (see *Handbook for Treatment of Attachment-Trauma Problems in*

Children by James) such as attending church, singing together at home, attending sports events, building and work projects, and helping others.

22. Accept physical contact with family members without withdrawal. (38)

38. Assign the family the homework exercise of 10 minutes of physical touching twice daily for 2 weeks (see *Handbook for Treatment of Attachment-Trauma Problems in Children* by James) to decrease the client's barriers to others. (This can take the form of snuggling with the parent while watching television, feet or shoulder massage, being held in a rocking chair, or physical recreational games.) Process the experience with the therapist at the end of 2 weeks.

23. Parents use respite care to protect selves from burnout. (39, 40)

39. Assist the parents in finding care providers; then encourage and monitor the parents' use of respite care on a scheduled basis to avoid burnout and to keep their energy level high, as well as to build trust with the client through the natural process of leaving and returning.

40. Meet with the parents conjointly on a regular basis to allow them to vent their concerns and frustrations in dealing day in and day out with the client. Also, provide the parents with specific suggestions to handle difficult situations when they feel stuck.

24. Parents respond calmly but firmly to the client's detachment behavior. (41, 42)

41. Educate the parents to understand the psychological meaning and purpose for the client's detachment, and train them to implement appropriate interventions to deal day to day with the behavior in a

therapeutic way (e.g., calmly reflecting on the client's feelings, ignoring negative behavior as much as is reasonably possible, rewarding any approximation of prosocial behavior, practicing unconditional positive regard).

42. Monitor the parents' implementation of interventions for detachment behavior and evaluate the effectiveness of their interventions; assist in making adjustments to interventions so that the client's feelings do not get out of hand.

25. Parents give the client choices and allow him/her to make own decisions. (43)

43. Ask the parents to give the client as many choices as is reasonable and possible to impart a sense of control and empowerment to him/her.

26. Complete a psychotropic medication evaluation and comply with all recommendations. (44)

44. Arrange for the client to have a psychiatric evaluation for medication, and if psychotropic medication is prescribed, monitor the client for compliance, side effects, and overall effectiveness of the medication.

27. Report a completion to the process of mourning losses in life. (45)

45. Assist, guide, and support the client in working through each stage of the grief process (see the Grief/Loss Unresolved chapter in this *Planner*).

—. _____
   _____
—. _____
   _____
—. _____
   _____

—. _____
   _____
—. _____
   _____
—. _____
   _____

DIAGNOSTIC SUGGESTIONS

Using DSM-IV/ICD-9-CM:

Axis I:	313.89	Reactive Attachment Disorder of Infancy and Early Childhood
	314.9	Attention-Deficit/Hyperactivity Disorder NOS
	296.3x	Major Depressive Disorder, Recurrent
	300.4	Dysthymic Disorder
	309.4	Adjustment Disorder With Mixed Disturbance of Emotions and Conduct
	309.81	Posttraumatic Stress Disorder
	300.3	Obsessive-Compulsive Disorder
	313.81	Oppositional Defiant Disorder
	_____	_____
	_____	_____
Axis II:	V71.09	No Diagnosis
	_____	_____
	_____	_____

Using DSM-5/ICD-9-CM/ICD-10-CM:

ICD-9-CM	ICD-10-CM	DSM-5 Disorder, Condition, or Problem
313.89	F94.1	Reactive Attachment Disorder
313.89	F94.2	Disinhibited Social Engagement Disorder
314.01	F90.9	Unspecified Attention-Deficit/Hyperactivity Disorder
314.01	F90.8	Other Specified Attention-Deficit/Hyperactivity Disorder
296.3x	F33.x	Major Depressive Disorder, Recurrent Episode
300.4	F34.1	Persistent Depressive Disorder
309.4	F43.25	Adjustment Disorder, With Mixed Disturbance of Emotions and Conduct
309.81	F43.10	Posttraumatic Stress Disorder
300.3	F42	Obsessive-Compulsive Disorder
313.81	F91.3	Oppositional Defiant Disorder

Note: The ICD-9-CM codes are to be used for coding purposes in the United States through September 30, 2014. ICD-10-CM codes are to be used starting October 1, 2014. Some ICD-9-CM codes are associated with more than one ICD-10-CM and *DSM-5* disorder, condition, or problem. In addition, some ICD-9-CM disorders have been discontinued resulting in multiple ICD-9-CM codes being replaced by one ICD-10-CM code. Some discontinued ICD-9-CM codes are not listed in this table. See *Diagnostic and Statistical Manual of Mental Disorders* (2013) for details.

ATTENTION-DEFICIT/HYPERACTIVITY DISORDER (ADHD)

BEHAVIORAL DEFINITIONS

1. Short attention span; difficulty sustaining attention on a consistent basis.
2. Susceptibility to distraction by extraneous stimuli and internal thoughts.
3. Gives impression that he/she is not listening well.
4. Repeated failure to follow through on instructions or complete school assignments or chores in a timely manner.
5. Poor organizational skills as demonstrated by forgetfulness, inattention to details, and losing things necessary for tasks.
6. Hyperactivity as evidenced by a high energy level, restlessness, difficulty sitting still, or loud or excessive talking.
7. Impulsivity as evidenced by difficulty awaiting turn in group situations, blurting out answers to questions before the questions have been completed, and frequent intrusions into others' personal business.
8. Frequent disruptive, aggressive, or negative attention-seeking behaviors.
9. Tendency to engage in carelessness or potentially dangerous activities.
10. Difficulty accepting responsibility for actions, projecting blame for problems onto others, and failing to learn from experience.
11. Low self-esteem and poor social skills.

—. _____
   _____
—. _____
   _____
—. _____
   _____

LONG-TERM GOALS

1. Sustain attention and concentration for consistently longer periods of time.
2. Increase the frequency of on-task behaviors.
3. Demonstrate marked improvement in impulse control.
4. Parents and/or teachers successfully utilize a reward system, contingency contract, or token economy to reinforce positive behaviors and deter negative behaviors.
5. Parents set firm, consistent limits and maintain appropriate parent-child boundaries.
6. Develop positive social skills to help maintain lasting peer friendships.

—. _____

_____

—. _____

_____

—. _____

_____

SHORT-TERM OBJECTIVES

1. Client and parents describe the nature of the ADHD including specific behaviors, triggers, and consequences. (1, 2, 3)

THERAPEUTIC INTERVENTIONS

1. Actively build the level of trust with the client and parents through consistent eye contact, active listening, unconditional positive regard, and warm acceptance to help increase his/her ability to identify and express feelings.

2. Thoroughly assess the various stimuli (e.g., situations, people, thoughts) that have triggered the client's ADHD behavior; the thoughts, feelings, and actions that have characterized his/her responses; and the consequences of the behavior (e.g., reinforcements, punishments), toward identifying target behaviors, antecedents,

consequences, and the appropriate placement of interventions (e.g., school-based, home-based, peer-based).

3. Rule out alternative conditions/causes of inattention, hyperactivity, and impulsivity (e.g., other behavioral, physical, emotional problems, or normal developmental behavioral).

2. Complete psychological testing to measure the nature and extent of ADHD and/or rule out other possible contributors. (4)

4. Arrange for psychological testing and/or objectives measures to assess the features of ADHD (e.g., the *Disruptive Behavior Disorder Rating Scale*; the *ADHD Rating Scale*); rule out emotional problems that may be contributing to the client's inattentiveness, impulsivity, and hyperactivity; and/or measure the behavior and stimuli associated with its appearance; give feedback to the client and his/her parents regarding the testing results.

3. Provide behavioral, emotional, and attitudinal information toward an assessment of specifiers relevant to a *DSM* diagnosis, the efficacy of treatment, and the nature of the therapy relationship.
(5, 6, 7, 8, 9)

5. Assess the client's level of insight (syntonic versus dystonic) toward the "presenting problems" (e.g., demonstrates good insight into the problematic nature of the "described behavior," agrees with others' concern, and is motivated to work on change; demonstrates ambivalence regarding the "problem described" and is reluctant to address the issue as a concern; or demonstrates resistance regarding acknowledgment of the "problem described," is not concerned, and has no motivation to change).

6. Assess the client for evidence of research-based correlated disorders (e.g., oppositional defiant behavior with ADHD, depression secondary to an anxiety disorder) including vulnerability to suicide, if appropriate (e.g., increased suicide risk when comorbid depression is evident).

7. Assess for any issues of age, gender, or culture that could help explain the client's currently defined "problem behavior" and factors that could offer a better understanding of the client's behavior.

8. Assess for the severity of the level of impairment to the client's functioning to determine appropriate level of care (e.g., the behavior noted creates mild, moderate, severe, or very severe impairment in social, relational, vocational, or occupational endeavors); continuously assess this severity of impairment as well as the efficacy of treatment (e.g., the client no longer demonstrates severe impairment but the presenting problem now is causing mild or moderate impairment).

9. Assess the client's home, school, and community for pathogenic care (e.g., persistent disregard for the child's emotional needs or physical needs, repeated changes in primary caregivers, limited opportunities for stable attachments, persistent harsh punishment or other grossly inept parenting).

▽ 4. Take prescribed medication as directed by the physician. (10, 11)

10. Arrange for the client to have an evaluation by a physician to assess the appropriateness of prescribing ADHD medication. ▽

11. Monitor the client for psychotropic medication prescription compliance, side effects, and effectiveness; consult with the prescribing physician at regular intervals. ▽

▽ 5. Parents and the client demonstrate increased knowledge about ADHD and its treatment. (12, 13, 14, 15)

12. Educate the client's parents and siblings about the symptoms of ADHD. ▽

13. Discuss with parents the various treatment options for ADHD (e.g., behavioral parent training, classroom-based behavioral management programs, peer-based programs, medication), discussing risks and benefits to fully inform the parents' decision-making. ▽

14. Assign the parents readings to increase their knowledge of ADHD (e.g., *Taking Charge of ADHD* by Barkley; *The ADD/ADHD Checklist: A Practical Reference for Parents and Teachers* by Rief; *The Family ADHD Solution: A Scientific Approach to Maximizing Your Child's Attention and Minimizing Parental Stress* by Bertin). ▽

15. Assign the client readings to increase his/her knowledge about ADHD and ways to manage related behavior (e.g., *Putting on the Brakes* by Quinn and Stern; *Sometimes I Drive My Mom Crazy, but I Know She's Crazy about Me* by Shapiro; *The ADHD Workbook for Kids* by Shapiro). ▽

▽ 6. Parents learn and implement Parent Management Training to increase prosocial behavior and decrease disruptive behavior of their child/children. (16, 17, 18, 19, 20)

16. Educate the parents about a Behavioral Parent Management Training approach, explaining how parent and child behavioral interactions can reduce the frequency of impulsive, disruptive, and negative attention-seeking behaviors and increase desired prosocial behavior through prompting and reinforcing positive behaviors as well as use of clear instruction, time-out, and other loss-of-privilege practices for problem behavior (recommend *The Kazdin Method for Parenting the Defiant Child* by Kazdin; *Parenting the Strong-Willed Child* by Forehand and Long; *Living with Children* by Patterson). ▽

17. Teach the parents how to specifically define and identify problem behaviors, identify their reactions to the behavior, determine whether the reaction encourages or discourages the behavior, and generate alternatives to the problem behavior. ▽

18. Teach parents about the possible functions of the ADHD behavior (e.g., avoidance, attention, to gain a desire object/activity, regulate sensory stimulation); how to test which function(s) is being served by the behavior, and how to use parent training methods to manage the behavior. ▽

19. Assign the parents home exercises in which they implement and record results of implementation exercises

(or assign "Clear Rules, Positive Reinforcement, Appropriate Consequences" in the *Adolescent Psychotherapy Homework Planner* by Jongsma, Peterson, and McInnis); review in session, providing corrective feedback toward improved, appropriate, and consistent use of skills.▽

20. Refer parents to a Parent Management Training Course.▽

▽ 7. Parents work with therapist and school to implement a behavioral classroom management program. (21, 22)

21. Consult with the client's teachers to implement strategies to improve school performance, such as sitting in the front row during class, using a prearranged signal to redirect the client back to task, scheduling breaks from tasks, providing frequent feedback, calling on the client often, arranging for a listening buddy, and implementing a daily behavioral report card.▽

22. Consult with parents and pertinent school personnel to implement a Behavioral Classroom Management Intervention (see *ADHD in the Schools* by DuPaul and Stoner) that rewards/reinforces appropriate behavior at school and at home, uses time-out for undesirable behavior, and uses a daily behavioral report card to monitor progress; (or employ the "Getting It Done" exercise in the *Child Psychotherapy Homework Planner* by Jongsma, Peterson, and McInnis).▽

▽ 8. Complete a peer-based treatment program focused on improving social interaction skills. (23)

23. Conduct or refer the client to a Behavioral Peer Intervention (e.g., Summer Treatment Program or after school/weekend

version) that involves brief social skills training, followed by coached group play in recreational activities guided by contingency management systems (e.g., point system, time-out) and utilizing objective observations, frequency counts, and adult ratings of social behaviors as outcome measures (see *Children's Summer Treatment Program Manual* by Pelham, Greiner, and Gnagy). ▽

9. Parents develop and utilize an organized system to keep track of the client's school assignments, chores, and household responsibilities. (24, 25)

24. Assist the parents in developing and implementing an organizational system to increase the client's on-task behaviors and completion of school assignments, chores, or household responsibilities through the use of calendars, charts, notebooks, and class syllabi (see *Homework Success for Children With ADHD: A Family-School Intervention Program* by Power, Karustis, and Habboushe).

25. Assist the parents in developing a routine schedule to increase the client's compliance with school, household, or work-related responsibilities.

10. Utilize effective study and test-taking skills on a regular basis to improve academic performance. (26, 27, 28)

26. Teach the client more effective study skills (e.g., clearing away distractions, studying in quiet places, and scheduling breaks in studying).

27. Teach the client more effective test-taking strategies (e.g., reviewing material regularly, reading directions twice, and rechecking work).

28. Assign the client to read *13 Steps to Better Grades* by Silverman to improve organizational and study skills; process the material read and identify ways to implement new practices.

11. Increase frequency of completion of school assignments, chores, and household responsibilities. (29)

29. Assist the parents in developing a routine schedule to increase the client's compliance with school, household, or work-related responsibilities (or assign "Establish a Homework Routine" in the *Child Psychotherapy Homework Planner* by Jongsma, Peterson, and McInnis).

12. Delay instant gratification in favor of achieving meaningful long-term goals. (30, 31)

30. Teach the client mediational and self-control strategies (e.g., "stop, look, listen, and think") to delay the need for instant gratification and inhibit impulses to achieve more meaningful, longer-term goals.

31. Assist the parents in increasing structure to help the client learn to delay gratification for longer-term goals (e.g., completing homework or chores before playing).

13. Learn and implement social skills to reduce anxiety and build confidence in social interactions. (32, 33)

32. Use instruction, modeling, and role-playing to build the client's general and developmentally appropriate social and/or communication skills.

33. Assign the client to read about general social and/or communication skills in books or treatment manuals on building social skills (e.g., or assign the "Social Skills Exercise" or "Greeting Peers" in the *Child Psychotherapy Homework Planner* by Jongsma, Peterson, and McInnis).

14. Identify and implement effective problem-solving strategies. (34, 35)

34. Teach older clients effective problem-solving skills through identifying the problem, brainstorming alternative solution options, listing pros and cons of each solution option, selecting an option, implementing a course of action, and evaluating the outcome (or assign the "Problem-Solving Exercise" in the *Child Psychotherapy Homework Planner* by Jongsma, Peterson, and McInnis).

35. Utilize role-playing and modeling to teach the older child how to implement effective problem-solving techniques in his/her daily life (or assign "Stop, Think, and Act" in the *Child Psychotherapy Homework Planner* by Jongsma, Peterson, and McInnis, or use the therapeutic game, Stop, Relax, and Think by Bridges [available from Childswork/Childsplay]).

15. Increase the frequency of positive interactions with parents. (36, 37, 38)

36. Explore for periods of time when the client demonstrated good impulse control and engaged in fewer disruptive behaviors; process his/her responses and reinforce positive coping mechanisms that he/she used to deter impulsive or disruptive behaviors.

37. Instruct the parents to observe and record three to five positive behaviors by the client in between therapy sessions; reinforce positive behaviors and encourage him/her to continue to exhibit these behaviors.

38. Encourage the parents to spend 10 to 15 minutes daily of

one-on-one time with the client to create a closer parent-child bond; allow the client to take the lead in selecting the activity or task.

16. Increase the frequency of socially appropriate behaviors with siblings and peers. (39, 40)

39. Give homework assignments where the client identifies 5 to 10 strengths or interests; review the list in the following session and encourage him/her to utilize strengths or interests to establish friendships (or assign "Show Your Strengths" exercise in the *Child Psychotherapy Homework Planner* by Jongsma, Peterson, and McInnis).

40. Assign the client the task of showing empathy, kindness, or sensitivity to the needs of others (e.g., allowing sibling or peer to take first turn in a video game, helping with a school fundraiser).

17. Increase verbalizations of acceptance of responsibility for misbehavior. (41, 42)

41. Firmly confront the client's impulsive behaviors, pointing out consequences for him/her and others.

42. Confront statements in which the client blames others for his/her annoying or impulsive behaviors and fails to accept responsibility for his/her actions.

18. Identify stressors or painful emotions that an trigger increase in hyperactivity and impulsivity. (43, 44, 45)

43. Explore and identify stressful events or factors that contribute to an increase in impulsivity, hyperactivity, and distractibility.

44. Explore possible stressors, roadblocks, or hurdles that might cause impulsive and acting-out behaviors to increase in the future.

45. Identify coping strategies (e.g., "stop, look, listen, and think,"

19. Parents and the client regularly attend and actively participate in group therapy. (46)

20. Complete a course of biofeedback to improve concentration and attention. (47)

21. Identify and list constructive ways to utilize energy. (48)

guided imagery, utilizing "I messages" to communicate needs) that the client and his/her family can use to cope with or overcome stressors, roadblocks, or hurdles.

46. Encourage the client's parents to participate in an ADHD support group.

47. Conduct or refer the client to a trial of EEG biofeedback (neurotherapy) for ADHD.

48. Give a homework assignment where the client lists the positive and negative aspects of his/her high energy level; review the list in the following session and encourage him/her to channel energy into healthy physical outlets and positive social activities.

___ . _____   ___ . _____
_____   _____
___ . _____   ___ . _____
_____   _____
___ . _____   ___ . _____
_____   _____

DIAGNOSTIC SUGGESTIONS

Using DSM-IV/ICD-9-CM:

Axis I:	314.01	Attention-Deficit/Hyperactivity Disorder, Combined Type
	314.00	Attention-Deficit/Hyperactivity Disorder, Predominantly Inattentive Type
	314.01	Attention-Deficit/Hyperactivity Disorder, Predominantly Hyperactive-Impulsive Type
	314.9	Attention-Deficit/Hyperactivity Disorder NOS
	312.81	Conduct Disorder, Childhood-Onset Type

312.82	Conduct Disorder, Adolescent-Onset Type	
313.81	Oppositional Defiant Disorder	
312.9	Disruptive Behavior Disorder NOS	
296.xx	Bipolar I Disorder	
_____	_____	
_____	_____	

Axis II:	V71.09	No Diagnosis
	_____	_____
	_____	_____

Using DSM-5/ICD-9-CM/ICD-10-CM:

ICD-9-CM	ICD-10-CM	*DSM-5* Disorder, Condition, or Problem
314.01	F90.2	Attention-Deficit/Hyperactivity Disorder, Combined Presentation
314.00	F90.0	Attention-Deficit/Hyperactivity Disorder, Predominately Inattentive Presentation
314.01	F90.1	Attention-Deficit/Hyperactivity Disorder, Predominately Hyperactive /Impulsive Presentation
314.01	F90.9	Unspecified Attention-Deficit/Hyperactivity Disorder
314.01	F90.8	Other Specified Attention-Deficit/Hyperactivity Disorder
312.81	F91.1	Conduct Disorder, Childhood-Onset Type
313.81	F91.3	Oppositional Defiant Disorder
312.9	F91.9	Unspecified Disruptive, Impulse Control, and Conduct Disorder
312.89	F91.8	Other Specified Disruptive, Impulse Control, and Conduct Disorder

Note: The ICD-9-CM codes are to be used for coding purposes in the United States through September 30, 2014. ICD-10-CM codes are to be used starting October 1, 2014. Some ICD-9-CM codes are associated with more than one ICD-10-CM and *DSM-5* disorder, condition, or problem. In addition, some ICD-9-CM disorders have been discontinued resulting in multiple ICD-9-CM codes being replaced by one ICD-10-CM code. Some discontinued ICD-9-CM codes are not listed in this table. See *Diagnostic and Statistical Manual of Mental Disorders* (American Psychiatric Association, 2013) for details.

▼ Indicates that the Objective/Intervention is consistent with those found in evidence-based treatments.

AUTISM SPECTRUM DISORDER

BEHAVIORAL DEFINITIONS

1. Shows a pervasive lack of interest in or responsiveness to other people.
2. Demonstrates a chronic failure to develop social relationships appropriate to the developmental level.
3. Lacks spontaneity and emotional or social reciprocity.
4. Exhibits a significant delay in or total lack of spoken language development.
5. Is impaired in sustaining or initiating conversation.
6. Demonstrates oddities in speech and language such as echolalia, pronominal reversal, or metaphorical language.
7. Rigidly adheres to repetition of nonfunctional rituals or stereotyped motor mannerisms.
8. Shows persistent preoccupation with objects, parts of objects, or restricted areas of interest.
9. Exhibits a marked impairment or extreme variability in intellectual and cognitive functioning.
10. Demonstrates extreme resistance or overreaction to minor changes in routines or environment.
11. Exhibits emotional constriction or blunted affect.
12. Demonstrates a recurrent pattern of self-abusive behaviors (e.g., head banging, biting, burning himself/herself).

—. _____
_____

—. _____
_____

—. _____
_____

LONG-TERM GOALS

1. Develop basic language skills and the ability to communicate simply with others.
2. Establish and maintain a basic emotional bond with primary attachment figures.
3. Family members develop acceptance of the client's overall capabilities and place realistic expectations on his/her behavior.
4. Parents become experts in their child's strengths and limitations, facilitating the child's ability to accomplish her/his goals.
5. Engage in reciprocal and cooperative interactions with others on a regular basis.
6. Stabilize mood and tolerate changes in routine or environment.
7. Eliminate all self-abusive behaviors.
8. Attain and maintain the highest realistic level of independent functioning.

—. _____
   _____
—. _____
   _____
—. _____
   _____

SHORT-TERM OBJECTIVES	THERAPEUTIC INTERVENTIONS
1. Participate in a thorough diagnostic evaluation, following recommendations for additional assessment(s) if needed. (1, 2)	1. Actively build the level of trust with the client and parents through consistent eye contact, active listening, attention and interest, unconditional positive regard, warm acceptance, and genuineness to facilitate increased communication.
	2. Conduct an initial clinical interview with the child and parents assessing the history of the autism and the possible need for additional assessment(s).
2. Cooperate with an intellectual and cognitive evaluation. (3)	3. Conduct or arrange for an intellectual and cognitive

assessment to identify the client's strengths and weaknesses with attention to any school requirements; provide feedback to the parents and inform the Individualized Educational Planning Committee (IEPC) with results, if indicated.

3. Cooperate with a vision/hearing examination. (4)

4. Refer the client in early childhood years for vision and/or hearing examination to rule out vision or hearing problems that may be interfering with his/her social and speech/language development.

4. Attend a medical evaluation. (5)

5. Refer the client for comprehensive medical examination to rule out health problems or general medical conditions that may be accounting for speech/language/behavioral problems or need to be addressed as part of the overall treatment plan.

5. Participate in a speech/ language evaluation and attend speech and language therapy sessions, if advised. (6)

6. Refer the client for speech/ language evaluation; consult with speech/language pathologist about evaluation findings; if indicated, refer the client to a speech/language pathologist for ongoing services to improve his/her speech and language abilities.

6. Cooperate with a neurological evaluation. (7)

7. Arrange for a neurological evaluation of the client to rule out neurological conditions that possibly contribute to the client's presenting problems.

7. Provide behavioral, emotional, and attitudinal information toward an assessment of specifiers relevant to a *DSM* diagnosis, the efficacy of treatment, and the nature

8. Assess the client's level of insight (syntonic versus dystonic) toward the "presenting problems" (e.g., demonstrates good insight into the problematic nature of the

of the therapy relationship. (8, 9, 10, 11, 12)

"described behavior," agrees with others' concern, and is motivated to work on change; demonstrates ambivalence regarding the "problem described" and is reluctant to address the issue as a concern; or demonstrates resistance regarding acknowledgment of the "problem described," is not concerned, and has no motivation to change).

9. Assess the client for evidence of research-based correlated disorders (e.g., oppositional defiant behavior with ADHD, depression secondary to an anxiety disorder) including vulnerability to suicide, if appropriate (e.g., increased suicide risk when comorbid depression is evident).

10. Assess for any issues of age, gender, or culture that could help explain the client's currently defined "problem behavior" and factors that could offer a better understanding of the client's behavior.

11. Assess for the severity of the level of impairment to the client's functioning to determine appropriate level of care (e.g., the behavior noted creates mild, moderate, severe, or very severe impairment in social, relational, vocational, or occupational endeavors); continuously assess this severity of impairment as well as the efficacy of treatment (e.g., the client no longer demonstrates severe impairment but the presenting problem now is

causing mild or moderate impairment).

12. Assess the client's home, school, and community for pathogenic care (e.g., persistent disregard for the child's emotional needs or physical needs, repeated changes in primary caregivers, limited opportunities for stable attachments, persistent harsh punishment or other grossly inept parenting).

▽ 8. Participate in a psychiatric evaluation regarding the need for psychotropic medication. (13)

13. Arrange for psychiatric evaluation of the client to assess the need for psychotropic medication. ▽

▽ 9. Parents verbalize increased knowledge and understanding of autism spectrum disorders. (14, 15)

14. Supportively educate the client's parents and family members about autism spectrum disorders, including the nature of the disorder, treatment options, the challenges involved in caring for the child, and supports; allow parents to share their thoughts and feelings about their child having autism (or assign "Initial Reaction to Diagnosis of Autism" in the *Child Psychotherapy Homework Planner* by Jongsma, Peterson, and McInnis). ▽

15. Assign the parents to view the videotape, *Straight Talk About Autism With Parents and Kids* (available from the A.D.D. Warehouse) to increase their knowledge about autism.

10. Parents, child, and school personnel comply with an intensive, in-home, behaviorally-based therapy program.

16. Consult with parents, school officials, and mental health professionals about establishing intensive, in-home, behaviorally-based therapy as early as possible after a diagnosis is made; if necessary, refer the parents to a

▽ 11. Parents work with the therapist toward ensuring coordination of care across the child's treatment providers. (17)

▽ 12. Comply fully with the recommendations offered by the assessment(s) and individualized educational planning committee (IEPC). (18, 19)

▽ 13. Participate in treatment based on the Lovaas method. (20)

specialist in providing this intensive treatment.

17. Maintain ongoing communication with the child's primary care physician(s) and other involved providers (e.g., school-based providers, audiologists, neurologists, home-based therapists/tutors) to assure that the child's current needs are being met in all areas: medical, psychological, and educational; provide information as needed that will assist the primary physician(s) in determining when referral to other health professionals is needed, and follow up with other professionals to assure that care is coordinated.▽

18. Attend an IEPC review to establish the client's eligibility for special education services, to update and revise educational interventions, and to establish new behavioral and educational goals.▽

19. Consult with the parents, teachers, and other appropriate school officials about designing effective learning programs, classroom assignments, or interventions that build on the client's strengths and compensate for weaknesses.▽

20. Conduct or refer to a provider trained in the Lovaas Model of Applied Behavior Analysis for autism—an intensive, comprehensive program that uses parent training, positive reinforcement, shaping and chaining, functional behavior assessment, and peer integration to develop skills (e.g., communication, speech and language,

academic, self-help, and play), generalize their use across various settings, and eventually integrate the child into the school environment (see *Teaching Individuals with Developmental Delays* by Lovass). ▽

▽ 14. Increase the frequency of appropriate, self-initiated verbalizations toward the therapist, family members, and others. (21, 22, 23)

21. Teach the parents skills consistent with Pivotal Response Training or PRT (see *Pivotal Response Treatments for Autism* and *The PRT Pocket Guide* by Koegel and Koegel) in which they are taught how to use behavioral management skills to increase their child's motivation to respond and to self-initiate social interactions in the context of play using natural reinforcers and child-selected stimulus materials; provide feedback toward improvement. ▽

22. Train the parents to use the Power Card Strategy to help increase the child's motivation by incorporating the child's special interests in various skill-building activities (see *Power Cards* by Gagnon). ▽

23. Have the parents and client practice PRT and Power Card techniques at a high frequency throughout the day and across multiple settings until parents reach an 80% correct-use criterion. ▽

▽ 15. Decrease the frequency of unwanted behavior and replace with appropriate, functional behavior. (24, 25, 26, 27)

24. Conduct a functional analysis to determine the function(s) of unwanted behavior (e.g., off-task, self-stimulation) followed by the development of a positive plan for teaching appropriate, functional (e.g., communicative) skills that serve as replacement

behaviors for the unwanted behavior (or assign "Reaction to Change and Excessive Stimulation" in the *Child Psychotherapy Homework Planner* by Jongsma, Peterson, and McInnis). ▽

25. Teach the parents behavior management techniques (e.g., interruption of unwanted behavior, prompting wanted behavior, reinforcement of alternative behaviors, reinforcement schedules, use of ignoring off-task behavior to promote compliance during joint action interactions). ▽

26. Assess and train tailored social skills, including parents in the training, and then transferring the training role to the parents to conduct in various settings to facilitate generalization (see *Social Skills Training* by Baker). ▽

27. Assist parents in arranging meaningful (to the child as well as others), age-appropriate learning activities in which behavioral management techniques can be practiced while the child learns social/communication skills that are functional in multiple settings; use naturalistic teaching methods as well as didactic, massed trial, adult-directed, one-on-one teaching approaches that begin with child choice and use intrinsic reinforcers to foster child motivation and generalization. ▽

▽ 16. Decrease the frequency and severity of temper outbursts and aggressive behaviors. (28, 29, 30)

28. Teach the parents to apply behavior management techniques (e.g., prompting

behavior, reinforcement and reinforcement schedules, use of ignoring for off-task behavior) to decrease the client's temper outbursts and self-abusive behaviors (or assign "Clear Rules, Positive Reinforcement, Appropriate Consequences" in the *Adolescent Psychotherapy Homework Planner* by Jongsma, Peterson, and McInnis). ▽

29. Design a token economy or other reward system for use in the home, classroom, or residential program to improve the client's social skills, anger/aggression management, impulse control, and speech/language abilities. ▽

30. Develop a contingency contract to improve the client's social skills and impulse control. ▽

▽ 17. Decrease the frequency and severity of self-abusive behaviors. (31)

31. Teach the parents to apply behavior management techniques (e.g., prompting behavior, reinforcement and reinforcement schedules, use of ignoring for off-task behavior) to decrease the client's self-abusive behaviors such as scratching or hitting self (or assign "Clear Rules, Positive Reinforcement, Appropriate Consequences" in the *Adolescent Psychotherapy Homework Planner* by Jongsma, Peterson, and McInnis). ▽

▽ 18. Demonstrate essential self-care and independent living skills. (32, 33, 34)

32. Counsel the parents about teaching the client essential self-care skills (e.g., combing hair, bathing, brushing teeth). ▽

33. Use modeling and operant techniques (e.g., shaping) to help the client develop self-help skills

(e.g., dressing self, making bed, fixing sandwich) and improve personal hygiene.▽

34. Encourage the parents to use the "Activities of Daily Living Program" in the *Child Psychotherapy Homework Planner* (Jongsma, Peterson, and McInnis) to improve the client's personal hygiene and self-help skills.

▽ 19. Increase the frequency of positive interactions with parents and siblings. (35, 36, 37)

35. Encourage the family members to include the client in structured work or play activities daily.▽

36. Instruct the parents to sing songs (e.g., nursery rhymes, lullabies, popular hits, songs related to the client's interests) with the client to help establish a closer parent-child bond and increase verbalizations in home environment.

37. Encourage detached parents to increase their involvement in the client's daily life, leisure activities, or schoolwork.

▽ 20. Parents and siblings report feeling a closer bond with the client. (38, 39, 40)

38. Conduct family therapy sessions to provide the parents and siblings with the opportunity to share and work through their feelings pertaining to the client's autism spectrum disorder.▽

39. To facilitate a closer parent-child bond, use filial play therapy approaches (i.e., parental involvement in session) with a higher-functioning client to increase the parents' awareness of the client's thoughts, feelings, and needs.

40. Assign the client and his/her parents tasks (e.g., swimming,

riding a bike) that will help build trust and mutual dependence.

⛛ 21. Increase the frequency of positive interactions with peers. (41)

41. Consult with the client's parents and teachers about increasing the frequency of his/her social contacts with peers to promote social growth and skill development (e.g., play dates, working with student aide in class, attending Sunday school, participating in Special Olympics, refer to summer camp). ⛛

⛛ 22. Expand the number and type of social activities with others. (42)

42. Facilitate the generalization of new social skills by arranging and facilitating their use in a variety of different activities and settings as well as with multiple adults and children throughout the day. ⛛

⛛ 23. Parents monitor the ongoing progress of their child, working with the treatment team to inform continuing treatment with the data. (43)

43. Teach the parents how to monitor the child's progress and incorporate the data into ongoing clinical decision making; include the frequency and severity of unwanted behaviors, disruptions in sleep and eating, and measures reflecting the acquisition and generalization of new skills. ⛛

⛛ 24. Parents and family members identify and use supportive resources for managing the stress of raising a child with autism. (44, 45, 46, 47)

44. Provide nonjudgmental and empathic support to the parents and siblings; assist parents in balancing the needs of each member of the family toward increasing family well-being (recommend the parents read *Parenting Your Child with Autism: Practical Solutions, Strategies, and Advice for Helping Your Family* by Sastry and Aguirre; or *Helping Your Child with Autism Spectrum Disorder: A Step-by-Step Workbook for Families* by

Lockshin, Gillis, and Romanczyk).▽

45. Assist the parents and family members in managing relevant stressors through supportive stress management interventions (e.g., calming, cognitive, time management, and conflict resolution skills training) and facilitating use of social support (e.g., parent support groups, making time with friends).▽

46. Direct the parents to join an autism group or organization (e.g., Autism Society of America) to expand their social network, to gain additional knowledge of the disorder, and to give them support and encouragement.▽

47. Refer the parents to, and encourage them to use, respite care on a periodic basis.▽

25. Identify and express basic emotions. (48, 49)

48. Use art therapy (e.g., drawing, painting, sculpting) with the higher-functioning client to help him/her express basic needs or emotions and facilitate a closer relationship with the parents, caretakers, and therapist.

49. Use a Feelings Poster (available from Childswork/Childsplay) to help the higher functioning client identify and express basic emotions.

—. _____   —. _____
   _____   _____
—. _____   —. _____
   _____   _____
—. _____   —. _____
   _____   _____

DIAGNOSTIC SUGGESTIONS

Using DSM-IV/ICD-9-CM:

Axis I:	299.00	Autistic Disorder
	299.80	Pervasive Developmental Disorder NOS
	299.80	Rett's Disorder
	299.10	Childhood Disintegrative Disorder
	299.80	Asperger's Disorder
	313.89	Reactive Attachment Disorder of Infancy or Early Childhood
	307.3	Stereotypic Movement Disorder
	295.xx	Schizophrenia
	_____	_____
	_____	_____
Axis II:	317	Mild Mental Retardation
	319	Mental Retardation, Severity Unspecified
	V71.09	No Diagnosis
	_____	_____
	_____	_____

Using DSM-5/ICD-9-CM/ICD-10-CM:

ICD-9-CM	ICD-10-CM	*DSM-5* Disorder, Condition, or Problem
299.00	F84	Autistic Spectrum Disorder
315.9	F89	Unspecified Neurodevelopmental Disorder
315.8	F88	Other Specified Neurodevelopmental Disorder
313.89	F94.1	Reactive Attachment Disorder
307.3	F98.4	Stereotypic Movement Disorder
295.xx	F20.9	Schizophrenia
317	F70	Intellectual Disability, Mild
319	F79	Unspecified Intellectual Disability

Note: The ICD-9-CM codes are to be used for coding purposes in the United States through September 30, 2014. ICD-10-CM codes are to be used starting October 1, 2014. Some ICD-9-CM codes are associated with more than one ICD-10-CM and *DSM-5* disorder, condition, or problem. In addition, some ICD-9-CM disorders have been discontinued resulting in multiple ICD-9-CM codes being replaced by one ICD-10-CM code. Some discontinued ICD-9-CM codes are not listed in this table. See *Diagnostic and Statistical Manual of Mental Disorders* (2013) for details.

▽ Indicates that the Objective/Intervention is consistent with those found in evidence-based treatments.

BLENDED FAMILY

BEHAVIORAL DEFINITIONS

1. Children from a previous union are united into a single family unit, resulting in interpersonal conflict, anger, and frustration.
2. Resistance and defiance expressed toward the new stepparent.
3. Open conflict evident between siblings from different parents now residing in the same family system.
4. A child makes verbal threats to one biological parent of reporting abuse if not allowed to go to live with the other parent.
5. Interference exhibited by former spouse in the daily life of the new family system.
6. Anxiety and concern expressed by both new partners regarding bringing their two families together.
7. No clear lines of communication established or responsibilities assigned within the blended family, making for confusion, frustration, and unhappiness.

—. _____
   _____
—. _____
   _____
—. _____
   _____

LONG-TERM GOALS

1. Achieve a reasonable level of family connectedness and harmony whereby members support, help, and are concerned for each other.
2. Become an integrated, blended family system that is functional and bonded to each other.

3. Accept stepparent and/or stepsiblings and treat them with respect, kindness, and cordiality.
4. Establish a new family identity in which each member feels he/she belongs and is valued.
5. Accept the new blended family system as not inferior to the nuclear family, just different.
6. Establish a strong bond between the couple as a parenting team that is free from triangulation and able to stabilize the family.

—. _____
   _____
   _____

—. _____
   _____
   _____

—. _____
   _____

SHORT-TERM OBJECTIVES

1. Each family member openly shares thoughts and feelings regarding the blended family. (1, 2, 3)

THERAPEUTIC INTERVENTIONS

1. Within family therapy sessions, actively build the level of trust with each family member through consistent eye contact, active listening, unconditional positive regard, and acceptance to allow each to identify and express openly his/her thoughts and feelings regarding the blended family.

2. In a family session, use a set of markers and a large sheet of drawing paper for the following exercise: The therapist begins a drawing by making a scribble line on the paper, then each family member adds to the line using a colored marker of his/her choice. When the drawing is complete, the family can be given the choice to either each interpret the drawing or to develop a mutual story based on

the drawing (see "Scribble Art" by Lowe).

3. Conduct individual, family, sibling, and/or marital sessions to explore and assess the issues of loss, conflict negotiation, parenting, stepfamily psychoeducation, joining, rituals, and relationship building in the newly developing stepfamily (or assign the client to complete "Blended Family Sentence Completion" from the *Child Psychotherapy Homework Planner* by Jongsma, Peterson, and McInnis).

2. Provide behavioral, emotional, and attitudinal information toward an assessment of specifiers relevant to a *DSM* diagnosis, the efficacy of treatment, and the nature of the therapy relationship. (4, 5, 6, 7, 8)

4. Assess the client's level of insight (syntonic versus dystonic) toward the "presenting problems" (e.g., demonstrates good insight into the problematic nature of the "described behavior," agrees with others' concern, and is motivated to work on change; demonstrates ambivalence regarding the "problem described" and is reluctant to address the issue as a concern; or demonstrates resistance regarding acknowledgment of the "problem described," is not concerned, and has no motivation to change).

5. Assess the client for evidence of research-based correlated disorders (e.g., oppositional defiant behavior with ADHD, depression secondary to an anxiety disorder) including vulnerability to suicide, if appropriate (e.g., increased suicide risk when comorbid depression is evident).

6. Assess for any issues of age, gender, or culture that could help explain the client's currently defined "problem behavior" and factors that could offer a better understanding of the client's behavior.

7. Assess for the severity of the level of impairment to the client's functioning to determine appropriate level of care (e.g., the behavior noted creates mild, moderate, severe, or very severe impairment in social, relational, vocational, or occupational endeavors); continuously assess this severity of impairment as well as the efficacy of treatment (e.g., the client no longer demonstrates severe impairment but the presenting problem now is causing mild or moderate impairment).

8. Assess the client's home, school, and community for pathogenic care (e.g., persistent disregard for the child's emotional needs or physical needs, repeated changes in primary caregivers, limited opportunities for stable attachments, persistent harsh punishment or other grossly inept parenting).

3. Participate in play therapy sessions to express thoughts and feelings about the family. (9, 10, 11)

9. Use child-centered play therapy approaches (e.g., providing unconditional positive regard, reflecting feelings in a nonjudgmental manner, displaying trust in the child's capacity to resolve issues) to assist the client in adjusting to changes, grieving losses, and cooperating with the new stepfamily.

10. Conduct individual play therapy sessions to provide the client an opportunity to express feelings about losses and changes in his/her family life.

11. Seize opportunities in play therapy (especially when the client is playing with groups of animals, army figures, dollhouse, puppets), as well as in sibling and family sessions, to emphasize the need for everyone within the family to respect and cooperate with each other.

4. Family members verbalize realistic expectations and rejection of myths regarding stepfamilies. (12, 13, 14)

12. In a family session, ask the members to list their expectations for the new family; ask the members to share and process their lists with the whole family and the therapist.

13. Remind family members that instant love of new family members is a myth. It is unrealistic to expect children to immediately like (much less love) the partner who is serving in the new-parent role.

14. Help family members accept the position that siblings from different biological families need not like or love one another, but that they should be mutually respectful and kind.

5. Identify losses/changes in each of their lives. (15, 16)

15. Instruct the family to read *Changing Families: An Interactive Guide for Kids and Grownups* by Fassler, Lash, and Ives; after reading is finished, help them identify the changes within their family and ways to adjust and thrive.

16. Assign sibling members in a session to complete a list of

losses and changes that each has experienced over the last year and then for all years. Give empathic confirmation while they share the list in the session, and help them to see the similarities of their experiences to those of their siblings.

6. Family members demonstrate increased skills in recognizing and expressing feelings. (17, 18, 19)

17. Have family or siblings play The Ungame (available from The Ungame Company) or The Talking, Feeling, Doing Game (available from Childswork/ Childsplay) to promote each family member's awareness of self and his/her feelings.

18. Using feelings charts, a feelings felt board, or a feelings card, educate the family on identifying, labeling, and expressing feelings appropriately.

19. In a family session, help the family to practice identifying and expressing feelings by doing a feelings exercise (e.g., "I feel sad when _____," "I feel excited when _____"). The therapist should affirm and acknowledge each member as he/she shares during the exercise.

7. Family members verbalize expanded knowledge of stepfamilies. (20, 21)

20. Assign parents or teens to read material to expand their knowledge of stepfamilies and their development (e.g., *Stepfamily Realities* by Newman; *How to Win as a Stepfamily* by Visher and Visher; *Stepfamilies Stepping Ahead* by Burt); process key concepts that they gathered from the reading.

21. Refer the parents to the Stepfamily Association of

America (1-800-735-0329) to obtain additional information and resources on stepfamilies.

8. Family members demonstrate increased negotiating skills. (22, 23, 24)

22. Conduct the following exercise in a sibling session: Place several phone books and/or Sunday papers in the center of a room and instruct the clients to tear the paper into small pieces and throw the shredded paper into the air. The only two rules are that the paper must be thrown *up* in the air, not *at* anyone, and that the participants must clean up afterward. Process the experience around releasing energy and emotion. Give positive feedback for following through and cooperating in cleaning up (see *Tearing Paper* by Daves).

23. Train family members in building problem-solving skills (e.g., identifying and pinpointing problems, brainstorming solutions, evaluating pros and cons, compromising, agreeing on a solution, making an implementation plan), and have them practice these skills on issues that present in family sessions (or assign "Problem-Solving Exercise" in the *Child Psychotherapy Homework Planner* by Jongsma, Peterson, and McInnis).

24. Assign siblings to write a list of their conflicts and suggest solutions (or assign the exercise "Negotiating a Peace Treaty" from the *Child Psychotherapy Homework Planner* by Jongsma, Peterson, and McInnis).

9. Family members report a reduced level of tension between all members. (25, 26, 27)

25. Inject humor whenever appropriate in a family or sibling session to decrease tensions/conflict and to model balance and perspective. Give positive feedback to members who create appropriate humor.

26. Hold a family sibling session in which each child focuses on listing and developing an appreciation of each sibling's differences/uniqueness (or assign the exercise "Cloning the Perfect Sibling" from the *Adolescent Psychotherapy Homework Planner* by Jongsma, Peterson, and McInnis; or "Interviewing My New Family Member" from the *Child Psychotherapy Homework Planner* by Jongsma, Peterson, and McInnis).

27. In a brief, solution-focused intervention, reframe or normalize the conflictual situation to show the clients that it's a stage the family needs to get through. Identify the next stage as the coming-together stage, and talk about when they might be ready to move there and how they could begin (see *A Guide to Possibility Land* by O'Hanlon and Beadle).

10. Family members report increased trust of each other. (28, 29)

28. Ask the client to express his/her feelings about the bioparent's new partner (spouse) and how these feelings could be changed to be more positive (or assign "Thoughts and Feelings About Parent's Live-In Partner" from the *Child Psychotherapy Homework Planner* by Jongsma, Peterson, and McInnis).

29. In a family session, read Dr. Seuss's *The Sneetches and Other Stories* to show members the folly of top dog, wunderdog, one-upmanship, and insider-outsider attitudes.

11. Each parent takes the primary role of disciplining own children. (30)

30. Encourage each parent to take the primary role in disciplining his/her own children, and have each refrain from all negative references to former spouses.

12. Parents attend a stepparenting didactic group to increase parenting skills. (31)

31. Refer the parents to a parenting group for stepparents.

13. Family members attend weekly family meetings in the home to express feelings. (32)

32. Assist the parents in implementing a once-a-week family meeting in which issues can be raised and resolved and members are encouraged to share their thoughts, complaints, and compliments.

14. Parents create and institute new family rituals. (33, 34, 35)

33. Assist the parents in creating and implementing daily rituals (e.g., mealtimes, bedtime stories, household chores, time alone with parents, times together) in order to give structure and connection to the system.

34. Conduct a family session in which rituals from both former families are examined. Then encourage the family to retain the rituals that are appropriate and will work in the new system and combine them with new rituals.

35. Give the family the assignment to create birthday rituals for the new blended unit.

15. Parents identify and eliminate triangulation within the system. (36)

36. Educate the parents on patterns of interactions within families by creating a genogram that denotes

the family's patterns of interactions and focuses on the pattern of triangulation and its dysfunctional aspects.

16. Parents report a strengthening of their marital bond. (37, 38, 39)

37. Refer the couple to skills-based marital therapy based on strengthening avenues of responsibilities, communication, and conflict resolution (see *Fighting for Your Marriage* by Markman, Stanley, and Blumberg).

38. Work with the dyad in conjoint sessions to deal with issues of having time away alone, privacy, and individual space; develop specific ways for these things to occur regularly.

39. Hold conjoint session(s) with the couple to process the issue of showing affection toward each other. Help the couple to develop appropriate boundaries and ways of showing affection that do not give rise to unnecessary anger in their children.

17. Family members report an increased sense of loyalty and connectedness. (40, 41, 42)

40. Conduct family sessions in which a genogram is developed for the entire new family system to show how everyone is interconnected.

41. Refer the family to an initiatives camp weekend to increase cooperation, conflict resolution, and sense of trust. Process the experiences with the family in the next family session.

42. In a family session, assign the family to design on poster board a coat of arms for the family that reflects where they came from and where they are now. Process this experience when completed

and have the family display it in their home.

18. Report the development of a bond between each family member. (43, 44)

43. Assist the parents in scheduling one-on-one time with each child and stepchild in order to give them undivided attention and to build/maintain relationships.

44. Emphasize and model in family, sibling, and couple sessions the need for the family to build their new relationships slowly, allowing everyone time and space to adjust and develop a level of trust with each other.

—·_____   —·_____
_____   _____
—·_____   —·_____
_____   _____
—·_____   —·_____
_____   _____

DIAGNOSTIC SUGGESTIONS

Using DSM-IV/ICD-9-CM:

Axis I:	309.0	Adjustment Disorder With Depressed Mood
	309.3	Adjustment Disorder With Disturbance of Conduct
	309.24	Adjustment Disorder With Anxiety
	309.81	Posttraumatic Stress Disorder
	300.4	Dysthymic Disorder
	V62.81	Relational Problem NOS
	_____	_____
	_____	_____
Axis II:	V71.09	No Diagnosis
	_____	_____
	_____	_____

Using DSM-5/ICD-9-CM/ICD-10-CM:

ICD-9-CM	ICD-10-CM	*DSM-5* Disorder, Condition, or Problem
309.0	F43.21	Adjustment Disorder, With Depressed Mood
309.3	F43.24	Adjustment Disorder, With Disturbance of Conduct
309.24	F43.22	Adjustment Disorder, With Anxiety
309.81	F43.10	Posttraumatic Stress Disorder
300.4	F34.1	Persistent Depressive Disorder
V62.81	Z62.891	Sibling Relational Problem

Note: The ICD-9-CM codes are to be used for coding purposes in the United States through September 30, 2014. ICD-10-CM codes are to be used starting October 1, 2014. Some ICD-9-CM codes are associated with more than one ICD-10-CM and *DSM-5* disorder, condition, or problem. In addition, some ICD-9-CM disorders have been discontinued resulting in multiple ICD-9-CM codes being replaced by one ICD-10-CM code. Some discontinued ICD-9-CM codes are not listed in this table. See *Diagnostic and Statistical Manual of Mental Disorders* (2013) for details.

BULLYING/INTIMIDATION PERPETRATOR

BEHAVIORAL DEFINITIONS

1. Makes verbal threats to younger or weaker peers.
2. Engages in intimidating behavior only when reinforced by friends.
3. Engages in intimidating behavior even when alone and not reinforced by friends.
4. Uses mild, physically aggressive behavior to reinforce the verbal intimidation (e.g., pushing, grabbing and holding, throwing things at the victim).
5. Breaks or takes objects belonging to the victim of the bullying.
6. Has fits of rage in front of peers that include screaming, shouting, threatening, or name-calling.
7. Family of origin has provided models of threatening, intimidating, aggressive behavior.

—. _____
_____

—. _____
_____

—. _____
_____

LONG-TERM GOALS

1. Terminate intimidating behavior and treat others with respect and kindness.
2. Develop empathy and compassion for others.

3. Parents/caregivers terminate the use of aggressive means of control and implement positive parenting methods.

—. _____

_____

—. _____

_____

—. _____

_____

SHORT-TERM OBJECTIVES

1. Describe the type of behavioral interaction that occurs with peers when the goal is to get own way or control the other peer. (1)

2. Parents/caregivers and teachers describe the client's pattern of bullying or intimidating his/her peers. (2)

3. Provide behavioral, emotional, and attitudinal information toward an assessment of specifiers relevant to a *DSM* diagnosis, the efficacy of treatment, and the nature of the therapy relationship. (3, 4, 5, 6, 7)

THERAPEUTIC INTERVENTIONS

1. Gather data from the client regarding his/her pattern of interaction with peers, especially when he/she is trying to control the situation or intimidate others.

2. Meet with the client's parents/caregivers and schoolteachers to ask for their input regarding his/her pattern of bullying or intimidating peers.

3. Assess the client's level of insight (syntonic versus dystonic) toward the "presenting problems" (e.g., demonstrates good insight into the problematic nature of the "described behavior," agrees with others' concern, and is motivated to work on change; demonstrates ambivalence regarding the "problem described" and is reluctant to address the issue as a concern; or demonstrates resistance regarding acknowledgment of the "problem described," is not concerned, and has no motivation to change).

4. Assess the client for evidence of research-based correlated disorders (e.g., oppositional defiant behavior with ADHD, depression secondary to an anxiety disorder) including vulnerability to suicide, if appropriate (e.g., increased suicide risk when comorbid depression is evident).

5. Assess for any issues of age, gender, or culture that could help explain the client's currently defined "problem behavior" and factors that could offer a better understanding of the client's behavior.

6. Assess for the severity of the level of impairment to the client's functioning to determine appropriate level of care (e.g., the behavior noted creates mild, moderate, severe, or very severe impairment in social, relational, vocational, or occupational endeavors); continuously assess this severity of impairment as well as the efficacy of treatment (e.g., the client no longer demonstrates severe impairment but the presenting problem now is causing mild or moderate impairment).

7. Assess the client's home, school, and community for pathogenic care (e.g., persistent disregard for the child's emotional needs or physical needs, repeated changes in primary caregivers, limited opportunities for stable attachments, persistent harsh punishment or other grossly inept parenting).

4. Acknowledge, without denial, that bullying has been used against peers. (8, 9)

8. Confront the client with facts reported by others that indicate that he/she does engage in intimidating behavior toward peers (or assign "Bullying Incident Report" in the *Child Psychotherapy Homework Planner* by Jongsma, Peterson, and McInnis).

9. Role-play several social interactions with peers in which the therapist, playing the role of the client, uses bullying behavior to intimidate others; ask the client to acknowledge that he/she does behave in this manner.

5. Verbalize an understanding of the feelings of the victim of intimidating behavior. (10, 11, 12, 13)

10. Teach the client empathy for the victim of his/her intimidating behavior by asking him/her to list the feelings generated in the victim due to the client's bullying such as fear, rejection, anger, helplessness, or social withdrawal (or assign "Apology Letter for Bullying" in the *Child Psychotherapy Homework Planner* by Jongsma, Peterson, and McInnis).

11. Engage the client in a role-playing session in which he/she is the victim of bullying from a peer (played by the therapist); stop the role-playing periodically to explore and identify the victim's feelings.

12. Assign the client to be alert to observing instances of bullying perpetrated by others and to note the feelings of the victim; process these experiences.

13. Explore the client's capacity for empathy; assess whether cruelty toward animals or other

	indicators of Conduct Disorder are present (see the Conduct Disorder chapter in this *Planner*).
6. Identify feelings toward self. (14, 15)	14. Ask the client to write a list of words that are self-descriptive; assess his/her perception of himself/herself (e.g., low self-esteem, aggressive, isolated, unloved).
	15. Administer or refer the client for psychological testing to determine his/her self-perception, emotional state, and relationship style; provide feedback of the test results to the client and his/her parents.
7. Identify the goal or intent of bullying or intimidating behavior. (16, 17, 18)	16. Assist the client in exploring his/her goal when he/she engages in intimidation of others (e.g., impress peers to gain acceptance; seek to control others; resolve a conflict using aggression).
	17. Role-play social interactions in which the client is the bully; stop the action periodically to have him/her verbalize his/her goal or intent.
	18. Read book passages or view videos with the client in which bullying is taking place; ask him/her to identify the goal of the intimidator and the feelings of the victim.
8. Implement prosocial assertiveness to attain social interaction goals and to resolve disputes. (19, 20)	19. Assist the client in identifying prosocial means of attaining healthy social interaction goals such as attaining respect by being kind, honest, and trustworthy; attaining leadership through assertiveness and respect, not aggression; using effective problem-solving

techniques, rather than intimidation (recommend *Cool, Calm, and Confident: A Workbook to Help Kids Learn Assertiveness Skills* by Schab).

20. Role-play peer conflict situations with the client in which bullying is used first, then where assertiveness and problem-solving techniques are used (or assign the "Problem-Solving Exercise" in the *Child Psychotherapy Homework Planner* by Jongsma, Peterson, and McInnis).

9. Family members acknowledge the presence of intimidation in family interactions. (21, 22)

21. In a family therapy session, assign the family the task of resolving a conflict (or assign the "Problem-Solving Exercise" in the *Child Psychotherapy Homework Planner* by Jongsma, Peterson, and McInnis); assess for the use of effective and respectful problem-solving techniques versus authoritarianism and aggression.

22. Explore with the family members whether aggression, intimidation, and threats are often a part of family interaction, especially during times of conflict.

10. Family members demonstrate respect for each other's rights and feelings during conflict resolution. (23, 24)

23. Teach the family respectful conflict resolution techniques in which the parents' authority is recognized but not flaunted without regard to the feelings of others.

24. During a role-playing session, guide the family in the use of prosocial problem-solving techniques that respect each person's rights and feelings.

11. Attend a social skills training group. (25, 26)

25. Refer the client to a social skills training group that emphasizes demonstrating respect and compassion for peers.

26. Review and process what the client has learned in attending the social skills training group.

12. Increase socially appropriate behavior with peers and siblings. (27, 28)

27. Play The Social Conflict Game (Berg) with the client to assist him/her in developing behavioral skills to decrease interpersonal antisocialism with others.

28. Use The Anger Control Game (Berg) or a similar game to expand the client's ways to manage aggressive feelings.

13. Attend and freely participate in play therapy sessions. (29, 30, 31, 32)

29. Employ the ACT model (Landreth) in play therapy sessions to *acknowledge* the client's feelings, to *communicate* limits, and to *target* more appropriate alternatives to ongoing conflicts and aggression with peers and/or siblings.

30. Employ psychoanalytic play therapy approaches (e.g., explore and gain an understanding of the etiology of unconscious conflicts, fixations, or arrests; interpret resistance, transference, or core anxieties) to help the client work through and resolve peer conflicts.

31. Interpret the client's feelings expressed in play therapy and relate them to anger and aggressive behaviors toward peers.

32. Create scenarios with puppets, dolls, or stuffed animals that model and/or suggest constructive ways for the client

14. Read books and play therapeutic games to increase sensitivity to the causes and effects of bullying. (33)

15. Identify family issues that contribute to bullying/intimidating behavior. (34)

16. Identify and verbally express feelings that are associated with past neglect, abuse, separation, or abandonment. (35, 36)

to handle/manage conflicts with peers.

33. Read books and play games with the client that focus on bullying to teach its causes and effects (e.g., *Sometimes I Like to Fight, but I Don't Do It Much Anymore* by Shapiro; *The Very Angry Day That Amy Didn't Have* by Shapiro; No More Bullies Game [available from Courage to Change]; The Anti-Bullying Game [Searle and Streng]; process the application of principles learned to the client's daily life.

34. Conduct family therapy sessions to explore the dynamics (e.g., parental modeling of aggressive behavior; sexual, verbal, or physical abuse of family members; substance abuse in the home; neglect) that contribute to the emergence of the client's bullying/intimidating behavior.

35. Encourage and support the client in expressing his/her feelings associated with neglect, abuse, separation, or abandonment (see the Attachment Disorder, Sexual Abuse Victim, and Physical/ Emotional Abuse Victim chapters in this *Planner*).

36. Give the client permission to cry about past losses, separation, or abandonment; educate him/her about the healing nature of crying (i.e., provides an opportunity to express sadness, takes the edge off anger, helps to induce calmness after crying subsides).

—. _____   —. _____
   _____   _____
—. _____   —. _____
   _____   _____
—. _____   —. _____
   _____   _____

DIAGNOSTIC SUGGESTIONS

Using DSM-IV/ICD-9-CM:

Axis I:	313.81	Oppositional Defiant Disorder
	312.xx	Conduct Disorder
	312.9	Disruptive Behavior Disorder NOS
	314.01	Attention-Deficit/Hyperactivity Disorder, Predominantly Hyperactive-Impulsive Type
	314.9	Attention-Deficit/Hyperactivity Disorder NOS
	V62.81	Relational Problem NOS
	V71.02	Child or Adolescent Antisocial Behavior
	_____	_____
	_____	_____
Axis II:	V71.09	No Diagnosis
	_____	_____
	_____	_____

Using DSM-5/ICD-9-CM/ICD-10-CM:

<u>ICD-9-CM</u>	<u>ICD-10-CM</u>	<u>*DSM-5* Disorder, Condition, or Problem</u>
313.81	F91.3	Oppositional Defiant Disorder
312.xx	F91.1	Conduct Disorder, Childhood-Onset Type
312.9	F91.9	Unspecified Disruptive, Impulse Control, and Conduct Disorder
312.89	F91.8	Other Specified Disruptive, Impulse Control, and Conduct Disorder
314.01	F90.1	Attention-Deficit/Hyperactivity Disorder, Predominately Hyperactive /Impulsive Presentation
314.01	F90.9	Unspecified Attention-Deficit/Hyperactivity Disorder
314.01	F90.8	Other Specified Attention-Deficit/Hyperactivity Disorder

| V62.81 | Z62.891 | Sibling Relational Problem |
| V71.02 | Z72.810 | Child or Adolescent Antisocial Behavior |

Note: The ICD-9-CM codes are to be used for coding purposes in the United States through September 30, 2014. ICD-10-CM codes are to be used starting October 1, 2014. Some ICD-9-CM codes are associated with more than one ICD-10-CM and *DSM-5* disorder, condition, or problem. In addition, some ICD-9-CM disorders have been discontinued resulting in multiple ICD-9-CM codes being replaced by one ICD-10-CM code. Some discontinued ICD-9-CM codes are not listed in this table. See *Diagnostic and Statistical Manual of Mental Disorders* (2013) for details.

CONDUCT DISORDER/DELINQUENCY

BEHAVIORAL DEFINITIONS

1. Persistent refusal to comply with rules or expectations in the home, school, or community.
2. Excessive fighting, intimidation of others, cruelty or violence toward people or animals, and destruction of property.
3. History of stealing at home, at school, or in the community.
4. School adjustment characterized by disrespectful attitude toward authority figures, frequent disruptive behaviors, and detentions or suspensions for misbehavior.
5. Repeated conflict with authority figures at home, at school, or in the community.
6. Impulsivity as manifested by poor judgment, taking inappropriate risks, and failing to stop and think about consequences of actions.
7. Numerous attempts to deceive others through lying, conning, or manipulating.
8. Consistent failure to accept responsibility for misbehavior accompanied by a pattern of blaming others.
9. Little or no remorse for misbehavior.
10. Lack of sensitivity to the thoughts, feelings, and needs of other people.

—. _____

_____

—. _____

_____

—. _____

_____

LONG-TERM GOALS

1. Consistently comply with rules and expectations in the home, school, and community.
2. Eliminate all illegal and antisocial behavior.
3. Terminate all acts of violence or cruelty toward people or animals and the destruction of property.
4. Demonstrate empathy, concern, and sensitivity for the thoughts, feelings, and needs of others on a regular basis.
5. Parents establish and maintain appropriate parent-child boundaries, setting firm, consistent limits when the client acts out in an aggressive or rebellious manner.
6. Parents learn and implement good child behavioral management skills.

—. _____

_____

—. _____

_____

—. _____

_____

SHORT-TERM OBJECTIVES

THERAPEUTIC INTERVENTIONS

1. Identify situations, thoughts, and feelings that trigger antisocial feelings, problem behaviors, and the targets of those actions. (1)

1. Conduct clinical interviews with the client and parents focused on specifying the nature, severity, and history of the child's misbehavior; thoroughly assess the various stimuli (e.g., situations, people, thoughts) that have triggered the client's antisocial thoughts, feelings, and actions.

2. Identify major concerns regarding the child's misbehavior and the associated parenting approaches that have been tried. (2)

2. Assess how the parents have attempted to respond to the child's misbehavior, what triggers and reinforcements there may be contributing to the behavior, the parents' consistency in their approach to the child, and whether they have

experienced conflicts between themselves over how to react to the child.

3. Parents and child cooperate with psychological assessment to further delineate the nature of the presenting problem. (3)

3. Administer psychological instruments designed to assess whether a comorbid condition(s) (e.g., bipolar disorder, depression, ADHD) is contributing to disruptive behavior problems and/or objectively assess parent-child relational conflict (e.g., the *Parent-Child Relationship Inventory*; follow up accordingly with the client and parents regarding treatment options; readminister as needed to assess treatment outcome.

4. Provide behavioral, emotional, and attitudinal information toward an assessment of specifiers relevant to a *DSM* diagnosis, the efficacy of treatment, and the nature of the therapy relationship. (4, 5, 6, 7, 8)

4. Assess the client's level of insight (syntonic versus dystonic) toward the "presenting problems" (e.g., demonstrates good insight into the problematic nature of the "described behavior," agrees with others' concern, and is motivated to work on change; demonstrates ambivalence regarding the "problem described" and is reluctant to address the issue as a concern; or demonstrates resistance regarding acknowledgment of the "problem described," is not concerned, and has no motivation to change).

5. Assess the client for evidence of research-based correlated disorders (e.g., oppositional defiant behavior with ADHD, depression secondary to an anxiety disorder) including vulnerability to suicide, if

appropriate (e.g., increased suicide risk when comorbid depression is evident).

6. Assess for any issues of age, gender, or culture that could help explain the client's currently defined "problem behavior" and factors that could offer a better understanding of the client's behavior.

7. Assess for the severity of the level of impairment to the client's functioning to determine appropriate level of care (e.g., the behavior noted creates mild, moderate, severe, or very severe impairment in social, relational, vocational, or occupational endeavors); continuously assess this severity of impairment as well as the efficacy of treatment (e.g., the client no longer demonstrates severe impairment but the presenting problem now is causing mild or moderate impairment).

8. Assess the client's home, school, and community for pathogenic care (e.g., persistent disregard for the child's emotional needs or physical needs, repeated changes in primary caregivers, limited opportunities for stable attachments, persistent harsh punishment or other grossly inept parenting).

5. Cooperate with the recommendations or requirements mandated by the criminal justice system. (9, 10, 11)

9. Assess the child's illegal behavior patterns (or assign "Childhood Patterns of Stealing" in the *Child Psychotherapy Homework Planner* by Jongsma, Peterson, and McInnis) and consult with criminal justice officials about the appropriate consequences for

the client's destructive or aggressive behaviors (e.g., pay restitution, community service, probation, intensive surveillance).

10. Consult with parents, school officials, and criminal justice officials about the need to place the client in an alternative setting (e.g., foster home, group home, residential program, juvenile detention facility).

11. Encourage and challenge the parents not to protect the client from the natural or legal consequences of his/her destructive or aggressive behaviors.

6. Cooperate with an evaluation for possible treatment with psychotropic medications to assist in anger and behavioral control and take medications consistently, if prescribed. (12)

12. Assess the client for the need for psychotropic medication to assist in control of anger and other misbehaviors; refer him/her to a physician for an evaluation for prescription medication; monitor prescription compliance, effectiveness, and side effects; provide feedback to the prescribing physician. ▽

7. Increase the number of statements that reflect an understanding of the consequences of disruptive behavior and acceptance of responsibility for it. (13, 14, 15)

13. Actively build the level of trust with the client through consistent eye contact, active listening, unconditional positive regard, and genuineness.

14. Therapeutically confront statements in which the client lies and/or blames others for his/her misbehaviors and fails to accept responsibility for his/her actions; explore and process the factors that contribute to the client's pattern of blaming others (e.g., harsh punishment experiences, family pattern of blaming others).

▽ 8. Verbalize alternative ways to think about and manage anger and misbehavior. (16, 17)

▽ 9. Learn and implement calming strategies as part of a new way to manage reactions to frustration. (18)

▽ 10. Identify, challenge, and replace self-talk that leads to anger and misbehavior with self-talk that facilitates more constructive reactions. (19)

15. Use techniques derived from motivational interviewing to move the client away from externalizing and blaming toward accepting responsibility from his/her actions and motivation to change.

16. Assist the client in making a connection between his/her feelings and reactive behaviors (or assign "Risk Factors Leading to Child Behavior Problems" in the *Child Psychotherapy Homework Planner* by Jongsma, Peterson, and McInnis). ▽

17. Assist the client in conceptualizing his/her disruptive behavior as involving different components (cognitive, physiological, affective, and behavioral) that go through predictable phases that can be managed (e.g., demanding expectations not being met leading to increased arousal and anger which leads to acting out). ▽

18. Teach the client calming techniques (e.g., muscle relaxation, paced breathing, calming imagery) as part of a more comprehensive, tailored skill set for responding appropriately to angry feelings when they occur (or assign "Deep Breathing Exercise" in the *Child Psychotherapy Homework Planner* by Jongsma, Peterson, and McInnis). ▽

19. Explore the client's self-talk that mediates his/her angry feelings and actions (e.g., demanding expectations reflected in *should*, *must*, or *have to* statements);

identify and challenge biases, assisting him/her in generating appraisals and self-talk that corrects for the biases and facilitates a more flexible and temperate response to frustration (or assign "Replace Negative Thoughts with Positive Self-Talk" in the *Child Psychotherapy Homework Planner* by Jongsma, Peterson, and McInnis). ▽

▽ 11. Learn and implement thought-stopping to manage intrusive unwanted thoughts that trigger anger and acting out. (20)

20. Teach the client the "thought-stopping" technique and assign implementation on a daily basis between sessions; review implementation, reinforcing success and providing corrective feedback toward improvement. ▽

▽ 12. Verbalize feelings of frustration, disagreement, and anger in a controlled, assertive way. (21)

21. Use instruction, videotaped or live modeling, and/or role-playing to help develop the client's anger control and assertiveness skills, such as calming, self-statements, assertion skills; if indicated, refer him/her to an anger control or assertiveness group for further instruction (see *Anger Control Training for Aggressive Youths* by Lochman et al.). ▽

▽ 13. Implement problem-solving and/or conflict resolution skills to manage interpersonal problems constructively. (22)

22. Teach the client conflict resolution skills (e.g., empathy, active listening, "I messages," respectful communication, assertiveness without aggression, compromise; problem-solving steps) and recommend the child and parents read *Cool, Calm, and Confident: A Workbook to Help Kids Learn Assertiveness Skills* by Schab; use modeling, role-playing, and behavior rehearsal to work through

several current conflicts (or assign "Problem-Solving Exercise" in the *Child Psychotherapy Homework Planner* by Jongsma, Peterson, and McInnis).▽

▽ 14. Practice using new calming, communication, conflict resolution, and thinking skills in group or individual therapy. (23, 24)

23. Assist the client in constructing and consolidating a client-tailored strategy for managing anger that combines any of the somatic, cognitive, communication, problem-solving, and/or conflict resolution skills relevant to his/her needs.▽

24. Use any of several techniques (e.g., relaxation, imagery, behavioral rehearsal, modeling, role-playing, feedback of videotaped practice) in increasingly challenging situations to help the client consolidate the use of his/her new anger management skills (see *Problem-Solving Skills Training and Parent Management Training for Conduct Disorder* by Kazdin).▽

▽ 15. Practice using new calming, communication, conflict resolution, and thinking skills in homework exercises. (25)

25. Assign the client homework exercises to help him/her practice newly learned calming, problem-solving, assertion, conflict resolution, and/or cognitive restructuring skills as needed; review and process toward the goal of consolidation (see *Problem-Solving Skills Training and Parent Management Training for Conduct Disorder* by Kazdin).▽

▽ 16. Decrease the number, intensity, and duration of angry outbursts, while increasing the use of new skills for managing anger. (26)

26. Monitor the client's reports of angry outbursts toward the goal of decreasing their frequency, intensity, and duration through

the client's use of new anger management skills (or assign "Anger Control" or "Child Anger Checklist" in the *Child Psychotherapy Homework Planner* by Jongsma, Peterson, and McInnis); review progress, reinforcing success and providing corrective feedback toward improvement. ▽

▽ 17. Identify social supports that will help facilitate the implementation of new skills. (27)

27. Encourage the client to discuss and/or use his/her new anger and conduct management skills with trusted peers, family, or otherwise significant others who are likely to support his/her change. ▽

▽ 18. Parents learn and implement Parent Management Training skills to recognize and manage problem behavior of the client. (28, 29, 30, 31, 32)

28. Use a Parent Management Training approach beginning with teaching the parents how parent and child behavioral interactions can encourage or discourage positive or negative behavior and that changing key elements of those interactions (e.g., prompting and reinforcing positive behaviors) can be used to promote positive change (e.g., *Parent Management Training* by Forgatch and Patterson; *Parenting the Strong-Willed Child* by Forehand and Long; *Living With Children* by Patterson). ▽

29. Ask the parents to read material consistent with a parent training approach to managing disruptive behavior (e.g., *The Kazdin Method for Parenting the Defiant Child* by Kazdin; *Living With Children* by Patterson).

30. Teach the parents how to specifically define and identify problem behaviors, identify their

reactions to the behavior, determine whether the reaction encourages or discourages the behavior, and generate alternatives to the problem behavior. ▽

31. Teach parents how to implement key parenting practices consistently, including establishing realistic age-appropriate rules for acceptable and unacceptable behavior, prompting of positive behavior in the environment, use of positive reinforcement to encourage behavior (e.g., praise), use of clear direct instruction, time out, and other loss-of-privilege practices for problem behavior. ▽

32. Assign the parents home exercises in which they implement and record results of implementation exercises (or assign "Clear Rules, Positive Reinforcement, Appropriate Consequences" in the *Adolescent Psychotherapy Homework Planner* by Jongsma, Peterson, and McInnis); review in session, providing corrective feedback toward improved, appropriate, and consistent use of skills. ▽

▽ 19. Parents and client participate in play sessions in which they use their new rules for appropriate conduct. (33)

33. Conduct Parent-Child Interaction Therapy in which child-directed and parent-directed sessions focus on teaching appropriate child behavior, and parental behavioral management skills (e.g., clear commands, consistent consequences, positive reinforcement) are developed (see *Parent-Child Interaction*

Therapy by McNeil and Humbree-Kigin).▽

▽ 20. Parents enroll in an evidence-based parent training program. (34)

34. Refer parents to an evidence-based parent training program such as The Incredible Years (see www.incredibleyears.com) or the Positive Parenting Program (Triple P; see www.triple-america.com).▽

▽ 21. Increase compliance with rules at home and school. (35)

35. Design a reward system and/or contingency contract for the client and meet with school officials to reinforce identified positive behaviors at home and school and deter impulsive or rebellious behaviors (or assign "Clear Rules, Positive Reinforcement, Appropriate Consequences" in the *Adolescent Psychotherapy Homework Planner* by Jongsma, Peterson, and McInnis).▽

▽ 22. Parents verbalize appropriate boundaries for discipline to prevent further occurrences of abuse and to ensure the safety of the client and his/her siblings. (36, 37)

36. Explore the client's family background for a history of neglect and physical or sexual abuse that may contribute to his/her behavioral problems; confront the client's parents to cease physically abusive or overly punitive methods of discipline.▽

37. Implement the steps necessary to protect the client and siblings from further abuse (e.g., report abuse to the appropriate agencies; remove the client or perpetrator from the home).▽

▽ 23. Increase verbalizations of empathy and concern for other people. (38)

38. Use role-playing and role reversal techniques to help the client develop sensitivity to the feelings of others in reaction to his/her antisocial behaviors (or assign "Apology Letter for

▽ 24. Increase the frequency of responsible and positive social behaviors. (39, 40, 41)

25. Client and family participate in family therapy. (42)

Bullying" or "Building Empathy" in the *Child Psychotherapy Homework Planner* by Jongsma, Peterson, and McInnis).▽

39. Direct the client to engage in three altruistic or benevolent acts (e.g., read to a developmentally disabled student, mow grandmother's lawn) before the next session to increase his/her empathy and sensitivity to the needs of others.▽

40. Assign homework designed to increase the client's empathy and sensitivity toward the thoughts, feelings, and needs of others (or assign "Building Empathy" in the *Child Psychotherapy Homework Planner* by Jongsma, Peterson, and McInnis).▽

41. Place the client in charge of tasks at home (e.g., preparing and cooking a special dish for a family get-together, building shelves in the garage, changing oil in the car) to demonstrate confidence in his/her ability to act responsibly.▽

42. Refer the family to an evidence-based family therapy such as Functional Family Therapy (see www.fftinc.com) or Brief Strategic Family Therapy (see *Brief Strategic Family Therapy for Hispanic Youth* by Robbins et al.) in which problematic interactions within the family system are assessed and changed through the use of family systems and social learning interventions to support more adaptive communication and functioning.▽

▽ 26. Client and family participate in a Multisystemic Therapy program. (43)

43. Refer the client with severe conduct problems to a Multisystemic Therapy program that uses cognitive behavioral and family interventions to target factors in the youth's social network that are contributing to his or her antisocial behavior and/or substance abuse in an effort to improve caregiver discipline practices, enhancing family affective relations, decreasing youth association with deviant peers and increasing youth association with prosocial peers, improving youth school or vocational performance, engaging youth in prosocial recreational outlets, and developing an indigenous support network (see *Multisystemic Therapy for Antisocial Behavior in Children and Adolescents* by Henggeler et al.). ▽

▽ 27. Verbalize an understanding of the difference between a lapse and relapse. (44, 45, 46)

44. Provide a rationale for relapse prevention that discusses the risk and introduces strategies for preventing it. ▽

45. Discuss with the parent/child the distinction between a lapse and relapse, associating a lapse with a temporary setback and relapse with a return to a sustained pattern thinking, feeling and behaving that is characteristic of oppositional defiant disorder/conduct disorder. ▽

46. Identify and rehearse with the parent/child the management of future situations or circumstances in which lapses could occur.

▽ 28. Implement strategies learned in therapy to counter lapses and prevent relapse. (47, 48, 49)

29. Identify and verbally express feelings associated with past neglect, abuse, separation, or abandonment. (50)

30. Parents participate in marital therapy. (51)

47. Instruct the parent/child to routinely use strategies learned in therapy (e.g., parent training techniques, problem-solving, anger management), building them into his/her life as much as possible. ▽

48. Develop a "coping card" on which coping strategies and other important information can be kept (e.g., steps in problem-solving, positive coping statements, reminders that were helpful to the client during therapy). ▽

49. Schedule periodic maintenance or "booster" sessions to help the parent/child maintain therapeutic gains and problem-solve challenges. ▽

50. Encourage and support the client in expressing feelings associated with neglect, abuse, separation, or abandonment and help process (e.g., assign the task of writing a letter to an absent parent, use the empty-chair technique, or assign "The Lesson of Salmon Rock . . . Fighting Leads to Loneliness" in the *Child Psychotherapy Homework Planner* by Jongsma, Peterson, and McInnis).

51. Assess the marital dyad for possible substance abuse, conflict, or triangulation that shifts the focus from marriage issues to the client's acting out behaviors (or assign "Concerns About Parent's Drug or Alcohol Problem" in the *Child Psychotherapy Homework Planner* by Jongsma, Peterson,

and McInnis); refer for
appropriate treatment, if needed.

—— . ————————————   —— . ————————————
————————————   ————————————
—— . ————————————   —— . ————————————
————————————   ————————————
—— . ————————————   —— . ————————————
————————————   ————————————

DIAGNOSTIC SUGGESTIONS

Using DSM-IV/ICD-9-CM:

Axis I:	312.81	Conduct Disorder, Childhood-Onset Type
	312.82	Conduct Disorder, Adolescent-Onset Type
	313.81	Oppositional Defiant Disorder
	312.9	Disruptive Behavior Disorder NOS
	314.01	Attention-Deficit/Hyperactivity Disorder, Predominantly Hyperactive-Impulsive Type
	314.9	Attention-Deficit/Hyperactivity Disorder NOS
	312.34	Intermittent Explosive Disorder
	V71.02	Child Antisocial Behavior
	V61.20	Parent-Child Relational Problem
	————	————————————————
	————	————————————————
Axis II:	V71.09	No Diagnosis
	————	————————————————
	————	————————————————

Using DSM-5/ICD-9-CM/ICD-10-CM:

ICD-9-CM	ICD-10-CM	*DSM-5* Disorder, Condition, or Problem
312.81	F91.1	Conduct Disorder, Childhood-Onset Type
313.81	F91.3	Oppositional Defiant Disorder
312.9	F91.9	Unspecified Disruptive, Impulse Control, and Conduct Disorder
312.89	F91.8	Other Specified Disruptive, Impulse Control, and Conduct Disorder

314.01	F90.1	Attention-Deficit/Hyperactivity Disorder, Predominately Hyperactive /Impulsive Presentation
314.01	F90.9	Unspecified Attention-Deficit/Hyperactivity Disorder
314.01	F90.8	Other Specified Attention-Deficit/Hyperactivity Disorder
312.34	F63.81	Intermittent Explosive Disorder
V71.02	Z72.810	Child or Adolescent Antisocial Behavior
V61.20	Z62.820	Parent-Child Relational Problem

Note: The ICD-9-CM codes are to be used for coding purposes in the United States through September 30, 2014. ICD-10-CM codes are to be used starting October 1, 2014. Some ICD-9-CM codes are associated with more than one ICD-10-CM and *DSM-5* disorder, condition, or problem. In addition, some ICD-9-CM disorders have been discontinued resulting in multiple ICD-9-CM codes being replaced by one ICD-10-CM code. Some discontinued ICD-9-CM codes are not listed in this table. See *Diagnostic and Statistical Manual of Mental Disorders* (2013) for details.

▼ Indicates that the Objective/Intervention is consistent with those found in evidence-based treatments.

DEPRESSION

BEHAVIORAL DEFINITIONS

1. Demonstrates sad or flat affect.
2. Reports a preoccupation with the subject of death.
3. Reports suicidal thoughts and/or actions.
4. Exhibits moody irritability.
5. Isolates self from family and/or peers.
6. Deterioration in academic performance.
7. Lacks interest in previously enjoyed activities.
8. Refuses to communicate openly.
9. Demonstrates low energy.
10. Makes little or no eye contact.
11. Frequently expresses statements reflecting low self-esteem.
12. Exhibits a reduced appetite.
13. Demonstrates an increased need for sleep.
14. Exhibits poor concentration and indecision.
15. Expresses feelings of hopelessness, worthlessness, or inappropriate guilt.
16. Reports unresolved feelings of grief.
17. Uses street drugs to elevate mood.

—. _____

_____

—. _____

_____

—. _____

_____

LONG-TERM GOALS

1. Elevate mood and show evidence of usual energy, activities, and socialization level.
2. Renew typical interest in academic achievement, social involvement, and eating patterns as well as occasional expressions of joy and zest for life.
3. Reduce irritability and increase normal social interaction with family and friends.
4. Develop healthy cognitive patterns and beliefs about self and the world that lead to alleviation and help prevent the relapse of depression symptoms.
5. Develop healthy interpersonal relationships that lead to alleviation and help prevent the relapse of depression symptoms.
6. Appropriately grieve the loss in order to normalize mood and to return to previous adaptive level of functioning.

—. _____

—. _____

—. _____

SHORT-TERM OBJECTIVES

1. Describe current and past experiences with depression complete with its impact on function and attempts to resolve it. (1)

2. Verbally identify, if possible, the source of depressed mood. (2)

THERAPEUTIC INTERVENTIONS

1. Assess current and past mood episodes including their features, frequency, intensity, and duration (e.g., clinical interview supplemented by the *Inventory to Diagnose Depression.*

2. Ask the client to make a list of what he/she is depressed about (or assign the "Childhood Depression Survey" in the *Child Psychotherapy Homework Planner* by Jongsma, Peterson, and McInnis); process the list content.

3. Complete psychological testing to assess the depth of depression, the need for antidepressant medication, and suicide prevention measures. (3)

3. Arrange for the administration of an objective assessment instrument for evaluating the client's depression and suicide risk (e.g., *Beck Depression Inventory for Youth*; *The Children's Depression Inventory*); evaluate results and give feedback to the parents/client; readminister as needed to assess progress.

4. Provide behavioral, emotional, and attitudinal information toward an assessment of specifiers relevant to a *DSM* diagnosis, the efficacy of treatment, and the nature of the therapy relationship. (4, 5, 6, 7, 8)

4. Assess the client's level of insight (syntonic versus dystonic) toward the "presenting problems" (e.g., demonstrates good insight into the problematic nature of the "described behavior," agrees with others' concern, and is motivated to work on change; demonstrates ambivalence regarding the "problem described" and is reluctant to address the issue as a concern; or demonstrates resistance regarding acknowledgment of the "problem described," is not concerned, and has no motivation to change).

5. Assess the client for evidence of research-based correlated disorders (e.g., oppositional defiant behavior with ADHD, depression secondary to an anxiety disorder) including vulnerability to suicide, if appropriate (e.g., increased suicide risk when comorbid depression is evident).

6. Assess for any issues of age, gender, or culture that could help explain the client's currently defined "problem behavior" and factors that could offer a better understanding of the client's behavior.

7. Assess for the severity of the level of impairment to the client's functioning to determine appropriate level of care (e.g., the behavior noted creates mild, moderate, severe, or very severe impairment in social, relational, vocational, or occupational endeavors); continuously assess this severity of impairment as well as the efficacy of treatment (e.g., the client no longer demonstrates severe impairment but the presenting problem now is causing mild or moderate impairment).

8. Assess the client's home, school, and community for pathogenic care (e.g., persistent disregard for the child's emotional needs or physical needs, repeated changes in primary caregivers, limited opportunities for stable attachments, persistent harsh punishment or other grossly inept parenting).

5. Verbalize any history of suicide attempts and any current suicidal urges. (9)

9. Assess the client's history and current thoughts about, desire for, or plans for suicide.

6. Comply with recommendations for reducing urges to harm self. (10)

10. Arrange for hospitalization, as necessary, when the client is judged to be harmful to self.

▽ 7. Take prescribed psychotropic medications responsibly at times ordered by physician. (11, 12)

11. Evaluate the client's possible need for psychotropic medication and arrange for a medication evaluation by a physician, if needed. ▽

12. Monitor and evaluate the client's psychotropic medication compliance, effectiveness, and side effects (including possible increased suicide risk); communicate with prescribing physician. ▽

▽ 8. Participate in cognitive behavioral therapy for depression. (13, 14)

13. Conduct or refer the child to a cognitive behavioral group therapy for depression (or treat individually if necessary) involving psychoeducation, cognitive restructuring, behavioral activation, as well as calming, personal, and interpersonal skills building (see *Treating Depressed Youth: Therapist's Manual for ACTION* by Stark et al.; *Depression: Cognitive Behavior Therapy With Children and Adolescents* by Verduyn, Rogers, and Wood).

14. Arrange for monthly meetings of the child's parents to encourage and teach parents how to assist their child in applying newly learned skills outside of group sessions and to increase the frequency of positive family activities; prescribe selected reading to support therapy (see *Parent's Workbook for ACTION* by Stark et al.). ▽

▽ 9. Parents and child learn about depression, factors that influence its development and continuance, and methods for overcoming and preventing its relapse. (15)

15. Provide psychoeducation and explain the rationale for cognitive behavioral treatment of depression that discusses how cognitive, behavioral, and interpersonal factors can contribute to depression and how changes in these factors can help overcome and prevent it; prescribe reading to support therapy (see *Children's Workbook for ACTION* by Stark et al. or *My Feeling Better Workbook: Help for Kids Who are Sad and Depressed* by Hamil). ▽

▽ 10. Identify and replace depressive thinking that leads to depressive feelings and actions. (16, 17, 18, 19)

16. Educate the client about cognitive restructuring including self-monitoring of automatic thoughts reflecting depressogenic beliefs; challenging depressive thinking patterns by examining evidence for and against them and replace them with reality-based alternatives, and testing through behavioral experiments (or assign "Replace Negative Thoughts with Positive Self-Talk" in the *Child Psychotherapy Homework Planner* by Jongsma, Peterson, and McInnis). ▽

17. Assign the client to keep a daily journal of automatic thoughts associated with depressive feelings (e.g., "Daily Record of Dysfunctional Thoughts" in *Cognitive Therapy of Depression* by Beck et al.); process the journal material to identify and challenge depressive thinking patterns and replace them with reality-based alternatives. ▽

18. Design age-appropriate "behavioral experiments" in which depressive automatic thoughts are treated as hypotheses/predictions, reality-based alternative hypotheses/ predictions are generated, and both are tested against the client's past, present, and/or future experiences. ▽

19. Conduct attribution retraining in which the client is taught to identify pessimistic explanations for events and generate more optimistic and realistic alternatives; reinforce the client's positive, reality-based cognitive

messages that enhance self-confidence and increase adaptive action; (supplement with "Recognizing Your Abilities, Traits, and Accomplishments" in the *Adolescent Psychotherapy Homework Planner* or "Positive Self-Statements" in the *Child Psychotherapy Homework Planner* by Jongsma, Peterson, and McInnis).▽

▽ 11. Learn and implement calming skills to reduce overall tension and moments of increased anxiety, tension, or arousal. (20, 21)

20. Teach the client cognitive and somatic calming skills (e.g., calming breathing; cognitive distancing, decatastrophizing, distraction; progressive muscle relaxation; guided imagery); rehearse with the client how to apply these skills to his/her daily life (or assign "Deep Breathing Exercise" in the *Child Psychotherapy Homework Planner* by Jongsma, Peterson, and McInnis); review and reinforce success while providing corrective feedback toward consistent implementation.▽

21. Assign the client and/or parents to read and discuss progressive muscle relaxation and other calming strategies in relevant books or treatment manuals (e.g., *The Relaxation and Stress Reduction Workbook for Kids* by Shapiro and Sprague; the *Coping C.A.T. Series* at workbookpublishing.com).▽

▽ 12. Learn and implement personal skills for managing stress, solving daily problems, and resolving conflicts effectively. (22)

22. Teach the client tailored, age-appropriate personal skills including calming skills (e.g., cognitive and somatic), problem-solving skills (e.g., specifying problem, generating options, listing pros and cons of each

option, plan development, implementation, and refining), and conflict resolution skills (e.g., empathy, active listening, "I messages," respectful communication, assertiveness without aggression, compromise), to manage daily stressors, improve personal and interpersonal functioning, and help alleviate depression; use modeling, role-playing, behavior rehearsal, and corrective feedback to develop skills and resolve any current conflicts (see the *Penn Resiliency Project* at ppc.sas.upenn.edu/prpsum.htm).▽

▽ 13. Learn new ways to overcome depression through activity. (23)

23. Engage the client in "behavioral activation" by scheduling activities that have a high likelihood for pleasure and mastery, are worthwhile to the client, and/or make him/her feel good about self; use behavioral techniques (e.g., modeling, role-playing, role reversal, rehearsal, and corrective feedback) as needed, to assist adoption in the client's daily life (or assign to the client along with parents "Identify and Schedule Pleasant Activities" in the *Adult Psychotherapy Homework Planner* by Jongsma); reinforce advances. ▽

▽ 14. Learn and implement social skills to reduce anxiety and build confidence in social interactions. (24)

24. Use instruction, modeling, and role-playing to build the client's general social and/or communication skills (see *Social Effectiveness Therapy for Children and Adolescents* by Beidel, Turner, and Morris).▽

▽ 15. Initiate and respond actively to social communication with family and peers. (25, 26)

25. Encourage the client to participate in social/recreational activities that increase social communication and interactions, enrich his/her life, and expand social network (or assign "Greeting Peers" or "Show Your Strengths" in the *Child Psychotherapy Homework Planner* by Jongsma, Peterson, and McInnis). ▽

26. Use therapeutic feelings games (e.g., The Talking, Feeling, and Doing Game by Gardner) to assist the client in being more verbal.

16. Discuss current personal and/or interpersonal conflicts/problems with therapist. (27, 28)

27. Use a nondirective, client-centered approach to help client clarify current conflicts/problems and client-generated solutions to them; support the client's efforts.

28. Conduct Individual Psycho-dynamic Psychotherapy with a focus on interpersonal relationships, life stresses, and dysfunctional attachments (see *Basic Principles and Techniques in Short-Term Dynamic Psychotherapy* by Davanloo).

17. Verbalize any unresolved grief issues that may be contributing to depression. (29)

29. Explore the role of unresolved grief issues as they contribute to the client's current depression (see the Grief/Loss Unresolved chapter in this *Planner*).

18. Implement a routine of physical exercise. (30)

30. Develop and reinforce a routine of physical exercise for the client.

19. Learn and implement relapse prevention skills. (31)

31. Build the client's relapse prevention skills by helping him/her identify early warning signs of relapse, reviewing skills learned during therapy, and developing a plan for managing challenges.

20. State the connection between rebellion, self-destruction, or withdrawal and the underlying depression. (32, 33, 34)

32. Assess the client's level of understanding about self-defeating behaviors linked to the depression.

33. Interpret and confront the client's acting out behaviors as avoidance of the real conflict involving his/her unmet emotional needs and reflection of the depression.

34. Teach the client the connection between angry, irritable behaviors and feelings of hurt and sadness (or assign the exercise "Surface Behavior/Inner Feelings" in the *Child Psychotherapy Homework Planner* by Jongsma, Peterson, and McInnis).

21. Specify what is missing from life to cause the unhappiness. (35, 36)

35. Explore the client's fears regarding abandonment or loss of love from others.

36. Explore with the client what is missing from his/her life that contributes to the unhappiness (or assign "Three Wishes Game" in the *Child Psychotherapy Homework Planner* by Jongsma, Peterson, and McInnis).

22. Specify what in the past or present life contributes to sadness. (37, 38)

37. Explore the emotional pain from the client's past that contributes to the feelings of hopelessness and low self-esteem.

38. Assist the client in identifying his/her current unmet emotional needs and specifying ways to meet those needs (or assign the exercise "Unmet Emotional Needs—Identification and Satisfaction" from the *Adolescent Psychotherapy Homework Planner* by Jongsma, Peterson, and McInnis).

23. Express negative feelings through artistic modalities. (39, 40)

39. Use art therapy (e.g., drawing, coloring, painting, collage, sculpture) to help the client express depressive feelings; use his/her artistic products as a springboard for further elaboration of emotions and their causes (or assign "Three Ways to Change the World" in the *Child Psychotherapy Homework Planner* by Jongsma, Peterson, and McInnis).

40. Ask the client to produce a family drawing to help assess the factors contributing to his/her depression.

24. Participate in family therapy to improve relationships and support among members. (41)

41. Conduct family therapy to facilitate better expression and communication within the family system while facilitating encouragement, support, and tolerance among family members (see *Rewriting Family Scripts* by Byng-Hall).

25. Improve academic performance as evidenced by better grades and positive teacher reports. (42)

42. Challenge and encourage the client's academic effort; arrange for a tutor, if needed, to increase the client's sense of academic mastery (or assign "Establish a Homework Routine" in the *Child Psychotherapy Homework Planner* by Jongsma, Peterson, and McInnis).

26. Adjust sleep hours to those typical of the developmental stage. (43)

43. Assess and monitor the client's sleep patterns and the restfulness of sleep (or assign to the parents "Childhood Sleep Problems" in the *Child Psychotherapy Homework Planner* by Jongsma, Peterson, and McInnis).

27. Eat nutritional meals regularly without strong urging from others. (44)

44. Assess the child's eating habits and as the depression lifts, monitor and encourage the client's food consumption.

28. Express feelings of sadness, hurt, and anger in play therapy sessions. (45, 46)

45. Arrange for a play therapy session that allows for the client to express feelings toward himself/herself and others.

46. Interpret the feelings expressed in play therapy as those of the client toward real life circumstances.

29. Verbalize the changes that would result in a reduction of sadness and an increase in hope and meaningfulness in life. (47)

47. Assign the client the homework of writing three ways he/she would like to change the world to bring increased feelings of joy, peace, and security (or assign the exercise "Three Ways to Change the World" in the *Child Psychotherapy Homework Planner* by Jongsma, Peterson, and McInnis).

__. _____   __. _____

   _____   _____

__. _____   __. _____

   _____   _____

__. _____   __. _____

   _____   _____

DIAGNOSTIC SUGGESTIONS

Using DSM-IV/ICD-9-CM:

Axis I:	309.0	Adjustment Disorder With Depressed Mood
	296.xx	Bipolar I Disorder
	296.89	Bipolar II Disorder
	300.4	Dysthymic Disorder
	296.2x	Major Depressive Disorder, Single Episode
	296.3x	Major Depressive Disorder, Recurrent
	V62.82	Bereavement
	_____	_____
	_____	_____

Axis II: V71.09   No Diagnosis

_____   _____

_____   _____

Using DSM-5/ICD-9-CM/ICD-10-CM:

ICD-9-CM	ICD-10-CM	*DSM-5* Disorder, Condition, or Problem
309.0	F43.21	Adjustment Disorder, With Depressed Mood
296.xx	F31.xx	Bipolar I Disorder
296.89	F31.81	Bipolar II Disorder
300.4	F34.1	Persistent Depressive Disorder
296.xx	F32.x	Major Depressive Disorder, Single Episode
296.xx	F33.x	Major Depressive Disorder, Recurrent Episode
V62.82	Z63.4	Uncomplicated Bereavement

Note: The ICD-9-CM codes are to be used for coding purposes in the United States through September 30, 2014. ICD-10-CM codes are to be used starting October 1, 2014. Some ICD-9-CM codes are associated with more than one ICD-10-CM and *DSM-5* disorder, condition, or problem. In addition, some ICD-9-CM disorders have been discontinued resulting in multiple ICD-9-CM codes being replaced by one ICD-10-CM code. Some discontinued ICD-9-CM codes are not listed in this table. See *Diagnostic and Statistical Manual of Mental Disorders* (2013) for details.

▽ Indicates that the Objective/Intervention is consistent with those found in evidence-based treatments.

DISRUPTIVE/ATTENTION-SEEKING

BEHAVIORAL DEFINITIONS

1. Repeated attempts to draw attention to self through silly, immature, or regressive behaviors, loud talking, and making inappropriate noises or gestures.
2. Frequent disruptions in the classroom by interrupting the teacher and/or interfering with classmates' attention and concentration by talking excessively, blurting out remarks, speaking without permission, and laughing or making noises at inappropriate times.
3. Strained sibling and peer relationships due to annoying or antagonistic behaviors (e.g., teasing, mocking, name-calling, picking on others).
4. Fails to follow agreed-upon rules in play or game activities, refusing to share or cooperate, and demanding that others do things his/her way.
5. Obstinate refusal to comply with reasonable requests by authority figures in home or school settings.
6. Unwillingness to back down or bend during an argument with family members, peers, or adult authority figures.
7. Lack of sensitivity to or awareness of how attention-seeking behaviors impact other people.
8. Lack of awareness of important social cues and/or failure to follow expected social norms.
9. Numerous complaints by siblings or peers of annoying physical contact and intrusions into personal space.

—. _____
   _____
—. _____
   _____
   _____
—. _____
   _____

LONG-TERM GOALS

1. Terminate disruptive attention-seeking behaviors, and increase cooperative, prosocial interactions.
2. Gain attention, approval, and acceptance from other people through appropriate verbalizations and positive social behaviors.
3. Establish and maintain positive sibling relationships and lasting peer friendships.
4. React appropriately to important social cues and follow expected rules of engagement in play, classroom, extracurricular, or social activities.
5. Parents set firm, consistent limits on the client's disruptive or negative attention-seeking behaviors and maintain appropriate parent-child boundaries.

—. _____
   _____
   _____
—. _____
   _____
   _____
—. _____
   _____

SHORT-TERM OBJECTIVES

1. Cooperate with a psychological assessment to rule out diagnosable conditions contributing to disruptive behavior. (1, 2)

THERAPEUTIC INTERVENTIONS

1. Arrange for psychological testing of the client to assess whether emotional factors or Attention-Deficit/Hyperactivity Disorder (ADHD) are contributing to his/her disruptive, antagonistic, annoying, or negative attention-seeking behaviors; provide feedback to the client and his/her parents.

2. Assess the client for the presence of symptom patterns that indicate the presence of oppositional defiant disorder or conduct disorder and treat appropriately if positive for either of these conditions (see the chapters on Conduct Disorder/Delinquency

and Oppositional Defiant in this *Planner*).

2. Complete a psychoeducational evaluation. (3)

3. Arrange for a psychoeducational evaluation of the client to rule out the presence of a learning disability that may be contributing to his/her disruptive and negative attention-seeking behaviors in the school setting; provide feedback to the client's parents or school officials.

3. Provide behavioral, emotional, and attitudinal information toward an assessment of specifiers relevant to a *DSM* diagnosis, the efficacy of treatment, and the nature of the therapy relationship. (4, 5, 6, 7, 8)

4. Assess the client's level of insight (syntonic versus dystonic) toward the "presenting problems" (e.g., demonstrates good insight into the problematic nature of the "described behavior," agrees with others' concern, and is motivated to work on change; demonstrates ambivalence regarding the "problem described" and is reluctant to address the issue as a concern; or demonstrates resistance regarding acknowledgment of the "problem described," is not concerned, and has no motivation to change).

5. Assess the client for evidence of research-based correlated disorders (e.g., oppositional defiant behavior with ADHD, depression secondary to an anxiety disorder) including vulnerability to suicide, if appropriate (e.g., increased suicide risk when comorbid depression is evident).

6. Assess for any issues of age, gender, or culture that could help explain the client's currently defined "problem behavior" and factors that could offer a better

understanding of the client's behavior.

7. Assess for the severity of the level of impairment to the client's functioning to determine appropriate level of care (e.g., the behavior noted creates mild, moderate, severe, or very severe impairment in social, relational, vocational, or occupational endeavors); continuously assess this severity of impairment as well as the efficacy of treatment (e.g., the client no longer demonstrates severe impairment but the presenting problem now is causing mild or moderate impairment).

8. Assess the client's home, school, and community for pathogenic care (e.g., persistent disregard for the child's emotional needs or physical needs, repeated changes in primary caregivers, limited opportunities for stable attachments, persistent harsh punishment or other grossly inept parenting).

4. Parents and teachers establish appropriate boundaries, develop clear rules, and follow through consistently with consequences for the client's disruptive or annoying behaviors. (9, 10, 11, 12, 13)

9. Assist the parents in establishing clearly defined boundaries and consequences for the client's disruptive, antagonistic, annoying, and negative attention-seeking behaviors (or assign "Being a Consistent Parent" from the *Child Psychotherapy Homework Planner* by Jongsma, Peterson, and McInnis).

10. Establish clear rules for the client in home and school; ask him/her to repeat the rules to demonstrate an understanding of the expectations.

11. Consult with the parents about increasing structure in the home to help the client delay gratification for longer-term goals (e.g., completing homework or chores before playing video games or socializing with peers).

12. Consult with the parents, teachers, and school officials to design and implement interventions (e.g., sitting in the front row during class, providing frequent feedback, calling on the client often, using a teacher's aide to assist with learning problems) to deter the client's impulsivity, improve academic performance, and increase positive behaviors in the classroom.

13. Assign the parents readings to increase their knowledge about effective disciplinary techniques (e.g., *The Kazdin Method for Parenting the Defiant Child* by Kazdin; *1-2-3 Magic: Effective Discipline for Children 2–12* by Phelan; *Assertive Discipline for Parents* by Canter and Canter).

5. Parents increase the frequency of praise and positive reinforcement to the client. (14, 15)

14. Encourage the parents to provide frequent praise and positive reinforcement for the client's positive social behaviors and good impulse control (recommend *Parents are Teachers: A Child Management Program* by Becker).

15. Design a reward system and/or contingency contract for the client to reinforce identified positive behaviors, completion of school and homework assignments, and to reduce the

6. Reduce the frequency and severity of disruptive or negative attention-seeking behaviors at home and/or school. (16, 17, 18, 19)

frequency of disruptive and negative attention-seeking behaviors.

16. Design and implement a token economy to increase the client's positive social behaviors and deter disruptive and negative attention-seeking behaviors.

17. Teach mediational and self-control strategies (e.g., relaxation; "stop, look, listen, and think") to help the client to delay the impulse to act out and engage in negative attention-seeking behaviors.

18. Encourage the client to use self-monitoring checklists at home or school to improve impulse control and social skills.

19. Assign the client to read material that will help him/her learn to improve impulse control and attain the ability to stop and think about possible consequences of negative social behaviors (see *How I Learned to Think Things Through* by Shapiro; or assign "Reasons for Negative Attention-Seeking Behaviors" from the *Child Psychotherapy Homework Planner* by Jongsma, Peterson, and McInnis).

7. Verbalize an awareness of how disruptive behaviors negatively affect self and others. (20, 21, 22)

20. Firmly confront the client's annoying and disruptive behaviors, pointing out consequences for himself/herself and others.

21. Help the client develop an awareness of how disruptive behaviors lead to negative consequences for himself/herself and others.

8. Recognize and verbalize how unpleasant or negative emotions are connected to disruptive behaviors. (23)

9. Identify and implement appropriate ways to elicit attention from family members, authority figures, or peers. (24, 25, 26, 27)

22. Confront statements in which the client blames others for his/her annoying or disruptive behaviors and fails to accept responsibility for his/her actions.

23. Help the client to make a connection between unpleasant or negative emotions and annoying or disruptive behaviors (or assign "Surface Behavior/Inner Feelings" from the *Child Psychotherapy Homework Planner* by Jongsma, Peterson, and McInnis).

24. Teach effective communication and assertiveness skills to help the client to meet his/her needs for attention and approval through appropriate verbalizations and positive social behaviors (or assign "Social Skills" from the *Child Psychotherapy Homework Planner* by Jongsma, Peterson, and McInnis).

25. Instruct the parents and teachers to observe and record positive behaviors by the client in between therapy sessions; reinforce and encourage the client to continue to engage in the positive behaviors.

26. Assess periods of time during which the client displays positive social behaviors; reinforce any strengths or resources used to gain approval and acceptance from peers.

27. Introduce the idea that the client can change the pattern of engaging in disruptive or negative attention-seeking behaviors by asking the following question: "What will

you be doing when you stop getting into trouble?" Process the client's responses and help him/her develop an action plan to accomplish goals or desired behavior changes (or assign "Finding Ways to Get Positive Attention" from the *Child Psychotherapy Homework Planner* by Jongsma, Peterson, and McInnis).

10. Identify and list stressors that contribute to the emergence of disruptive and negative attention-seeking behaviors. (28, 29)

28. Explore with the client possible stressors or frustrations (e.g., lengthy separation from parent, learning problems, failure experiences) that might cause negative behaviors to reappear in the future; help him/her and family members identify how to manage stressors or frustrations.

29. Conduct family therapy sessions to explore the dynamics that contribute to the emergence of the client's disruptive and negative attention-seeking behaviors.

11. Increase parental time spent with the client in positive and rewarding activities. (30, 31, 32)

30. Conduct filial play therapy sessions (i.e., parental involvement in session) to help improve the quality of the parent-child relationship and increase the parent's awareness of the factors contributing to the client's disruptive or annoying behaviors.

31. Give a directive to uninvolved or disengaged parent(s) to spend more time with the client in leisure, school, or household activities.

32. Prescribe a symptom by directing the client to engage in annoying or disruptive behaviors for a

specific length of time or at a set time each day to help disrupt established patterns of negative behaviors. (This intervention seeks to diffuse the client's power of gaining negative attention through the annoying and disruptive behaviors.)

12. Identify and verbally express feelings associated with past neglect, abuse, separation, or abandonment. (33, 34, 35, 36)

33. Explore the client's family background for a history of physical, sexual, or substance abuse, which may contribute to his/her disruptive behaviors.

34. Encourage and support the client in expressing feelings associated with neglect, abuse, separation, or abandonment.

35. Use child-centered play therapy approaches (e.g., provide unconditional, positive regard, offer nonjudgmental reflection of feelings, display trust in child's capacity to act responsibly) to help the client express and work through feelings surrounding past neglect, abuse, separation, or abandonment.

36. Use the empty-chair technique to assist the client in expressing and working through feelings of anger and sadness about past neglect, abuse, separation, or abandonment.

13. Increase the frequency of socially appropriate behaviors with siblings and peers. (37, 38, 39)

37. Encourage the client to participate in extracurricular or positive peer group activities to improve social skills, get positive attention, and increase self-esteem (or assign "Finding Ways to Get Positive Attention" from the *Child Psychotherapy Homework Planner* by Jongsma, Peterson, and McInnis).

38. Refer the client for group therapy to improve his/her social judgment and interpersonal skills.

39. Play the game, You & Me: A Game of Social Skills (Shapiro) to help the client develop positive social skills.

14. Increase verbalizations of empathy and concern for other people. (40)

40. Assign the client the task of showing empathy, kindness, or sensitivity to the needs of others (e.g., reading a bedtime story to a sibling, helping a classmate with reading or math problems).

15. Express feelings in therapeutic games or individual play therapy sessions. (41, 42, 43)

41. Play The Helping, Sharing, and Caring Game (Gardner) with the client to promote his/her greater expression of empathy and concern for other people.

42. Interpret the feelings expressed in individual play therapy sessions, and relate them to the client's negative attention-seeking behaviors.

43. Employ psychoanalytic play therapy principles (e.g., explore and gain an understanding of the etiology of unconscious conflicts, fixations, or arrests; interpret resistance, transference, or core anxieties) to help the client work through and resolve issues contributing to disruptive behaviors.

16. Express feelings through art therapy and mutual storytelling. (44, 45)

44. Use puppets, dolls, or stuffed animals to create a story that models appropriate ways to gain approval and acceptance from peers; then ask the client to create a story with similar characters or themes.

45. Use the Color-Your-Life technique (O'Connor) to

improve the client's ability to
identify and verbalize feelings
instead of acting them out: Ask
the client to match colors to
different emotions (e.g., red-
anger, blue-sad, black-very sad,
yellow-happy), and then fill up a
blank page with colors that
reflect his/her feelings about
different life events.

17. Take medication as prescribed
by the physician. (46)

46. Arrange for a medication
evaluation to improve the client's
impulse control and stabilize
his/her moods.

—. _____

—. _____

   _____

—. _____

—. _____

   _____

—. _____

—. _____

   _____

—. _____

DIAGNOSTIC SUGGESTIONS

Using DSM-IV/ICD-9-CM:

Axis I:	312.9	Disruptive Behavior Disorder NOS
	314.01	Attention-Deficit/Hyperactivity Disorder, Predominantly Hyperactive-Impulsive Type
	314.01	Attention-Deficit/Hyperactivity Disorder, Combined Type
	312.81	Conduct Disorder, Childhood-Onset Type
	313.81	Oppositional Defiant Disorder
	309.3	Adjustment Disorder With Disturbance of Conduct
	309.4	Adjustment Disorder With Mixed Disturbance of Emotions and Conduct
	V71.02	Child Antisocial Behavior
	V61.20	Parent-Child Relational Problem
	_____	_____
	_____	_____

Axis II:	V71.09	No Diagnosis
	_____	_____
	_____	_____

Using DSM-5/ICD-9-CM/ICD-10-CM:

ICD-9-CM	ICD-10-CM	*DSM-5* Disorder, Condition, or Problem
312.9	F91.9	Unspecified Disruptive, Impulse Control, and Conduct Disorder
312.89	F91.8	Other Specified Disruptive, Impulse Control, and Conduct Disorder
314.01	F90.1	Attention-Deficit/Hyperactivity Disorder, Predominately Hyperactive /Impulsive Presentation
314.01	F90.2	Attention-Deficit/Hyperactivity Disorder, Combined Presentation
312.81	F91.1	Conduct Disorder, Childhood-Onset Type
313.81	F91.3	Oppositional Defiant Disorder
309.3	F43.24	Adjustment Disorder, With Disturbance of Conduct
309.4	F43.25	Adjustment Disorder, With Mixed Disturbance of Emotions and Conduct
V71.02	Z72.810	Child or Adolescent Antisocial Behavior
V61.20	Z62.820	Parent-Child Relational Problem

Note: The ICD-9-CM codes are to be used for coding purposes in the United States through September 30, 2014. ICD-10-CM codes are to be used starting October 1, 2014. Some ICD-9-CM codes are associated with more than one ICD-10-CM and *DSM-5* disorder, condition, or problem. In addition, some ICD-9-CM disorders have been discontinued resulting in multiple ICD-9-CM codes being replaced by one ICD-10-CM code. Some discontinued ICD-9-CM codes are not listed in this table. See *Diagnostic and Statistical Manual of Mental Disorders* (2013) for details.

DIVORCE REACTION

BEHAVIORAL DEFINITIONS

1. Infrequent contact or loss of contact with a parental figure due to separation or divorce.
2. Intense emotional reaction (e.g., crying, begging, pleading, temper outbursts) associated with separation of parental figures and/or when making the transfer from one parent's home to another.
3. Persistent fears and worries about being abandoned or separated from a parent.
4. Strong feelings of grief and sadness combined with feelings of low self-worth, lack of confidence, social withdrawal, and loss of interest in activities that normally bring pleasure.
5. Feelings of guilt accompanied by unreasonable belief regarding behaving in some manner to cause parents' divorce and/or failing to prevent their divorce from occurring.
6. Marked increase in frequency and severity of acting-out, oppositional, and aggressive behaviors since the onset of parents' marital problems, separation, or divorce.
7. Significant decline in school performance and lack of interest or motivation in school-related activities.
8. Appearance of regressive behaviors (e.g., thumb-sucking, baby talk, rocking, bed-wetting).
9. Pseudomaturity as manifested by denying or suppressing painful emotions about parents' divorce and often assuming parental roles or responsibilities.
10. Numerous psychosomatic complaints in response to anticipated separations, stress, or frustration.
11. Loss of contact with positive support network due to geographic move.

—. _____

_____

—. _____
   _____
—. _____
   _____

LONG-TERM GOALS

1. Accept parents' separation or divorce with understanding and control of feelings and behavior.
2. Alleviate anger, sadness, and fear of abandonment and establish loving, secure relationship with the parents.
3. Eliminate feelings of guilt and statements that reflect self-blame for parents' divorce.
4. Parents establish and maintain appropriate parent-child boundaries in discipline and assignment of responsibilities.
5. Parents consistently demonstrate mutual respect for one another, especially in front of the children.

—. _____
   _____
—. _____
   _____
   _____
—. _____
   _____

SHORT-TERM OBJECTIVES

1. Tell the story of parents' separation or divorce. (1, 2)

THERAPEUTIC INTERVENTIONS

1. Actively build the level of trust with the client through consistent eye contact, active listening, unconditional positive regard, and warm acceptance to improve his/her ability to identify and express feelings connected to parents' separation or divorce.

2. Explore, encourage, and support the client in verbally expressing

and clarifying his/her feelings associated with the separation or divorce (or assign "My Thoughts and Feelings about My Parents' Divorce" or "Petey's Journey Through Sadness" from the *Child Psychotherapy Homework Planner* by Jongsma, Peterson, and McInnis).

2. Identify and express feelings related to parents' separation or divorce. (3, 4, 5, 6)

3. Read books with the client to assist him/her in expressing his/her feelings about the parents' divorce and changes in the family system (e.g., *What Can I Do?: A Book for Children of Divorce* by Lowry; *The Divorce Workbook for Children* by Schab; *Was It the Chocolate Pudding?: A Story for Little Kids about Divorce* by Levins).

4. Create a photo album by first instructing the client to gather a diverse collection of photographs covering many aspects of his/her life (or assign "Create a Memory Album" from the *Child Psychotherapy Homework Planner* by Jongsma, Peterson, and McInnis); then place the pictures in a photo album during a session while allowing him/her to verbalize his/her feelings about changes in the family system.

5. Use the Color-Your-Life Technique (O'Connor) to improve the client's ability to identify and verbalize feelings: Ask the client to match colors with different emotions (e.g., red-anger, purple-rage, yellow-happy, blue-sad, black-very sad), and then instruct him/her to fill a blank page with colors that

reflect his/her feelings about his/her parents' separation or divorce.

6. Ask the client to first draw pictures of different emotions on blank faces and then share time when he/she experienced those emotions about parents' separation or divorce (or use the "Feelings and Faces Game" exercise from the *Child Psychotherapy Homework Planner* by Jongsma, Peterson, and McInnis).

3. Describe how parents' separation or divorce has impacted his/her personal and family life. (7)

7. Use the empty-chair technique to help the client express mixed emotions he/she feels toward both parents about changes in personal or family life due to separation or divorce.

4. Provide behavioral, emotional, and attitudinal information toward an assessment of specifiers relevant to a *DSM* diagnosis, the efficacy of treatment, and the nature of the therapy relationship. (8, 9, 10, 11, 12)

8. Assess the client's level of insight (syntonic versus dystonic) toward the "presenting problems" (e.g., demonstrates good insight into the problematic nature of the "described behavior," agrees with others' concern, and is motivated to work on change; demonstrates ambivalence regarding the "problem described" and is reluctant to address the issue as a concern; or demonstrates resistance regarding acknowledgment of the "problem described," is not concerned, and has no motivation to change).

9. Assess the client for evidence of research-based correlated disorders (e.g., oppositional defiant behavior with ADHD, depression secondary to an anxiety disorder) including

vulnerability to suicide, if appropriate (e.g., increased suicide risk when comorbid depression is evident).

10. Assess for any issues of age, gender, or culture that could help explain the client's currently defined "problem behavior" and factors that could offer a better understanding of the client's behavior.

11. Assess for the severity of the level of impairment to the client's functioning to determine appropriate level of care (e.g., the behavior noted creates mild, moderate, severe, or very severe impairment in social, relational, vocational, or occupational endeavors); continuously assess this severity of impairment as well as the efficacy of treatment (e.g., the client no longer demonstrates severe impairment but the presenting problem now is causing mild or moderate impairment).

12. Assess the client's home, school, and community for pathogenic care (e.g., persistent disregard for the child's emotional needs or physical needs, repeated changes in primary caregivers, limited opportunities for stable attachments, persistent harsh punishment or other grossly inept parenting).

5. Express thoughts and feelings within the family system regarding parental separation or divorce. (13, 14)

13. Hold family therapy sessions to allow the client and siblings to express feelings about separation or divorce in presence of parents.

14. Encourage the parents to provide opportunities

(e.g., family meetings) at home to allow the client and siblings to express feelings about separation/divorce and subsequent changes in family system.

6. Recognize and affirm self as not being responsible for parents' separation or divorce. (15, 16)

15. Explore the factors contributing to the client's feelings of guilt and self-blame about parents' separation/divorce; assist him/her in realizing that his/her negative behaviors did not cause parents' divorce to occur (recommend *It's Not Your Fault, Koko Bear: A Read-Together Book for Parents and Young Children During Divorce* by Lansky).

16. Assist the client in realizing that he/she does not have the power or control to bring parents back together.

7. Parents verbalize an acceptance of the responsibility for dissolution of the marriage. (17, 18)

17. Conduct family therapy sessions where the parents affirm the client and siblings as not being responsible for separation or divorce.

18. Challenge and confront statements by the parents that place blame or responsibility for separation or divorce on the children.

8. Identify positive and negative aspects of parents' separation or divorce. (19)

19. Give homework assignment in which the client lists both positive and negative aspects of parents' divorce; process this list in the next session and allow him/her to express different emotions.

9. Identify and verbalize unmet need to parents. (20, 21)

20. Give parents the directive of spending 10 to 15 minutes of one-on-one time with the client and siblings on a regular daily

basis to identify and meet the children's needs.

21. Consult with the client and his/her parents about establishing routine or ritual (e.g., snuggling and reading books together, playing board games, watching a favorite video) to help decrease his/her emotional distress around periods of separation or transfer from one parent's home to another.

10. Reduce the frequency and severity of angry, depressed, and anxious moods. (22, 23)

22. Empower the client by reinforcing his/her ability to cope with divorce and make healthy adjustments.

23. Assist the client in making a connection between underlying painful emotions about divorce and angry outbursts or aggressive behaviors (or assign "Surface Behavior/Inner Feelings" from the *Child Psychotherapy Homework Planner* by Jongsma, Peterson, and McInnis).

11. Express feelings of anger about the parents' separation or divorce through controlled, respectful verbalizations and healthy physical outlets. (24, 25)

24. Identify appropriate and inappropriate ways for the client to express anger about the parents' separation or divorce.

25. Use the Angry Tower technique (Saxe) to help the client identify and express feelings of anger about divorce: Build a tower out of plastic containers; place a small object (representing anger) on top of the tower; instruct the client to throw a small fabric ball at the tower while verbalizing feelings of anger connected to the divorce.

12. Parents verbally recognize how their guilt and failure to follow through with limits contributes to the client's acting-out or aggressive behaviors. (26, 27)

26. Encourage and challenge the parents not to allow guilt feelings about divorce to interfere with the need to impose consequences for acting out or oppositional behaviors.

27. Assist the parents in establishing clearly defined rules, boundaries, and consequences for acting out, oppositional, or aggressive behaviors (or assign "Being a Consistent Parent" from the *Child Psychotherapy Homework Planner* by Jongsma, Peterson, and McInnis).

13. Reduce the frequency and severity of acting-out, oppositional, and aggressive behaviors. (28, 29, 30)

28. Help the client to recognize how an increase in acting-out behaviors is connected to emotional pain surrounding the parents' divorce (or assign the "Surface Behavior/Inner Feelings" exercise in the *Child Psychotherapy Homework Planner* by Jongsma, Peterson, and McInnis).

29. Assign the parents to read a book to learn to manage the client's increased acting-out, oppositional, and aggressive behaviors (e.g., *The Kazdin Method for Parenting the Defiant Child* by Kazdin; *1-2-3 Magic: Effective Discipline for Children 2–12* by Phelan); process the reading with the therapist.

30. Design a reward system and/or contingency contract with the client to reinforce good anger control and deter acting-out, oppositional, or aggressive behaviors.

14. Complete school and homework assignments on a regular basis. (31, 32)

31. Assist the parents in establishing a new study routine to help the client complete school or homework assignments.

15. Decrease the frequency of somatic complaints. (33)

16. Noncustodial parent verbally recognizes pattern of overindulgence and begins to set limits on money spending and/or time spent in leisure or recreational activities. (34)

17. Noncustodial parent begins to assign household responsibilities and/or require the client to complete homework during visits. (35)

18. Reduce the frequency of regressive, immature, and irresponsible behaviors. (36, 37)

19. Parents cease making unnecessary, hostile, or overly critical remarks about the other parent in the presence of their child(ren). (38)

20. Parents recognize and agree to cease the pattern of soliciting information and/or sending

32. Design and implement a reward system and/or contingency contract to reinforce completion of school and homework assignments or good academic performance.

33. Refocus the client's discussion from physical complaints to emotional conflicts and the expression of feelings.

34. Encourage the noncustodial parent to set limits on the client's misbehavior and refrain from overindulging the client during visits.

35. Give a directive to the noncustodial parent to assign a chore of having the client complete a school or homework assignment during a visit.

36. Teach how enmeshed or overly protective parents reinforce the client's regressive, immature, or irresponsible behaviors by failing to set necessary limits.

37. Have the client and his/her parents identify age-appropriate ways for him/her to meet needs for attention, affection, and acceptance; process the list and encourage him/her to engage in age-appropriate behaviors.

38. Challenge and confront the parents to cease making unnecessary hostile or overly critical remarks about the other parent in the presence of the child(ren).

39. Counsel the parents about not placing the child(ren) in the middle by soliciting information

messages to the other parent through the child(ren). (39, 40)

about the other parent or sending messages through the child(ren) to the other parent about adult matters.

40. Challenge and confront the client about playing one parent against the other to meet needs, obtain material goods, or avoid responsibility.

21. Disengaged or uninvolved parent follows through with recommendations to spend greater quality time with the client. (41, 42, 43)

41. Hold individual and/or family therapy session to challenge and encourage noncustodial parent to maintain regular visitation and involvement in the client's life.

42. Give a directive to the disengaged or distant parent to spend more time or perform a specific task with the client (e.g., going on an outing to the zoo, assisting the client with homework, working on a project around the home).

43. Use family theraplay principles (e.g., active involvement by the parent in the session, with him/her responding empathically to the client's feelings or needs) to strengthen or facilitate a closer parent-child relationship.

22. Identify and express feelings through mutual storytelling and artwork. (44, 45, 46)

44. Use a mutual storytelling technique whereby the therapist and client alternate telling stories through the use of puppets, dolls, or stuffed animals: The therapist first models appropriate ways to express emotions related to the parents' separation or divorce; the client then follows by creating a story with similar characters or themes.

45. Have the client draw a variety of pictures reflecting his/her feelings

about his/her parents' divorce or how divorce has impacted his/her life; place these pictures in a notebook that is given to him/her at the end of therapy as a keepsake.

46. Instruct the client to draw pictures of both his/her mother's and father's homes, and then have him/her share what it is like to live in or visit each home to assess the quality of his/her relationship with each parent.

23. Increase participation in a positive peer group and extracurricular or school-related activities. (47)

47. Encourage the client to participate in school, extracurricular, or positive peer group activities to offset the loss of time spent with his/her parents.

24. Participate in a support group with other children of divorce. (48)

48. Refer the client to a children-of-divorce group to assist him/her in expressing feelings and to help him/her understand that he/she is not alone in going through the divorce process.

25. Increase contacts with adults and build a support network outside the family. (49)

49. Identify a list of adult individuals (e.g., school counselor, neighbor, uncle or aunt, Big Brother or Big Sister, member of clergy) outside the family to whom the client can turn for support, guidance, and nurturance to help him/her cope with divorce, family move, or a change in schools.

—. _____
_____
—. _____
_____
—. _____
_____

—. _____
_____
—. _____
_____
—. _____
_____

DIAGNOSTIC SUGGESTIONS

Using DSM-IV/ICD-9-CM:

Axis I:	309.0	Adjustment Disorder With Depressed Mood
	309.24	Adjustment Disorder With Anxiety
	309.28	Adjustment Disorder With Mixed Anxiety and Depressed Mood
	309.3	Adjustment Disorder With Disturbance of Conduct
	309.4	Adjustment Disorder With Mixed Disturbance of Emotions and Conduct
	300.4	Dysthymic Disorder
	300.02	Generalized Anxiety Disorder
	309.21	Separation Anxiety Disorder
	313.81	Oppositional Defiant Disorder
	300.81	Undifferentiated Somatoform Disorder
	_____	_____
	_____	_____
Axis II:	V71.09	No Diagnosis
	_____	_____
	_____	_____

Using DSM-5/ICD-9-CM/ICD-10-CM:

ICD-9-CM	ICD-10-CM	*DSM-5* Disorder, Condition, or Problem
309.0	F43.21	Adjustment Disorder, With Depressed Mood
309.24	F43.22	Adjustment Disorder, With Anxiety
309.28	F43.23	Adjustment Disorder, With Mixed Anxiety and Depressed Mood
309.3	F43.24	Adjustment Disorder, With Disturbance of Conduct
309.4	F43.25	Adjustment Disorder, With Mixed Disturbance of Emotions and Conduct
300.4	F34.1	Persistent Depressive Disorder
300.02	F41.1	Generalized Anxiety Disorder
309.21	F93.0	Separation Anxiety Disorder
313.81	F91.3	Oppositional Defiant Disorder
300.81	F45.1	Somatic Symptom Disorder
V61.03	Z63.5	Disruption of Family by Separation or Divorce

Note: The ICD-9-CM codes are to be used for coding purposes in the United States through September 30, 2014. ICD-10-CM codes are to be used starting October 1, 2014. Some ICD-9-CM codes are associated with more than one ICD-10-CM and *DSM-5* disorder, condition, or problem. In addition, some ICD-9-CM disorders have been discontinued resulting in multiple ICD-9-CM codes being replaced by one ICD-10-CM code. Some discontinued ICD-9-CM codes are not listed in this table. See *Diagnostic and Statistical Manual of Mental Disorders* (2013) for details.

ENURESIS/ENCOPRESIS

BEHAVIORAL DEFINITIONS

1. Repeated pattern of voluntary or involuntary voiding of urine into bed or clothes during the day or at night after age 5, when continence is expected.
2. Repeated passage of feces, whether voluntary or involuntary, in inappropriate places (e.g., clothing, floor) after age 5, when continence is expected.
3. Feelings of shame associated with enuresis or encopresis that cause the avoidance of situations (e.g., overnight visits with friends) that might lead to further embarrassment.
4. Social ridicule, isolation, or ostracism by peers because of enuresis or encopresis.
5. Frequent attempts to hide feces or soiled clothing because of shame or fear of further ridicule, criticism, or punishment.
6. Excessive anger, rejection, or punishment by the parents or caretakers centered on toilet-training practices, which contributes to low self-esteem.
7. Strong feelings of fear or hostility, which are channeled into acts of enuresis and encopresis.
8. Poor impulse control, which contributes to lack of responsibility with toilet-training practices.
9. Deliberate smearing of feces.

__. _____
   _____
__. _____
   _____
__. _____
   _____

LONG-TERM GOALS

1. Eliminate all diurnal and/or nocturnal episodes of enuresis.
2. Terminate all episodes of encopresis, whether voluntary or involuntary.
3. Resolve the underlying core conflicts contributing to the emergence of enuresis or encopresis.
4. Parents eliminate rigid or coercive toilet-training practices.
5. Cease all incidents of smearing feces.
6. Increase self-esteem and successfully work through feelings of shame or humiliation associated with past enuresis or encopresis.

—. _____

_____

—. _____

_____

—. _____

_____

SHORT-TERM OBJECTIVES

1. Parents and client discuss the nature of the problem and its consequences. (1, 2)

2. Comply with a physician's orders for medical tests and evaluations, including possible medication use. (3, 4)

THERAPEUTIC INTERVENTIONS

1. Build rapport with the client and parents through use of active listening, empathic reflection, unconditional regard, acceptance, and genuineness.

2. Conduct a thorough assessment of the elimination problem including its nature, frequency, environmental stimuli, child and parental responses and management efforts; assess for the presence of other psychological or psychiatric conditions that may account for the problem or warrant additional treatment attention.

3. Refer the client for a medical examination to rule out general medical conditions that may be causing the enuresis or encopresis (e.g., urinary tract

infection, imperforate anus, Hirschsprung's Disease).

3. Cooperate with psychological testing. (5)

4. Arrange for a medication evaluation of the client.

5. Conduct psychological testing or use objective measures to assess for other psychological or psychiatric conditions that may warrant treatment attention (e.g., Attention-Deficit/Hyperactivity Disorder (ADHD), impulse-control disorder, or serious underlying emotional problems); provide relevant feedback from the testing to the client and his/her parents.

4. Provide behavioral, emotional, and attitudinal information toward an assessment of specifiers relevant to a *DSM* diagnosis, the efficacy of treatment, and the nature of the therapy relationship. (6, 7, 8, 9, 10)

6. Assess the client's level of insight (syntonic versus dystonic) toward the "presenting problems" (e.g., demonstrates good insight into the problematic nature of the "described behavior," agrees with others' concern, and is motivated to work on change; demonstrates ambivalence regarding the "problem described" and is reluctant to address the issue as a concern; or demonstrates resistance regarding acknowledgment of the "problem described," is not concerned, and has no motivation to change).

7. Assess the client for evidence of research-based correlated disorders (e.g., oppositional defiant behavior with ADHD, depression secondary to an anxiety disorder) including vulnerability to suicide, if appropriate (e.g., increased suicide risk when comorbid depression is evident).

8. Assess for any issues of age, gender, or culture that could help explain the client's currently defined "problem behavior" and factors that could offer a better understanding of the client's behavior.

9. Assess for the severity of the level of impairment to the client's functioning to determine appropriate level of care (e.g., the behavior noted creates mild, moderate, severe, or very severe impairment in social, relational, vocational, or occupational endeavors); continuously assess this severity of impairment as well as the efficacy of treatment (e.g., the client no longer demonstrates severe impairment but the presenting problem now is causing mild or moderate impairment).

10. Assess the client's home, school, and community for pathogenic care (e.g., persistent disregard for the client's emotional needs or physical needs, repeated changes in primary caregivers, limited opportunities for stable attachments, persistent harsh punishment or other grossly inept parenting).

▽ 5. Take prescribed medication as directed by the physician. (11)

11. Monitor the client for medication compliance, side effects, and effectiveness; consult with the prescribing physician at regular intervals and be alert for relapse after discontinuation. ▽

▽ 6. Parents verbally recognize how rigid toilet-training practices or hostile, critical remarks contribute to the client's enuresis

12. Explore parent-child interactions to assess whether the parents' toilet-training practices are excessively rigid or whether the

or encopresis and agree to discontinue them. (12, 13, 14)

7. Parents consistently comply with the use of an alarm-based behavioral treatment (e.g., bell-and-pad conditioning procedures) to treat nocturnal enuresis. (15, 16)

parents make frequent hostile, critical remarks about the client. ▽

13. Counsel the client's parents on effective, nonabusive, reward-based toilet-training practices; get parental agreement to change from a punishment- to a reward-based system. ▽

14. Conduct family therapy sessions to assess and address negative interactions that contribute to the emergence or reinforcement of the client's enuresis, encopresis, or smearing of feces. ▽

15. Contract or otherwise secure agreement with the parents and client for a trial of alarm-based biobehavioral treatment, discussing its features and rationale (see *Elimination Disorders in Children and Adolescents* by Christopherson and Friman). ▽

16. Train the client and his/her parents to treat enuresis by using a bed-based or pajama-based alarm that sounds when involuntary wetting occurs (or assign the parents "Dry Bed Training Program" in the *Child Psychotherapy Homework Planner* by Jongsma, Peterson, and McInnis); follow an alarm with a procedure of fully awakening the child, instructing him/her to go to the bathroom to complete (or attempt) urination, change bedding and pajamas (responsibility training), reset the alarm, and go back to bed; ensure that alarm can be heard by child and parents. ▽

▼ 8. Parents and client measure the effect of treatment as instructed by the therapist. (17)

▼ 9. Parents and client learn and implement the overlearning technique to build upon success gained using the alarm. (18, 19)

17. Teach and employ a measurement system that parents use to measure the frequency of wetting and size of urine stain. ▼

18. Continue alarm-based treatment until criteria for improvement is met (e.g., 14 consecutive "dry days"). ▼

19. Once initial criteria for improvement is met, employ overlearning method (e.g., require the client to drink a gradually increasing, but small, amount of fluid shortly before bedtime) along with the use of the alarm-based procedures used in latter stages of treatment to help prevent the client's relapse of nocturnal enuresis. ▼

▼ 10. Parents implement reward-based system for increasing successful bladder control while decreasing the frequency of enuretic behavior. (20)

20. Design and counsel the parents on the use of positive reinforcement procedures during the alarm-based technique to increase the client's bladder control, simultaneously eliminating use of punishment; use larger awards when the client reaches major milestones (e.g., a video game for successful completion of the training). ▼

▼ 11. Parents assist the client in practicing urine-retention control techniques. (21)

21. Teach the client and his/her parents an effective urine-retention training technique that increases the client's awareness of the sensation or need to urinate by having the client drink extra fluid (e.g., 16 oz. water or juice) and gets rewards for holding urine for increasingly longer periods of time before voiding (or assign "Bladder Retention Training Program" in the *Child Psychotherapy*

▽ 12. Participate in a scheduled awakening. (22)

Homework Planner by Jongsma, Peterson, and McInnis). ▽

22. Train the client's parents or caretakers in the use of an awakening procedure in which the child is awakened at the parents' normal bedtime to control nocturnal enuresis. ▽

▽ 13. Learn and practice Kegel and stream-interruption exercises. (23)

23. Teach the client Kegel exercises in which he/she purposefully contracts muscles involved in terminating elimination (urine or feces); prescribe a "stream-interruption" exercise in which the client practices terminating the flow of urine at least once a day. ▽

▽ 14. Parents and client participate in a systematic biobehavioral approach to reduce the frequency of encopretic behavior. (24, 25)

24. Conduct a biobehavioral approach to encopresis beginning with education of the client and parents about the elimination process, including difficulties; explain the components and rationale for treatment (see *Elimination Disorders in Children and Adolescents* by Christopherson and Friman). ▽

25. Debunk myths that personality characteristics such as stubbornness, immaturity, or laziness are the cause of encopresis, discouraging parents from shaming and blaming their children. ▽

▽ 15. Read books recommended by the therapist on overcoming toileting problems. (26)

26. Facilitate therapy by recommending reading consistent with the therapeutic approach (see *It's No Accident* by Hodges and Schlosberg; *Waking Up Dry* by Bennett; *Toilet Training in Less Than a Day* by Azrin; resources at

▽ 16. Comply with use of techniques for cleansing the bowel. (27)

▽ 17. Comply with dietary recommendations designed to improve bowel function. (28)

▽ 18. Establish a regular time to attempt bowel movements. (29, 30)

▽ 19. Parents implement a reward system for successful bowel movements and unsuccessful efforts. (31)

▽ 20. Develop and implement a plan for responding to toileting accidents. (32)

pottymd.com, encopresis.com, and/or pottytrainingconcepts .com). ▽

27. Begin the process of establishing regular bowel movements by first cleansing the bowel completely of fecal matter (e.g., through supervised enema and/or laxative use). ▽

28. Implement a diet with a high level of dietary fiber to increase colonic motility and moisture, thus facilitating easier and more regular bowel movements. ▽

29. Work with parents to choose one or two regular times for the child to attempt bowel movements that is not during school hours and is guided by the child's typical habits and child-parent time constraints; have child sit no longer than 10 minutes to avoid increasing the aversive properties of the toileting experience. ▽

30. Make toileting a relaxed, pleasant experience by allowing the child to listen to music, read, or talk with the parent while attempting to have a bowel movement. ▽

31. Reward successful bowel movement in the toilet with praise and/or other reward system; if the child does not have a bowel movement, his/her effort should be praised and another session should be scheduled for later in the day. ▽

32. Respond to accidents without punishment or criticism, although involve the child in clean-up in an age-appropriate

manner (e.g., older children clean the mess; younger children just bring soiled clothing to the laundry area and allow themselves to be cleaned by the parent).▽

▽ 21. Parents monitor client's progress through therapy. (33)

33. Teach parents how to monitor progress using pants checks with praise for accident-free checks and ongoing recording of toileting successes, accidents, and the size and consistency of both; review routinely, reinforcing successes and problem-solving obstacles.▽

▽ 22. Client and/or parents increase responsibility for developing bowel control. (34, 35)

34. Encourage the client to assume active responsibility for achieving mastery of bladder and/or bowel control (e.g., keeping a record of wet and dry days, setting an alarm clock for voiding times, cleaning soiled underwear or linens) and reward appropriately; or assign the "Bowel Control Training Program" in the *Child Psychotherapy Homework Planner* by Jongsma, Peterson, and McInnis.▽

35. Inquire into what the client does differently on days when he/she demonstrates good bladder/ bowel control and does not have any enuretic or encopretic incidents; process his/her responses and reinforce any effective strategies that are used to gain bladder/bowel control.▽

23. Verbalize how anxiety or fears associated with toilet-training practices are unfounded. (36, 37)

36. Explore the client's irrational cognitive messages that produce fear or anxiety associated with toilet training; replace the irrational messages with realistic messages.

24. Understand and verbally recognize the secondary gain that results from enuresis or encopresis. (38, 39, 40)

37. Use cognitive therapy techniques to assist the client in realizing how his/her anxiety or fears associated with toilet training are unfounded.

38. Assist the client and his/her parents in developing an insight into the secondary gain (e.g., parental attention; avoidance of separation from the parents; physician or counselor attention) received from enuresis or encopresis.

39. Use a strategic family therapy approach in which the therapist does not talk about enuresis or encopresis, but discusses what might surface if this problem were resolved (i.e., camouflaged problems may be revealed).

40. Use Ericksonian therapy intervention of prescribing the symptom, whereby the client is instructed to pick out a specific night of the week when he/she will deliberately wet the bed. (Paradoxical intervention allows the client to control enuresis by making the unconscious behavior a conscious maneuver.)

25. Identify and express feelings associated with past separation, loss, trauma, or rejection experiences and how they are connected to current encopresis/enuresis. (41, 42, 43)

41. Determine whether the client's enuresis, encopresis, or smearing of feces is associated with past separation, loss, traumatization, or rejection experiences.

42. Explore, encourage, and support the client in verbally expressing and clarifying feelings associated with past separation, loss, trauma, or rejection experiences.

43. Employ psychoanalytic play therapy approaches (e.g., explore

and gain understanding of the etiology of unconscious conflicts, fixations, or arrests; interpret resistance, transference, or core anxieties) to help the client work through and resolve issues contributing to bladder/bowel control problems.

26. Express feelings through artwork and mutual storytelling. (44)

44. Instruct the client to draw a picture that reflects how enuretic or encopretic incidents affect self-esteem.

27. Increase the frequency of positive self-descriptive statements that reflect improved self-esteem. (45, 46)

45. Assist the client in identifying and listing his/her positive characteristics to help decrease feelings of shame and embarrassment; reinforce his/her positive self-statements.

46. Assign the client to make one positive self-statement daily and record that in a journal.

28. Appropriately express anger verbally and physically rather than channeling anger through enuresis, encopresis, or smearing of feces. (47, 48)

47. Teach the client effective communication and assertiveness skills to improve his/her ability to express thoughts and feelings through appropriate verbalizations.

48. Teach the client appropriate physical outlets that allow the expression of anger in a constructive manner, rather than through inappropriate wetting or soiling.

—. _____

_____

—. _____

_____

—. _____

_____

—. _____

_____

—. _____

_____

—. _____

_____

DIAGNOSTIC SUGGESTIONS

Using DSM-IV/ICD-9-CM:

Axis I:	307.6	Enuresis (Not Due to a General Medical Condition)
	787.6	Encopresis, With Constipation and Overflow Incontinence
	307.7	Encopresis, Without Constipation and Overflow Incontinence
	300.4	Dysthymic Disorder
	296.xx	Major Depressive Disorder
	299.80	Pervasive Developmental Disorder NOS
	309.81	Posttraumatic Stress Disorder
	313.81	Oppositional Defiant Disorder
	314.01	Attention-Deficit/Hyperactivity Disorder, Combined Type
	_____	_____
	_____	_____
Axis II:	V71.09	No Diagnosis
	_____	_____
	_____	_____

Using DSM-5/ICD-9-CM/ICD-10-CM:

ICD-9-CM	ICD-10-CM	*DSM-5* Disorder, Condition, or Problem
307.6	F98.0	Enuresis (Specify: Nocturnal Only, Diurnal Only, Nocturnal and Diurnal)
307.7	F98.1	Encopresis (Specify: With Constipation and Overflow Incontinence, Without Constipation and Overflow Incontinence)
300.4	F34.1	Persistent Depressive Disorder
296.xx	F32.x	Major Depressive Disorder, Single Episode
296.xx	F33.x	Major Depressive Disorder, Recurrent Episode
315.9	F89	Unspecified Neurodevelopmental Disorder
315.8	F88	Other Specified Neurodevelopmental Disorder
309.81	F43.10	Posttraumatic Stress Disorder
313.81	F91.3	Oppositional Defiant Disorder
314.01	F90.2	Attention-Deficit/Hyperactivity Disorder, Combined Presentation

Note: The ICD-9-CM codes are to be used for coding purposes in the United States through September 30, 2014. ICD-10-CM codes are to be used starting October 1, 2014. Some ICD-9-CM codes are associated with more than one ICD-10-CM and *DSM-5* disorder, condition, or problem. In addition, some ICD-9-CM disorders have been discontinued resulting in multiple ICD-9-CM codes being replaced by one ICD-10-CM code. Some discontinued ICD-9-CM codes are not listed in this table. See *Diagnostic and Statistical Manual of Mental Disorders* (2013) for details.

▼ Indicates that the Objective/Intervention is consistent with those found in evidence-based treatments.

FIRE SETTING

BEHAVIORAL DEFINITIONS

1. Has set one or more fires in the past 6 months.
2. Has been regularly observed playing with fire, fireworks, or combustible substances.
3. Is around fire whenever possible.
4. Consistently has matches, lighters, candles, and so forth in his/her possession.
5. Has an easily discernible fascination and/or preoccupation with fire.
6. Does not experience tension or sexual arousal prior to fire-setting behavior, or gratification or relief when witnessing the fire.

—. _____
   _____
—. _____
   _____
—. _____
   _____

LONG-TERM GOALS

1. Establish safety of self, the family, and the community.
2. Terminate the fascination and preoccupation with fire.
3. Redirect or rechannel fascination with fire into constructive arenas.
4. Establish the existence of a psychotic process or major affective disorder and procure placement in an appropriate treatment program.
5. Parents responsibly monitor and supervise the client's behaviors and whereabouts.

—. _____
   _____
—. _____
   _____
—. _____
   _____

SHORT-TERM OBJECTIVES

1. Provide information regarding the history of fire setting behavior and the thoughts and feelings accompanying the behavior. (1, 2, 3)

2. Provide behavioral, emotional, and attitudinal information toward an assessment of specifiers relevant to a *DSM* diagnosis, the efficacy of treatment, and the nature of the therapy relationship. (4, 5, 6, 7, 8)

THERAPEUTIC INTERVENTIONS

1. Ask the client to describe his/her history of the fascination with fire and how this has included fire setting.

2. Probe the client's thoughts and feelings that occur prior to, during, and after being close to fire or setting a fire; assess the role of anger in fire setting behavior.

3. Interview the parents as to their knowledge and understanding of the child's history of fire fascination and fire-setting behavior.

4. Assess the client's level of insight (syntonic versus dystonic) toward the "presenting problems" (e.g., demonstrates good insight into the problematic nature of the "described behavior," agrees with others' concern, and is motivated to work on change; demonstrates ambivalence regarding the "problem described" and is reluctant to address the issue as a concern; or demonstrates resistance regarding acknowledgment of the "problem described," is not concerned, and has no motivation to change).

5. Assess the client for evidence of research-based correlated disorders (e.g., oppositional defiant behavior with ADHD, depression secondary to an anxiety disorder) including vulnerability to suicide, if appropriate (e.g., increased suicide risk when comorbid depression is evident).

6. Assess for any issues of age, gender, or culture that could help explain the client's currently defined "problem behavior" and factors that could offer a better understanding of the client's behavior.

7. Assess for the severity of the level of impairment to the client's functioning to determine appropriate level of care (e.g., the behavior noted creates mild, moderate, severe, or very severe impairment in social, relational, vocational, or occupational endeavors); continuously assess this severity of impairment as well as the efficacy of treatment (e.g., the client no longer demonstrates severe impairment but the presenting problem now is causing mild or moderate impairment).

8. Assess the client's home, school, and community for pathogenic care (e.g., persistent disregard for the child's emotional needs or physical needs, repeated changes in primary caregivers, limited opportunities for stable attachments, persistent harsh punishment or other grossly inept parenting).

3. Parents consistently guide and supervise the client's behavior, including monitoring him/her for possessing articles connected with fire (e.g., matches, lighters). (9, 10, 11)

9. Teach the parents to consistently structure and supervise the client's behavior.

10. Monitor the parents' efforts to structure, set limits on, and supervise the client, giving support, encouragement, and redirection as appropriate (or assign "Being a Consistent Parent" from the *Child Psychotherapy Homework Planner* by Jongsma, Peterson, and McInnis).

11. Assist the client and parents in developing ways to increase his/her impulse control through use of positive reinforcement at times of apparent control.

4. Identify the constructive and destructive aspects of fires. (12, 13)

12. Assign and work with the client and parents to create two collages, one that emphasizes fire's positive aspects and one that focuses on fire's destructive aspects; discuss with the client as the collages are presented.

13. Construct with the client and his/her parents a list of questions for the client to ask a firefighter or a nurse in a local burn unit. Then help arrange an interview with one of these individuals. Afterward, process the experience and information gathered.

5. Report a decrease in the impulse to set fires. (14, 15, 16)

14. Assign the family an operant-based intervention in which the parent allows the client to strike up to 40 matches under supervision, noting a need for safety with fire. A sum of money will be placed next to the pack and the client will receive a predetermined sum as well as

warm praise for each match left unstruck (or assign "Fireproofing Your Home and Family" from the *Child Psychotherapy Homework Planner* by Jongsma, Peterson, and McInnis); repeat this exercise at least three times per week and chart matches lit, unlit, and money earned.

15. Assign the mother to give the child a monetary reward for turning in any fire setting material (e.g., matches, lighters, etc.) found around the house and for not having any such material in his/her room or in clothing (or assign the exercise "Fireproofing Your Home and Family" from the *Child Psychotherapy Homework Planner* by Jongsma, Peterson, and McInnis); ask the mother to purposely leave matches where they can be found by the child and keep a chart of how much money is earned.

16. Assist and coach the dad to teach the child a safe way to build a fire and an effective way to put it out while talking about the constructive as well as potential destructive power of fire (or assign the exercise "Fireproofing Your Home and Family" from the *Child Psychotherapy Homework Planner* by Jongsma, Peterson, and McInnis); process the assignment in the next family session.

6. Increase the frequency of positive interactions and connectedness between family members. (17, 18)

17. Use a family system approach to address fire setting behavior; require the entire family to attend an agreed-upon number

of sessions during which the family's roles, ways of communicating, and conflicts will be explored and confronted.

18. Assign each family member to list the positive or supportive and negative or conflictual aspects of the family (or within the session use the exercise "When a Fire Has No Fuel" from the *Child Psychotherapy Homework Planner* by Jongsma, Peterson, and McInnis); process the exercise.

7. The client and his/her family demonstrate the ability to identify, express, and tolerate unpleasant feelings. (19, 20)

19. Assist the family members in learning to identify, express, and tolerate their own feelings and those of other family members.

20. Gently probe the client's emotions in order to help him/her become better able to identify and express his/her feelings.

8. Parents and caregivers identify and implement ways of satisfying the client's unmet emotional needs. (21, 22, 23)

21. Assess the client's unmet needs for attention, nurturance, and affirmation; assist all caregivers (parents, siblings, teachers, babysitters, and extended family) in identifying the child's maladaptive actions (e.g., loud talk, acts of showing off, making up stories) that are used to meet unmet needs (or utilize "Reasons for Negative Attention-Seeking Behaviors" from the *Child Psychotherapy Homework Planner* by Jongsma, Peterson, and McInnis).

22. Brainstorm with parents, child, and/or caregivers ways to meet the child's unmet emotional needs to prevent the child's acting out in a maladaptive

manner (or utilize the exercise "Unmet Emotional Needs—Identification and Satisfaction" from the *Adolescent Psychotherapy Homework Planner* by Jongsma, Peterson, and McInnis).

23. Assess the degree of chaos and/or violence in family leading to the client's desire for power or control over his/her environment. Encourage more structure, predictability, and respect within the family.

9. Increase positive time spent with the father or another significant male figure in the client's life. (24, 25)

24. Ask the father or other caregiving male figure to identify three things he could do to relate more to the client; ask him to implement two of the three, and monitor the results.

25. Assist the mother or other caregiving person in obtaining an older companion for the client through the Big Brother or Big Sister program.

10. Verbalize feelings of rejection and anger. (26)

26. Explore with the child and parents as to possible sources of anger within the child such as abandonment, rejection, abuse, neglect, or criticism (or utilize the "Child Anger Checklist" from the *Child Psychotherapy Homework Planner* by Jongsma, Peterson, and McInnis; or *Helping Your Angry Child: A Workbook for You and Your Family* by Nemeth, Ray, and Schexnayder); interpret fire setting as an expression of rage.

11. Identify instances of physical or sexual abuse. (27)

27. Assess whether the client's fire setting is associated with his/her being a victim of sexual and/or physical abuse (see the Sexual

Abuse Victim chapter in this *Planner*).

12. Cooperate with an evaluation for psychotropic medication or Attention-Deficit/ Hyperactivity Disorder (ADHD). (28, 29)

28. Assess whether the client's fire setting is associated with a psychotic process or major affective disorder that may need psychotropic medication treatment; refer him/her to a physician for evaluation, if necessary.

29. Assess the client for the presence of ADHD and how it may contribute to fire setting behavior (see the ADHD chapter in this *Planner*).

13. Comply with all recommendations of the psychiatric or ADHD evaluation. (30, 31)

30. Support and monitor the family's follow-through with all the recommendations from the psychiatric or ADHD evaluations.

31. Assist the family in placing the client in a residential treatment program for intense treatment of a serious psychiatric disturbance, if indicated.

—. _____
_____
—. _____
_____
—. _____
_____

—. _____
_____
—. _____
_____
—. _____
_____

DIAGNOSTIC SUGGESTIONS

Using DSM-IV/ICD-9-CM:

| **Axis I:** | 312.xx | Conduct Disorder |
| | 314.9 | Attention-Deficit/Hyperactivity Disorder NOS |

309.3	Adjustment Disorder With Disturbance of Conduct
309.4	Adjustment Disorder With Mixed Disturbance of Emotions and Conduct
312.30	Impulse-Control Disorder NOS
298.9	Psychotic Disorder NOS
296.xx	Major Depressive Disorder

_____   _____

_____   _____

Axis II: V71.09   No Diagnosis

_____   _____

_____   _____

Using DSM-5/ICD-9-CM/ICD-10-CM:

ICD-9-CM	ICD-10-CM	_DSM-5_ Disorder, Condition, or Problem
312.xx	F91.1	Conduct Disorder, Childhood-Onset Type
314.01	F90.9	Unspecified Attention-Deficit/Hyperactivity Disorder
314.01	F90.8	Other Specified Attention-Deficit/Hyperactivity Disorder
309.3	F43.24	Adjustment Disorder, With Disturbance of Conduct
309.4	F43.25	Adjustment Disorder, With Mixed Disturbance of Emotions and Conduct
312.9	F91.9	Unspecified Disruptive, Impulse Control, and Conduct Disorder
312.89	F91.8	Other Specified Disruptive, Impulse Control, and Conduct Disorder
298.9	F29	Unspecified Schizophrenia Spectrum and Other Psychotic Disorder
298.8	F28	Other Specified Schizophrenia Spectrum and Other Psychotic Disorder
296.xx	F32.x	Major Depressive Disorder, Single Episode
296.xx	F33.x	Major Depressive Disorder, Recurrent Episode

Note: The ICD-9-CM codes are to be used for coding purposes in the United States through September 30, 2014. ICD-10-CM codes are to be used starting October 1, 2014. Some ICD-9-CM codes are associated with more than one ICD-10-CM and _DSM-5_ disorder, condition, or problem. In addition, some ICD-9-CM disorders have been discontinued resulting in multiple ICD-9-CM codes being replaced by one ICD-10-CM code. Some discontinued ICD-9-CM codes are not listed in this table. See _Diagnostic and Statistical Manual of Mental Disorders_ (2013) for details.

GENDER DYSPHORIA

BEHAVIORAL DEFINITIONS

1. Repeatedly states the desire to be, or feels he/she is, the opposite sex.
2. Preference for dressing in clothes typically worn by the other sex.
3. Prefers the roles of the opposite sex in make-believe play or fantasies.
4. Insists on participating in games and pastimes typical of the other sex.
5. Prefers playmates of the opposite sex.
6. Frequently passes as the opposite sex.
7. Insists that he/she was born the wrong sex.
8. Verbalizes a disgust with or rejection of his/her sexual anatomy.

__. _____
   _____

LONG-TERM GOALS

1. Resolve the confusion regarding gender and/or sexual identity.
2. As transgender desire desists, behave consistent with one's birth-sex gender role as defined by oneself.
3. As transgender desires persist and intensify accept self as a person with opposite sex gender identity.
4. Parents accept and affirm their child as exploration of gender identity progresses.

__. _____
   _____

SHORT-TERM OBJECTIVES

1. Openly express thoughts, feelings, and desires, regarding gender identity and identify the causes for rejection of gender identity. (1, 2)

THERAPEUTIC INTERVENTIONS

1. Using a nonjudgmental interview or play therapy technique encourage the client to disclose the history and current status of

his/her thoughts, feelings, and desires regarding his/her gender; assess gender identity, gender role behavior, and gender dysphoria.

2. Share self-perception of general mood state, areas of conflict, relationships that are enjoyable, and comfort with authority figures. (3, 4)

2. Explore the client's reasons for and history of his/her attraction to an opposite-sex identity.

3. Assess the client for any clinically significant co-occurring psychological conditions such as depression, anxiety, ADHD, autism, or ODD; develop and implement appropriate treatment plan to address any evident conditions.

4. Assess the client's perception and feelings regarding acceptance on the part of peers and family members; be alert to possible bullying by peers, criticism by family members or parents, and stigmatized labeling related to gender typicality in behavior, dress, or grooming.

3. Provide behavioral, emotional, and attitudinal information toward an assessment of specifiers relevant to a DSM diagnosis, the efficacy of treatment, and the nature of the therapy relationship. (5, 6, 7, 8, 9)

5. Assess the client's level of insight (syntonic versus dystonic) toward the "presenting problems" (e.g., demonstrates good insight into the problematic nature of the "described behavior," agrees with others' concern, and is motivated to work on change; demonstrates ambivalence regarding the "problem described" and is reluctant to address the issue as a concern; or demonstrates resistance acknowledging the "problem described," is not concerned, and has no motivation to change).

6. Assess the client for evidence of research-based correlated disorders (e.g., oppositional defiant behavior with ADHD,

depression secondary to an anxiety disorder) including vulnerability to suicide, if appropriate (e.g., increased suicide risk when comorbid depression is evident).

7. Assess for any issues of age, gender, or culture that could help explain the client's currently defined "problem behavior" and factors that could offer a better understanding of the client's behavior.

8. Assess for the severity of the level of impairment to the client's functioning to determine appropriate level of care (e.g., the behavior noted creates mild, moderate, severe, or very severe impairment in social, relational, vocational, or occupational endeavors); continuously assess this severity of impairment as well as the efficacy of treatment (e.g., the client no longer demonstrates severe impairment but the problem now is causing mild or moderate impairment).

9. Assess the client's home, school, and community for pathogenic care (e.g., persistent disregard for the child's emotional needs or physical needs, repeated changes in primary caregivers, limited opportunities for stable attachments, harsh punishment or other grossly inept parenting).

4. Parents share their view of the history and current status of the client's gender identity conflict. (10, 11, 12)

10. Explore the parents' perception of client's gender-related thoughts, feelings, behaviors, and expressed desires; assess for time of onset as well as persistence, intensity, and pervasiveness of client's gender dysphoria or transgender revelations.

11. Assess the parents' attitude, behavior, and feelings regarding the client's nonconformity in gender identity and behavior; process their feelings.

12. Encourage parents to be affirming of their child's exploration of gender nonconformity; suggest reading material that may help them understand and be non-judgmental about the client's gender dysphoria and transgender behavior.

5. Parents discuss their thoughts about a decision concerning the direction of counseling for their child. (13, 14)

13. Disclose to the parents the range of treatment options that are available if the gender dysphoria persists (e.g., noninvasive social transitioning to a cross gender role, adolescent endocrine treatment to suppress puberty and secondary sex characteristics), pointing out that research evidence is very limited to inform treatment outcome; facilitate the decision making process from a position of neutrality.

14. Offer to refer the parents and client to a multidisciplinary team of psychologist, physician, and education specialist who have been trained and are experienced in working with gender diverse and transgender children.

6. Identify and replace negative, distorted cognitive messages regarding gender identity and self-esteem. (15, 16, 17)

15. Teach the child cognitive restructuring techniques to give himself/herself positive and self affirming messages to counteract social rejection; encourage the child to be patient and persistent in being true to self-identity.

16. Use the Positive Thinking game within sessions to promote healthy self-talk and thought patterns; encourage the family to play the game at home.

7. Demonstrate an increased self-esteem as evidenced by positive statements made about talents, traits, and appearance. (18, 19)

8. Verbalize an understanding that gender exploration may be threatening to others (but is not "bad") and therefore may generate fearful or critical reactions by others. (20, 21)

9. All family members verbalize an increased understanding of the client's need for affirmation and acceptance during his/her gender role exploration. (22, 23, 24, 25,)

17. Assist the client in identifying positive, realistic self-talk that can replace negative cognitions regarding gender identity.

18. Assign a mirror exercise in which the client talks positively to himself/herself regarding his/her gender identity.

19. Reinforce the client's positive self-descriptive statements.

20. Affirm the client and nonjudgmentally neutralize his/her gender exploration as opposed to being critical and attempting to reverse or suppress the verbal or behavioral expressions of gender variance.

21. Help the client understand that his/her behavior will probably trigger negative reactions (e.g., rejection, teasing, shunning) from others due to a lack of under-standing and their expectations of culturally typical sexual role behavior; teach the client to use self-affirming statements to counteract this hostility and to report problems to adults.

22. Meet with family members to explore their thoughts and feelings regarding the client's gender variant behavior; explain that the client's gender identity cannot be altered by their reactions but self-esteem may be damaged by a lack of unconditional acceptance.

23. Encourage family members to be patient and affirming of the client while living with the uncertainty about the client's gender and sexual identity development, realizing that the gender dysphoria will most likely desist.

24. Discuss whether parents are open to allowing the client to engage in a social transitioning experiment with opposite gender behavior (e.g., name, dress, actions, play) while in a social setting apart from his/her neighborhood (e.g., while on vacation); process all the family members' thoughts and feelings before the experiment is implemented (or not).

25. Process the feelings of the client and family members that resulted from the experiment with social transitioning while in a setting apart from his/her neighborhood or school; assess the comfort level of family members and discuss impact on future gender role behavior for the client.

10. Parent take steps to inform the client's school personnel of the client's exploration of gender identity and possible social sex role transitions that may occur. (26)

26. Encourage parents to meet with the client's school personnel (and offer to join them) to explain client's gender identity struggles and transgender desires; urge parents to ask teachers to be accepting of the client's gender identity exploration, to nuture acceptance from the client's school peers, and to be intolerant of any bullying.

11. Parents and/or client attend a support group for parents and children coping with gender dysphoria and transgender issues. (27)

27. Refer family members to support groups composed of others who are coping with gender identity variances and transgender preferences (e.g. PFLAG.com, TransYouth Family Allies).

12. Parents express thoughts and feelings about social gender transitioning with their child in home, school, and neighborhood. (28, 29)

28. Explore the parents' willingness to support the client's persistent and intense desires for gender variance by allowing fully reversible social gender transitioning in school and neighbourhood, including cross-gender clothing, name

change, pronoun change, hairstyle alteration; process their thoughts and feelings regarding implementing (or not) this intervention in small steps.

29. Implement fully reversible social gender transitioning of client in home, school, and neighborhood settings; process feelings of client and family members.

13. Disclose any physical or sexual abuse victimization history. (30)

30. Explore the possibility that the client was physically or sexually abused (see the Physical/ Emotional Abuse Victim and Sexual Abuse Victim chapters in this *Planner*).

14. Verbalize whether and to what degree of intensity and frequency thoughts of sexual attraction to same-sex peers may be present. (31)

31. Explore whether the child's confusion over gender identity may be the beginning of a gay or lesbian identity; reassure the child of acceptance and self-worth as a gay person if this is the outcome and assist the parents in accepting this possibility (suggest *All I Want to Be Is Me* by Rothblatt).

DIAGNOSTIC SUGGESTIONS

Using DSM-IV/ICD-9-CM:

Axis I:	302.6	Gender Identity Disorder in Children
	302.6	Gender Identity Disorder NOS
Axis II:	V71.09	No Diagnosis

Using DSM-5/ICD-9-CM/ICD-10-CM:

ICD-9-CM	ICD-10-CM	*DSM-5* Disorder, Condition, or Problem
302.6	F64.2	Gender Dysphoria in Children
302.6	F64.9	Unspecified Gender Disorder
302.6	F64.8	Other Specified Gender Disorder

GRIEF/LOSS UNRESOLVED

BEHAVIORAL DEFINITIONS

1. Loss of contact with a parent due to the parent's death.
2. Loss of contact with a parent figure due to termination of parental rights.
3. Loss of contact with a parent due to the parent's incarceration.
4. Loss of contact with a positive support network due to a geographic move.
5. Loss of meaningful contact with a parent figure due to the parent's emotional abandonment.
6. Strong emotional response experienced when the loss is mentioned.
7. Lack of appetite, nightmares, restlessness, inability to concentrate, irritability, tearfulness, or social withdrawal that began subsequent to a loss.
8. Marked drop in school grades, and an increase in angry outbursts, hyperactivity, or clinginess when separating from parents.
9. Feelings of guilt associated with the unreasonable belief in having done something to cause the loss or not having prevented it.
10. Avoidance of talking at length or in any depth about the loss.

—. _____
   _____
—. _____
   _____
—. _____
   _____

LONG-TERM GOALS

1. Begin a healthy grieving process around the loss.
2. Complete the process of letting go of the lost significant other.

3. Work through the grieving and letting-go process and reach the point of emotionally reinvesting in life.
4. Successfully grieve the loss within a supportive emotional environment.
5. Resolve the loss and begin reinvesting in relationships with others and in age-appropriate activities.
6. Resolve feelings of guilt, depression, or anger that are associated with the loss and return to the previous level of functioning.

—. _____
   _____
—. _____
   _____
—. _____
   _____

SHORT-TERM OBJECTIVES

1. Develop a trusting relationship with the therapist as evidenced by the open communication of feelings and thoughts associated with the loss. (1, 2)

2. Provide behavioral, emotional, and attitudinal information toward an assessment of specifiers relevant to a *DSM* diagnosis, the efficacy of treatment, and the nature of the therapy relationship. (3, 4, 5, 6, 7)

THERAPEUTIC INTERVENTIONS

1. Actively build the level of trust with the client through consistent eye contact, active listening, unconditional positive regard, and warm acceptance while asking him/her to identify and express feelings associated with the loss.

2. Read with the client a story about death and loss (e.g., *Where Is Daddy?* by Gof; *Emma Says Goodbye* by Nystrom) and afterward discuss the story.

3. Assess the client's level of insight (syntonic versus dystonic) toward the "presenting problems" (e.g., demonstrates good insight into the problematic nature of the "described behavior," agrees with others' concern, and is motivated to work on change; demonstrates ambivalence

regarding the "problem described" and is reluctant to address the issue as a concern; or demonstrates resistance regarding acknowledgment of the "problem described," is not concerned, and has no motivation to change).

4. Assess the client for evidence of research-based correlated disorders (e.g., oppositional defiant behavior with ADHD, depression secondary to an anxiety disorder) including vulnerability to suicide, if appropriate (e.g., increased suicide risk when comorbid depression is evident).

5. Assess for any issues of age, gender, or culture that could help explain the client's currently defined "problem behavior" and factors that could offer a better understanding of the client's behavior.

6. Assess for the severity of the level of impairment to the client's functioning to determine appropriate level of care (e.g., the behavior noted creates mild, moderate, severe, or very severe impairment in social, relational, vocational, or occupational endeavors); continuously assess this severity of impairment as well as the efficacy of treatment (e.g., the client no longer demonstrates severe impairment but the presenting problem now is causing mild or moderate impairment).

7. Assess the client's home, school, and community for pathogenic care (e.g., persistent disregard for

the child's emotional needs or physical needs, repeated changes in primary caregivers, limited opportunities for stable attachments, persistent harsh punishment or other grossly inept parenting).

3. Attend and freely participate in art and play therapy sessions. (8, 9, 10)

8. Using child-centered play therapy approaches (e.g., providing unconditional positive regard, reflecting feelings in a nonjudgmental manner, displaying trust in the child's capacity to act responsibly), assist the client in working through his/her loss.

9. Conduct individual play therapy sessions with the client to provide the environment for expressing and working through feelings connected to his/her loss.

10. Use various art therapy techniques with Play-Doh, clay, fingerpaints, and/or markers to help the client creatively express his/her feelings connected to his/her loss; ask him/her to give an explanation of his/her creation.

4. Tell the story of the loss. (11, 12, 13)

11. Use the Mutual Storytelling Technique (Gardner) in which the client tells his/her story. The therapist interprets the story for its underlying meaning and then tells a story using the same characters in a similar setting, but weaves into the story a healthy way to adapt to and resolve the loss.

12. Use a before and after drawing technique (see the "Before and After Drawing Technique" by Cangelosi) to help guide the

client in telling the story, through drawings, of how he/she was before and after the loss; work through the connected feelings.

13. Suggest that the client act out or tell about the loss by using puppets or felt figures on a board.

5. Identify feelings connected with the loss. (14, 15, 16)

14. Assist the client in identifying his/her feelings by using the Five Faces technique (see *Helping Children Cope with Separation and Loss* by Jewett).

15. Play either the Goodbye Game (available from Childswork/Childsplay) or The Good Mourning Game (Bisenius and Norris) with the client to assist him/her in exploring grief.

16. Ask the client to write a letter to the lost person describing his/her feelings and read this letter to the therapist (or assign "Grief Letter" in the *Child Psychotherapy Homework Planner* by Jongsma, Peterson, and McInnis).

6. Verbalize and experience feelings connected with the loss. (17, 18, 19)

17. Conduct a play therapy session around the use of "Art or Verbal Metaphor for Children Experiencing Loss" (see Short) in which the client is asked to talk about what his/her life was like prior to and after the loss using stories and drawings. Mirror, acknowledge, and validate the client's feelings.

18. Assist the client in identifying, labeling, and expressing feelings connected with the loss (or assign "Petey's Journey Through Sadness" in the *Child*

Psychotherapy Homework Planner by Jongsma, Peterson, and McInnis).

19. Assign the client to keep a daily grief journal of drawings representing thoughts and feelings associated with the loss; review the journal in therapy sessions.

7. Attend a grief support group. (20)

20. Refer the client to a grief support group for children.

8. Verbalize questions about the loss, and work to obtain answers for each question. (21, 22)

21. Expand the client's understanding of death by reading to him/her a book on death and dying (e.g., *The Fall of Freddie the Leaf* by Buscaglia or *The Next Place* by Hanson or *I Miss You: A First Look at Death* by Thomas); discuss all questions that arise from the reading.

22. Assist the client in developing a list of questions about a specific loss; then try to direct him/her to resources (e.g., books, member of clergy, parent, counselor) for possible answers for each question.

9. Verbalize an increase in understanding the process of grieving and letting go. (23, 24)

23. Use *The Empty Place: A Child's Guide Through Grief* (Temes) to work the client through his/her grief process.

24. Read to the client *Don't Despair on Thursdays!* (Moser) and process the various suggestions given to handle the feelings connected to his/her grief.

10. Decrease the expression of feelings of guilt and blame for the loss. (25, 26, 27)

25. Explore the client's thoughts and feelings of guilt and blame surrounding the loss, replacing irrational thoughts with realistic thoughts (see *Why Did You Die?:*

Activities to Help Children Cope With Grief and Loss by Leeuwenburgh and Goldring).

26. Use a Despart Fable (see *Helping Children Cope with Separation and Loss* by Jewett) or a similar variation to help the client communicate blame for the loss (e.g., the therapist states, "A child says softly to himself, 'Oh, I did wrong.' What do you suppose the child believes he/she did wrong?").

27. Help the client lift the self-imposed curse that he/she believes he/she is the cause for the loss by asking the person who is perceived as having imposed the curse to take it back or by using a pretend phone conversation in which the client apologizes for the behavior that he/she believes is the cause for the curse.

11. Identify positive things about the deceased loved one and/or the lost relationship and discuss how these things may be remembered. (28, 29)

28. Ask the client to list positive things about the deceased and how he/she plans to remember each; then process the list.

29. Ask the client to bring to a session pictures or mementos connected with the loss and to talk about them with the therapist (or assign "Create a Memory Album" in the *Child Psychotherapy Homework Planner* by Jongsma, Peterson, and McInnis).

12. Verbalize and resolve feelings of anger or guilt focused on self, on God, or on the deceased loved one that block the grief process. (30, 31)

30. Encourage and support the client in sessions to look angry, then to act angry, and finally to verbalize the anger.

31. Use behavioral techniques (e.g., kneading clay, kicking a paper

bag stuffed with newsprint, using foam bats to hit objects without damage) in order to encourage the client to release repressed feelings of anger; explore the target causes for anger.

13. Say goodbye to the lost loved one. (32, 33)

32. Assign the client to write a goodbye letter to a significant other or to make a goodbye drawing, and then process the letter or drawing within the session (or assign the "Grief Letter" exercise in the *Child Psychotherapy Homework Planner* by Jongsma, Peterson, and McInnis.)

33. Assign the client to visit the grave of the loved one with an adult to communicate feelings and say goodbye, perhaps by leaving a letter or drawing; process the experience.

14. Parents verbalize an increase in their understanding of the grief process. (34, 35)

34. Educate the parents about the stages of the grieving process, and teach the parents how to answer any of the client's questions (recommend *Waterbugs and Dragonflies: Explaining Death to Young Children* by Stickney, *Caring for Your Grieving Child: A Parent's Guide* by Wakenshaw, or *Good Grief* by Westberg).

35. Teach the parents specific ways to provide comfort, consolation, love, companionship, and support to the client in grief such as bringing up the loss occasionally for discussion, encouraging the client to talk freely of the loss, suggesting photographs of the loved one be displayed, spending one-on-one time with the client in quiet

activities that may foster sharing of feelings, spending time with the client in diversion activities (see *Help Me Say Goodbye: Activities for Helping Kids Cope When a Special Person Dies* by Silverman).

15. Parents increase their verbal openness about the loss. (36, 37)

36. Conduct family sessions in which each member of the client's family talks about his/her experience related to the loss.

37. Refer the client's parents to a grief/loss support group.

16. Participate in memorial services, funeral services, or other grieving rituals. (38)

38. Encourage the parents to allow the client to participate in the rituals and customs of grieving if he/she is willing to be involved.

17. Parents and the client attend and participate in a formal session to say goodbye to the parents whose parental rights are being terminated. (39, 40)

39. Conduct a session with the parents who are losing custody of the client to prepare them to say goodbye to him/her in a healthy, affirming way.

40. Facilitate a goodbye session with the client and the parents who are losing custody to give the client permission to move on with his/her life. If the parents who are losing custody or the current parents are not available, ask them to write a letter that can be read at the session, or conduct a role-playing session in which the client says goodbye to each parent.

18. Verbalize positive memories of the past and hopeful statements about the future. (41, 42)

41. Assist the client in making a record of his/her life in a book format to help visualize past, present, and future life. When it is completed, have the client keep a copy and give another to the current parents.

42. Encourage the client to express positive memories of the lost loved one (or assign "Petey's Journey Through Sadness" in the *Child Psychotherapy Homework Planner* by Jongsma, Peterson, and McInnis).

— . _____   — . _____
   _____   _____
— . _____   — . _____
   _____   _____
— . _____   — . _____
   _____   _____

DIAGNOSTIC SUGGESTIONS

Using DSM-IV/ICD-9-CM:

Axis I:	296.2x	Major Depressive Disorder, Single Episode
	296.3x	Major Depressive Disorder, Recurrent
	V62.82	Bereavement
	309.0	Adjustment Disorder With Depressed Mood
	309.4	Adjustment Disorder With Mixed Disturbance of Emotions and Conduct
	300.4	Dysthymic Disorder
	_____	_____
	_____	_____
Axis II:	V71.09	No Diagnosis
	_____	_____
	_____	_____

Using DSM-5/ICD-9-CM/ICD-10-CM:

ICD-9-CM	ICD-10-CM	*DSM-5* Disorder, Condition, or Problem
296.2x	F32.x	Major Depressive Disorder, Single Episode
296.3x	F33.x	Major Depressive Disorder, Recurrent Episode
V62.82	Z63.4	Uncomplicated Bereavement
309.0	F43.21	Adjustment Disorder, With Depressed Mood

| 309.4 | F43.25 | Adjustment Disorder, With Mixed Disturbance of Emotions and Conduct |
| 300.4 | F34.1 | Persistent Depressive Disorder |

Note: The ICD-9-CM codes are to be used for coding purposes in the United States through September 30, 2014. ICD-10-CM codes are to be used starting October 1, 2014. Some ICD-9-CM codes are associated with more than one ICD-10-CM and *DSM-5* disorder, condition, or problem. In addition, some ICD-9-CM disorders have been discontinued resulting in multiple ICD-9-CM codes being replaced by one ICD-10-CM code. Some discontinued ICD-9-CM codes are not listed in this table. See *Diagnostic and Statistical Manual of Mental Disorders* (2013) for details.

INTELLECTUAL DEVELOPMENTAL DISORDER

BEHAVIORAL DEFINITIONS

1. Significantly subaverage intellectual functioning as demonstrated by an IQ score of 70 or below on an individually administered intelligence test.
2. Significant impairments in academic functioning, communication, self-care, home living, and social skills.
3. Difficulty understanding and following complex directions in home, school, or community settings.
4. Short- and long-term memory impairment.
5. Concrete thinking or impaired abstract reasoning abilities.
6. Impoverished social skills as manifested by frequent use of poor judgment, limited understanding of the antecedents and consequences of social actions, and lack of reciprocity in peer interactions.
7. Lack of insight and repeated failure to learn from experience or past mistakes.
8. Low self-esteem as evidenced by frequent self-derogatory remarks (e.g., "I'm so stupid").
9. Recurrent pattern of acting out or engaging in disruptive behaviors without considering the consequences of the actions.

__. _____

_____

__. _____

_____

__. _____

_____

LONG-TERM GOALS

1. Achieve all academic goals identified on the client's individualized educational plan (IEP).
2. Function at full potential of independence in home, residential, educational, or community settings.
3. Develop an awareness and acceptance of intellectual and cognitive limitations but consistently verbalize feelings of self-worth.
4. Parents and/or caregivers develop an awareness and acceptance of the client's intellectual and cognitive capabilities so that they facilitate the client reaching his/her full potential.
5. Consistently comply and follow through with simple directions in a daily routine at home, in school, or in a residential setting.
6. Significantly reduce the frequency and severity of socially inappropriate or acting-out behaviors.

—. _____

_____

—. _____

_____

—. _____

_____

SHORT-TERM OBJECTIVES

1. Complete a comprehensive intellectual and cognitive assessment. (1)

2. Complete psychological testing. (2)

THERAPEUTIC INTERVENTIONS

1. Arrange for an intellectual and cognitive assessment to determine the presence of an intellectual developmental disorder and gain greater insight into the client's learning strengths and weaknesses; provide feedback to the client, parents, and school officials.

2. Arrange for psychological testing to assess whether emotional factors or Attention-Deficit/ Hyperactivity Disorder (ADHD) are interfering with the client's intellectual and academic functioning; provide feedback to the client and parents.

3. Complete neuropsychological testing. (3)

3. Arrange for a neurological examination or neuropsychological testing to specify organic factors that may be contributing to the client's intellectual or cognitive deficits.

4. Complete an evaluation by physical and occupational therapists. (4)

4. Refer the client to physical and occupational therapists to assess perceptual or sensory-motor deficits and determine the need for ongoing physical and/or occupational therapy.

5. Complete a speech/language evaluation. (5)

5. Refer the client to a speech/language pathologist to assess deficits and determine the need for appropriate therapy.

6. Provide behavioral, emotional, and attitudinal information toward an assessment of specifiers relevant to a *DSM* diagnosis, the efficacy of treatment, and the nature of the therapy relationship.
   (6, 7, 8, 9, 10)

6. Assess the client's level of insight (syntonic versus dystonic) toward the "presenting problems" (e.g., demonstrates good insight into the problematic nature of the "described behavior," agrees with others' concern, and is motivated to work on change; demonstrates ambivalence regarding the "problem described" and is reluctant to address the issue as a concern; or demonstrates resistance regarding acknowledgment of the "problem described," is not concerned, and has no motivation to change).

7. Assess the client for evidence of research-based correlated disorders (e.g., oppositional defiant behavior with ADHD, depression secondary to an anxiety disorder) including vulnerability to suicide, if appropriate (e.g., increased suicide risk when comorbid depression is evident).

8. Assess for any issues of age, gender, or culture that could help explain the client's currently defined "problem behavior" and factors that could offer a better understanding of the client's behavior.

9. Assess for the severity of the level of impairment to the client's functioning to determine appropriate level of care (e.g., the behavior noted creates mild, moderate, severe, or very severe impairment in social, relational, vocational, or occupational endeavors); continuously assess this severity of impairment as well as the efficacy of treatment (e.g., the client no longer demonstrates severe impairment but the presenting problem now is causing mild or moderate impairment).

10. Assess the client's home, school, and community for pathogenic care (e.g., persistent disregard for the child's emotional needs or physical needs, repeated changes in primary caregivers, limited opportunities for stable attachments, persistent harsh punishment or other grossly inept parenting).

7. The client and his/her parents comply with recommendations made by a multidisciplinary evaluation team at school regarding educational interventions. (11, 12)

11. Attend an Individualized Educational Planning Committee (IEPC) meeting with the client's parents, teachers, and other appropriate professionals to determine his/her eligibility for special education services, design educational interventions, and establish goals.

12. Consult with the client, his/her parents, teachers, and other

appropriate school officials about designing effective learning programs or interventions that build on the client's strengths and compensate for weaknesses.

8. Move to an appropriate residential setting. (13)

13. Consult with the client's parents, school officials, or mental health professionals about the client's need for placement in a foster home, group home, or residential program.

9. Parents maintain regular communication with the client's teachers and other appropriate school officials. (14)

14. Encourage the parents to maintain regular communication with the client's teachers or school officials to monitor his/her academic, behavioral, emotional, and social progress.

10. Parents, teachers, and caregivers implement a token economy in the classroom or placement setting. (15)

15. Design a token economy for the classroom or residential program to reinforce on-task behaviors, completion of school assignments, good impulse control, and positive social skills.

11. Parents increase praise and other positive reinforcement toward the client regarding his/her academic performance or social behaviors. (16, 17, 18)

16. Conduct filial play therapy sessions (i.e., parents are present) to increase the parents' awareness of the client's thoughts and feelings and to strengthen the parent-child bond.

17. Encourage the parents to provide frequent praise and other reinforcement for the client's positive social behaviors and academic performance.

18. Design a reward system or contingency contract to reinforce the client's adaptive or prosocial behaviors (or utilize the exercise "Activities of Daily Living Program" from the *Child Psychotherapy Homework*

12. Parents and family cease verbalizations of denial about the client's intellectual and cognitive deficits. (19, 20)

13. Parents recognize and verbally acknowledge their unrealistic expectations of or excessive pressure on the client. (21, 22)

14. Parents recognize and verbally acknowledge that their pattern of overprotectiveness interferes with the client's intellectual, emotional, and social development. (23, 24)

Planner by Jongsma, Peterson, and McInnis).

19. Educate the parents about the symptoms and characteristics of Intellectual Developmental Disorder.

20. Confront and challenge the parents' denial surrounding their child's intellectual deficits so they cooperate with recommendations regarding placement and educational interventions.

21. Conduct family therapy sessions to assess whether the parents are placing excessive pressure on the client to function at a level that he/she is not capable of achieving.

22. Confront and challenge the parents about placing excessive pressure on the client.

23. Observe parent-child interactions to assess whether the parents' overprotectiveness or infantilization of the client interferes with his/her intellectual, emotional, or social development (recommend the book *Life Skills Activities for Special Children* by Mannix).

24. Assist the parents or caregivers in developing realistic expectations of the client's intellectual capabilities and level of adaptive functioning such that the client can reach his/her full potential (recommend *Steps to Independence: Teaching Everyday Skills to Children With Special Needs* by Baker and Brightman).

15. Increase participation in family activities or outings. (25, 26, 27, 28)

25. Encourage the parents and family members to regularly include the client in outings or activities (e.g., attend sporting events, go ice skating, visit a children's museum).

26. Encourage family members to observe and reinforce positive behaviors by the client between therapy sessions; during the session, praise the client's positive behaviors performed at home and encourage the client to continue to exhibit these behaviors.

27. Assign the client homework of being placed in charge of a routine or basic task at home designed to promote his/her feelings of acceptance and a sense of belonging in the family system, school setting, or community (or assign the "A Sense of Belonging" exercise from the *Child Psychotherapy Homework Planner* by Jongsma, Peterson, and McInnis).

28. Instruct the client to complete a family kinetic drawing to assess how he/she perceives his/her role or place in the family system; process this perception within a family session.

16. Perform chores at school or residential program on a daily or regular basis. (29)

29. Consult with school officials or the residential staff about the client performing a job (e.g., raising the flag, helping to run video equipment) to build self-esteem and provide him/her with a sense of responsibility.

17. Parents agree to and implement an allowance program that helps the client learn to manage money more effectively. (30)

30. Counsel the parents about setting up an allowance plan that seeks to increase the client's responsibilities and help him/her

learn simple money management skills.

18. Take a bath or shower, dress self independently, comb hair, wash hands before meals, and brush teeth on a daily basis. (31)

31. Design and implement a reward system to reinforce desired self-care behaviors such as combing hair, washing dishes, or cleaning the bedroom (or assign the parents to use the "Activities of Daily Living Program" exercise from the *Child Psychotherapy Homework Planner* by Jongsma, Peterson, and McInnis).

19. Parents consistently implement behavior management techniques to reduce the frequency and severity of temper outbursts or disruptive and aggressive behaviors. (32, 33)

32. Teach the parents effective behavior management techniques (e.g., time-outs, removal of privileges) to decrease the frequency and severity of the client's temper outbursts, acting out, and aggressive behaviors.

33. Encourage the parents to utilize natural, logical consequences for the client's inappropriate social or maladaptive behaviors.

20. Decrease frequency of impulsive, disruptive, or aggressive behaviors. (34, 35)

34. Teach the client basic mediational and self-control strategies (e.g., "stop, look, listen, and think") to delay gratification and inhibit impulses.

35. Train the client in the use of guided imagery or relaxation techniques to calm himself/herself down and develop greater control of anger (see *The Relaxation and Stress Reduction Workbook for Kids* by Shapiro and Sprague).

21. Recognize and verbally identify appropriate and inappropriate social behaviors. (36)

36. Utilize role-playing and modeling in individual sessions to teach the client positive social skills (consider the use of the "Social Skills Exercise" from the *Child Psychotherapy Homework*

Planner by Jongsma, Peterson, and McInnis); reinforce new or emerging prosocial behaviors.

22. Increase the frequency of identifying and expressing feelings. (37, 38, 39, 40, 41)

37. Educate the client about how to identify and label different emotions.

38. Tell the client to draw faces of basic emotions; then have him/her share times when he/she experienced the different emotions.

39. Teach the client effective communication skills (i.e., proper listening, good eye contact, "I statements") to improve his/her ability to express thoughts, feelings, and needs more clearly.

40. Use puppets, dolls, or stuffed animals to model socially appropriate ways of expressing emotions or relating to others.

41. Use a Feelings Poster (Bureau for At-Risk Youth, available from Childswork/Childsplay) to help the client identify and express different emotions.

23. Express feelings of sadness, anxiety, and insecurity that are related to cognitive and intellectual limitations. (42, 43)

42. Assist the client in coming to an understanding and acceptance of the limitations surrounding his/her intellectual deficits and adaptive functioning.

43. Explore the client's feelings of depression, anxiety, and insecurity that are related to cognitive or intellectual limitations. Provide encouragement and support for the client.

24. Increase the frequency of positive self-statements. (44, 45)

44. Encourage the client to participate in the Special Olympics to build self-esteem.

45. Explore times when the client achieved success or accomplished a goal; reinforce positive steps that the client took to successfully accomplish goals.

25. Express feelings through artwork. (46)

46. Use art therapy (e.g., drawing, painting, sculpting) with the client in foster care or residential program to help him/her express basic emotions related to issues of separation, loss, or abandonment by parental figures.

___ . _____   ___ . _____
      _____   _____

___ . _____   ___ . _____
      _____   _____

___ . _____   ___ . _____
      _____   _____

DIAGNOSTIC SUGGESTIONS

Using DSM-IV/ICD-9-CM:

Axis I:	299.00	Autistic Disorder
	299.80	Rett's Disorder
	299.80	Asperger's Disorder
	299.10	Childhood Disintegrative Disorder
	_____	_____
	_____	_____
Axis II:	317	Mild Intellectual Developmental Disorder
	318.0	Moderate Intellectual Developmental Disorder
	318.1	Severe Intellectual Developmental Disorder
	318.2	Profound Intellectual Developmental Disorder
	319	Intellectual Developmental Disorder, Severity Unspecified
	V62.89	Borderline Intellectual Functioning
	V71.09	No Diagnosis
	_____	_____
	_____	_____

Using DSM-5/ICD-9-CM/ICD-10-CM:

ICD-9-CM	ICD-10-CM	*DSM-5* Disorder, Condition, or Problem
299.00	F84	Autistic Spectrum Disorder
317	F70	Intellectual Disability, Mild
318.0	F71	Intellectual Disability, Moderate
318.1	F72	Intellectual Disability, Severe
318.2	F73	Intellectual Disability, Profound
319	F79	Unspecified Intellectual Disability
V62.89	R41.83	Borderline Intellectual Functioning

Note: The ICD-9-CM codes are to be used for coding purposes in the United States through September 30, 2014. ICD-10-CM codes are to be used starting October 1, 2014. Some ICD-9-CM codes are associated with more than one ICD-10-CM and *DSM-5* disorder, condition, or problem. In addition, some ICD-9-CM disorders have been discontinued resulting in multiple ICD-9-CM codes being replaced by one ICD-10-CM code. Some discontinued ICD-9-CM codes are not listed in this table. See *Diagnostic and Statistical Manual of Mental Disorders* (2013) for details.

LOW SELF-ESTEEM

BEHAVIORAL DEFINITIONS

1. Verbalizes self-disparaging remarks, seeing self as unattractive, worthless, stupid, a loser, a burden, unimportant, and so on.
2. Takes blame easily.
3. Inability to accept compliments.
4. Refuses to take risks associated with new experiences, as she/he expects failure.
5. Avoids social contact with adults and peers.
6. Seeks excessively to please or receive attention/praise of adults and/or peers.
7. Unable to identify or accept positive traits or talents about self.
8. Fears rejection from others, especially peer group.
9. Acts out in negative, attention-seeking ways.
10. Difficulty saying no to others; fears not being liked by others.

—. _____

_____

—. _____

_____

—. _____

_____

LONG-TERM GOALS

1. Elevate self-esteem.
2. Increase social interaction, assertiveness, confidence in self, and reasonable risk taking.
3. Build a consistently positive self-image.

4. Demonstrate improved self-esteem by accepting compliments, by identifying positive characteristics about self, by being able to say no to others, and by eliminating self-disparaging remarks.
5. See self as lovable and capable.
6. Increase social skill level.

—. _____

_____

—. _____

_____

—. _____

_____

SHORT-TERM OBJECTIVES

1. Parents and client describe the client's thoughts, feelings, and behaviors reflective of how the client views himself/herself alone and in relationship to others. (1)

2. Attend and actively participate in play therapy sessions. (2, 3, 4)

THERAPEUTIC INTERVENTIONS

1. Interview the client and parents to assess the client's patterns of verbalizations and other behaviors that are self-disparaging and reflective of a lack of self-confidence.

2. Employ psychoanalytic play therapy approaches (e.g., allow the client to take the lead with the therapist in exploring the source of unconscious conflicts, fixations, or developmental arrests) to assist the client in developing trust in the therapist and in disclosing negative thought patterns/beliefs or fears that impact his/her level of self-esteem.

3. Assess the client's self-esteem using puppets in a directed or nondirected way to allow the client to play out scenes involving self-esteem (e.g., making friends, starting conversations, trying something new, working out a conflict,

expressing feelings, asking for something that he/she needs).

4. Assess the client's feelings toward himself/herself and in relationship to others using an expressive clay technique, either directed (see *Clayscapes* by Hadley) or nondirected, to assist the client's expression and communication of significant issues related to self-esteem.

3. Provide behavioral, emotional, and attitudinal information toward an assessment of specifiers relevant to a *DSM* diagnosis, the efficacy of treatment, and the nature of the therapy relationship. (5, 6, 7, 8, 9)

5. Assess the client's level of insight (syntonic versus dystonic) toward the "presenting problems" (e.g., demonstrates good insight into the problematic nature of the "described behavior," agrees with others' concern, and is motivated to work on change; demonstrates ambivalence regarding the "problem described" and is reluctant to address the issue as a concern; or demonstrates resistance regarding acknowledgment of the "problem described," is not concerned, and has no motivation to change).

6. Assess the client for evidence of research-based correlated disorders (e.g., oppositional defiant behavior with ADHD, depression secondary to an anxiety disorder) including vulnerability to suicide, if appropriate (e.g., increased suicide risk when comorbid depression is evident).

7. Assess for any issues of age, gender, or culture that could help explain the client's currently defined "problem behavior" and factors that could offer a better

understanding of the client's behavior.

8. Assess for the severity of the level of impairment to the client's functioning to determine appropriate level of care (e.g., the behavior noted creates mild, moderate, severe, or very severe impairment in social, relational, vocational, or occupational endeavors); continuously assess this severity of impairment as well as the efficacy of treatment (e.g., the client no longer demonstrates severe impairment but the presenting problem now is causing mild or moderate impairment).

9. Assess the client's home, school, and community for pathogenic care (e.g., persistent disregard for the child's emotional needs or physical needs, repeated changes in primary caregivers, limited opportunities for stable attachments, persistent harsh punishment or other grossly inept parenting).

4. Verbalize an increased awareness of self-disparaging statements. (10, 11)

10. Confront and reframe the client's self-disparaging comments.

11. Assist the client in becoming aware of how he/she expresses or acts out (e.g., lack of eye contact, social withdrawal, expectation of failure or rejection) negative feelings about self.

5. Decrease frequency of negative self-statements. (12, 13)

12. Refer the client to a group therapy that is focused on ways to build self-esteem.

13. Probe the parents' interactions with the client in family sessions, and redirect or rechannel any

patterns of discipline that are negative or critical of the client.

6. Decrease verbalized fear of rejection while increasing statements of self-acceptance. (14, 15)

14. Ask the client to make one positive statement about himself/ herself daily, and record it on a chart or in a journal (or recommend "Positive Self-Statements" from the *Child Psychotherapy Homework Planner* by Jongsma, Peterson, and McInnis).

15. Assist the client in developing positive self-talk as a way of boosting his/her confidence and positive self-image.

7. Identify positive traits and talents about self. (16, 17, 18)

16. Develop with the client a list of positive affirmations about himself/herself, and ask that it be read three times daily (or recommend "Symbols of Self-Worth" from the *Child Psychotherapy Homework Planner* by Jongsma, Peterson, and McInnis).

17. Use the Positive Attitude Ball (available from Childswork/ Childsplay) or a similar aid to identify and affirm with the client positive things about him/her for the first 5 minutes of each session.

18. Reinforce verbally the client's use of positive statements of confidence or identification of positive attributes about himself/herself.

8. Identify and verbalize feelings. (19, 20, 21)

19. Use a therapeutic game (e.g., The Talking, Feeling, and Doing Game, available from CreativeTherapeutics; Let's See About Me, available from Childswork/Childsplay; The Ungame, available from The

Ungame Company) to promote the client becoming more aware of himself/herself and his/her feelings.

20. Use a feelings chart, feelings felt board, or a card game to enhance the client's ability to identify specific feelings (or use the "Feelings and Faces Game" from the *Child Psychotherapy Homework Planner* by Jongsma, Peterson, and McInnis).

21. Educate the client in the basics of identifying and labeling feelings, and assist him/her in beginning to identify what he/she is feeling.

9. Increase eye contact with others. (11, 22, 23)

11. Assist the client in becoming aware of how he/she expresses or acts out (e.g., lack of eye contact, social withdrawal, expectation of failure or rejection) negative feelings about himself/herself.

22. Focus attention on the client's lack of eye contact; encourage and reinforce increased eye contact within sessions.

23. Ask the client to increase eye contact with teachers, parents, and other adults; review and process reports of attempts and the feelings associated with them.

10. Identify actions that can be taken to improve self-image. (24, 25, 26)

24. Read with the client *Don't Feed the Monster on Tuesdays!* (Moser). Afterward, assist him/her in identifying things from the book that can be used to keep the monster of self-critical messages away. Then help the client make a chart containing self-esteem-building activities and have him/her record progress on each; monitor and provide

encouragement and affirmation for reported progress.

25. Ask the client to read *Happy to Be Me!: A Kid Book About Self-Esteem* by Adams and Butch and then make a list of good qualities about himself/herself to share with therapist.

26. Encourage the client to try new activities and to see failure as a learning experience (or assign the exercises "Dixie Overcomes Her Fears" and "Learn From Your Mistakes" from the *Child Psychotherapy Homework Planner* by Jongsma, Peterson, and McInnis).

11. Identify and verbalize needs. (27, 28, 29)

27. Assist the client in identifying and verbalizing his/her emotional needs; brainstorm ways to increase the chances of his/her needs being met.

28. Conduct a family session in which the client expresses his/her needs to family and vice versa.

29. Use therapeutic stories (e.g., *Dr. Gardner's Fairy Tales for Today's Children* by Gardner) to help the client identify feelings or needs and to build self-esteem.

12. Increase the frequency of speaking up with confidence in social situations. (30, 31, 32)

30. Use role-playing and behavioral rehearsal to improve the client's assertiveness and social skills (or assign "Social Skills Exercise" from the *Child Psychotherapy Homework Planner* by Jongsma, Peterson, and McInnis).

31. Encourage the client to use the Pretending to Know How (Theiss) method in attempting tasks and facing new situations. Process the client's results,

acknowledging his/her competence in following through and reinforcing the self-confidence gained from each experience.

32. Assign the parents to read with the client *Good Friends Are Hard to Find* by Frankel to help the client build social skills.

13. Identify instances of emotional, physical, or sexual abuse that have damaged self-esteem. (33)

33. Explore for incidents of abuse (emotional, physical, and sexual) and how they have impacted feelings about self (see Sexual Abuse Victim and/or Physical/Emotional Abuse Victim chapters in this *Planner*).

14. Identify negative automatic thoughts and replace them with positive self-talk messages to build self-esteem. (34, 35, 36)

34. Help the client identify his/her distorted negative beliefs about himself/herself and the world.

35. Help the client to identify, and reinforce the use of, more realistic, positive messages about himself/herself and life events (or recommend "Replace Negative Thoughts With Positive Self-Talk" from the *Child Psychotherapy Homework Planner* by Jongsma, Peterson, and McInnis).

36. Use the Positive Thinking game (available from Childswork/ Childsplay) to promote healthy self-talk and thought patterns. Allow the client to take the game home to play with his/her parent(s).

15. Take responsibility for daily self-care and household tasks that are developmentally age-appropriate. (37)

37. Help the client find and implement daily self-care and household or academic responsibilities that are age-appropriate. Monitor follow-through and give positive feedback when warranted.

16. Identify changes in self that can bring positive feelings about self. (38)

38. Have conversation(s) on phone with the client about some recent accomplishment, allowing him/her to initiate the call if he/she chooses and tell about the accomplishment (or work together on "Three Ways to Change Yourself" from the *Child Psychotherapy Homework Planner* by Jongsma, Peterson, and McInnis); give positive feedback, praise, and compliments.

17. Positively acknowledge and verbally accept praise or compliments from others. (39, 40, 41)

39. Ask the client to participate in The Yarn Drawing Game (see *Directive Group Play Therapy* by Leben), in which a ball of yarn/string is shaped into words, numbers, objects, or a complete picture. The therapist will offer the directive that there is no wrong design to empower the client, and will also give encouragement and perspective on the various designs created.

40. Use a projective exercise, such as Magic Art (Walker), whereby the client selects a colored piece of paper and uses at least three colors of paint to make dots, lines, or a picture. The paper is then folded lengthwise and flattened, with the therapist saying, "Magic picture, what will the client draw today?" The client unfolds the paper and tells what he/she sees in the design. The therapist will emphasize that there is no possible way to make a bad picture.

41. Use neurolinguistic programming or reframing techniques in which messages about self are changed to assist

the client in accepting compliments from others (see *Introducing NLP: Psychological Skills for Understanding and Influencing People* by O'Connor and Seymour.

18. Parents attend a didactic series on positive parenting. (42)

42. Ask the parents to attend a didactic series on positive parenting, afterward processing how they can begin to implement some of these techniques.

19. Parents verbalize realistic expectations and discipline methods for the client. (43, 44)

43. Explore the parents' expectations of the client. Assist, if necessary, in making them more realistic.

44. Train the parents in the three R's (related, respectful, and reasonable) discipline techniques (see *Raising Self-Reliant Children in a Self-Indulgent World* by Glenn and Nelson) in order to eliminate discipline that results in rebellion, revenge, or reduced self-esteem. Assist in implementation, and coach the parents as they develop and improve their skills using this method.

20. Parents identify specific activities for the client that will facilitate development of positive self-esteem. (45)

45. Ask the parents to involve the client in esteem-building activities (e.g., scouting, experiential camps, music, sports, youth groups, enrichment programs).

__. _____   __. _____
   _____   _____
__. _____   __. _____
   _____   _____
__. _____   __. _____
   _____   _____

DIAGNOSTIC SUGGESTIONS

Using DSM-IV/ICD-9-CM:

Axis I:	300.4	Dysthymic Disorder
	314.01	Attention-Deficit/Hyperactivity Disorder, Predominantly Hyperactive-Impulsive Type
	300.23	Social Anxiety Disorder (Social Phobia)
	296.xx	Major Depressive Disorder
	307.1	Anorexia Nervosa
	309.21	Separation Anxiety Disorder
	300.02	Generalized Anxiety
	995.54	Physical Abuse of Child (Victim)
	V61.21	Sexual Abuse of Child
	V61.21	Neglect of Child
	995.52	Neglect of Child (Victim)
	995.53	Sexual Abuse of Child (Victim)

_____   _____

_____   _____

Axis II:	317	Mild Mental Retardation
	V62.89	Borderline Intellectual Functioning
	V71.09	No Diagnosis

_____   _____

_____   _____

Using DSM-5/ICD-9-CM/ICD-10-CM:

ICD-9-CM	ICD-10-CM	*DSM-5* Disorder, Condition, or Problem
300.4	F34.1	Persistent Depressive Disorder
314.01	F90.1	Attention-Deficit/Hyperactivity Disorder, Predominately Hyperactive /Impulsive Presentation
300.23	F40.10	Social Anxiety Disorder (Social Phobia)
296.xx	F32.x	Major Depressive Disorder, Single Episode
296.xx	F33.x	Major Depressive Disorder, Recurrent Episode
307.1	F50.02	Anorexia Nervosa, Binge-Eating/Purging Type
307.1	F50.01	Anorexia Nervosa, Restricting Type
309.21	F93.0	Separation Anxiety Disorder
300.02	F41.1	Generalized Anxiety Disorder
995.54	T74.12XA	Child Physical Abuse, Confirmed, Initial Encounter
995.54	T74.12XD	Child Physical Abuse, Confirmed, Subsequent Encounter

V61.22	Z69.011	Encounter for Mental Health Services for Perpetrator of Parental Child Sexual Abuse
V62.83	Z69.021	Encounter for Mental Health Services for Perpetrator of Nonparental Child Sexual Abuse
V61.21	Z69.011	Encounter for Mental Health Services for Perpetrator of Parental Child Neglect
995.52	T74.02XA	Child Neglect, Confirmed, Initial Encounter
995.52	T74.02XD	Child Neglect, Confirmed, Subsequent Encounter
995.53	T74.22XA	Child Sexual Abuse, Confirmed, Initial Encounter
995.53	T74.22XD	Child Sexual Abuse, Confirmed, Subsequent Encounter
317	F70	Intellectual Disability, Mild
V62.89	R41.83	Borderline Intellectual Functioning

Note: The ICD-9-CM codes are to be used for coding purposes in the United States through September 30, 2014. ICD-10-CM codes are to be used starting October 1, 2014. Some ICD-9-CM codes are associated with more than one ICD-10-CM and *DSM-5* disorder, condition, or problem. In addition, some ICD-9-CM disorders have been discontinued resulting in multiple ICD-9-CM codes being replaced by one ICD-10-CM code. Some discontinued ICD-9-CM codes are not listed in this table. See *Diagnostic and Statistical Manual of Mental Disorders* (2013) for details.

LYING/MANIPULATIVE

BEHAVIORAL DEFINITIONS

1. Repeated pattern of lying to satisfy personal needs or obtain material goods/desired objects.
2. Chronic problem with lying to escape consequences or punishment for misbehavior.
3. Frequent lying to avoid facing responsibilities or performing work or chores.
4. Increase in lying after experiencing a threat to or loss of self-esteem.
5. Numerous lies or exaggerations about deeds or performance in order to boost self-esteem or elevate status in the eyes of peers.
6. Willingness to manipulate or exploit others in order to satisfy personal needs or avoid consequences for misbehavior.
7. Repeated attempts to pit parents and/or peers against each other in order to gratify personal needs or escape punishment.
8. Desire to seek thrills, excitement, or pleasure through acts of manipulation or deception.
9. Persistent refusal to accept responsibility for deceitful or manipulative behavior.
10. Verbal expressions give evidence of underlying feelings of insecurity or low self-esteem that contribute to the need to lie, falsify information, or manipulate others.
11. Distinction between fantasy and reality is blurred by repeated lies or exaggerations.

—. _____

_____

—. _____

_____

—. _____

_____

LONG-TERM GOALS

1. Significantly reduce the frequency of lying.
2. Eliminate manipulative and deceptive behavior.
3. Consistently tell the truth, even when facing possible consequences for wrongful actions or irresponsible behavior.
4. Verbalize an acceptance of responsibility for actions or behavior on a regular basis.
5. Elevate self-esteem, and maintain positive self-image, thus decreasing the need to lie to impress and deceive others.
6. Establish and maintain trusting relationships that provide a sense of security and belonging.

—. _____
   _____
—. _____
   _____
—. _____
   _____

SHORT-TERM OBJECTIVES

1. Parents and client describe the client's history of lying and the circumstances surrounding or prompting such deceit as well as the consequences following the discovery of lying. (1)

2. Provide behavioral, emotional, and attitudinal information toward an assessment of specifiers relevant to a DSM diagnosis, the efficacy of treatment, and the nature of the therapy relationship. (2, 3, 4, 5, 6)

THERAPEUTIC INTERVENTIONS

1. Assess the client's history of lying and what may be motivating such behavior (e.g., escape punishment, gratify desires, boost self-esteem, avoid responsibility, promote a fantasy; etc.); probe the client's feelings about his/her lying behavior and the parent's typical responses to the child's lies.

2. Assess the client's level of insight (syntonic versus dystonic) toward the "presenting problems" (e.g., demonstrates good insight into the problematic nature of the "described behavior," agrees with others' concern, and is motivated to work on change; demonstrates ambivalence

regarding the "problem described" and is reluctant to address the issue as a concern; or demonstrates resistance regarding acknowledgment of the "problem described," is not concerned, and has no motivation to change).

3. Assess the client for evidence of research-based correlated disorders (e.g., oppositional defiant behavior with ADHD, depression secondary to an anxiety disorder) including vulnerability to suicide, if appropriate (e.g., increased suicide risk when comorbid depression is evident).

4. Assess for any issues of age, gender, or culture that could help explain the client's currently defined "problem behavior" and factors that could offer a better understanding of the client's behavior.

5. Assess for the severity of the level of impairment to the client's functioning to determine appropriate level of care (e.g., the behavior noted creates mild, moderate, severe, or very severe impairment in social, relational, vocational, or occupational endeavors); continuously assess this severity of impairment as well as the efficacy of treatment (e.g., the client no longer demonstrates severe impairment but the presenting problem now is causing mild or moderate impairment).

6. Assess the client's home, school, and community for pathogenic care (e.g., persistent disregard for

the child's emotional needs or physical needs, repeated changes in primary caregivers, limited opportunities for stable attachments, persistent harsh punishment or other grossly inept parenting).

3. Identify prior life events that have fostered lying and manipulative behavior. (7, 8, 9)

7. Gather a detailed developmental and family history of the client to gain insight into the emotional factors, family dynamics, or environmental stressors that contribute to the emergence of his/her lying and manipulative behavior.

8. Assist the client in developing an awareness of prior life events or significant relationships that encouraged or reinforced lying and manipulative behavior (e.g., parents or family members who lie regularly, overly rigid or punitive parenting, affiliation with peers or siblings who reinforced lying).

9. Explore periods of time when the client demonstrated an increase in lying or acts of manipulation to identify factors that contributed to the emergence of such behavior.

4. Verbally identify current situations and/or people that trigger lying and manipulative behavior. (10)

10. Help the client and his/her parents to identify current life situations or people that trigger lying and manipulative behavior (e.g., threat of being punished, failure experiences, facing criticism).

5. Record incidents of lying, deception, or manipulation. (11, 12, 13)

11. Help the client identify examples of his/her deceitful and manipulative behavior (or assign "Truthful/Lying Incident Reports" in the *Child*

Psychotherapy Homework Planner by Jongsma, Peterson, and McInnis).

12. Assist the client in increasing his/her awareness of deceitful and manipulative behavior by instructing him/her to keep a log of interactions with individuals whom he/she has attempted to deceive or manipulate.

13. Instruct the parents or caregivers to keep a log of times when the client has been caught lying or engaging in manipulative behavior; process entries to explore the factors that contribute to his/her willingness to lie or manipulate.

6. Recognize and list irrational or distorted thoughts that maintain lying and manipulative behavior. (14, 15, 16)

14. Probe the client's thoughts that precede and follow lying or manipulative behavior; assist him/her to correct faulty thinking or irrational thoughts.

15. Identify irrational or distorted thoughts that contribute to the emergence of lying or manipulative behavior (e.g., "I deserve this toy, so it doesn't matter if I take advantage of anyone"; "Nobody will ever catch me lying"; "This person is weak and deserves to be taken advantage of").

16. Counsel the client about replacing irrational or distorted thoughts with reality-based or more adaptive ways of thinking (e.g., "I could get caught lying, and it would only create more problems for me"; "It is best to be honest"; "My friends won't want to play with me if I lie or take advantage of them").

7. Identify negative consequences that deceitful/manipulative behavior has for self and others. (17, 18, 19)

17. Confront the client firmly about the impact of his/her lying or manipulative behavior, pointing out consequences for himself/herself and others (or assign "Truthful/Lying Incident Reports" in the *Child Psychotherapy Homework Planner* by Jongsma, Peterson, and McInnis).

18. Direct the client to list the negative effects that lying and manipulative behavior has on himself/herself and others (e.g., creates mistrust, provokes anger and hurt in others, leads to social isolation).

19. Use guided imagery techniques to help the client visualize the long-term effects that continued lying and acts of manipulation will have on his/her interpersonal relationships (e.g., termination of friendships, loss of respect, frequent arguments with parents and authority figures).

8. Verbally identify the benefits of honesty. (20)

20. Teach the client the value of honesty as a basis for building trust and mutual respect in all relationships (or assign "The Value of Honesty" in the *Child Psychotherapy Homework Planner* by Jongsma, Peterson, and McInnis).

9. Verbalize an increased sensitivity and/or empathy toward individuals being deceived or manipulated. (21, 22, 23)

21. Inquire into how the client would likely feel if he/she were deceived or manipulated by others; process his/her responses and help him/her empathize with others whom he/she has deceived in the past (recommend *Don't Tell a Whopper on Fridays!: The Children's Truth-Control Book* by Moser).

22. Use role reversal or role-playing techniques to help the client become aware of how deceitful or manipulative behavior negatively impacts others.

23. Assign the client the task of observing instances between therapy sessions where others have lied to or manipulated others; instruct him/her to notice the feelings of individuals who have been taken advantage of or manipulated (or ask the parents and child to work on "Bad Choice—Lying to Cover Up Another Lie" in the *Child Psychotherapy Homework Planner* by Jongsma, Peterson, and McInnis).

10. Increase the frequency of honest and truthful verbalizations. (24, 25)

24. Teach the client mediational and self-control strategies (e.g., "stop, look, listen, and think"; thought-stopping; assertive communication techniques) to help him/her resist the urge to lie or manipulate others in order to meet needs or avoid consequences.

25. Encourage the parents to praise and reinforce the client for accepting "no" or unfavorable responses to his/her requests without attempting to lie or manipulate.

11. Parents develop clear rules and follow through with consequences for lying and manipulative behavior. (26, 27, 28, 29)

26. Assist the parents in establishing clearly defined rules and consequences for lying and manipulative behavior; inform the client and have him/her repeat the consequences to demonstrate an understanding of the rules and expectations.

27. Establish a contingency contract with the client and his/her parents that clearly outlines the consequences if he/she is caught lying or manipulating others; have him/her sign the contract, and ask the parents to post it in a visible place in the home.

28. Challenge the parents to remain firm and not give into the client's lies or attempts to manipulate; instruct the parents to assign additional consequences (e.g., time-out, removal of privileges or desired objects) if he/she is caught attempting to lie or manipulate to get out of trouble for other misbehaviors.

29. Counsel the parents on how their failure to follow through consistently with limits or consequences reinforces the client's deceptive and manipulative behavior because it communicates a message to him/her that he/she can possibly control the situation or get away with his/her misbehavior (or assign "Being a Consistent Parent" in the *Child Psychotherapy Homework Planner* by Jongsma, Peterson, and McInnis).

12. Verbalize an acceptance of responsibility for lying and manipulation by publicly acknowledging and apologizing for deceitful actions. (30, 31)

30. Instruct the parents to require the client to undo lies and manipulation by publicly acknowledging his/her wrongdoings to the individual(s) to whom he/she has lied or manipulated.

31. Direct the client to apologize, either verbally or in writing, to individuals to whom he/she has lied or manipulated.

13. Parents refrain from responding in ways that reinforce the client's lying and manipulative behavior. (32, 33)

32. Counsel the parents and family members to withdraw attention from the client when he/she attempts to manipulate a situation in the home.

33. Urge the parents to present a united front and prevent splitting by making each other aware of the client's attempts to deceive or manipulate (e.g., self-pity, somatic complaints, inappropriate jokes, lying); encourage the parents to reach a mutually agreed-upon consequence for the deceitful or manipulative behavior (recommend to the parents *Why Kids Lie: How Parents Can Encourage Truthfulness* by Ekman).

14. Parents and family members identify factors or stressors that promote or reinforce the client's deceptive and manipulative behavior. (34, 35)

34. Conduct family therapy sessions to explore the dynamics and stressors that promote or reinforce the client's deceptive or manipulative behavior (e.g., modeling of deception, severe criticism, harsh punishment, rejection of the client, substance abuse by the parent).

35. Challenge and confront the parents to cease modeling inappropriate behavior to the client through their own acts of deception or manipulation.

15. Verbalize an understanding of the connection between unmet needs or rejection experiences and a history of lying or manipulation. (36, 37, 38)

36. Explore the connection between the client's unmet needs or past rejection experiences and his/her history of lying and manipulation; assist him/her in identifying more adaptive ways to meet his/her needs for love, affection, or closeness other than through lying or manipulating others (or assign "Unmet Emotional Needs—Identification

and Satisfaction" in the *Adolescent Psychotherapy Homework Planner* by Jongsma, Peterson, and McInnis).

37. Encourage the client to express his/her feelings of rejection or deprivation; provide support to him/her in directly verbalizing his/her needs for love and affection to his/her parents and significant others.

38. Assist the client in identifying a list of resource people to whom he/she can turn for support and help in meeting unmet needs; encourage him/her to reach out to these individuals for support or help, rather than using deception or manipulation to meet these needs.

16. Identify negative or painful emotions that trigger lying and manipulative behavior. (39, 40)

39. Assist the client in making a connection between his/her underlying painful emotions (e.g., depression, anxiety, insecurity, anger) and lying or manipulative behavior (or assign "Surface Behavior/Inner Feelings" in the *Child Psychotherapy Homework Planner* by Jongsma, Peterson, and McInnis).

40. Teach the client effective communication and assertiveness skills to express his/her painful emotions to others in a more direct and constructive fashion.

17. Increase the frequency of positive social behaviors that help rebuild trust in relationships. (41, 42, 43, 44)

41. Give the client the homework assignment of identifying 5 to 10 positive social behaviors that can help him/her rebuild trust; review the list and encourage him/her to engage in these behaviors.

42. Instruct the parents to observe and record from 3 to 5 prosocial

or responsible behaviors by the client that help to rebuild trust; encourage the parents to praise and reinforce him/her.

43. Use puppets, dolls, or stuffed animals to create a story that teaches the value of honesty and/or models appropriate ways to rebuild trust; then ask the client to create a story with similar characters or themes.

44. Brainstorm with the client socially appropriate ways to be sneaky or manipulative (e.g., learn a magic trick; ask peers to solve riddles; design a trick play for a basketball team); assign him/her the task of exercising the socially appropriate skill at least once before the next therapy session.

18. Verbally recognize the connection between feelings of low self-esteem and the need to lie or exaggerate about performance or deeds. (45, 46, 47)

45. Assist the client in realizing the connection between underlying feelings of low self-esteem and his/her desire to lie or exaggerate about performance or deeds; help him/her identify more effective ways to improve self-esteem, other than through lying and exaggerated claims.

46. Point out to the client how lies and exaggerated claims are self-defeating as they interfere with his/her ability to establish and maintain close, trusting relationships.

47. Instruct the client to draw pictures of symbols or objects that reflect his/her interests or strengths (or assign "Symbols of Self-Worth" in the *Child Psychotherapy Homework Planner* by Jongsma, Peterson,

and McInnis); encourage him/her to use talents and strengths to improve self-esteem and meet deeper needs for closeness and intimacy.

19. Identify socially appropriate ways to use intelligence to meet needs. (48)

48. Challenge the client to cease channeling intellectual abilities into self-defeating acts of deception and manipulation; encourage him/her to use intelligence in socially appropriate ways (e.g., learn to play chess; play the villain in a school play; make up a story for language arts class).

—. _____   —. _____

_____   _____

—. _____   —. _____

_____   _____

—. _____   —. _____

_____   _____

DIAGNOSTIC SUGGESTIONS

Using DSM-IV/ICD-9-CM:

Axis I:	313.81	Oppositional Defiant Disorder
	312.81	Conduct Disorder, Childhood-Onset Type
	312.82	Conduct Disorder, Adolescent-Onset Type
	312.9	Disruptive Behavior Disorder NOS
	314.01	Attention-Deficit/Hyperactivity Disorder, Combined Type
	309.3	Adjustment Disorder With Disturbance of Conduct
	V71.02	Child or Adolescent Antisocial Behavior
	V61.20	Parent-Child Relational Problem
	300.4	Dysthymic Disorder
	_____	_____
	_____	_____

Axis II: V71.09 No Diagnosis

_____ _____

_____ _____

Using DSM-5/ICD-9-CM/ICD-10-CM:

ICD-9-CM	ICD-10-CM	*DSM-5* Disorder, Condition, or Problem
313.81	F91.3	Oppositional Defiant Disorder
312.81	F91.1	Conduct Disorder, Childhood-Onset Type
312.9	F91.9	Unspecified Disruptive, Impulse Control, and Conduct Disorder
312.89	F91.8	Other Specified Disruptive, Impulse Control, and Conduct Disorder
314.01	F90.2	Attention-Deficit/Hyperactivity Disorder, Combined Presentation
309.3	F43.24	Adjustment Disorder, With Disturbance of Conduct
V71.02	Z72.810	Child or Adolescent Antisocial Behavior
V61.20	Z62.820	Parent-Child Relational Problem
300.4	F34.1	Persistent Depressive Disorder

Note: The ICD-9-CM codes are to be used for coding purposes in the United States through September 30, 2014. ICD-10-CM codes are to be used starting October 1, 2014. Some ICD-9-CM codes are associated with more than one ICD-10-CM and *DSM-5* disorder, condition, or problem. In addition, some ICD-9-CM disorders have been discontinued resulting in multiple ICD-9-CM codes being replaced by one ICD-10-CM code. Some discontinued ICD-9-CM codes are not listed in this table. See *Diagnostic and Statistical Manual of Mental Disorders* (2013) for details.

MEDICAL CONDITION

BEHAVIORAL DEFINITIONS

1. A diagnosis of a chronic illness that is not life-threatening but necessitates changes in living.
2. A diagnosis of an acute, serious illness that is life-threatening.
3. A diagnosis of a chronic illness that eventually will lead to an early death.
4. Sad affect, social withdrawal, anxiety, loss of interest in activities, and low energy.
5. Suicidal ideation.
6. Denial of the seriousness of the medical condition.
7. Refusal to cooperate with recommended medical treatments.

__. _____
   _____
__. _____
   _____
__. _____
   _____

LONG-TERM GOALS

1. Accept the illness and adapt life to necessary changes.
2. Resolve emotional crisis and face the implications of the terminal illness.
3. Work through the grieving process and face the reality of own death with peace.
4. Accept emotional support from those who care without pushing them away in anger.
5. Resolve depression, fear, and anxiety, finding peace of mind despite the illness.

6. Live life to the fullest extent possible even though time may be limited.
7. Cooperate with the medical treatment regimen without passive-aggressive or active resistance.

—. _____

_____

—. _____

_____

—. _____

_____

SHORT-TERM OBJECTIVES

1. Describe history, symptoms, and treatment of the medical condition. (1, 2, 3)

▽ 2. Share fearful or depressed feelings regarding the medical condition and develop a plan for addressing them. (4, 5, 6)

THERAPEUTIC INTERVENTIONS

1. Establish rapport and a working alliance with the child and parents using appropriate process skills (e.g., active listening, reflective empathy, support, and instillation of hope).

2. Gather a history of the facts regarding the client's medical condition, including symptoms, treatment, and prognosis.

3. With informed consent and appropriate releases, contact the treating physician and family members for additional medical information regarding the client's diagnosis, treatment, and prognosis.

4. Explore and process the client's fears associated with deterioration of physical health, death, and dying. ▽

5. Normalize the client's feelings of grief, sadness, or anxiety associated with his/her medical condition; encourage verbal expression of these emotions. ▽

3. Provide behavioral, emotional, and attitudinal information toward an assessment of specifiers relevant to a *DSM* diagnosis, the efficacy of treatment, and the nature of the therapy relationship. (7, 8, 9, 10, 11)

6. Assess the client for and treat his/her depression and anxiety using relevant cognitive, physiological, and/or behavioral aspects of treatments for those conditions (see the Depression and Anxiety chapters in this *Planner*). ▽

7. Assess the client's level of insight (syntonic versus dystonic) toward the "presenting problems" (e.g., demonstrates good insight into the problematic nature of the "described behavior," agrees with others' concern, and is motivated to work on change; demonstrates ambivalence regarding the "problem described" and is reluctant to address the issue as a concern; or demonstrates resistance regarding acknowledgment of the "problem described," is not concerned, and has no motivation to change).

8. Assess the client for evidence of research-based correlated disorders (e.g., oppositional defiant behavior with ADHD, depression secondary to an anxiety disorder) including vulnerability to suicide, if appropriate (e.g., increased suicide risk when comorbid depression is evident).

9. Assess for any issues of age, gender, or culture that could help explain the client's currently defined "problem behavior" and factors that could offer a better understanding of the client's behavior.

10. Assess for the severity of the level of impairment to the client's functioning to determine

appropriate level of care (e.g.,
the behavior noted creates mild,
moderate, severe, or very severe
impairment in social, relational,
vocational, or occupational
endeavors); continuously assess
this severity of impairment as
well as the efficacy of treatment
(e.g., the client no longer
demonstrates severe impairment
but the presenting problem now
is causing mild or moderate
impairment).

11. Assess the client's home, school,
and community for pathogenic
care (e.g., persistent disregard
for the child's emotional needs
or physical needs, repeated
changes in primary caregivers,
limited opportunities for stable
attachments, persistent harsh
punishment or other grossly
inept parenting).

▽ 4. Verbalize an understanding of
the medical condition, its
consequences, and effective
cognitive behavioral coping. (12)

12. Encourage and facilitate the
client and parents in learning
about the medical condition,
cognitive behavioral factors
that facilitate or interfere with
effective coping and symptom
reduction, the realistic course
of the illness, pain management
options, and chance for
recovery.

▽ 5. Comply with the medication
regimen and necessary medical
procedures, reporting any side
effects or problems to physicians
or therapists. (13, 14, 15)

13. Monitor and reinforce the
client's compliance with the
medical treatment regimen.▽

14. Explore and address the client's
misconceptions, fears, and
situational factors that interfere
with medical treatment
compliance.▽

15. Therapeutically confront any
manipulation, passive-aggressive,

▽ 6. Adjust sleep hours to those typical of the developmental stage. (16)

16. Assess and monitor the client's sleep patterns and sleep hygiene; intervene accordingly to promote good sleep hygiene and sleep cycle (or assign to the parents "Childhood Sleep Problems" in the *Child Psychotherapy Homework Planner* by Jongsma, Peterson, and McInnis). ▽

and denial mechanisms that interfere with the client's compliance with the medical treatment regimen. ▽

▽ 7. Eat nutritious meals regularly. (17)

17. Assess the child's eating habits and intervene accordingly to establish a well-balanced and nutritious eating schedule. ▽

▽ 8. Share feelings triggered by the knowledge of the medical condition and its consequences. (18)

18. Assist the client in identifying, sorting through, and verbalizing the various feelings and stresses generated by his/her medical condition (or assign "Gaining Acceptance of Physical Handicap or Illness" or "Dealing With Childhood Asthma" in the *Child Psychotherapy Homework Planner* by Jongsma, Peterson, and McInnis). ▽

▽ 9. Verbalize acceptance of the reality of the medical condition and its consequences while decreasing denial. (19, 20)

19. Gently confront the client's denial of the seriousness of his/her condition and of the need for compliance with medical treatment procedures. ▽

20. Reinforce the client's acceptance of his/her medical condition. ▽

▽ 10. Family members share with each other the feelings that are triggered by the client's medical condition. (21)

21. Meet with family members to facilitate their clarifying and sharing possible feelings of guilt, anger, helplessness, and/or sibling attention jealousy associated with the client's medical condition (or assign "Coping With a Sibling's Health

▽ 11. Family members share any conflicts that have developed between or among them. (22, 23, 24)

▽ 12. Family members verbalize an understanding of the power of one's own personal positive presence with the sick child. (25)

▽ 13. Identify and grieve the losses or limitations that have been experienced due to the medical condition. (26, 27, 28, 29)

Problems" in the *Adolescent Psychotherapy Homework Planner* by Jongsma, Peterson, and McInnis). ▽

22. Explore how each parent is dealing with the stress related to the client's illness and whether conflicts have developed between the parents because of differing response styles. ▽

23. Assess family conflicts using conflict resolution approach to addressing them. ▽

24. Facilitate a spirit of tolerance for individual difference in each person's internal resources and response styles in the face of threat. ▽

25. Stress the healing power in the family's constant presence with the ill child and emphasize that there is strong healing potential in creating a warm, caring, supportive, positive environment for the child. ▽

26. Ask the client to list his/her perception of changes, losses, or limitations that have resulted from the medical condition. ▽

27. Educate the client on the stages of the grieving process and answer any questions (or suggest that the child read *Don't Despair on Thursdays!* by Moser). ▽

28. Suggest that the client's parents read a book on grief and loss (e.g., *Good Grief* by Westberg; *How Can It Be All Right When Everything Is All Wrong?* by Smedes; *When Bad Things Happen to Good People* by Kushner; *Caring for Your*

Grieving Child: A Parent's Guide by Wakenshaw) to help them understand and support their child in the grieving process.▽

29. Assign the client to keep a daily grief journal to be shared in therapy sessions.▽

▽ 14. Parents implement consistent positive parenting practices to facilitate adaptive responding of child to the medical condition. (30)

30. Assess the parents understanding and use of positive reinforcement principles in child rearing practices; if necessary, teach the parents operant-based child management techniques (see the Parenting chapter in this *Planner*).▽

▽ 15. Identify and replace negative self-talk and catastrophizing that is associated with the medical condition. (31, 32)

31. Assist the client in identifying the cognitive distortions and negative automatic thoughts that contribute to his/her negative attitude and hopeless feelings associated with the medical condition (or assign "Bad Thoughts Lead to Depressed Feelings" in the *Adolescent Psychotherapy Homework Planner* by Jongsma, Peterson, and McInnis).▽

32. Generate with the client a list of positive, realistic self-talk that can replace cognitive distortions and catastrophizing regarding his/her medical condition and its treatment (or assign "Replace Negative Thoughts With Positive Self-Talk" in the *Child Psychotherapy Homework Planner* by Jongsma, Peterson, and McInnis).▽

▽ 16. Decrease time spent focused on the negative aspects of the medical condition. (33, 34)

33. Suggest that the client set aside a specific time-limited period each day to focus on mourning the medical condition; after the time period is up, have the client

resume regular daily activities with agreement to put off thoughts until next scheduled time.▽

34. Challenge the client to focus his/her thoughts on the positive aspects of his/her life and time remaining, rather than on the losses associated with his/her medical condition; reinforce instances of such a positive focus.▽

▽ 17. Learn and implement calming skills to reduce overall tension and moments of increased anxiety, tension, or arousal. (35, 36, 37)

35. Teach the client cognitive and somatic calming skills (e.g., calming breathing; cognitive distancing, de-catastrophizing, distraction; progressive muscle relaxation; guided imagery); rehearse with the client how to apply these skills to his/her daily life (or assign "Deep Breathing Exercise" in the *Child Psychotherapy Homework Planner* by Jongsma, Peterson, and McInnis); review and reinforce success while providing corrective feedback toward consistent implementation.▽

36. Utilize electromyography (EMG) biofeedback to monitor, increase, and reinforce the client's depth of relaxation.▽

37. Assign the client and/or parents to read and discuss progressive muscle relaxation and other calming strategies in relevant books or treatment manuals (e.g., *The Relaxation and Stress Reduction Workbook for Kids* by Shapiro and Sprague; the *Coping C.A.T. Series* at workbookpublishing.com).▽

▽ 18. Parents and child learn and implement social skills for resolving conflicts effectively. (38)

38. Teach the client and parents tailored, age-appropriate social skills including problem-solving skills (e.g., specifying problem, generating options, listing pros and cons of each option, selecting an option, implementation, and refining), and conflict resolution skills (e.g., empathy, active listening, "I messages," respectful communication, assertiveness without aggression, compromise) to improve interpersonal functioning; use behavioral skills-building techniques (e.g., modeling, role-playing, and behavior rehearsal, corrective feedback) to develop skills and work through several current conflicts. ▽

▽ 19. Engage in social, productive, and recreational activities that are possible despite the medical condition. (39, 40, 41, 42)

39. Sort out with the client activities that can still be enjoyed alone and with others. ▽

40. Assess the effects of the medical condition on the client's social network (or assign "Effects of Physical Handicap or Illness on Self-Esteem and Peer Relations" in the *Adolescent Psychotherapy Homework Planner* by Jongsma, Peterson, and McInnis); facilitate the social support available through the client's family and friends. ▽

41. Solicit a commitment from the client to increase his/her activity level by engaging in enjoyable and challenging activities (or assign "Show Your Strengths" in the *Child Psychotherapy Homework Planner* by Jongsma, Peterson, and McInnis); reinforce such engagement. ▽

42. Engage the client in "behavioral activation" by scheduling activities that have a high likelihood for pleasure and mastery, are worthwhile to the client, and/or make him/her feel good about self; use behavioral techniques (e.g., modeling, role-playing, role reversal, rehearsal, and corrective feedback) as needed, to assist adoption in the client's daily life (or assign to the client along with parents "Identify and Schedule Pleasant Activities" in the *Adult Psychotherapy Homework Planner* by Jongsma); reinforce advances. ▽

▽ 20. Establish a regular exercise schedule. (43)

43. Develop and encourage a routine of physical exercise for the client. ▽

22. Learn and implement relapse prevention skills. (44)

44. Build the client's relapse prevention skills by helping him/her identify early warning signs of relapse into negative thoughts, feelings, and actions, reviewing skills learned during therapy, and developing a plan for managing challenges.

24. Attend a support group of others diagnosed with a similar illness, if desired. (45)

45. Refer the client to a support group of others living with a similar medical condition.

23. Parents and family members attend a support group, if desired. (46)

46. Refer family members to a community-based support group associated with the client's medical condition.

24. Client and family identify the sources of emotional support that have been beneficial and additional sources that could be sought. (47, 48)

47. Probe and evaluate the client's, siblings', and parents' sources of emotional support.

48. Encourage the parents and siblings to reach out for support from each other, church leaders,

extended family, hospital social services, community support groups, and personal religious beliefs.

25. Implement faith-based activities as a source of comfort and hope. (49, 50)

49. Draw out the parents' unspoken fears about the client's possible death; empathize with their panic, helplessness, frustration, and anxiety; reassure them of their God's presence as the giver and supporter of life.

50. Encourage the client to rely upon his/her spiritual faith promises, activities (e.g., prayer, meditation, worship, music) and fellowship as sources of support and peace of mind.

__ . _____   __ . _____

_____   _____

__ . _____   __ . _____

_____   _____

__ . _____   __ . _____

_____   _____

DIAGNOSTIC SUGGESTIONS

Using DSM-IV/ICD-9-CM:

Axis I:	316	Psychological Symptoms Affecting (Axis III Disorder)
	309.0	Adjustment Disorder With Depressed Mood
	309.24	Adjustment Disorder With Anxiety
	309.28	Adjustment Disorder With Mixed Anxiety and Depressed Mood
	309.3	Adjustment Disorder With Disturbance of Conduct
	309.4	Adjustment Disorder With Mixed Disturbance of Emotions and Conduct
	296.xx	Major Depressive Disorder
	311	Depressive Disorder NOS

	300.02	Generalized Anxiety Disorder
	_____	_____
	_____	_____
Axis II:	V71.09	No Diagnosis
	_____	_____
	_____	_____

Using DSM-5/ICD-9-CM/ICD-10-CM:

ICD-9-CM	ICD-10-CM	*DSM-5* Disorder, Condition, or Problem
316	F54	Psychological Factors Affecting Other Medical Conditions
309.0	F43.21	Adjustment Disorder, With Depressed Mood
309.24	F43.22	Adjustment Disorder, With Anxiety
309.28	F43.23	Adjustment Disorder, With Mixed Anxiety and Depressed Mood
309.3	F43.24	Adjustment Disorder, With Disturbance of Conduct
309.4	F43.25	Adjustment Disorder, With Mixed Disturbance of Emotions and Conduct
296.xx	F32.x	Major Depressive Disorder, Single Episode
296.xx	F33.x	Major Depressive Disorder, Recurrent Episode
311	F32.9	Unspecified Depressive Disorder
311	F32.8	Other Specified Depressive Disorder
300.02	F41.1	Generalized Anxiety Disorder
300.09	F41.8	Other Specified Anxiety Disorder
300.00	F41.9	Unspecified Anxiety Disorder

Note: The ICD-9-CM codes are to be used for coding purposes in the United States through September 30, 2014. ICD-10-CM codes are to be used starting October 1, 2014. Some ICD-9-CM codes are associated with more than one ICD-10-CM and *DSM-5* disorder, condition, or problem. In addition, some ICD-9-CM disorders have been discontinued resulting in multiple ICD-9-CM codes being replaced by one ICD-10-CM code. Some discontinued ICD-9-CM codes are not listed in this table. See *Diagnostic and Statistical Manual of Mental Disorders* (2013) for details.

$\overline{\underline{\triangledown}}$ Indicates that the Objective/Intervention is consistent with those found in evidence-based treatments.

OBSESSIVE-COMPULSIVE DISORDER (OCD)

BEHAVIORAL DEFINITIONS

1. Recurrent and persistent ideas, thoughts, or impulses that are viewed as intrusive, senseless, and time-consuming, or that interfere with the client's daily routine, school performance, or social relationships.
2. Failed attempts to ignore or control these thoughts or impulses or neutralize them with other thoughts and actions.
3. Recognition that obsessive thoughts are a product of his/her own mind.
4. Excessive concerns about dirt or unfounded fears of contracting a dreadful disease or illness.
5. Obsessions related to troubling aggressive or sexual thoughts, urges, or images.
6. Persistent and troubling thoughts about religious issues; excessive concern about morality and right or wrong.
7. Repetitive and intentional behaviors and/or mental acts that are done in response to obsessive thoughts or increased feelings of anxiety or fearfulness.
8. Repetitive and excessive behaviors and/or mental acts that are done to neutralize or prevent discomfort or some dreaded event; however, these behaviors or mental acts are not connected in a realistic way with what they are designed to neutralize or prevent, or are clearly excessive.
9. Recognition of repetitive behaviors as excessive and unreasonable.
10. Cleaning and washing compulsions (e.g., excessive hand washing, bathing, showering, cleaning of household items).
11. Hoarding or collecting compulsions.
12. Checking compulsions (e.g., repeatedly checking to see if door is locked, rechecking homework to make sure it is done correctly, checking to make sure that no one has been harmed).
13. Compulsions about having to arrange objects or things in proper order (e.g., stacking coins in certain order, laying out clothes each evening at same time, wearing only certain clothes on certain days).

—. _____
_____
—. _____
_____
—. _____
_____

LONG-TERM GOALS

1. Significantly reduce time involved with or interference from obsessions.
2. Significantly reduce frequency of compulsive or ritualistic behaviors.
3. Function daily at a consistent level with minimal interference from obsessions and compulsions.
4. Resolve key life conflicts and the emotional stress that fuels obsessive-compulsive behavior patterns.
5. Let go of key thoughts, beliefs, and past life events in order to maximize time free from obsessions and compulsions.

—. _____
_____
—. _____
_____
—. _____
_____

SHORT-TERM OBJECTIVES

1. Describe the nature, history, and severity of obsessive thoughts and/or compulsive behavior. (1, 2)

THERAPEUTIC INTERVENTIONS

1. Establish rapport and a working alliance with the client and parents using appropriate process skills (e.g., active listening, reflective empathy, support, and instillation of hope).

2. Assess the nature, severity, and history of the client's obsessions and compulsions using clinical interview with the client and the

2. Comply with psychological testing evaluation to assess the nature and severity of the obsessive-compulsive problem. (3)

3. Provide behavioral, emotional and attitudinal information toward an assessment of specifiers relevant to a DSM diagnosis, the efficacy of treatment, and the nature of the therapy relationship. (4, 5, 6, 7, 8)

parents (or assign the exercise "Concerns, Feelings, and Hopes about OCD" in the *Child Psychotherapy Homework Planner* by Jongsma, Peterson, and McInnis).

3. Arrange for psychological testing or use objective measures to further evaluate the nature and severity of the client's obsessive-compulsive problem (e.g., *Children's Yale-Brown Obsessive Compulsive Scale*).

4. Assess the client's level of insight (syntonic versus dystonic) toward the "presenting problems" (e.g., demonstrates good insight into the problematic nature of the "described behavior," agrees with others' concern, and is motivated to work on change; demonstrates ambivalence regarding the "problem described" and is reluctant to address the issue as a concern; or demonstrates resistance regarding acknowledgment of the "problem described," is not concerned, and has no motivation to change).

5. Assess the client for evidence of research-based correlated disorders (e.g., oppositional defiant behavior with ADHD, depression secondary to an anxiety disorder) including vulnerability to suicide, if appropriate (e.g., increased suicide risk when comorbid depression is evident).

6. Assess for any issues of age, gender, or culture that could help explain the client's currently

defined "problem behavior" and factors that could offer a better understanding of the client's behavior.

7. Assess for the severity of the level of impairment to the client's functioning to determine appropriate level of care (e.g., the behavior noted creates mild, moderate, severe, or very severe impairment in social, relational, vocational, or occupational endeavors); continuously assess this severity of impairment as well as the efficacy of treatment (e.g., the client no longer demonstrates severe impairment but the presenting problem now is causing mild or moderate impairment).

8. Assess the client's home, school, and community for pathogenic care (e.g., persistent disregard for the child's emotional needs or physical needs, repeated changes in primary caregivers, limited opportunities for stable attachments, persistent harsh punishment or other grossly inept parenting).

▽ 4. Cooperate with an evaluation by a physician for psychotropic medication. (9, 10)

9. Arrange for an evaluation for a prescription of psychotropic medications (e.g., serotonergic medications). ▽

10. Monitor the client for prescription compliance, side effects, and overall effectiveness of the medication; consult with the prescribing physician at regular intervals. ▽

▽ 5. Verbalize an understanding of OCD and the rationale for its treatment. (11, 12)

11. Provide the client and parents with initial and ongoing psychoeducation about OCD,

a cognitive behavioral conceptualization of OCD, biopsychosocial factors influencing its development, how fear and avoidance serve to maintain the disorder, and other information relevant to therapeutic goals. ▽

12. Discuss a rationale in which treatment serves as an arena to desensitize learned fear, reality test obsessive fears and underlying beliefs (e.g., seeing obsessive fears as "false alarms"), and build confidence in managing fears without compulsions (see *Cognitive Behavioral Treatment of Childhood OCD: It's Only a False Alarm–Therapist Guide* by Piacentini, Langley, and Roblek). ▽

▽ 6. Express an intent to participate in cognitive behavioral therapy for OCD. (13)

13. Confirm the client's motivation to participate in treatment; use motivational interviewing techniques, a pros/cons analysis, and/or other motivational interventions to help move the client toward committed engagement in therapy. ▽

▽ 7. Participate in exposure and ritual prevention therapy for obsessions and compulsions in individual or small group format, with or without family. (14)

14. Enroll the client in exposure and (response) ritual prevention therapy for obsessions and compulsions in an intensive (e.g., daily) or non-intensive (e.g., weekly) level of care; individual (preferred) or small (closed enrollment) group; with or without family involvement (e.g., see *Treatment of OCD in Children and Adolescents* by Wagner; *OCD in Children and Adolescents* by March and Mulle; *Cognitive Behavioral Treatment of Childhood OCD: It's Only a False Alarm–Therapist*

⧊ 8. Complete a daily journal of obsessions and compulsions as guided by the therapist. (15)

⧊ 9. Identify and replace biased, fearful self-talk and beliefs. (16)

⧊ 10. Learn cognitive coping strategies to manage obsessions therapeutically. (17)

⧊ 11. Learn about OCD and its treatment through media recommended by the therapist (e.g., books, DVDs). (18)

Guide by Piacentini, Langley, and Roblek).⧊

15. Instruct and ask the client to self-monitor and record obsessions and compulsions including triggers, specific fears, and mental and/or behavioral compulsions; involve parents if needed; review to facilitate psychoeducation and/or assess response to treatment.⧊

16. Explore the client's biased cognitive self-talk, beliefs, and underlying assumptions that mediate his/her obsessive fears and compulsive behavior (e.g., distorted risk appraisals, inflated sense of responsibility for harm, excessive self-doubt, thought-action fusion—thinking of a harmful act is the same as actually doing it); assist him/her in generating thoughts/beliefs that correct for the biases.⧊

17. Teach cognitive skills such as constructive self-talk, "bossing back" obsessions, distancing and nonattachment (letting obsessive thoughts, images, and/or impulses come and go) to improve the client's personal efficacy in managing obsessions.⧊

18. Prescribe reading or other sources of information (e.g., CDs, DVDs) on OCD and exposure and ritual prevention therapy to facilitate psychoeducation done in session (e.g., *It's Only a False Alarm: A Cognitive Behavioral Treatment Program–Client Workbook* by Piacentini, Langley, & Roblek; *Brain Lock: Free Yourself from Obsessive-Compulsive Behavior* by Schwartz; *Obsessive-Compulsive*

▽ 12. Participate in imaginary exposure to feared external and/or internal triggers of obsessions without use of compulsive rituals. (19, 20, 21)

Disorder: Help for Children and Adolescents by Waltz). ▽

19. Assess the nature of any external cues (e.g., persons, objects, situations) and internal cues (thoughts, images, and impulses) that precipitate the client's obsessions and compulsions. ▽

20. Direct and assist the client in construction of a hierarchy of feared internal and external fear cues. ▽

21. Select initial imaginary exposures to the internal and/or external OCD cues that have a high likelihood of being a successful experience for the client; do cognitive restructuring during and after the exposure. ▽

▽ 13. Participate in live (*in vivo*) exposure to feared external and/or internal triggers of obsessions without use of compulsive rituals. (22, 23, 24)

22. Teach the client to use coping strategies (e.g., constructive self-talk, distraction, distancing) to resist engaging in compulsive behaviors invoked to reduce the obsession-triggered distress; ask client to record attempts to resist compulsions (or assign the parents to help the client through the exercise); assign "Reducing the Strength of Compulsive Behaviors" in the *Adult Psychotherapy Homework Planner* by Jongsma); review during next session, reinforcing success and providing corrective feedback toward improvement. ▽

23. Design a reward system for the parents to reinforce the client for attempts to complete exposures while resisting the urge to engage in compulsive behavior. ▽

24. Assign an exposure homework exercise in which the client

gradually reduces time given per day to obsessions and/or compulsions, encouraging him/her to use coping strategies and the parents to use reinforcement of the child's success (or assign "Ritual Exposure and Response Prevention" in the *Child Psychotherapy Homework Planner* by Jongsma, Peterson, and McInnis). ▽

▽ 14. Implement relapse prevention strategies to help maintain gain achieved through therapy. (25, 26, 27, 28)

25. Discuss with the client the distinction between a lapse and relapse, associating a lapse with an initial and reversible return of symptoms, fear, or urges to avoid and relapse with the decision to return to fearful and avoidant patterns. ▽

26. Identify and rehearse with the client the management of future situations or circumstances in which lapses could occur. ▽

27. Instruct the client to routinely use strategies learned in therapy (e.g., continued exposure to previously feared external or internal cues that arise) to prevent relapse into obsessive-compulsive patterns. ▽

28. Schedule periodic "maintenance" sessions to help the client maintain therapeutic gains and adjust to life without OCD (see *A Relapse Prevention Program for Treatment of Obsessive Compulsive Disorder* by Hiss, Foa, and Kozak for a description of relapse prevention strategies for OCD). ▽

▽ 15. Parents participate in therapy to provide appropriate support, facilitate the client's advancement in therapy, and help manage

29. Include family in sessions to identify specific, positive ways that the parents can help the client manage his/her obsessions

stresses encountered in the process. (29, 30, 31, 32)

or compulsions (see *Family-Based Treatment for Young Children With OCD, Therapist Guide* by Freeman and Garcia). $\overline{\underline{\triangledown}}$

30. Teach parents how to remain calm, patient, and supportive when faced with the client's obsessions or compulsions, discouraging parents from reacting strongly with anger or frustration. $\overline{\underline{\triangledown}}$

31. Teach family members their appropriate role in helping the client adhere to treatment; assist them in identifying and changing tendencies to reinforce the client's OCD (or assign "Refocusing" in the *Child Psychotherapy Homework Planner* by Jongsma, Peterson, and McInnis). $\overline{\underline{\triangledown}}$

32. Teach family members stress management techniques (e.g., calming, problem-solving, and communication skills) to manage stress and resolve problems encountered through therapy. $\overline{\underline{\triangledown}}$

16. Identify support persons or resources that can help the client manage obsessions/ compulsions. (33, 34)

33. Encourage and instruct the client to involve support person(s) or a "coach" who can help him/her adhere to therapeutic recommendations in managing OCD.

34. Refer the client and parents to support group(s) to help maintain and support the gains made in therapy.

17. Participate in an Acceptance and Commitment Therapy for OCD. (35)

35. Use an acceptance and commitment-based approach to help the client change from experiential avoidance of obsessions and compulsions to a more psychologically flexible approach of acceptance of thoughts, images, and/or impulses and

commitment to valued action (see *Acceptance and Mindfulness Treatments for Children and Adolescents* by Greco and Hayes).

18. Participate in an Ericksonian task that involves facing the OCD. (36)

36. Develop and design an Ericksonian task (e.g., if obsessed with a loss, give the client the task to visit, send a card, or bring flowers to someone who has lost someone) for the client that is centered on the facing the obsession or compulsion and process the results with the client (see *Uncommon Therapy: The Psychiatric Techniques of Milton H. Erickson, M.D.* by Haley).

19. Engage in a strategic ordeal to overcome OCD impulses. (37)

37. Create and promote a strategic ordeal that offers a guaranteed cure to help the client with the obsession or compulsion (e.g., instruct client to perform an aversive chore each time an obsessive thought or compulsive behavior occurs). Note that Haley emphasizes that the "cure" offers an intervention to achieve a goal and is not a promise to cure the client in beginning of therapy (see *Ordeal Therapy* by Haley).

20. Participate in family therapy, addressing family dynamics that contribute to the emergence, maintenance, or exacerbation of OCD symptoms. (38, 39)

38. Obtain detailed family history of important past and present interpersonal relationships and experiences; identify dynamics that may contribute to the emergence, maintenance, or exacerbation of OCD symptoms.

39. Conduct family therapy sessions to address past and/or present conflicts, as well as the dynamics contributing to the emergence, maintenance, or exacerbation of OCD symptoms (see *Family-Based Treatment for Young*

Children with OCD–Workbook or Therapist Guide by Freeman and Garcia).

21. Participate in play therapy with the therapist to reduce OCD symptoms. (40)

40. Conduct psychodynamically-oriented play therapy to address issues such as resistance, shame, negative self-concept, and to facilitate social adjustment (see *Integrating Play Therapy Into the Treatment of Children With OCD* by Gold-Steinberg and Logan).

—. _____   —. _____

_____   _____

—. _____   —. _____

_____   _____

—. _____   —. _____

_____   _____

DIAGNOSTIC SUGGESTIONS

Using DSM-IV/ICD-9-CM:

Axis I:	300.3	Obsessive-Compulsive Disorder
	300.00	Anxiety Disorder NOS
	300.02	Generalized Anxiety Disorder
	296.xx	Major Depressive Disorder
	_____	_____
	_____	_____
Axis II:	V71.09	No Diagnosis
	_____	_____
	_____	_____

Using DSM-5/ICD-9-CM/ICD-10-CM:

ICD-9-CM	ICD-10-CM	*DSM-5* Disorder, Condition, or Problem
300.3	F42	Obsessive-Compulsive Disorder
300.09	F41.8	Other Specified Anxiety Disorder
300.00	F41.9	Unspecified Anxiety Disorder
300.02	F41.1	Generalized Anxiety Disorder
296.xx	F32.x	Major Depressive Disorder, Single Episode
296.xx	F33.x	Major Depressive Disorder, Recurrent Episode

Note: The ICD-9-CM codes are to be used for coding purposes in the United States through September 30, 2014. ICD-10-CM codes are to be used starting October 1, 2014. Some ICD-9-CM codes are associated with more than one ICD-10-CM and *DSM-5* disorder, condition, or problem. In addition, some ICD-9-CM disorders have been discontinued resulting in multiple ICD-9-CM codes being replaced by one ICD-10-CM code. Some discontinued ICD-9-CM codes are not listed in this table. See *Diagnostic and Statistical Manual of Mental Disorders* (2013) for details.

▽ Indicates that the Objective/Intervention is consistent with those found in evidence-based treatments.

OPPOSITIONAL DEFIANT

BEHAVIORAL DEFINITIONS

1. Displays a pattern of negativistic, hostile, and defiant behavior toward most adults.
2. Often acts as if parents, teachers, and other authority figures are the "enemy."
3. Erupts in temper tantrums (e.g., screaming, crying, throwing objects, thrashing on ground, refusing to move) in defiance of direction from an adult caregiver.
4. Consistently argues with adults.
5. Often defies or refuses to comply with requests and rules, even when they are reasonable.
6. Deliberately annoys people and is easily annoyed by others.
7. Often blames others for own mistakes or misbehavior.
8. Consistently is angry and resentful.
9. Often is spiteful or vindictive.
10. Has experienced significant impairment in social or academic functioning.

—. _____
_____

—. _____
_____

—. _____
_____

LONG-TERM GOALS

1. Display a marked reduction in the intensity and frequency of hostile and defiant behaviors toward adults.

2. Terminate temper tantrums and replace with controlled, respectful compliance with directions from authority figures.
3. Replace hostile, defiant behaviors toward adults with those of respect and cooperation.
4. Resolution of the conflict that underlies the anger, hostility, and defiance.
5. Reach a level of reduced tension, increased satisfaction, and improved communication with family and/or other authority figures.
6. Parents learn and implement good child behavioral management skills.

__. _____
   _____
__. _____
   _____
__. _____
   _____

SHORT-TERM OBJECTIVES

1. Parents, client, and others identify situations, thoughts, and feelings that trigger angry feelings, defiant behavior, and the targets of those actions. (1)

2. Parents and client cooperate with psychological assessment to further delineate the nature of the presenting problem. (2)

THERAPEUTIC INTERVENTIONS

1. Thoroughly assess the various stimuli (e.g., situations, people, thoughts) that have triggered the client's defiant behavior and the thoughts, feelings, and actions that have characterized his/her defiant responses; consult others (e.g., family members, teachers) and/or use parent/teacher rating scales (e.g., *Child Behavior Checklist*; *Eyberg Child Behavior Inventory*; *Sutter-Eyberg Student Behavior Inventory–Revised*) to supplement assessment as necessary.

2. Administer psychological instruments designed to assess whether a comorbid condition(s) (e.g., bipolar disorder, depression, ADHD) is contributing to disruptive behavior problems and/or

objectively assess parent-child relational conflict (e.g., the *Parent-Child Relationship Inventory*); follow up accordingly with client and parents regarding treatment options; readminister as needed to assess treatment outcome.

3. Provide behavioral, emotional, and attitudinal information toward an assessment of specifiers relevant to a *DSM* diagnosis, the efficacy of treatment, and the nature of the therapy relationship. (3, 4, 5, 6, 7)

3. Assess the client's level of insight (syntonic versus dystonic) toward the "presenting problems" (e.g., demonstrates good insight into the problematic nature of the "described behavior," agrees with others' concern, and is motivated to work on change; demonstrates ambivalence regarding the "problem described" and is reluctant to address the issue as a concern; or demonstrates resistance regarding acknowledgment of the "problem described," is not concerned, and has no motivation to change).

4. Assess the client for evidence of research-based correlated disorders (e.g., oppositional defiant behavior with ADHD, depression secondary to an anxiety disorder) including vulnerability to suicide, if appropriate (e.g., increased suicide risk when comorbid depression is evident).

5. Assess for any issues of age, gender, or culture that could help explain the client's currently defined "problem behavior" and factors that could offer a better understanding of the client's behavior.

6. Assess for the severity of the level of impairment to the client's functioning to determine appropriate level of care (e.g., the behavior noted creates mild, moderate, severe, or very severe impairment in social, relational, vocational, or occupational endeavors); continuously assess this severity of impairment as well as the efficacy of treatment (e.g., the client no longer demonstrates severe impairment but the presenting problem now is causing mild or moderate impairment).

7. Assess the client's home, school, and community for pathogenic care (e.g., persistent disregard for the child's emotional needs or physical needs, repeated changes in primary caregivers, limited opportunities for stable attachments, persistent harsh punishment or other grossly inept parenting).

▽ 4. Cooperate with a physician evaluation for possible treatment with psychotropic medications and take medications consistently, if prescribed. (8, 9)

8. Assess the client for the need for psychotropic medication to assist in anger and behavioral control, referring him/her, if indicated, to a physician for an evaluation for prescription medication. ▽

9. Monitor the client's prescription compliance, effectiveness, and side effects; provide feedback to the prescribing physician. ▽

▽ 5. Recognize and verbalize how feelings are connected to misbehavior. (10)

10. Actively build the level of trust with the client through consistent eye contact, active listening, unconditional positive regard, and warm acceptance to help increase his/her ability to identify and express feelings

▽ 6. Increase the number of statements that reflect an understanding of the consequences of disruptive behavior and acceptance of responsibility for it. (11, 12)

instead of acting them out; assist the client in making a connection between his/her feelings and reactive behaviors (or assign "Risk Factors Leading to Child Behavior Problems" in the *Child Psychotherapy Homework Planner* by Jongsma, Peterson, and McInnis). ▽

11. Therapeutically confront statements in which the client lies and/or blames others for his/her misbehaviors and fails to accept responsibility for hurt caused by his/her actions (or assign "Building Empathy" or "The Lesson of Salmon Rock . . . Fighting Leads to Loneliness" in the *Child Psychotherapy Homework Planner* by Jongsma, Peterson, and McInnis); explore and process the factors that contribute to the client's pattern of blaming others (e.g., harsh punishment experiences, family pattern of blaming others). ▽

12. Use techniques derived from motivational interviewing to move the client away from externalizing and blaming toward accepting responsibility for his/her actions and motivation to change. ▽

▽ 7. Agree to learn alternative ways to think about and manage anger and misbehavior. (13)

13. Assist the client in identifying the positive consequences of managing anger and misbehavior (e.g., respect from others and self, cooperation from others, improved physical health); ask the client to agree to learn new ways to conceptualize and manage anger and misbehavior. ▽

▽ 8. Verbalize alternative ways to think about and manage anger and misbehavior. (14, 15)

14. Assist the client in conceptualizing his/her oppositional behavior as involving different components (cognitive, physiological, affective, and behavioral) that go through predictable phases that can be managed (e.g., demanding expectations not being met leading to increased arousal and anger which leads to acting out). ▽

15. Discuss a rationale for treatment explaining how changes in the different factors contributing to oppositional behavior (e.g., cognitive, physiological, affective, and behavioral) can change interactions with others that minimize negative consequences and increase positive ones. ▽

▽ 9. Learn and implement calming strategies as part of a new way to manage reactions to frustration. (16)

16. Teach the client calming techniques (e.g., muscle relaxation, paced breathing, calming imagery) as part of a more comprehensive, tailored skill set for responding appropriately to angry feelings when they occur (or assign "Deep Breathing Exercise" in the *Child Psychotherapy Homework Planner* by Jongsma, Peterson, and McInnis). ▽

▽ 10. Identify, challenge, and replace self-talk that leads to anger and misbehavior with self-talk that facilitates more constructive reactions. (17)

17. Explore the client's self-talk that mediates his/her angry feelings and actions (e.g., demanding expectations reflected in *should*, *must*, or *have to* statements); identify and challenge biases, assisting him/her in generating appraisals and self-talk that corrects for the biases and facilitates a more flexible and temperate response to frustration

(or assign "Replace Negative Thoughts with Positive Self-Talk" in the *Child Psychotherapy Homework Planner* by Jongsma, Peterson and McInnis). ▽

11. Learn and implement thought-stopping to manage intrusive unwanted thoughts that trigger anger and acting out. (18)

18. Teach the client the thought-stopping technique and assign implementation on a daily basis between sessions; review implementation, reinforcing success and providing corrective feedback toward improvement. ▽

12. Verbalize feelings of frustration, disagreement, and anger in a controlled, assertive way. (19)

19. Use instruction, videotaped or live modeling, and/or role-playing to help develop the client's anger control and assertiveness skills, such as calming, self-statements, assertion skills; if indicated, refer him/her to an anger control or assertiveness group for further instruction (see *Anger Control Training for Aggressive Youths* by Lochman et al.). ▽

13. Implement problem-solving and/or conflict resolution skills to manage interpersonal problems constructively. (20)

20. Teach the client conflict resolution skills (e.g., empathy, active listening, "I messages," respectful communication, assertiveness without aggression, compromise; problem-solving steps) and recommend the child and parents read *Cool, Calm, and Confident: A Workbook to Help Kids Learn Assertiveness Skills* by Schab; use modeling, role-playing, and behavior rehearsal to work through several current conflicts (or assign "Problem-Solving Exercise" in the *Child Psychotherapy Homework Planner* by Jongsma, Peterson and McInnis). ▽

▽ 14. Practice using new calming, communication, conflict resolution, and thinking skills in group or individual therapy. (21, 22)

21. Assist the client in constructing and consolidating a client-tailored strategy for managing anger that combines any of the somatic, cognitive, communication, problem-solving, and/or conflict resolution skills relevant to his/her needs. ▽

22. Use any of several techniques (e.g., relaxation, imagery, behavioral rehearsal, modeling, role-playing, feedback of videotaped practice) in increasingly challenging situations to teach the client to consolidate the use of his/her new anger management skills; encourage the client to practice these skills *in vivo* (see *Problem-Solving Skills Training and Parent Management Training for Conduct Disorder* by Kazdin). ▽

▽ 15. Decrease the number, intensity, and duration of angry outbursts, while increasing the use of new skills for managing anger. (23)

23. Monitor the client's reports of angry outbursts toward the goal of decreasing their frequency, intensity, and duration through the client's use of new anger management skills (or assign "Anger Control" or "Child Anger Checklist" in the *Child Psychotherapy Homework Planner* by Jongsma, Peterson, and McInnis); review progress, reinforcing success and providing corrective feedback toward improvement. ▽

▽ 16. Identify social supports that will help facilitate the implementation of new skills. (24)

24. Encourage the client to discuss and/or use his/her new anger and conduct management skills with trusted peers, family, or otherwise significant others who are likely to support his/her change. ▽

▽ 17. Parents learn and implement Parent Management Training skills to recognize and manage problem behavior of the client. (25, 26, 27, 28, 29)

25. Use a Parent Management Training approach beginning with teaching the parents how parent and child behavioral interactions can encourage or discourage positive or negative behavior and that changing key elements of those interactions (e.g., prompting and reinforcing positive behaviors) can be used to promote positive change (e.g., *Parent Management Training* by Forgatch and Patterson; *Parenting the Strong-Willed Child* by Forehand and Long; *Living with Children* by Patterson). ▽

26. Ask the parents to read material consistent with a parent training approach to managing disruptive behavior (e.g., *The Kazdin Method for Parenting the Defiant Child* by Kazdin; *Living with Children* by Patterson).

27. Teach the parents how to specifically define and identify problem behaviors, identify their reactions to the behavior, determine whether the reaction encourages or discourages the behavior, and generate alternatives to the problem behavior. ▽

28. Teach parents how to implement key parenting practices consistently, including establishing realistic age-appropriate rules for acceptable and unacceptable behavior, prompting of positive behavior in the environment, use of positive reinforcement to encourage behavior (e.g., praise), use of clear direct instruction,

time-out, and other loss-of-privilege practices for problem behavior.▽

29. Assign the parents home exercises in which they implement and record results of behavior reinforcement (or assign "Clear Rules, Positive Reinforcement, Appropriate Consequences" in the *Adolescent Psychotherapy Homework Planner* by Jongsma, Peterson, and McInnis); review in session, providing corrective feedback toward improved, appropriate, and consistent use of skills.▽

▽ 18. Parents and client participate in play sessions in which they use their new rules for appropriate conduct. (30)

30. Conduct Parent-Child Interaction Therapy in which child-directed and parent-directed sessions focus on teaching appropriate child behavior, and parental behavioral management skills (e.g., clear commands, consistent consequences, positive reinforcement) are developed (see *Parent-Child Interaction Therapy by* McNeil and Humbree-Kigin).▽

▽ 19. Parents enroll in an evidence-based parent-training program. (31)

31. Refer parents to an evidence-based parent-training program such as Incredible Years (see www.incredibleyears.com) or the Positive Parenting Program (Triple P; see www.triplep-america.com).▽

▽ 20. Increase compliance with rules at home and school. (32)

32. Design a reward system and/or contingency contract for the client and meet with school officials to reinforce identified positive behaviors at home and school and deter impulsive or rebellious behaviors (or assign "Clear Rules, Positive

Reinforcement, Appropriate Consequences" in the *Adolescent Psychotherapy Homework Planner* by Jongsma, Peterson, and McInnis). ▽

21. Parents verbalize appropriate boundaries for discipline to prevent further occurrences of abuse and to ensure the safety of the client and his/her siblings. (33, 34)

33. Explore the client's family background for a history of neglect and physical or sexual abuse that may contribute to his/her behavioral problems; confront the client's parents to cease physically abusive or overly punitive methods of discipline. ▽

34. Implement the steps necessary to protect the client and siblings from further abuse (e.g., report abuse to the appropriate agencies; remove the client or perpetrator from the home). ▽

22. Verbalize an understanding of the difference between a lapse and relapse. (35, 36)

35. Provide a rationale for relapse prevention that discusses the risk and introduces strategies for preventing it. ▽

36. Discuss with the parent/client the distinction between a lapse and relapse, associating a lapse with a temporary setback and relapse with a return to a sustained pattern of thinking, feeling and behaving that is characteristic of oppositional defiant disorder or conduct disorder. ▽

23. Implement strategies learned in therapy to counter lapses and prevent relapse. (37, 38, 39, 40)

37. Identify and rehearse with the parent/client the management of future situations or circumstances in which lapses could occur. ▽

38. Instruct the parent/client to routinely use strategies learned in therapy (e.g., parent training techniques, problem-solving, anger management), building

them into his/her life as much as possible. ▽

39. Develop a "coping card" on which coping strategies and other important information can be kept (e.g., steps in problem-solving, positive coping statements, reminders that were helpful to the client during therapy). ▽

40. Schedule periodic maintenance or "booster" sessions to help the parent/child maintain therapeutic gains and problem-solve challenges. ▽

24. Increase the frequency of civil, respectful interactions with parents/adults. (41)

41. Teach the client the principle of reciprocity, asking him/her to agree to treat everyone in a respectful manner for a one-week period to see if others will reciprocate by treating him/her with more respect.

25. Demonstrate the ability to play by the rules in a cooperative fashion. (42)

42. Play a game (e.g., checkers), first with the client determining the rules (and the therapist holding the client to those rules) and then with rules determined by the therapist. Process the experience and give positive verbal praise to the client for following established rules.

26. Increase the frequency of responsible and positive social behaviors. (43, 44)

43. Direct the client to engage in three altruistic or benevolent acts (e.g., read to a developmentally disabled student, mow grandmother's lawn) before the next session to increase his/her empathy and sensitivity to the needs of others.

44. Place the client in charge of tasks at home (e.g., preparing and cooking a special dish for a family get-together, building

shelves in the garage, changing oil in the car) to demonstrate confidence in his/her ability to act responsibly (or assign "Share a Family Meal" in the *Child Psychotherapy Homework Planner* by Jongsma, Peterson, and McInnis).

27. Identify and verbally express feelings associated with past neglect, abuse, separation, or abandonment. (45)

45. Encourage and support the client in expressing feelings associated with neglect, abuse, separation, or abandonment and help process (e.g., assign the task of writing a letter to an absent parent, use the empty-chair technique).

28. Seek a resolution of conflicts in the family through respectful expression of complaints within a family therapy setting. (46)

46. Conduct family sessions in which all members express their thoughts and feelings respectfully and openly followed by offering suggestions for reasonable resolution of the complaints (or assign "Filing a Complaint" or "If I Could Run My Family" in the *Child Psychotherapy Homework Planner* by Jongsma, Peterson, and McInnis).

29. Parents participate in marital therapy. (47)

47. Assess the marital dyad for possible substance abuse, conflict, or triangulation that shifts the focus from marriage issues to the client's acting-out behaviors; refer for appropriate treatment, if needed.

__. _____

_____

__. _____

_____

__. _____

_____

__. _____

_____

__. _____

_____

__. _____

_____

DIAGNOSTIC SUGGESTIONS

Using DSM-IV/ICD-9-CM:

Axis I:	312.81	Conduct Disorder, Childhood-Onset Type
	312.82	Conduct Disorder, Adolescent-Onset Type
	313.81	Oppositional Defiant Disorder
	312.9	Disruptive Behavior Disorder NOS
	314.01	Attention-Deficit/Hyperactivity Disorder, Predominantly Hyperactive-Impulsive Type
	312.34	Intermittent Explosive Disorder
	V71.02	Child Antisocial Behavior
	V61.20	Parent-Child Relational Problem
	_____	_____
	_____	_____
Axis II:	V71.09	No Diagnosis
	_____	_____
	_____	_____

Using DSM-5/ICD-9-CM/ICD-10-CM:

ICD-9-CM	ICD-10-CM	*DSM-5* Disorder, Condition, or Problem
312.81	F91.1	Conduct Disorder, Childhood-Onset Type
313.81	F91.3	Oppositional Defiant Disorder
312.9	F91.9	Unspecified Disruptive, Impulse Control, and Conduct Disorder
312.89	F91.8	Other Specified Disruptive, Impulse Control, and Conduct Disorder
314.01	F90.1	Attention-Deficit/Hyperactivity Disorder, Predominately Hyperactive /Impulsive Presentation
314.01	F90.9	Unspecified Attention-Deficit/Hyperactivity Disorder
314.01	F90.8	Other Specified Attention-Deficit/Hyperactivity Disorder
312.34	F63.81	Intermittent Explosive Disorder
V71.02	Z72.810	Child or Adolescent Antisocial Behavior
V61.20	Z62.820	Parent-Child Relational Problem

Note: The ICD-9-CM codes are to be used for coding purposes in the United States through September 30, 2014. ICD-10-CM codes are to be used starting October 1, 2014. Some ICD-9-CM codes are associated with more than one ICD-10-CM and *DSM-5* disorder, condition, or problem. In addition, some ICD-9-CM disorders have been discontinued resulting in multiple ICD-9-CM codes being replaced by one ICD-10-CM code. Some discontinued ICD-9-CM codes are not listed in this table. See *Diagnostic and Statistical Manual of Mental Disorders* (2013) for details.

▼ Indicates that the Objective/Intervention is consistent with those found in evidence-based treatments.

OVERWEIGHT/OBESITY

BEHAVIORAL DEFINITIONS

1. An excess of body weight, relative to height, that is attributed to an abnormally high proportion of body fat (Body Mass Index of 30 or more).
2. Episodes of binge eating (a large amount of food is consumed in a relatively short period of time and there is a sense of lack of control over the eating behavior).
3. Eating to manage troubling emotions.
4. Eating much more rapidly than normal.
5. Eating until feeling uncomfortably full.
6. Eating large amounts of food when not feeling physically hungry.
7. Eating alone because of feeling embarrassed by how much one is eating.
8. Feeling disgusted with oneself, depressed, or very guilty after eating too much.

—. _____
   _____
   _____
—. _____
   _____
   _____
—. _____
   _____

LONG-TERM GOALS

1. Terminate overeating and implement lifestyle changes (e.g., more exercise, eat more vegetables and fruits, eat healthy snacks) that lead to weight loss and improved health.
2. Develop healthy cognitive patterns and beliefs about self that lead to positive identity and prevent a relapse into unhealthy eating patterns.

3. Develop effective skills for managing personal and interpersonal stress without resorting to overeating or emotional eating.
4. Gain insight into past painful emotional experiences contributing to present overeating.

—. _____
_____

—. _____
_____

—. _____
_____

SHORT-TERM OBJECTIVES

1. Honestly describe the pattern of eating including types, amounts, frequency of food restricted and consumed; thoughts and feelings associated with food; lifestyle; as well as family and peer relationships. (1, 2)

2. Client and parents discuss any other personal, marital, or family problems. (3)

3. Complete psychological testing or objective questionnaires. (4)

THERAPEUTIC INTERVENTIONS

1. Establish rapport with the client and parents toward building a therapeutic alliance.

2. Conduct a comprehensive assessment of factors potentially influencing obesity including personal and family eating habits and patterns; thoughts, attitudes, and beliefs about food and diet; lifestyle; exercise; and relationships toward identifying targets for change.

3. Assess for the presence of problems/psychopathology in the parents, client, or both that may be contributing to overeating (e.g., client's depression, anxiety disorder, parents' marital conflict) or otherwise warrant treatment attention; treat accordingly if evident (see relevant chapter in this *Planner*).

4. Refer or conduct psychological testing to inform the overall assessment (e.g., confirm or rule

4. Provide behavioral, emotional, and attitudinal information toward an assessment of specifiers relevant to a *DSM* diagnosis, the efficacy of treatment, and the nature of the therapy relationship. (5, 6, 7, 8, 9)

out psychopathology); give the client feedback regarding the results of the assessment; readminister as needed to assess treatment outcome.

5. Assess the client's level of insight (syntonic versus dystonic) toward the "presenting problems" (e.g., demonstrates good insight into the problematic nature of the "described behavior," agrees with others' concern, and is motivated to work on change; demonstrates ambivalence regarding the "problem described" and is reluctant to address the issue as a concern; or demonstrates resistance regarding acknowledgment of the "problem described," is not concerned, and has no motivation to change).

6. Assess the client for evidence of research-based correlated disorders (e.g., oppositional defiant behavior with ADHD, depression secondary to an anxiety disorder) including vulnerability to suicide, if appropriate (e.g., increased suicide risk when comorbid depression is evident).

7. Assess for any issues of age, gender, or culture that could help explain the client's currently defined "problem behavior" and factors that could offer a better understanding of the client's behavior.

8. Assess for the severity of the level of impairment to the client's functioning to determine appropriate level of care

(e.g., the behavior noted creates mild, moderate, severe, or very severe impairment in social, relational, vocational, or occupational endeavors); continuously assess this severity of impairment as well as the efficacy of treatment (e.g., the client no longer demonstrates severe impairment but the presenting problem now is causing mild or moderate impairment).

9. Assess the client's home, school, and community for pathogenic care (e.g., persistent disregard for the child's emotional needs or physical needs, repeated changes in primary caregivers, limited opportunities for stable attachments, persistent harsh punishment or other grossly inept parenting).

5. Cooperate with a complete medical evaluation. (10)

10. Refer the client to a physician for a medical evaluation to assess possible negative consequences of obesity that may influence treatment planning (e.g., medical conditions secondary to obesity, approved types and amount of exercise, foods to avoid for health purposes) and to assess cholesterol level and blood sugar or hormone imbalances that could be contributing to weight problem.

6. Cooperate with an evaluation by a physician for psychotropic medication and, if indicated, take medications as prescribed. (11, 12)

11. Refer the client for a medication evaluation if warranted (e.g., presence of depression, anxiety).

12. Monitor the client's psychotropic medication prescription compliance, effectiveness, and side effects; stay in contact with prescriber as needed.

7. Verbalize an understanding of the relative risks and benefits of obesity. (13)

13. Discuss with the client and parents how the seeming (short-term) benefits of overeating increase the risk for more serious medical consequences (e.g., hypertension, heart disease, and the like); discuss the health benefits of good weight management practices.

8. Child and parents discuss motivation to participate in weight management treatment. (14)

14. Assess the client's and parents' motivation and readiness for change and intervene accordingly (e.g., defer treatment or conduct motivational interventions with the unmotivated, obtain consent for treatment with the motivated).

▼ 9. Keep a journal documenting food consumption and related factors. (15)

15. Ask the client and/or parents to monitor and record the child's food consumption including types, amounts, time of day, setting, and any other relevant factors (e.g., associated emotions, thoughts); review using data to reinforce psychoeducational objectives as needed (e.g., portion sizes, high and low calorie food, nutrition, food as stress management). ▼

▼ 10. Verbalize an accurate under-standing of factors influencing eating, health, overweight, and obesity. (16)

16. Conduct a Behavioral Weight Management approach to treatment beginning with discussion of obesity, factors influencing it; attend to the roles of lifestyle, exercise, attitudes or cognition/beliefs, relationships, and nutrition (see *The LEARN Program for Weight Management* by Brownell). ▼

▼ 11. Read recommended material to supplement information learned in therapy. (17)

17. Assign the client and parents to read psychoeducational material about obesity, factors influencing it, the rationale and various

emphases in treatment as they are introduced throughout therapy (e.g., *The LEARN Program for Weight Management* by Brownell).▽

▽ 12. Verbalize an understanding of the rationale of treatment. (18)

18. Review the primary emphases of the treatment program, confirming that the client understands and agrees with the rationale and approach.▽

▽ 13. Agree to reasonable weight goals and realistic expectations about how they can be achieved through the therapy. (19, 20, 21)

19. Discuss with the client and parents realistic expectations for what the therapy will entail, the challenges and benefits; emphasize the importance of adherence; instill hope for success and realistic expectations for the challenges.▽

20. Establish short-term (weekly), medium-term (monthly), and long-term (6 months to a year) goals; evaluate and update on a regular basis.▽

21. Discuss a flexible goal-setting strategy recognizing that lapses occur in behavior change and that a problem-solving approach is taken should a lapse occur (e.g., forgive self, identify triggers, generate and evaluate options for addressing risks, implement plan, get back on track with the established goals).▽

▽ 14. Track and chart weight on a routine interval throughout therapy. (22)

22. Routinely measure the client's weight and chart/graph to assess changes during treatment (e.g., weekly).▽

▽ 15. Learn and implement healthy nutritional practices. (23, 24)

23. Teach healthy nutritional practices involving concepts of balance and variety in obtaining necessary nutrients (recommend *The Monster Health Book: A*

Guide to Eating Healthy, Being Active & Feeling Great for Monsters & Kids! by Miller or *Good Enough to Eat: A Kid's Guide to Food and Nutrition* by Rockwell); outline a healthy food diet consistent with good nutritional practices and aimed at attaining the client's weight goals. ▽

24. Refer the client to a nutritionist to develop an appropriate diet aimed at attaining the client's weight goals. ▽

▽ 16. Learn and implement the principles of moderation and variety in food choices and diet. (25)

25. Work with the client and parents to develop an individualized diet that includes the child's preferred food choices while encouraging variety and allowing choice; teach the client and/or parents the principle of portion control for managing total caloric intake; emphasize that a family approach to healthy eating is most beneficial, that no food is prohibited, and that moderation of intake is a key to maintaining a healthy weight. ▽

▽ 17. As a lifestyle change, take steps to avoid and/or manage triggers of spontaneous food buying or eating. (26)

26. Use stimulus control techniques that reduce exposure to triggers of spontaneous food buying/ selection/eating and other poor eating practices (e.g., avoiding buying and eating high-calorie snacks after school; eat before shopping for food or going to a place where unhealthy food is readily available; shop for food from a list; no nonnutritional snack foods openly available in the home; prepare foods from a preplanned menu). ▽

▽ 18. Make changes in the environment and in one's approach to eating that facilitate adherence to moderation and portion size goals. (27)

▽ 19. Identify changes in daily lifestyle activity conducive to improved health and good weight management. (28, 29, 30)

▽ 20. Identify, challenge, and replace negative self-talk with positive, realistic, and empowering self-talk. (31, 32, 33)

27. Use stimulus control techniques such as serving on smaller plates, eating slowly, creating a pleasant mealtime ambience to create an eating routine conducive to pleasurable, moderated eating. ▽

28. Work with the parents and client to identify small, doable changes in activities consistent with therapeutic exercise goals (e.g., parking further away to promote walking, taking stairs, walking to school, staying active during recess; avoiding electronic games that are sedentary); monitor and record physical activity. ▽

29. Encourage parents and client to play games that require physical movement (e.g., running/throwing games, interactive computer games). ▽

30. Encourage participation in organized physical activities (e.g., physical education/gym at school, swimming, youth club sports). ▽

31. Explore the client's self-talk and beliefs that mediate his/her nontherapeutic eating habits (e.g., overeating, eating to manage emotions, poor self-concept); teach him/her how to challenge the biases; assist him/her in replacing the biased messages with reality-based, positive alternatives (e.g., eating for health; using character/values rather than weight in defining self). ▽

32. Assign the client a homework exercise in which he/she identifies self-talk and creates reality-based

alternatives (consider assigning "Replace Negative Thoughts With Positive Self-Talk" from the *Child Psychotherapy Homework Planner* by Jongsma, Peterson, and McInnis); review and reinforce success, providing corrective feedback for failure. ▽

33. Use behavioral techniques (e.g., modeling, corrective feedback, imaginal rehearsal, social reinforcement) to teach the client positive self-talk and self-reward to facilitate the child's new behavior change efforts (or assign "Positive Self-Statements" from the *Child Psychotherapy Homework Planner* by Jongsma, Peterson, and McInnis). ▽

▽ 21. Learn and implement skills for managing stress and effectively solving daily relationship problems previously managed through eating.
(34, 35, 36, 37, 38)

34. Use behavioral skill-building techniques (e.g., modeling, role-playing, and behavior rehearsal, corrective feedback) to teach the client tailored, age-appropriate cognitive and somatic calming skills (recommend *The Relaxation and Stress Reduction Workbook for Kids* by Shapiro; assign the "Deep Breathing Exercise" from the *Child Psychotherapy Homework Planner* by Jongsma, Peterson, and McInnis). ▽

35. Use behavioral skill-building techniques (e.g., modeling, role-playing, and behavior rehearsal, corrective feedback) to teach the client tailored, age-appropriate problem-solving skills (e.g., pinpointing the problem, generating options, listing pros and cons of each option, selecting an option,

implementing an option, and refining); assign homework to practice these skills (consider assigning "Problem-Solving Exercise" from the *Child Psychotherapy Homework Planner* by Jongsma, Peterson, and McInnis). ∇

36. Use behavioral skill-building techniques (e.g., modeling, role-playing, and behavior rehearsal, corrective feedback) to teach the client tailored, age-appropriate conflict resolution skills such as empathy, active listening, and "I messages" (or assign "Negotiating a Peace Treaty" from the *Child Psychotherapy Homework Planner* by Jongsma, Peterson, and McInnis). ∇

37. Use behavioral skill-building techniques (e.g., modeling, role-playing, and behavior rehearsal, corrective feedback) to teach the client tailored, age-appropriate respectful communication, assertiveness without aggression, compromise), develop skills and work through several current conflicts (recommend *Cool, Calm, and Confident: A Workbook to Help Kids Learn Assertiveness Skills* by Schab). ∇

38. Teach all family members stress management skills (e.g., calming, problem solving, communication, conflict resolution) to manage stress and facilitate the client's progress in treatment. ∇

∇ 22. Family members demonstrate support for the client as he/she participates in treatment. (39, 40, 41)

39. Teach parents how to prompt and reward treatment-consistent behavior, empathetically ignore excessive complaining, and

model the behavior being
prescribed to the child. ▽

40. Assist the family in overcoming
the tendency to reinforce the
client's poor eating habits and/or
misplaced motivations (e.g.,
eating to manage emotions);
teach them constructive ways to
reward the client's progress. ▽

41. Encourage and assist the parents
in arranging ongoing support for
weight management effort of the
child (e.g., email messages, phone
calls, website communication,
and postal mail notes) from
significant others that provide
maintenance support and
encouragement. ▽

▽ 23. Implement strategies for
preventing relapse.
(42, 43, 44, 45)

42. Discuss with the client the
distinction between a lapse and
relapse, associating a lapse with
a temporary and reversible
return to prior habits and relapse
with the decision to repeatedly
return to the pattern of behavior
associated with overweight or
obesity. ▽

43. Identify and rehearse with the
client the management of future
situations or circumstances in
which lapses could occur. ▽

44. Instruct the client to routinely
use strategies learned in therapy
(e.g., calming, cognitive
restructuring, stimulus control),
building them into his/her life as
much as possible. ▽

45. Develop a "coping card" on
which coping strategies and
other important information
(e.g., "One step at a time," "Eat
healthy," "Distract yourself from
urges," "Keep portions small,"

"You can manage it") are written for the client's later use. ▽

▽ 24. Attend a group behavioral weight loss program. (46)

46. Refer the client and parents to a group behavioral weight loss program (e.g., programs that emphasize changes in lifestyle, exercise, attitudes, relationships, and nutrition). ▽

25. Verbalize the feelings associated with a past emotionally painful situation connected with eating or food deprivation. (47, 48)

47. Using sensitive questioning, active listening, and unconditional regard, probe, discuss, and interpret the possible emotional neglect, abuse, and/or unmet emotional needs being met through eating.

48. Reinforce the client's insight into the past emotional pain and its connection to present overeating.

__. _____   __. _____
    _____   _____
__. _____   __. _____
    _____   _____
__. _____   __. _____
    _____   _____

DIAGNOSTIC SUGGESTIONS

Using DSM-IV/ICD-9-CM:

Axis I:	307.50	Eating Disorder NOS
	316	Personality Traits or Coping Style Affecting Obesity
	V61.20	Parent-Child Relational Problem
	_____	_____
	_____	_____
Axis II:	V71.09	No Diagnosis
	_____	_____
	_____	_____

Using DSM-5/ICD-9-CM/ICD-10-CM:

ICD-9-CM	ICD-10-CM	*DSM-5* Disorder, Condition, or Problem
278.00	E66.9	Overweight or Obesity
309.0	F43.21	Adjustment Disorder, With Depressed Mood
307.59	F50.8	Other Specified Feeding or Eating Disorder
307.50	F50.9	Unspecified Feeding or Eating Disorder
316	F54	Psychological Factors Affecting Other Medical Conditions, Obesity
V61.20	Z62.820	Parent-Child Relational Problem

Note: The ICD-9-CM codes are to be used for coding purposes in the United States through September 30, 2014. ICD-10-CM codes are to be used starting October 1, 2014. Some ICD-9-CM codes are associated with more than one ICD-10-CM and *DSM-5* disorder, condition, or problem. In addition, some ICD-9-CM disorders have been discontinued resulting in multiple ICD-9-CM codes being replaced by one ICD-10-CM code. Some discontinued ICD-9-CM codes are not listed in this table. See *Diagnostic and Statistical Manual of Mental Disorders* (2013) for details.

▽ Indicates that the Objective/Intervention is consistent with those found in evidence-based treatments.

PARENTING

BEHAVIORAL DEFINITIONS

1. Expression of feelings of inadequacy in setting effective limits with their child.
2. Lack knowledge regarding implementation of proven effective parenting techniques.
3. Frequently struggle to control their emotional reactions to their child's misbehavior.
4. Increasing conflict between spouses over how to parent/discipline their child.
5. A pattern of lax supervision and inadequate limit setting.
6. A pattern of overindulgence of the child's wishes and demands.
7. A pattern of harsh, rigid, and demeaning behavior toward the child.
8. A pattern of physically and emotionally abusive parenting.
9. One parent is perceived as overindulgent while the other is seen as too harsh.
10. One parent expresses resentment over feeling like the only one who is responsible for the child's supervision, nurture, and discipline.
11. Lack of knowledge regarding reasonable expectations for a child's behavior at a given developmental level.
12. Have been told by others (e.g., school officials, juvenile court, friends) that they need to do something to control their child's negative behavior pattern.
13. Have exhausted their ideas and resources in attempt to deal with their child's behavior.

—. _____
_____
—. _____
_____

—. _____

_____

LONG-TERM GOALS

1. Achieve an understanding and implementation of competent, effective parenting techniques.
2. Reach a realistic view of and approach to parenting and the child's developmental level.
3. Terminate ineffective and/or abusive parenting and implement positive, effective techniques.
4. Establish and maintain a healthy functioning parental team.
5. Resolve childhood issues that prevent effective parenting.
6. Achieve a level of greater family connectedness.

—. _____

_____

—. _____

_____

—. _____

_____

SHORT-TERM OBJECTIVES

THERAPEUTIC INTERVENTIONS

1. Provide information on the marital relationship, child behavior expectations, and style of parenting. (1)

1. Engage the parents through the use of empathy and normalization of their struggles with parenting and obtain information on their marital relationship, child behavior expectations, and parenting style.

2. Identify specific marital conflicts and work toward their resolution. (2, 3)

2. Analyze the data received from the parents about their relationship and parenting and establish or rule out the presence of marital conflicts.

3. Conduct or refer the parents to marital/relationship therapy to

3. Complete recommended evaluation instruments and receive the results. (4, 5, 6)

resolve the conflicts that are preventing them from being effective parents.

4. Administer or arrange for the parents to complete assessment instruments to evaluate their parenting strengths and weaknesses (e.g., the *Parenting Stress Index*, the *Parent-Child Relationship Inventory*).

5. Share results of assessment instruments with the parents and identify issues to begin working on to strengthen the parenting team.

6. Use testing results to identify parental strengths and begin to build the confidence and effectiveness level of the parental team.

4. Provide behavioral, emotional, and attitudinal information toward an assessment of specifiers relevant to a *DSM* diagnosis, the efficacy of treatment, and the nature of the therapy relationship. (7, 8, 9, 10, 11)

7. Assess the client's level of insight (syntonic versus dystonic) toward the "presenting problems" (e.g., demonstrates good insight into the problematic nature of the "described behavior," agrees with others' concern, and is motivated to work on change; demonstrates ambivalence regarding the "problem described" and is reluctant to address the issue as a concern; or demonstrates resistance regarding acknowledgment of the "problem described," is not concerned, and has no motivation to change).

8. Assess the client for evidence of research-based correlated disorders (e.g., oppositional defiant behavior with ADHD, depression secondary to an anxiety disorder) including

vulnerability to suicide, if appropriate (e.g., increased suicide risk when comorbid depression is evident).

9. Assess for any issues of age, gender, or culture that could help explain the client's currently defined "problem behavior" and factors that could offer a better understanding of the client's behavior.

10. Assess for the severity of the level of impairment to the client's functioning to determine appropriate level of care (e.g., the behavior noted creates mild, moderate, severe, or very severe impairment in social, relational, vocational, or occupational endeavors); continuously assess this severity of impairment as well as the efficacy of treatment (e.g., the client no longer demonstrates severe impairment but the presenting problem now is causing mild or moderate impairment).

11. Assess the client's home, school, and community for pathogenic care (e.g., persistent disregard for the child's emotional needs or physical needs, repeated changes in primary caregivers, limited opportunities for stable attachments, persistent harsh punishment or other grossly inept parenting).

5. Express feelings of frustration, helplessness, and inadequacy that each experiences in the parenting role. (12, 13, 14)

12. Create a compassionate, empathetic environment where the parents become comfortable enough to let their guard down and express the frustrations of parenting.

13. Educate the parents on the full scope of parenting by using humor and normalization.

14. Help the parents reduce their unrealistic expectations of themselves.

6. Identify unresolved childhood issues that affect parenting and work toward their resolution. (15, 16)

15. Explore each parent's childhood to identify any unresolved issues that are present and to identify how these issues are now affecting the ability to effectively parent.

16. Assist the parents in working through issues from childhood that are unresolved.

7. Identify the child's personality/temperament type that causes challenges and develop specific strategies to more effectively deal with that personality/temperament type. (17, 18, 19)

17. Have the parents read *The Challenging Child* (Greenspan) and then identify which type of difficult behavior pattern their child exhibits; encourage implementation of several of the parenting methods suggested for that type of child.

18. Expand the parents' repertoire of intervention options by having them read material on parenting difficult children (e.g., *The Difficult Child* by Turecki and Tonner; *The Explosive Child* by Greene; *How to Handle a Hard-to-Handle Kid* by Edwards; *The Kazdin Method for Parenting the Defiant Child* by Kazdin).

19. Support, empower, monitor, and encourage the parents in implementing new strategies for parenting their child, giving feedback and redirection as needed.

▼ 8. Decrease reactivity to the child's minor misbehaviors. (20, 21, 22)

20. Evaluate the level of the parental team's reactivity to the child's behavior and then help them to

learn to respond in a more modulated, thoughtful, planned manner (or assign "Picking Your Battles" in the *Child Psychotherapy Homework Planner* by Jongsma, Peterson, and McInnis). ▽

21. Help the parents become aware of the "hot buttons" they have that the child can push to get a quick negative response and how this overreactive response reduces their effectiveness as parents; encourage parents to ignore minor misbehaviors while praising positive behavior. ▽

22. Role-play reactive situations with the parents to help them learn to thoughtfully respond instead of automatically reacting to their child's demands or negative behaviors. ▽

▽ 9. Parents learn and implement Parent Management Training skills to recognize and manage problem behavior of the client. (23, 24, 25, 26, 27)

23. Use a Parent Management Training approach beginning with teaching the parents how parent and child behavioral interactions can encourage or discourage positive or negative behavior and that changing key elements of those interactions (e.g., prompting and reinforcing positive behaviors) can be used to promote positive change (e.g., *Parent Management Training* by Forgatch and Patterson; *Parenting the Strong-Willed Child* by Forehand and Long; *Living With Children* by Patterson). ▽

24. Ask the parents to read material consistent with a parent training approach to managing disruptive behavior (e.g., *The Kazdin Method for Parenting the Defiant*

Child by Kazdin; *Living With Children* by Patterson). ▽

25. Teach the parents how to specifically define and identify problem behaviors, identify their reactions to the behavior, determine whether the reaction encourages or discourages the behavior, and generate alternatives to the problem behavior. ▽

26. Teach parents how to implement key parenting practices consistently, including establishing realistic age-appropriate rules for acceptable and unacceptable behavior, prompting of positive behavior in the environment, use of positive reinforcement to encourage behavior (e.g., praise), use of clear direct instruction, time-out, and other loss-of-privilege practices for problem behavior. ▽

27. Assign the parents home exercises in which they implement and record results of implementation exercises (or assign "Clear Rules, Positive Reinforcement, Appropriate Consequences" in the *Adolescent Psychotherapy Homework Planner* by Jongsma, Peterson, and McInnis); review in session, providing corrective feedback toward improved, appropriate, and consistent use of skills. ▽

▽ 10. Learn and implement a time-out procedure for managing undesired behavior. (28)

28. Teach parents the rationale and use of the time-out technique as a consequence for inappropriate behavior; if possible, use a "signal seat" that has a battery-operated buzzer that serves as both a timer

and an alert that the child is not staying in the seat (see *Self-Administered Behavioral Parent Training* by Hamilton and MacQuiddy); teach parents to remain calm when administering time-out and keep time-out brief and immediate. ▽

▽ 11. Parents and client participate in play sessions in which they use their new rules for appropriate conduct. (29)

29. Conduct Parent-Child Interaction Therapy in which child-directed and parent-directed sessions focus on teaching appropriate child behavior, and parental behavioral management skills (e.g., clear commands, consistent consequences, positive reinforcement) are developed (see *Parent-Child Interaction Therapy by* McNeil and Humbree-Kigin). ▽

▽ 12. Parents enroll in an evidence-based parent-training program. (30)

30. Refer parents to an evidence-based parent-training program such as Incredible Years (see www.incredibleyears.com) or the Positive Parenting Program (Triple P; see www.triplep-america.com). ▽

▽ 13. Develop skills to talk openly and effectively with the children. (31, 32)

31. Use modeling and role-play to teach the parents to listen more than talk to their children and to use open-ended questions that encourage openness, sharing, and ongoing dialogue. ▽

32. Ask the parents to read material on parent-child communication (e.g., *How to Talk So Kids Will Listen and Listen So Kids Will Talk* by Faber and Mazlish; *Parent Effectiveness Training* by Gordon); help them to implement the new communication style in daily dialogue with their children

14. Parents implement a reward system designed to increase the client's compliance with rules at home and school. (33)

15. Verbalize an understanding of child developmental stages and the behaviors associated with them. (34)

16. Parents verbalize a sense of increased skill, effectiveness, and confidence in their parenting. (35, 36)

17. Parents enact appropriate boundaries for discipline, terminating all abusive behaviors. (37, 38)

and to see the positive responses each child had to it. ▽

33. Design a reward system and/or contingency contract for the client and assign parents to meet with school officials to reinforce identified positive behaviors at home and school and reduce impulsive or disruptive behaviors. ▽

34. Educate the parents on the numerous key developmental differences between boys and girls, such as rate of development, perspectives, impulse control, and anger, and how to handle these differences in the parenting process (recommend *Ages and Stages: A Parent's Guide to Normal Childhood Development* by Schaefer and DiGeronimo). ▽

35. Have the children complete the "Parent Report Card" (Berg-Gross) and then give feedback to the parents; support areas of parenting strength and identify weaknesses that need to be bolstered.

36. Assist the parental team in identifying areas of parenting weaknesses; help the parents improve their skills and boost their confidence and follow-through (or assign "Being a Consistent Parent" in the *Child Psychotherapy Homework Planner* by Jongsma, Peterson, and McInnis).

37. Explore the client's family background for a history of neglect and physical or sexual abuse that may contribute to

his/her behavioral problems; confront the client's parents to cease physically abusive or overly punitive methods of discipline and to ensure the safety of the client and his/her siblings.

38. Implement the steps necessary to protect the client or siblings from further abuse (e.g., report abuse to the appropriate agencies; remove the client or perpetrator from the home).

18. Partners express verbal support of each other in the parenting process. (39)

39. Help the parents identify and implement specific ways they can support each other as parents and in realizing the ways children work to keep the parents from cooperating in order to get their way.

▼ 19. Parents report a reduction in stress and an increase in satisfying activities. (40)

40. Encourage parents to use exercise, hobbies, social activities, entertainment, and relaxation techniques to reduce stress and increase feelings of life satisfaction apart from parenting (or assign "Identify and Schedule Pleasurable Activities" in the *Adult Psychotherapy Homework Planner* by Jongsma); recommend parents read *Working Parents, Thriving Families* by Palmiter. ▼

20. Decrease outside pressures, demands, and distractions that drain energy and time from the family. (41, 42)

41. Give the parents permission not to involve their child and themselves in too numerous activities, organizations, or sports; suggest setting aside time for family activities that involve one-on-one time with the children.

21. Parents verbalize a termination of their perfectionist expectations of the child. (43, 44)

22. Parents and client report an increased feeling of connectedness between them. (45)

42. Ask the parents to provide a weekly schedule of their entire family's activities and then evaluate the schedule with them, looking for which activities are valuable and which can possibly be eliminated to create a more focused and relaxed time to parent.

43. Help the parents recognize unreasonable and perfectionist expectations of their child that they hold and help them to modify these expectations.

44. Help the parents identify the negative consequences/outcomes that perfectionist expectations have on a child and on the relationship between the parents and the child.

45. Assist the parents in removing and resolving any barriers that prevent or limit connectedness between family members and in identifying activities that will promote connectedness such as games or one-on-one time (or assign "Share a Family Meal" in the *Child Psychotherapy Homework Planner* by Jongsma, Peterson, and McInnis).

—. _____
    _____
—. _____
    _____
—. _____
    _____

—. _____
    _____
—. _____
    _____
—. _____
    _____

DIAGNOSTIC SUGGESTIONS

Using DSM-IV/ICD-9-CM:

Axis I:	309.3	Adjustment Disorder With Disturbance of Conduct
	309.4	Adjustment Disorder With Mixed Disturbance of Emotions and Conduct
	V61.21	Neglect of Child
	V61.20	Parent-Child Relational Problem
	V61.1	Partner Relational Problem
	V61.21	Physical Abuse of Child
	V61.21	Sexual Abuse of Child
	_____	_____
	_____	_____
Axis II:	301.7	Antisocial Personality Disorder
	301.6	Dependent Personality Disorder
	301.81	Narcissistic Personality Disorder
	301.83	Borderline Personality Disorder
	799.9	Diagnosis Deferred
	V71.09	No Diagnosis
	_____	_____
	_____	_____

Using DSM-5/ICD-9-CM/ICD-10-CM:

ICD-9-CM	ICD-10-CM	*DSM-5* Disorder, Condition, or Problem
309.3	F43.24	Adjustment Disorder, With Disturbance of Conduct
309.4	F43.25	Adjustment Disorder, With Mixed Disturbance of Emotions and Conduct
V61.21	Z69.011	Encounter for Mental Health Services for Perpetrator of Parental Child Neglect
V61.20	Z62.820	Parent-Child Relational Problem
V61.21	Z69.011	Encounter for Mental Health Services for Perpetrator of Parental Child Abuse
V61.22	Z69.011	Encounter for Mental Health Services for Perpetrator of Parental Child Sexual Abuse
313.81	F91.3	Oppositional Defiant Disorder
312.9	F91.9	Unspecified Disruptive, Impulse Control, and Conduct Disorder
312.89	F91.8	Other Specified Disruptive, Impulse Control, and Conduct Disorder
312.82	F91.2	Conduct Disorder, Adolescent-Onset Type

312.81	F91.1	Conduct Disorder, Childhood-Onset Type (This is an added diagnosis to the chapter list)
314.01	F90.2	Attention-Deficit/Hyperactivity Disorder, Combined Presentation
301.7	F60.2	Antisocial Personality Disorder
301.6	F60.7	Dependent Personality Disorder
301.81	F60.81	Narcissistic Personality Disorder
301.83	F60.3	Borderline Personality Disorder

Note: The ICD-9-CM codes are to be used for coding purposes in the United States through September 30, 2014. ICD-10-CM codes are to be used starting October 1, 2014. Some ICD-9-CM codes are associated with more than one ICD-10-CM and *DSM-5* disorder, condition, or problem. In addition, some ICD-9-CM disorders have been discontinued resulting in multiple ICD-9-CM codes being replaced by one ICD-10-CM code. Some discontinued ICD-9-CM codes are not listed in this table. See *Diagnostic and Statistical Manual of Mental Disorders* (2013) for details.

EBT Indicates that the Objective/Intervention is consistent with those found in evidence-based treatments.

PEER/SIBLING CONFLICT

BEHAVIORAL DEFINITIONS

1. Frequent, overt, intense fighting (verbal and/or physical) with peers and/or siblings.
2. Projects responsibility for conflicts onto others.
3. Believes that he/she is treated unfairly and/or that parents favor sibling(s) over himself/herself.
4. Peer and/or sibling relationships are characterized by bullying, defiance, revenge, taunting, and incessant teasing.
5. Has virtually no friends, or a few who exhibit similar socially disapproved behavior.
6. Exhibits a general pattern of behavior that is impulsive, intimidating, and unmalleable.
7. Behaviors toward peers are aggressive and lack a discernible empathy for others.
8. Parents are hostile toward the client, demonstrating a familial pattern of rejection, quarreling, and lack of respect or affection.

—. _____
   _____
—. _____
   _____
—. _____
   _____

LONG-TERM GOALS

1. Compete, cooperate, and resolve conflict appropriately with peers and siblings.

2. Develop healthy mechanisms for handling anxiety, tension, frustration, and anger.
3. Terminate aggressive behavior and replace with assertiveness and empathy.
4. Form respectful, trusting peer and sibling relationships.
5. Parents acquire the necessary parenting skills to model respect, empathy, nurturance, and lack of aggression.
6. Demonstrate consistent prosocial behaviors with all peers and siblings.

—. _____
   _____

—. _____
   _____

—. _____
   _____

SHORT-TERM OBJECTIVES

1. Describe relationship with siblings and friends. (1, 2)

2. Provide behavioral, emotional, and attitudinal information toward an assessment of specifiers relevant to a *DSM* diagnosis, the efficacy of treatment, and the nature of the therapy relationship. (3, 4, 5, 6, 7)

THERAPEUTIC INTERVENTIONS

1. Actively build level of trust with client through consistent eye contact, active listening, unconditional positive regard, and warm acceptance to help increase the client's ability to identify and express feelings.

2. Explore the client's perception of the nature of his/her relationships with siblings and peers; assess the degree of denial regarding conflict and the projection of responsibility for conflict onto others.

3. Assess the client's level of insight (syntonic versus dystonic) toward the "presenting problems" (e.g., demonstrates good insight into the problematic nature of the "described behavior," agrees with others' concern, and is motivated to work on change;

demonstrates ambivalence regarding the "problem described" and is reluctant to address the issue as a concern; or demonstrates resistance regarding acknowledgment of the "problem described," is not concerned, and has no motivation to change).

4. Assess the client for evidence of research-based correlated disorders (e.g., oppositional defiant behavior with ADHD, depression secondary to an anxiety disorder) including vulnerability to suicide, if appropriate (e.g., increased suicide risk when comorbid depression is evident).

5. Assess for any issues of age, gender, or culture that could help explain the client's currently defined "problem behavior" and factors that could offer a better understanding of the client's behavior.

6. Assess for the severity of the level of impairment to the client's functioning to determine appropriate level of care (e.g., the behavior noted creates mild, moderate, severe, or very severe impairment in social, relational, vocational, or occupational endeavors); continuously assess this severity of impairment as well as the efficacy of treatment (e.g., the client no longer demonstrates severe impairment but the presenting problem now is causing mild or moderate impairment).

7. Assess the client's home, school, and community for pathogenic

care (e.g., persistent disregard for the child's emotional needs or physical needs, repeated changes in primary caregivers, limited opportunities for stable attachments, persistent harsh punishment or other grossly inept parenting).

3. Attend and freely participate in a play therapy session. (8, 9, 10, 11)

8. Employ psychoanalytic play therapy approaches (e.g., explore and gain understanding of the etiology of unconscious conflicts, fixations, or arrests; interpret resistance, transference, or core anxieties) to help the client work through and resolve issues with the sibling and/or peers.

9. Employ the ACT model (Landreth) in play therapy sessions to *acknowledge* the client's feelings, to *communicate* limits, and to *target* more appropriate alternatives to ongoing conflicts and aggression with peers and/or siblings.

10. Interpret the feelings expressed in play therapy and relate them to anger and aggressive behaviors toward siblings and/or peers.

11. Create scenarios with puppets, dolls, or stuffed animals that model and/or suggest constructive ways to handle/manage conflicts with siblings or peers.

4. Decrease the frequency and intensity of aggressive actions toward peers or siblings. (12, 13, 14, 15)

12. Guide the parents in utilizing the "Playing Baby Game" (Schaefer) in which the child is given an allotted time each day (30 minutes) to be a baby and have mother/parents cater to his/her every need. After the allotted time, client is again

treated in an age-appropriate manner as a regular member of the family.

13. Utilize the "Tearing Paper" exercise (Daves), in which the therapist places several phone books and Sunday papers in the center of the room and instructs the family to tear the paper into small pieces and throw them in the air. The only two conditions are that they must clean up and not throw paper at one another. During cleanup, the therapist reinforces verbally their follow through in cleaning up and processes how it felt for family/ siblings to release energy in this way and how could they do it in other situations at home.

14. Teach the client the "Stamping Feet and Bubble Popping" method (Wunderlich) of releasing angry and frustrating feelings that are part of everyday life and emphasize that what is important is how we choose to handle them. Then talk about how the "anger goes through his/her fingers into the air."

15. Instruct the parents and teachers in social learning techniques of ignoring the client's aggressive acts, except when there is danger of physical injury, while making a concerted effort to attend to and praise all nonaggressive, cooperative, and peaceful behavior.

5. Identify verbally and in writing how he/she would like to be treated by others. (16, 17, 18)

16. Educate the client about feelings, focusing on how others feel when they are the focus of aggressive actions and then asking how the client would like to be treated by

others (consider using "Building Empathy" or "The Lesson of Salmon Rock . . . Fighting Leads to Loneliness" from the *Child Psychotherapy Homework Planner* by Jongsma, Peterson, and McInnis).

17. Ask the client to list the problems that he/she has with siblings and to suggest concrete solutions (or assign the client and parents the exercise "Negotiating a Peace Treaty" from the *Child Psychotherapy Homework Planner* by Jongsma, Peterson, and McInnis).

18. Play The Helping, Sharing, and Caring Game (Gardner) with the client and/or family to develop and expand feelings of respect for self and others.

6. Recognize and verbalize the feelings of others as well as her/his own. (19, 20, 21)

19. Use therapeutic stories (e.g., *Dr. Gardner's Fairy Tales for Today's Children* by Gardner) to increase awareness of feelings and ways to cooperate with others.

20. Refer the client to a peer therapy group whose objectives are to increase social sensitivity and behavioral flexibility through the use of group exercises (strength bombardment, trusting, walking, expressing negative feelings, etc.).

21. Use The Talking, Feeling, and Doing game (Gardner; available from Creative Therapeutics) to increase the client's awareness of self and others.

7. Increase socially appropriate behavior with peers and siblings. (22, 23, 24)

22. Use The Anger Control Game (Berg) or a similar game to expose the client to new,

constructive ways to manage aggressive feelings.

23. Play with the client The Social Conflict Game (Berg) to assist him/her in developing behavior skills to decrease interpersonal antisocialism with others.

24. Conduct or refer the client to a behavioral contracting group therapy in which contracts for positive peer interaction are developed each week and reviewed. Positive reinforcers are verbal feedback and small concrete rewards.

8. Participate in peer group activities in a cooperative manner. (25, 26)

25. Direct the parents to involve the client in cooperative activities (sports, Scouts, etc.).

26. Refer the client to an alternative summer camp that focuses on self-esteem and cooperation with peers.

9. Parents facilitate the client's social network building. (27)

27. Have the parents read *Why Don't They Like Me? Helping Your Child Make and Keep Friends* by Sheridan; assist them in implementing several of the suggestions with the client to build his/her skills in connecting with others.

10. Identify feelings associated with the perception that parent(s) have special feelings of favoritism toward a sibling. (28)

28. Help the client work through his/her perception that his/her parents have a favorite child (or assign the "Joseph, His Amazing Technicolor Coat, and More" exercise from the *Child Psychotherapy Homework Planner* by Jongsma, Peterson, and McInnis).

11. Respond positively to praise and encouragement as evidenced by smiling and expressing gratitude. (29)

12. Parents increase verbal and physical demonstrations of affection and praise to the client. (30)

13. Verbalize an understanding of the pain that underlies the anger. (31)

14. Family members decrease the frequency of quarreling and messages of rejection. (32, 33, 34)

29. Use role-playing, modeling, and behavior rehearsal to teach the client to become open and responsive to praise and encouragement.

30. Assist the parents in developing their ability to verbalize affection and appropriate praise to the client in family sessions.

31. Probe whether the client has endured rejection experiences with family and friends as the cause for the client's anger.

32. Ask the parents and children to read *Siblings: You're Stuck With Each Other, So Stick Together* by Crist and Verdick and then coach them into implementing several of the suggestions. The therapist will follow up by monitoring, encouraging, and redirecting as needed.

33. Work with the parents in family sessions to reduce parental aggression, messages of rejection, and quarreling within the family.

34. Ask the parents to read *Siblings Without Rivalry* by Faber and Mazlish and process key concepts with the therapist; have the parents choose two suggestions from the reading and implement them with their children.

15. Parents attend a didactic series on positive parenting. (35)

16. Parents implement a behavior modification plan designed to increase the frequency of cooperative social behaviors. (36, 37)

35. Refer the parents to a positive parenting class.

36. Assist the parents in developing and implementing a behavior modification plan in which the client's positive interaction with peers and siblings is reinforced

immediately with tokens that can be exchanged for pre-established rewards; monitor and give feedback as indicated.

37. Conduct weekly contract sessions with the client and the parents in which the past week's behavior modification contract is reviewed and revised for the following week; give feedback and model positive encouragement when appropriate.

17. Parents terminate alliances with children that foster sibling conflict. (38)

38. Hold family therapy sessions to assess dynamics and alliances that may underlie peer or sibling conflict.

18. Family members engage in conflict resolution in a respectful manner. (39)

39. Confront disrespectful expression of feelings in family session and use modeling, role-playing, and behavior rehearsal to teach cooperation, respect, and peaceful resolution of conflict (consider using the "Problem-Solving Exercise" from the *Child Psychotherapy Homework Planner* by Jongsma, Peterson, and McInnis).

19. Complete the recommended psychiatric or psychological testing/evaluation. (40)

40. Assess and refer the client for a psychiatric or psychological evaluation.

20. Comply with the recommendations of the mental health evaluations. (41)

41. Assist and monitor the client and the parents in implementing the recommendations of the mental health assessment.

__ . _____   __ . _____
     _____   _____
__ . _____   __ . _____
     _____   _____
__ . _____   __ . _____
     _____   _____

DIAGNOSTIC SUGGESTIONS

Using DSM-IV/ICD-9-CM:

Axis I:	313.81	Oppositional Defiant Disorder
	312.xx	Conduct Disorder
	312.9	Disruptive Behavior Disorder NOS
	314.01	Attention-Deficit/Hyperactivity Disorder, Predominantly Hyperactive-Impulsive Type
	314.9	Attention-Deficit/Hyperactivity Disorder NOS
	V62.81	Relational Problem NOS
	V71.02	Child or Adolescent Antisocial Behavior
	315.00	Reading Disorder
	315.9	Learning Disorder NOS
	_____	_____
	_____	_____
Axis II:	V71.09	No Diagnosis
	_____	_____
	_____	_____

Using DSM-5/ICD-9-CM/ICD-10-CM:

ICD-9-CM	ICD-10-CM	*DSM-5* Disorder, Condition, or Problem
313.81	F91.3	Oppositional Defiant Disorder
312.xx	F91.1	Conduct Disorder, Childhood-Onset Type
312.9	F91.9	Unspecified Disruptive, Impulse Control, and Conduct Disorder
312.89	F91.8	Other Specified Disruptive, Impulse Control, and Conduct Disorder
314.01	F90.1	Attention-Deficit/Hyperactivity Disorder, Predominately Hyperactive /Impulsive Presentation
314.01	F90.9	Unspecified Attention-Deficit/ Hyperactivity Disorder
314.01	F90.8	Other Specified Attention-Deficit/ Hyperactivity Disorder
V62.81	Z62.891	Sibling Relational Problem
315.00	F81.0	Specific Learning Disorder With Impairment in Reading

Note: The ICD-9-CM codes are to be used for coding purposes in the United States through September 30, 2014. ICD-10-CM codes are to be used starting October 1, 2014. Some ICD-9-CM codes are associated with more than one ICD-10-CM and *DSM-5* disorder, condition, or problem. In addition, some ICD-9-CM disorders have been discontinued resulting in multiple ICD-9-CM codes being replaced by one ICD-10-CM code. Some discontinued ICD-9-CM codes are not listed in this table. See *Diagnostic and Statistical Manual of Mental Disorders* (2013) for details.

PHYSICAL/EMOTIONAL ABUSE VICTIM

BEHAVIORAL DEFINITIONS

1. Confirmed self-report or account by others of having been assaulted (e.g., hit, burned, kicked, slapped, tortured) by an older person.
2. Bruises or wounds as evidence of victimization.
3. Self-reports of being injured by a supposed caregiver coupled with feelings of fear and social withdrawal.
4. Significant increase in the frequency and severity of aggressive behaviors toward peers or adults.
5. Recurrent and intrusive distressing recollections of the abuse.
6. Feelings of anger, rage, or fear when in contact with the perpetrator.
7. Frequent and prolonged periods of depression, irritability, anxiety, and/or apathetic withdrawal.
8. Appearance of regressive behaviors (e.g., thumb-sucking, baby talk, bedwetting).
9. Sleep disturbances (e.g., difficulty falling asleep, refusal to sleep alone, night terrors, recurrent distressing nightmares).
10. Running away from home to avoid further physical assaults.

—. _____
   _____
—. _____
   _____
—. _____
   _____

LONG-TERM GOALS

1. Terminate the physical abuse.
2. Escape from the environment where the abuse is occurring and move to a safe haven.

3. Rebuild sense of self-worth and overcome the overwhelming sense of fear, shame, and sadness.
4. Resolve feelings of fear and depression while improving communication and the boundaries of respect within the family.
5. Caregivers establish limits on the punishment of the client such that no physical harm can occur and respect for his/her rights is maintained.
6. Client and his/her family eliminate denial, putting the responsibility for the abuse on the perpetrator and allowing the victim to feel supported.
7. Reduce displays of aggression that reflect abuse and keep others at an emotional distance.
8. Build self-esteem and a sense of empowerment as manifested by an increased number of positive self-descriptive statements and greater participation in extracurricular activities.

—. _____
   _____

—. _____
   _____

—. _____
   _____

SHORT-TERM OBJECTIVES

1. Tell the entire account of the most recent abuse as well as the history of the nature, frequency, and duration of the abuse. (1, 2, 3, 4, 5)

THERAPEUTIC INTERVENTIONS

1. Actively build the level of trust with the client through consistent eye contact, active listening, unconditional positive regard, and warm acceptance to help him/her increase the ability to identify and express facts and feelings about the abuse.

2. Explore, encourage, and support the client in verbally expressing and clarifying the facts associated with the abuse.

3. Use individual play therapy sessions to provide the client with the opportunity to reveal facts and feelings regarding the abuse.

    4. Report physical abuse to the appropriate child protection agency, criminal justice officials, or medical professionals.

    5. Consult with the family, a physician, criminal justice officials, or child protection case managers to assess the veracity of the physical abuse charges.

2. Agree to actions taken to protect self and provide boundaries against any future abuse or retaliation. (6, 7, 8)

    6. Assess whether the perpetrator or the client should be removed from the client's home.

    7. Implement the necessary steps (e.g., removal of the client from the home, removal of the perpetrator from the home) to protect the client and other children in the home from further physical abuse.

    8. Reassure the client repeatedly of concern and caring on the part of the therapist and others who will protect him/her from any further abuse.

3. Verbalize the effects that the abuse has had on emotional adjustment and behavior, including noticeable changes in emotional lability, daily activities, sleep, and feelings about self. (9)

    9. Assess the client for the presence of a psychiatric disorder(s) caused by the abuse (e.g., posttraumatic stress disorder, other anxiety disorder, depression) and inform treatment with an evidence-based approach to the relevant disorder (see relevant chapters in this *Planner*).

4. Identify and express the feelings connected to the abuse. (10)

    10. Explore, encourage, and support the client in expressing and clarifying his/her feelings toward the perpetrator and self (or assign the homework exercise "My Thoughts and Feelings" in the *Child Psychotherapy Homework Planner* by Jongsma, Peterson, and McInnis).

5. Provide behavioral, emotional, and attitudinal information toward an assessment of specifiers relevant to a *DSM* diagnosis, the efficacy of treatment, and the nature of the therapy relationship. (11, 12, 13, 14, 15)

11. Assess the client's level of insight (syntonic versus dystonic) toward the "presenting problems" (e.g., demonstrates good insight into the problematic nature of the "described behavior," agrees with others' concern, and is motivated to work on change; demonstrates ambivalence regarding the "problem described" and is reluctant to address the issue as a concern; or demonstrates resistance regarding acknowledgment of the "problem described," is not concerned, and has no motivation to change).

12. Assess the client for evidence of research-based correlated disorders (e.g., oppositional defiant behavior with ADHD, depression secondary to an anxiety disorder) including vulnerability to suicide, if appropriate (e.g., increased suicide risk when comorbid depression is evident).

13. Assess for any issues of age, gender, or culture that could help explain the client's currently defined "problem behavior" and factors that could offer a better understanding of the client's behavior.

14. Assess for the severity of the level of impairment to the client's functioning to determine appropriate level of care (e.g., the behavior noted creates mild, moderate, severe, or very severe impairment in social, relational, vocational, or occupational endeavors); continuously assess this severity of impairment as well as the efficacy of treatment (e.g.,

the client no longer demonstrates severe impairment).

15. Assess the client's home, school, and community for pathogenic care (e.g., persistent disregard for the child's emotional needs or physical needs, repeated changes in primary caregivers, limited opportunities for stable attachments, persistent harsh punishment or other grossly inept parenting).

6. Terminate verbalizations of denial or making excuses for the perpetrator. (16, 17, 18, 19)

16. Actively confront and challenge denial within the perpetrator and the entire family system.

17. Confront the client about making excuses for the perpetrator's abuse and accepting blame for it.

18. Reassure the client that he/she did not deserve the abuse but that he/she deserves respect and a controlled response even in punishment situations.

19. Reinforce any and all client statements that put responsibility clearly on the perpetrator for the abuse, regardless of any misbehavior by the client.

7. Perpetrator takes responsibility for the abuse. (20)

20. Hold a family therapy session in which the client and/or therapist confronts the perpetrator with the abuse.

8. Perpetrator asks for forgiveness and pledges respect for disciplinary boundaries. (21)

21. Conduct a family therapy session in which the perpetrator apologizes to the client and/or other family member(s) for the abuse.

9. Perpetrator agrees to seek treatment. (22, 23, 24)

22. Require the perpetrator to participate in a child abusers' psychotherapy group.

23. Refer the perpetrator for a psychological evaluation and treatment.

24. Evaluate the possibility of substance abuse with the perpetrator or within the family; refer the perpetrator and/or family member(s) for substance abuse treatment, if indicated.

10. Parents and caregivers verbalize the establishment of appropriate disciplinary boundaries to ensure protection of the client. (25, 26)

25. Counsel the client's family about appropriate disciplinary boundaries.

26. Ask the parents/caregivers to list appropriate means of discipline or correction; reinforce reasonable actions and appropriate boundaries that reflect respect for the rights and feelings of the child.

11. Family members identify the stressors or other factors that may trigger violence. (27, 28)

27. Construct a multigenerational family genogram that identifies physical abuse within the extended family to help the perpetrator recognize the cycle of violence.

28. Assess the client's family dynamics and explore for the stress factors or precipitating events that contributed to the emergence of the abuse.

12. Nonabusive parent and other key family members verbalize support and acceptance of the client. (29)

29. Elicit and reinforce support and nurturance of the client from the nonabusive parent and other key family members.

13. Reduce the expressions of rage and aggressiveness that stem from feelings of helplessness related to physical abuse. (30, 31)

30. Assign the client to write a letter expressing feelings of hurt, fear, and anger to the perpetrator; process the letter.

31. Interpret the client's generalized expressions of anger and aggression as triggered by feelings toward the perpetrator.

14. Decrease the statements of being a victim while increasing the statements that reflect personal empowerment. (32, 33)

32. Empower the client by identifying sources of help against abuse (e.g., phone numbers to call, a safe place to run to, asking for temporary alternate protective placement).

33. Assist the client in writing his/her thoughts and feelings regarding surviving the abuse, coping with it, and overcoming it (or assign the exercise "Letter of Empowerment" in the *Child Psychotherapy Homework Planner* by Jongsma, Peterson, and McInnis).

15. Increase the frequency of positive self-descriptive statements. (34, 35)

34. Assist the client in identifying a basis for self-worth by reviewing his/her talents, importance to others, and intrinsic spiritual value.

35. Reinforce positive statements that the client has made about himself/herself and the future.

16. Express forgiveness of the perpetrator and others connected with the abuse while insisting on respect for his/her own right to safety in the future. (21, 36, 37)

21. Conduct a family therapy session in which the perpetrator apologizes to the client and/or other family member(s) for the abuse.

36. Assign the client to write a forgiveness letter and/or complete a forgiveness exercise in which he/she verbalizes forgiveness to the perpetrator and/or significant family member(s) while asserting the right to safety; process this letter.

37. Assign the client a letting-go exercise in which a symbol of the abuse is disposed of or destroyed; process this experience.

17. Increase socialization with peers and family. (38, 39, 40)

38. Encourage the client to make plans for the future that involve

interacting with his/her peers and family.

39. Encourage the client to participate in positive peer groups or extracurricular activities.

40. Refer the client to a victim support group with other children to assist him/her in realizing that he/she is not alone in this experience.

18. Verbalize an understanding of the loss of trust in all relationships that results from abuse by a parent. (41)

41. Facilitate the client expressing loss of trust in adults and relate this loss to the perpetrator's abusive behavior and the lack of protection provided.

19. Increase the level of trust of others as shown by increased socialization and a greater number of friendships. (42, 43)

42. Assist the client in making discriminating judgments that allow for the trust of some people rather than a distrust of all.

43. Teach the client the share-check method of building trust, in which a degree of shared information is related to a proven level of trustworthiness.

20. Verbalize how the abuse has affected feelings toward self. (44, 45)

44. Assign the client to draw pictures that represent how he/she feels about himself/herself.

45. Ask the client to draw pictures of his/her own face that represent how he/she felt about himself/herself before, during, and after the abuse occurred.

21. Express feelings in play therapy sessions. (46)

46. Use child-centered play therapy approaches (e.g., demonstrate genuine interest, provide unconditional positive regard, reflect feelings, profess trust in the client's inner direction) to promote resolution of fear, grief, and rage.

— · _____   — · _____
   _____   _____
— · _____   — · _____
   _____   _____
— · _____   — · _____
   _____   _____

DIAGNOSTIC SUGGESTIONS

Using DSM-IV/ICD-9-CM:

Axis I:	309.81	Posttraumatic Stress Disorder
	308.3	Acute Stress Disorder
	995.54	Physical Abuse of Child (Victim)
	300.4	Dysthymic Disorder
	296.xx	Major Depressive Disorder
	300.02	Generalized Anxiety Disorder
	307.47	Nightmare Disorder
	313.81	Oppositional Defiant Disorder
	312.81	Conduct Disorder, Childhood-Onset Type
	300.6	Depersonalization Disorder
	300.15	Dissociative Disorder NOS
	_____	_____
	_____	_____
Axis II:	V71.09	No Diagnosis
	_____	_____
	_____	_____

Using DSM-5/ICD-9-CM/ICD-10-CM:

ICD-9-CM	ICD-10-CM	*DSM-5* Disorder, Condition, or Problem
309.81	F43.10	Posttraumatic Stress Disorder
308.3	F43.0	Acute Stress Disorder
995.54	T74.12XA	Child Physical Abuse, Confirmed, Initial Encounter
995.54	T74.12XD	Child Physical Abuse, Confirmed, Subsequent Encounter
995.51	T743.2XA	Child Psychological Abuse, Confirmed, Initial Encounter
995.51	T743.2XD	Child Psychological Abuse, Confirmed, Subsequent Encounter
300.4	F34.1	Persistent Depressive Disorder

296.xx	F32.x	Major Depressive Disorder, Single Episode
296.xx	F33.x	Major Depressive Disorder, Recurrent Episode
300.02	F41.1	Generalized Anxiety Disorder
307.47	F51.5	Nightmare Disorder
313.81	F91.3	Oppositional Defiant Disorder
312.81	F91.1	Conduct Disorder, Childhood-Onset Type
300.6	F48.1	Depersonalization/Derealization Disorder
300.15	F44.89	Other Specified Dissociative Disorder
300.15	F44.9	Unspecified Dissociative Disorder

Note: The ICD-9-CM codes are to be used for coding purposes in the United States through September 30, 2014. ICD-10-CM codes are to be used starting October 1, 2014. Some ICD-9-CM codes are associated with more than one ICD-10-CM and *DSM-5* disorder, condition, or problem. In addition, some ICD-9-CM disorders have been discontinued resulting in multiple ICD-9-CM codes being replaced by one ICD-10-CM code. Some discontinued ICD-9-CM codes are not listed in this table. See *Diagnostic and Statistical Manual of Mental Disorders* (2013) for details.

POSTTRAUMATIC STRESS DISORDER (PTSD)

BEHAVIORAL DEFINITIONS

1. Exposure to threats of death or serious injury, or subjection to actual injury that resulted in an intense emotional response of fear, helplessness, or horror.
2. Intrusive, distressing thoughts or images that recall the traumatic event.
3. Disturbing dreams associated with the traumatic event.
4. A sense that the event is recurring, as in illusions or flashbacks.
5. Intense distress when exposed to reminders of the traumatic event.
6. Physiological reactivity when exposed to internal or external cues that symbolize the traumatic event.
7. Avoidance of thoughts, feelings, or conversations about the traumatic event.
8. Avoidance of activities, places, or people associated with the traumatic event.
9. Inability to recall some important aspect of the traumatic event.
10. Lack of interest and participation in formerly meaningful activities.
11. A sense of detachment from others.
12. Inability to experience the full range of emotions, including love.
13. A pessimistic, fatalistic attitude regarding the future.
14. Sleep disturbance.
15. Irritability or angry outbursts.
16. Lack of concentration.
17. Hypervigilance.
18. Exaggerated startle response.
19. Symptoms have been present for more than one month.
20. Sad or guilty affect and other signs of depression.
21. Verbally and/or physically violent threats or behavior.

—. _____

_____

—. _____

_____

—. _____

_____

LONG-TERM GOALS

1. Recall the traumatic event without becoming overwhelmed with negative emotions.
2. Interact normally with friends and family without irrational fears or intrusive thoughts that control behavior.
3. Return to pretrauma level of functioning without avoiding people, places, thoughts, or feelings associated with the traumatic event.
4. Display a full range of emotions without experiencing loss of control.
5. Develop and implement effective coping skills that allow for carrying out normal responsibilities and participating in relationships and social activities.

—. _____

_____

—. _____

_____

—. _____

_____

SHORT-TERM OBJECTIVES

1. Describe the history and nature of the PTSD and any other reactions to the trauma. (1, 2)

THERAPEUTIC INTERVENTIONS

1. Establish rapport with the client and parents toward building a therapeutic alliance.

2. Conduct a thorough clinical interview including assessment of PTSD symptoms, other psychopathology/behavior problems, and their impact on functioning (or assign the "PTSD Incident Report" in the *Child Psychotherapy Homework*

Planner by Jongsma, Peterson, and McInnis; or "Describe Your PTSD Symptoms" in the *Adolescent Psychotherapy Homework Planner* by Jongsma, Peterson, and McInnis; or see *The Anxiety Disorders Interview Schedule for Children—Parent Version* or *Child Version* by Silverman and Albano).

2. Complete psychological tests designed to assess and/or track the nature and severity of PTSD symptoms. (3)

3. Administer or refer the client for psychological testing or objective measurement of PTSD and other relevant symptoms (e.g., *The Child PTSD Symptom Scale*; *Child Posttraumatic Stress Reaction Index*; *Clinician-Administered PTSD Scale for Children and Adolescents*).

3. Describe the traumatic event in as much detail as possible. (4)

4. Gently and sensitively explore the client's recollection of the facts of the traumatic incident and his/her emotional reactions at the time; begin with descriptions of neutral events then progressing to the trauma, if needed; (or utilize "Describe the Trauma and Your Feelings" in the *Adolescent Psychotherapy Homework Planner* by Jongsma, Peterson, and McInnis).

4. Discuss any feelings of depression, including any suicidal thoughts. (5)

5. Assess the client's depth of depression and suicide potential and treat appropriately, taking the necessary safety precautions as indicated (see the Depression chapter in this *Planner*).

5. Provide behavioral, emotional, and attitudinal information toward an assessment of specifiers relevant to a *DSM* diagnosis, the efficacy of

6. Assess the client's level of insight (syntonic versus dystonic) toward the "presenting problems" (e.g., demonstrates good insight into the

treatment, and the nature of the therapy relationship. (6, 7, 8, 9, 10)

problematic nature of the "described behavior," agrees with others' concern, and is motivated to work on change; demonstrates ambivalence regarding the "problem described" and is reluctant to address the issue as a concern; or demonstrates resistance regarding acknowledgment of the "problem described," is not concerned, and has no motivation to change).

7. Assess the client for evidence of research-based correlated disorders (e.g., oppositional defiant behavior with ADHD, depression secondary to an anxiety disorder) including vulnerability to suicide, if appropriate (e.g., increased suicide risk when comorbid depression is evident).

8. Assess for any issues of age, gender, or culture that could help explain the client's currently defined "problem behavior" and factors that could offer a better understanding of the client's behavior.

9. Assess for the severity of the level of impairment to the client's functioning to determine appropriate level of care (e.g., the behavior noted creates mild, moderate, severe, or very severe impairment in social, relational, vocational, or occupational endeavors); continuously assess this severity of impairment as well as the efficacy of treatment (e.g., the client no longer demonstrates severe impairment

but the presenting problem now is causing mild or moderate impairment).

10. Assess the client's home, school, and community for pathogenic care (e.g., persistent disregard for the child's emotional needs or physical needs, repeated changes in primary caregivers, limited opportunities for stable attachments, persistent harsh punishment or other grossly inept parenting).

▽ 6. Participate in an evaluation by a physician for psychotropic medication. (11, 12)

11. Assess the client's need for medication (e.g., selective serotonin reuptake inhibitors) and arrange for prescription, if appropriate. ▽

12. Monitor and evaluate the client's psychotropic medication prescription compliance and the effectiveness of the medication on his/her level of functioning. ▽

▽ 7. Participate, with or without parents, in individual or group therapy sessions focused on PTSD. (13)

13. Conduct group or individual therapy sessions consistent with Trauma-Focused Cognitive Behavioral Therapy—include parents as needed and if helpful (see *Trauma-Focused CBT for Children and Adolescents* by Cohen, Mannarino, and Deblinger; *Treating Trauma and Traumatic Grief in Children and Adolescents* by Cohen, Mannarino, and Deblinger). ▽

▽ 8. Client and parents verbalize an accurate understanding of PTSD and how it develops. (14, 15)

14. Discuss with the client and parents a biopsychosocial model of PTSD, including that it results from exposure to trauma and results in intrusive recollection, unwarranted fears, anxiety, and a vulnerability to other negative emotions such as shame, anger,

and guilt; normalize the client's experiences. ▽

15. Assign the client's parents to read psychoeducational chapters of books or treatment manuals on PTSD that explain its features and development. ▽

▽ 9. Verbalize an understanding of the rationale for treatment of PTSD. (16, 17)

16. Discuss how coping skills, cognitive restructuring, and exposure help build confidence, desensitize and overcome fears, and see one's self, others, and the world in a less fearful and/or depressing way. ▽

17. Assign the client's parents to read about anxiety management, stress inoculation, cognitive restructuring, and/or exposure-based therapy in chapters of books or treatment manuals on PTSD (e.g., *Prolonged Exposure Therapy for PTSD—Teen Workbook* by Chrestman, Gilboa-Schechtman, and Foa; *Think Good—Feel Good: A Cognitive Behaviour Therapy Workbook for Children* by Stallard; *The Relaxation and Stress Reduction Workbook for Kids* by Shapiro and Sprague). ▽

▽ 10. Parents learn and implement Parent Management Training skills to recognize and manage any problem behavior of the client. (18, 19, 20, 21, 22)

18. Use a Parent Management Training approach beginning with teaching the parents how parent and child behavioral interactions can encourage or discourage positive or negative behavior and that changing key elements of those interactions (e.g., prompting and reinforcing positive behaviors) can be used to promote positive change (e.g., *Parent Management Training* by Forgatch and Patterson;

Parenting the Strong-Willed Child by Forehand and Long; *Living With Children* by Patterson).▽

19. Ask the parents to read material consistent with a parent training approach to managing disruptive behavior (e.g., *The Kazdin Method for Parenting the Defiant Child* by Kazdin; *Living With Children* by Patterson).▽

20. Teach the parents how to specifically define and identify problem behaviors, identify their reactions to the behavior, determine whether the reaction encourages or discourages the behavior, and generate alternatives to the problem behavior.▽

21. Teach parents how to implement key parenting practices consistently, including establishing realistic age-appropriate rules for acceptable and unacceptable behavior, prompting of positive behavior in the environment, use of positive reinforcement to encourage behavior (e.g., praise), use of clear direct instruction, time out, and other loss-of-privilege practices for problem behavior.▽

22. Assign the parents home exercises in which they implement and record results of implementation exercises (or assign "Clear Rules, Positive Reinforcement, Appropriate Consequences" in the *Adolescent Psychotherapy Homework Planner* by Jongsma, Peterson, and McInnis); review in session,

providing corrective feedback toward improved, appropriate, and consistent use of skills. ▽

11. Learn and implement physical and mental calming and coping skills to manage emotional reactions related to trauma and other stressors. (23)

23. While building rapport, teach the client skills needed to progress in therapy including the identification and management of emotions such as anxiety, anger, and shame; use skill-building techniques (e.g., from Anxiety Management Training or Stress Inoculation Training) such as relaxation, breathing control, coping self-statements, covert modeling (i.e., imagining the successful use of the strategies), and/or role-playing (i.e., with therapist or trusted other) toward effective use of relevant skills (see relevant chapters such as Anxiety and Anger Control Problems in this *Planner*). ▽

12. Learn and implement skills for managing relationships with friends, family, and others. (24)

24. Teach the client interpersonal communication skills such as assertive communication, problem solving, and conflict resolution skills for mitigating and managing interpersonal conflicts; use behavioral skills training methods such as instruction, modeling, rehearsal, to develop skills and practice, review, and corrective feedback for refining and consolidating use. ▽

13. Identify, challenge, and replace fearful self-talk with reality-based, positive self-talk. (25, 26)

25. Work with the client to identify and explore the client's schema and self-talk that mediate his/her trauma-related fears; identify and challenge biases; assist him/her in generating appraisals that correct for the biases and build confidence (or assign

"Replace Negative Thoughts with Positive Self-Talk" in the *Child Psychotherapy Homework Planner* by Jongsma, Peterson, and McInnis). ▽

26. Assign the client a homework exercise in which he/she identifies fearful self-talk and creates reality-based alternatives; review and reinforce success, providing corrective feedback for failure. ▽

▽ 14. Participate in imaginal and *in vivo* exposure to trauma-related memories until talking or thinking about the trauma does not cause marked distress. (27, 28, 29)

27. Direct and assist the client in constructing a detailed narrative description of the trauma(s) for imaginal exposure (or assign "Finding My Triggers" in the *Child Psychotherapy Homework Planner* by Jongsma, Peterson, and McInnis); construct a fear and avoidance hierarchy of feared and avoided trauma-related stimuli for *in vivo* exposure. ▽

28. Have the client undergo imaginal exposure to the trauma by having him/her describe a traumatic experience at an increasing but client-chosen level of detail; use narrative, drawing, or other imaginal methods as needed; repeat exposure until associated anxiety reduces and stabilizes, recording the session for use in cognitive restructuring and further exposure in and/or between sessions (see *Trauma-Focused CBT for Children and Adolescents* by Cohen, Mannarino, and Deblinger; *Treating Trauma and Traumatic Grief in Children and Adolescents* by Cohen, Mannarino, and

Deblinger); review and reinforce progress, problem-solve obstacles. ▽

29. Assign the client a homework exercise in which he/she repeats the narrative exposure or does *in vivo* exposure to environmental stimuli as rehearsed in therapy; ask him/her to record responses; review and reinforce progress. ▽

▽ 15. Discuss feelings of grief/loss associated with the trauma. (30)

30. Assess the extent that traumatic grief is a consequence of the trauma experience encouraging expression and working toward acceptance and resolution. ▽

▽ 16. Learn and implement thought-stopping to manage intrusive unwanted thoughts. (31)

31. Teach the client thought-stopping in which he/she internally voices the word STOP and/or imagines something representing the concept of stopping (e.g., a stop sign or light) immediately upon noticing unwanted trauma or otherwise negative unwanted thoughts. ▽

▽ 17. Implement relapse prevention strategies for managing possible future trauma-related symptoms. (32, 33, 34, 35)

32. Discuss with the client the distinction between a lapse and relapse, associating a lapse with an initial and reversible return of symptoms, fear, or urges to avoid and relapse with the decision to return to fearful and avoidant patterns. ▽

33. Identify and rehearse with the client the management of future situations or circumstances in which lapses could occur. ▽

34. Instruct the client to routinely use strategies learned in therapy (e.g., cognitive restructuring, social skills, exposure) while building social interactions and relationships. ▽

35. Develop a "coping card" or other reminder on which coping strategies and other important information (e.g., "Pace your breathing," "Focus on the task at hand," "You can manage it," "It will go away") are recorded for the client's later use. ▽

▽ 18. Family members learn skills that strengthen and support the client's positive behavior change. (36, 37, 38)

36. Involve the family in the treatment of the client, teaching them developmentally appropriate treatment goals, how to give support as the client faces his/her fears, and how to prevent reinforcing the client's fear and avoidance; offer encouragement, support, and redirection as required. ▽

37. Assist the family members in recognizing and managing their own difficult emotional reactions to the client's experience of trauma. ▽

38. Encourage the family to model constructive skills they have learned and model and praise the therapeutic skills the client is learning (e.g., calming, cognitive restructuring, nonavoidance of unrealistic fears). ▽

▽ 19. Client and parents participate in conjoint sessions to review and enhance progress in therapy. (39)

39. Lead conjoint client-parent sessions to review shared therapeutic activities; facilitate open communication; model and encourage positive reinforcement of advancements; provide psychoeducation as needed. ▽

20. Cooperate with eye movement desensitization and reprocessing (EMDR) technique to reduce emotional reaction to the traumatic event. (40)

40. Utilize the EMDR technique to reduce the client's emotional reactivity to the traumatic event (see *Through the Eyes of a Child: EMDR with Children* by Tinker and Wilson).

21. Implement a regular exercise regimen as a stress release technique. (41)

22. Express facts and feelings surrounding the trauma through play therapy and mutual storytelling. (42, 43, 44)

41. Develop and encourage a routine of physical exercise for the client.

42. Use child-centered play therapy principles (e.g., provide unconditional positive regard, offer nonjudgmental reflection of feelings, display trust in the child's capacity for growth) to help the client identify and express feelings surrounding the traumatic incident.

43. Employ psychoanalytic play therapy approaches (e.g., allow the child to take the lead; explore etiology of unconscious conflicts, fixations, or developmental arrests; interpret resistance, transference, and core anxieties) to help the client express and work through feelings surrounding the traumatic incident.

44. Utilize a mutual storytelling technique (see *Therapeutic Communication with Children: The Mutual Storytelling Technique* by Gardner) whereby the client and therapist alternate telling stories through the use of puppets, dolls, or stuffed animals. Therapist first models constructive steps to take to protect self and feel empowered; the client follows by creating a story with similar characters or themes.

23. Express facts and feelings through painting or drawing. (45)

45. Provide the client with materials and ask him/her to draw/paint pictures depicting the trauma and of himself/herself depicting emotions associated with the trauma.

24. Sleep without being disturbed by dreams of the trauma. (46)

46. Monitor the client's sleep pattern and encourage use of relaxation, positive imagery, and sleep hygiene as aids to sleep (see the Sleep Disturbance chapter in this *Planner*).

25. Verbalize hopeful and positive statements regarding the future. (47)

47. Reinforce the client's positive, reality-based cognitive messages that enhance self-confidence and increase adaptive action.

__. _____

    _____

__. _____

    _____

__. _____

    _____

__. _____

    _____

__. _____

    _____

__. _____

    _____

DIAGNOSTIC SUGGESTIONS

Using DSM-IV/ICD-9-CM:

Axis I:	309.81	Posttraumatic Stress Disorder
	309.xx	Adjustment Disorder
	995.54	Physical Abuse of Child (Victim)
	995.53	Sexual Abuse of Child (Victim)
	308.3	Acute Stress Disorder
	296.xx	Major Depressive Disorder
	_____	_____
	_____	_____
Axis II:	V71.09	No Diagnosis
	_____	_____
	_____	_____

Using DSM-5/ICD-9-CM/ICD-10-CM:

ICD-9-CM	ICD-10-CM	*DSM-5* Disorder, Condition, or Problem
309.81	F43.10	Posttraumatic Stress Disorder
309.xx	F43.xx	Adjustment Disorder
995.54	T74.12XA	Child Physical Abuse, Confirmed, Initial Encounter
995.54	T74.12XD	Child Physical Abuse, Confirmed, Subsequent Encounter
995.53	T74.22XA	Child Sexual Abuse, Confirmed, Initial Encounter
995.53	T74.22XD	Child Sexual Abuse, Confirmed, Subsequent Encounter
308.3	F43.0	Acute Stress Disorder
296.xx	F32.x	Major Depressive Disorder, Single Episode
296.xx	F33.x	Major Depressive Disorder, Recurrent Episode

Note: The ICD-9-CM codes are to be used for coding purposes in the United States through September 30, 2014. ICD-10-CM codes are to be used starting October 1, 2014. Some ICD-9-CM codes are associated with more than one ICD-10-CM and *DSM-5* disorder, condition, or problem. In addition, some ICD-9-CM disorders have been discontinued resulting in multiple ICD-9-CM codes being replaced by one ICD-10-CM code. Some discontinued ICD-9-CM codes are not listed in this table. See *Diagnostic and Statistical Manual of Mental Disorders* (2013) for details.

⚕ Indicates that the Objective/Intervention is consistent with those found in evidence-based treatments.

SCHOOL REFUSAL

BEHAVIORAL DEFINITIONS

1. Persistent reluctance or refusal to attend school because of a desire to remain at home with the parents.
2. Marked emotional distress and repeated complaints (e.g., crying, temper outbursts, pleading with parents not to go to school) when anticipating separation from home to attend school or after arrival at school.
3. Frequent somatic complaints (e.g., headaches, stomachaches, nausea) associated with attending school or in anticipation of school attendance.
4. Excessive clinging or shadowing of parents when anticipating leaving home for school or after arriving at school.
5. Frequent negative comments about school and/or repeated questioning of the necessity of going to school.
6. Persistent and unrealistic expression of fear that a future calamity will cause a separation from his/her parents if he/she attends school (e.g., he/she or parent(s) will be lost, kidnapped, killed, or the victim of an accident).
7. Verbalizations of low self-esteem and lack of confidence that contribute to the fear of attending school and being separated from the parents.
8. Verbalization of a fear of failure, ridicule, or anxiety regarding academic achievement accompanying the refusal to attend school.
9. Excessive shrinking from or avoidance of contact with unfamiliar people for extended periods of time.

—. _____
_____
—. _____
_____
—. _____
_____

LONG-TERM GOALS

1. Attend school on a consistent, full-time basis.
2. Eliminate anxiety and the expression of fears prior to leaving home and after arriving at school.
3. Cease temper outbursts, regressive behaviors, complaints, and pleading associated with attending school.
4. Eliminate somatic complaints associated with attending school.
5. Increase the frequency of independent behaviors.
6. Parents establish and maintain appropriate parent-child boundaries, setting firm, consistent limits when the client exhibits temper tantrums and passive-aggressive behaviors associated with attending school.

—. _____
   _____

—. _____
   _____

—. _____
   _____

SHORT-TERM OBJECTIVES	THERAPEUTIC INTERVENTIONS
1. Parents and client describe the client's history of school attendance and express feelings associated with refusal to attend school. (1, 2)	1. Actively build the level of trust with the client through consistent eye contact, active listening, unconditional positive regard, and warm acceptance to increase his/her ability to identify and express feelings.
	2. Explore the client's feelings and behaviors regarding school attendance and any known reasons for his/her refusal to attend; interview the parents regarding their perceptions of the client's patterns of school attendance and refusal as well as the causes behind the refusal.
2. Complete psychological testing and an assessment interview. (3)	3. Arrange for psychological testing of the client to assess the severity of anxiety, depression, or gross

psychopathology and to gain greater insight into the underlying dynamics contributing to school refusal; provide feedback to the client and parents.

3. Complete psychoeducational testing. (4)

4. Arrange for psychoeducational testing of the client to rule out the presence of learning disabilities that may interfere with school attendance; provide feedback to the client, parents, and school officials.

4. Provide behavioral, emotional, and attitudinal information toward an assessment of specifiers relevant to a *DSM* diagnosis, the efficacy of treatment, and the nature of the therapy relationship. (5, 6, 7, 8, 9)

5. Assess the client's level of insight (syntonic versus dystonic) toward the "presenting problems" (e.g., demonstrates good insight into the problematic nature of the "described behavior," agrees with others' concern, and is motivated to work on change; demonstrates ambivalence regarding the "problem described" and is reluctant to address the issue as a concern; or demonstrates resistance regarding acknowledgment of the "problem described," is not concerned, and has no motivation to change).

6. Assess the client for evidence of research-based correlated disorders (e.g., oppositional defiant behavior with ADHD, depression secondary to an anxiety disorder) including vulnerability to suicide, if appropriate (e.g., increased suicide risk when comorbid depression is evident).

7. Assess for any issues of age, gender, or culture that could help explain the client's currently

defined "problem behavior" and factors that could offer a better understanding of the client's behavior.

8. Assess for the severity of the level of impairment to the client's functioning to determine appropriate level of care (e.g., the behavior noted creates mild, moderate, severe, or very severe impairment in social, relational, vocational, or occupational endeavors); continuously assess this severity of impairment as well as the efficacy of treatment (e.g., the client no longer demonstrates severe impairment but the presenting problem now is causing mild or moderate impairment).

9. Assess the client's home, school, and community for pathogenic care (e.g., persistent disregard for the child's emotional needs or physical needs, repeated changes in primary caregivers, limited opportunities for stable attachments, persistent harsh punishment or other grossly inept parenting).

▽ 5. Cooperate with a medical evaluation and take medication as prescribed by the physician. (10, 11)

10. Refer the client for a medical examination to rule out genuine health problems that may contribute to his/her school refusal and somatic complaints. ▽

11. Arrange for the client to be evaluated for psychotropic medication; monitor for medication prescription compliance, side effects, and effectiveness. ▽

▽ 6. Parents verbalize an understanding of and implement skills for managing the child's behavior while facilitating his/her return to school. (12)

12. Conduct parent/teacher training comprised of clinical sessions with parents and consultation with school personnel; teach parents behavior management strategies including the reduction of home-based reinforcement during school hours, planning the process for escorting the child to school, positive reinforcement of coping behavior and attendance; review and refine toward consistent school attendance by the child.▽

▽ 7. Parents and school officials implement a plan to facilitate the client's return to school, deal with temper tantrums, crying spells, or excessive clinging after arriving at school. (13, 14, 15, 16)

13. Consult with school personnel prior to school return and subsequently through telephone contact; discuss preparations for the client's return; helping the client settle into school on arrival; using positive reinforcement and planned ignoring; and accommodating the client academically, socially, and emotionally.▽

14. Consult with the parents and school officials to develop a plan to manage the client's emotional distress and negative outbursts after arriving at school (e.g., the parent ceases lengthy goodbyes, the client goes to the principal's office to calm down).▽

15. Consult with the teacher in the initial stages of treatment about planning an immediate assignment that will provide the client with an increased chance of success.▽

16. Use the teacher's aide or a positive peer role model to provide one-on-one attention for the client and decrease the fear and anxiety about attending school.▽

▽ 8. Verbally acknowledge how the fears related to attending school are irrational or unrealistic. (17, 18)

17. Explore the irrational, negative cognitive messages that produce the client's anxiety or fear; assist him/her in identifying the irrational or unrealistic nature of these fears. ▽

18. Assist the client in developing reality-based positive cognitive messages that increase his/her self-confidence to cope with anxiety or fear; teach parents to be supportive of these cognitive changes (recommend parents read *When Children Refuse School: A Cognitive-Behavioral Therapy Approach—Parent Workbook* by Kearney and Albano). ▽

▽ 9. Implement relaxation and guided imagery to reduce anxiety. (19)

19. Teach the client relaxation techniques or guided imagery as a coping skill (recommend *The Relaxation and Stress Reduction Workbook for Kids: Help for Children to Cope With Stress, Anxiety, and Transitions* by Shapiro and Sprague) when anxiety rises during school attendance (e.g., approaching the school grounds or being asked questions by peers at school); assign homework for implementing relaxation (e.g., "Deep Breathing Exercise" in the *Child Psychotherapy Homework Planner* by Jongsma, Peterson, and McInnis). ▽

▽ 10. Learn and implement skills for effectively managing social interactions at school. (20)

20. Teach the client social communication skills (e.g., common social "scripts," conversational, assertive, and conflict-resolution skills) for managing predictable social encounters at school (e.g., answering peers' questions

regarding their absence from school) and to otherwise improve general social competence; use homework exercises to practice skills (or assign "Greeting Peers" or "Show Your Strengths" in the *Child Psychotherapy Homework Planner* by Jongsma, Peterson, and McInnis).▽

11. Implement assertiveness in social situations that call for protection of self and personal rights. (21, 22)

21. Use the Stand Up for Yourself (Shapiro) game in therapy sessions to help teach the client assertiveness skills that can be used at school (or assign "Learn to be Assertive" in the *Child Psychotherapy Homework Planner* by Jongsma, Peterson, and McInnis).

22. Assign readings to teach the client effective ways to deal with aggressive or intimidating peers at school (e.g., *Why Is Everybody Always Picking on Me? A Guide to Understanding Bullies for Young People* by Webster-Doyle).

▽ 12. Comply with a systematic desensitization program and attend school for increasingly longer periods of time. (23)

23. Design and implement a systematic desensitization program involving imaginal then in vivo exposure to help the client manage his/her anxiety and gradually attend school for longer periods of time (or assign "Gradual Exposure to Fear" in the *Adolescent Psychotherapy Homework Planner* by Jongsma, Peterson, and McInnis).▽

▽ 13. Parents implement a reward system, contingency contract, or token economy focused on school attendance by the client. (24, 25)

24. Develop a reward system or contingency contract to reinforce the client's attending school for increasingly longer periods of time (or assign "School Fear Reduction" in the *Child Psychotherapy Homework*

▽ 14. Identify positive coping strategies to help decrease anxiety, fears, and emotional distress. (26, 27)

15. Increase positive statements about accomplishments and experiences at school. (28)

16. Decrease the frequency of verbalized somatic complaints. (29, 30, 31)

Planner by Jongsma, Peterson, and McInnis).▽

25. Design and implement a token economy to reinforce the client's school attendance.▽

26. Explore for days or periods of time in which the client was able to attend school without exhibiting significant distress. Identify and reinforce coping strategies that the client used to attend school without displaying excessive fear or anxiety.▽

27. Anticipate possible stressors or events (e.g., illness, school holidays, vacations) that might cause fears and anxiety about attending school to reappear. Identify coping strategies and contingency plans (e.g., relaxation techniques, positive self-talk, disengaged parent transporting the client to school) that the client and family can use to overcome fears or anxiety.▽

28. Assist the client in identifying and acknowledging his/her accomplishments and positive experiences in school.

29. Consult with the parents and school officials to develop a contingency plan to manage the client's somatic complaints (e.g., ignore them, take the client's temperature matter-of-factly, redirect the client to task, send the client to the nurse's office).

30. Refocus the client's discussion from physical complaints to emotional conflicts and the expression of feelings.

31. Conduct family therapy sessions to assess the dynamics, including secondary gain, that may be contributing to the emergence of the somatic complaints associated with school refusal.

17. Increase the time spent between the client and the disengaged parent in play, school, or work activities. (32, 33)

32. Ask the client to draw a picture of a house; then instruct him/her to pretend that he/she lives in the house and describe what it is like to live there; process the client's responses to assess family dynamics, focusing on the role of the disengaged parent.

33. Give a directive to the disengaged parent to transport the client to school in the morning (or assign "A Pleasant Journey" in the *Child Psychotherapy Homework Planner* by Jongsma, Peterson, and McInnis); contact the parent's employer, if necessary, to gain permission for this.

18. Parents reinforce the client's autonomous behaviors and set limits on overly dependent behaviors. (34, 35, 36)

34. Encourage the parents to reinforce the client's autonomous behaviors (e.g., attending school, working alone on school assignments) and set limits on overly dependent behaviors (e.g., client insisting that the parent enter the classroom).

35. Stress to the parents the importance of remaining calm and not communicating anxiety to the client.

36. Praise and reinforce the parents for taking positive steps to help the client overcome his/her fears or anxieties about attending school.

19. Parents cease sending inconsistent messages about school attendance and begin to set firm, consistent limits on excessive clinging, pleading, crying, and temper tantrums. (37, 38)

37. Counsel the parents about setting firm, consistent limits on the client's temper outbursts, manipulative behaviors, or excessive clinging.

38. Instruct the parents to write a letter to the client that sends a clear message about the importance of attending school and reminds him/her of coping strategies that he/she can use to calm fears or anxieties. Place the letter in a notebook and have the client read the letter at appropriate times during school day when he/she begins to feel afraid or anxious (or assign the parents to complete the "Letter of Encouragement" in the *Child Psychotherapy Homework Planner* by Jongsma, Peterson, and McInnis).

20. Enmeshed or overly protective parent identifies overly dependent behaviors. (39, 40)

39. Identify how enmeshed or overly protective parents reinforce the client's dependency and irrational fears.

40. Use a paradoxical intervention (e.g., instruct the enmeshed parent to spoon-feed the client each morning) to work around the family's resistance and disengage the client from an overly protective parent.

21. Identify and express the feelings connected with past unresolved separation, loss, or trauma. (41, 42, 43)

41. Assess whether the client's anxiety and fear about attending school are associated with a previously unresolved separation, loss, trauma, or unrealistic danger.

42. Explore, encourage, and support the client in verbally expressing and clarifying his/her feelings associated with a past

separation, loss, trauma, or realistic danger.

43. Assign the older child to write a letter to express his/her feelings about a past separation, loss, trauma, or danger; process it with the therapist.

22. Increase the frequency and duration of time spent in independent play or activities away from the parents or home. (44, 45, 46)

44. Encourage the client's assertive participation in extracurricular and positive peer group activities.

45. Give the client a directive to spend a specified period of time with his/her peers after school or on weekends.

46. Give the client a directive to initiate three social contacts per week with unfamiliar people or when placed in new social settings.

23. Express feelings about attending school through play, mutual storytelling, and art. (47, 48, 49, 50)

47. Employ psychoanalytic play therapy approaches (e.g., allow the client to take the lead; explore the etiology of unconscious conflicts, fixation, or developmental arrests; interpret resistance, transference, and core anxieties) to help the client work through and resolve issues contributing to school refusal.

48. Use mutual storytelling technique: The client and therapist alternate telling stories through the use of puppets, dolls, or stuffed animals. The therapist first models appropriate ways to overcome fears or anxieties to face separation or academic challenges; the client follows by creating a story with similar characters or themes (see

Therapeutic Communication with Children: The Mutual Storytelling Technique by Gardner).

49. Direct the client to draw a picture or create a sculpture about what he/she fears will happen when he/she goes to school; discuss whether his/her fears are realistic or unrealistic.

50. Use "The Angry Tower" technique (Saxe) to help the client identify and express underlying feelings of anger that contribute to school refusal: Build a tower out of plastic containers or buckets; place doll on top of tower (doll represents object of anger); instruct the client to throw small fabric ball at the tower while verbalizing feelings of anger.

24. Parent(s) follow through with recommendations regarding medication and therapeutic interventions. (51)

51. Assess overly enmeshed parent for the possibility of having either an anxiety or depressive disorder that may be contributing to the client's refusal to attend school. Refer the parent for a medication evaluation and/or individual therapy if it is found that the parent has an anxiety or a depressive disorder.

—___ . _____

_____

—___ . _____

_____

—___ . _____

_____

—___ . _____

_____

—___ . _____

_____

—___ . _____

_____

DIAGNOSTIC SUGGESTIONS

Using DSM-IV/ICD-9-CM:

Axis I:	309.21	Separation Anxiety Disorder
	300.02	Generalized Anxiety Disorder
	300.23	Social Anxiety Disorder (Social Phobia)
	296.xx	Major Depressive Disorder
	300.4	Dysthymic Disorder
	300.81	Somatization Disorder
	300.81	Undifferentiated Somatoform Disorder
	309.81	Posttraumatic Stress Disorder
	_____	_____
	_____	_____
Axis II:	V71.09	No Diagnosis
	_____	_____
	_____	_____

Using DSM-5/ICD-9-CM/ICD-10-CM:

ICD-9-CM	ICD-10-CM	*DSM-5* Disorder, Condition, or Problem
309.21	F93.0	Separation Anxiety Disorder
300.02	F41.1	Generalized Anxiety Disorder
300.23	F40.10	Social Anxiety Disorder (Social Phobia)
296.xx	F32.x	Major Depressive Disorder, Single Episode
296.xx	F33.x	Major Depressive Disorder, Recurrent Episode
300.4	F34.1	Persistent Depressive Disorder
300.81	F45.1	Somatic Symptom Disorder
309.81	F43.10	Posttraumatic Stress Disorder

Note: The ICD-9-CM codes are to be used for coding purposes in the United States through September 30, 2014. ICD-10-CM codes are to be used starting October 1, 2014. Some ICD-9-CM codes are associated with more than one ICD-10-CM and *DSM-5* disorder, condition, or problem. In addition, some ICD-9-CM disorders have been discontinued resulting in multiple ICD-9-CM codes being replaced by one ICD-10-CM code. Some discontinued ICD-9-CM codes are not listed in this table. See *Diagnostic and Statistical Manual of Mental Disorders* (2013) for details.

🖫 Indicates that the Objective/Intervention is consistent with those found in evidence-based treatments.

SEPARATION ANXIETY

BEHAVIORAL DEFINITIONS

1. Excessive emotional distress and repeated complaints (e.g., crying, regressive behaviors, pleading with parents to stay, temper tantrums) when anticipating separation from home or close attachment figures.
2. Persistent and unrealistic worry about possible harm occurring to close attachment figures or excessive fear that they will leave and not return.
3. Persistent and unrealistic fears expressed that a future calamity will separate the client from a close attachment figure (e.g., the client or his/her parent will be lost, kidnapped, killed, the victim of an accident).
4. Repeated complaints and heightened distress (e.g., pleading to go home, demanding to see or call a parent) after separation from home or the attachment figure has occurred.
5. Persistent fear and avoidance of being alone as manifested by excessive clinging and shadowing of a close attachment figure.
6. Frequent reluctance or refusal to go to sleep without being near a close attachment figure; refusal to sleep away from home.
7. Recurrent nightmares centering on the theme of separation.
8. Frequent somatic complaints (e.g., headaches, stomachaches, nausea) when separation from home or the attachment figure is anticipated or has occurred.
9. Excessive requests for reassurance about safety and protection from possible harm or danger.
10. Statements reflecting low self-esteem and lack of self-confidence that contribute to the fear of being alone or participating in social activities.

—. _____

_____

—. _____

_____

—. _____

_____

LONG-TERM GOALS

1. Tolerate separation from attachment figures without exhibiting heightened emotional distress, regressive behaviors, temper outbursts, or pleading.
2. Eliminate the somatic complaints associated with separation.
3. Manage nighttime fears effectively as evidenced by remaining calm, sleeping in own bed, and not attempting to go into the attachment figure's room at night.
4. Resolve the core conflicts or traumas contributing to the emergence of the separation anxiety.
5. Participate in extracurricular or peer group activities and spend time in independent play on a regular, consistent basis.
6. Parents maintain appropriate parent-child boundaries and set firm, consistent limits when the client exhibits temper outbursts or manipulative behaviors around separation points.

—. _____

_____

—. _____

_____

—. _____

_____

SHORT-TERM OBJECTIVES	THERAPEUTIC INTERVENTIONS
1. Describe current and past experiences with specific fears, prominent worries, and anxiety symptoms surrounding separation issues including their impact on functioning and attempts to resolve it. (1, 2)	1. Actively build a level of trust with the client that will promote the open sharing of thoughts and feelings, especially fearful ones attached to separation issues (or assign "Expressions of Fear Through Art" from the *Child Psychotherapy Homework Planner* by Jongsma, Peterson, and McInnis).

2. Assess the client's fear and avoidance of separation from parents or other caretakers, including the types of avoidance (e.g., distraction, escape, dependence on others), development, and disability (e.g., *The Anxiety Disorders Interview Schedule for Children—Parent Version* or *Child Version*).

2. Parents and/or client complete questionnaires designed to assess general and/or separation anxiety. (3)

3. Administer to the client and/or parents an objective assessment instrument to help assess the nature and degree of the client's fears, worries, and anxiety symptoms (e.g., *Revised Children's Manifest Anxiety Scale*; *The Multidimensional Anxiety Scale for Children*; *The Screen for Anxiety Related Emotional Disorders: Child* and/or *Parent Version*); repeat administration as desired to assess therapeutic progress.

3. Provide behavioral, emotional, and attitudinal information toward an assessment of specifiers relevant to a *DSM* diagnosis, the efficacy of treatment, and the nature of the therapy relationship. (4, 5, 6, 7, 8)

4. Assess the client's level of insight (syntonic versus dystonic) toward the "presenting problems" (e.g., demonstrates good insight into the problematic nature of the "described behavior," agrees with others' concern, and is motivated to work on change; demonstrates ambivalence regarding the "problem described" and is reluctant to address the issue as a concern; or demonstrates resistance regarding acknowledgment of the "problem described," is not concerned, and has no motivation to change).

5. Assess the client for evidence of research-based correlated disorders (e.g., oppositional defiant behavior with ADHD, depression secondary to an anxiety disorder) including vulnerability to suicide, if appropriate (e.g., increased suicide risk when comorbid depression is evident).

6. Assess for any issues of age, gender, or culture that could help explain the client's currently defined "problem behavior" and factors that could offer a better understanding of the client's behavior.

7. Assess for the severity of the level of impairment to the client's functioning to determine appropriate level of care (e.g., the behavior noted creates mild, moderate, severe, or very severe impairment in social, relational, vocational, or occupational endeavors); continuously assess this severity of impairment as well as the efficacy of treatment (e.g., the client no longer demonstrates severe impairment but the presenting problem now is causing mild or moderate impairment).

8. Assess the client's home, school, and community for pathogenic care (e.g., persistent disregard for the child's emotional needs or physical needs, repeated changes in primary caregivers, limited opportunities for stable attachments, persistent harsh punishment or other grossly inept parenting).

▽ 4. Cooperate with an evaluation by a physician for antianxiety medication. (9, 10)

9. Assess the need to refer the client to a physician for a psychotropic medication consultation. ▽

10. Monitor the client's psychotropic medication compliance, side effects, and effectiveness; confer regularly with the physician. ▽

▽ 5. Verbalize an understanding of how thoughts, physical feelings, and behavioral actions contribute to anxiety and its treatment. (11, 12)

11. Discuss how separation fears involve perceiving unrealistic threats, underestimating coping skills, feeling fear, and avoiding what is threatening, and that these fears interact to maintain the problem. ▽

12. Discuss how exposure serves as an arena to lessen fear, build confidence, and feel safer by building a new history of success experiences (see the *Coping C.A.T. Series* at workbookpublishing.com). ▽

▽ 6. Learn and implement calming skills to reduce and manage anxiety symptoms. (13, 14, 15)

13. Teach the client anxiety management skills (e.g., staying focused on behavioral goals, muscular relaxation, evenly paced diaphragmatic breathing, positive self-talk) to address anxiety symptoms that may emerge during encounters with phobic objects or situations (see *The Relaxation and Stress Reduction Workbook for Kids* by Shapiro and Sprague). ▽

14. Assign the client a homework exercise (e.g., "Deep Breathing Exercise" in the *Child Psychotherapy Homework Planner* by Jongsma, Peterson, and McInnis) by which he/she practices daily calming skills; review and reinforce success, providing corrective feedback for failure. ▽

15. Use biofeedback techniques to facilitate the client's success at learning calming skills. ▽

▽ 7. Identify, challenge, and replace fearful self-talk with positive, realistic, and empowering self-talk. (16, 17, 18)

16. Explore the client's schema and self-talk that mediates his/her fear response; challenge the biases; assist him/her in replacing the distorted messages with reality-based, positive self-talk. ▽

17. Use behavioral techniques (e.g., modeling, corrective feedback, imaginal rehearsal, social reinforcement) to train the client in positive self-talk that prepares him/her to endure anxiety symptoms without serious consequences. ▽

18. Assign the client a homework exercise in which he/she identifies fearful self-talk and creates reality-based alternatives (or assign "Replace Negative Thoughts with Positive Self-Talk" in the *Child Psychotherapy Homework Planner* by Jongsma, Peterson, and McInnis); review and reinforce success, providing corrective feedback for failure. ▽

▽ 8. Participate in gradual, repeated exposure to feared or avoided separation situations. (19, 20, 21, 22, 23)

19. Direct and assist the client in construction of a hierarchy of separation anxiety-producing situations. ▽

20. Select initial exposures that have a high likelihood of being a successful experience for the client; develop a plan for managing the symptoms and rehearse the plan (or assign "Gradually Facing a Phobic Fear" in the *Adolescent Psychotherapy Homework Planner* by Jongsma, Peterson, and McInnis). ▽

21. Assign parents to read about situational exposure in books or treatment manuals on separation anxiety (e.g., the *Coping C.A.T. Series* at workbookpublishing.com; *Helping Your Anxious Child* by Rapee et al.). ▽

22. Encourage the client to cooperate with a process of facing fear rather than using avoidance to cope (or assign "Maurice Faces His Fear" in the *Child Psychotherapy Homework Planner* by Jongsma, Peterson, and McInnis); conduct practice exposures in session with the client or client and attachment figures using graduated tasks, modeling, and reinforcement of the client's success. ▽

23. Assign the client a homework exercise in which he/she does situational exposures and records responses; review; reinforce success and provide corrective feedback toward improvement. ▽

▽ 9. Participate in a cognitive behavioral group treatment for anxiety to learn about anxiety, develop skills for managing it, and use the skills effectively in everyday life. (24)

24. Conduct cognitive behavioral group therapy (e.g., *Cognitive Behavioral Therapy for Anxious Children: Therapist Manual for Group Treatment* by Flannery-Schroeder and Kendall) in which participant youth are taught about the cognitive, behavioral, and emotional components of anxiety, learn and implement skills for coping with anxiety, and then practice their new skills in several anxiety-provoking situations toward consistent effective use. ▽

▽ 10. Participate in group cognitive behavioral therapy with parents to learn about anxiety and develop skills for managing it. (25, 26, 27)

25. Conduct cognitive behavioral group therapy with parents (e.g., *Cognitive Behavioral Therapy for Anxious Children: Therapist Manual for Group Treatment* by Flannery-Schroeder and Kendall) in which the parents are taught about the cognitive, behavioral, and emotional components of anxiety, learn and implement skills for coping with anxiety, and then practice their new skills in several anxiety-provoking situations toward consistent effective use. ▽

26. Teach parents constructive skills for managing their child's anxious behavior, including how to prompt and reward courageous behavior, empathetically ignore excessive complaining and other avoidant behaviors, manage their own anxieties, and model the behavior being taught in session (recommend *Helping Your Anxious Child* by Rapee et al.; *Helping Your Child Overcome Separation Anxiety or School Refusal: A Step-by-Step Guide for Parents* by Eison and Engler; or *The No-Cry Separation Anxiety Solution: Gentle Ways to Make Good-bye Easy From Six Months to Six Years* by Pantley). ▽

27. Teach family members anxiety management, problem-solving, and communication skills to reduce family conflict and assist the client's progress through therapy; review; reinforce success and provide corrective feedback toward improvement. ▽

▽ 11. Reduce the frequency and severity of crying, clinging, temper tantrums, and verbalized fears when separated from attachment figures. (28, 29, 30)

28. Teach parents about setting firm, consistent limits on the client's temper tantrums and excessive clinging or whining. ▽

29. Design a reward system and/or contingency contract that reinforces the client for being able to manage separation from his/her parents without displaying excessive emotional distress. ▽

30. Inquire into what the client does differently on days that he/she is able to separate from parents without displaying excessive clinging, pleading, crying, or protesting; process the client's response and reinforce any positive coping mechanisms that are used to manage separations (or assign "Parents' Time Away" in the *Child Psychotherapy Homework Planner* by Jongsma, Peterson, and McInnis). ▽

▽ 12. Increase the client's participation in extracurricular or positive peer group activities away from home. (31, 32)

31. Encourage participation in extracurricular or peer group activities (or assign "Show Your Strengths" in the *Child Psychotherapy Homework Planner* by Jongsma, Peterson, and McInnis). ▽

32. Use behavioral approaches (e.g., instruction, behavioral rehearsal, role-play of peer group interaction, reinforcement) to teach the client social skills and reduce social anxiety (or assign "Greeting Your Peers" in the *Child Psychotherapy Homework Planner* by Jongsma, Peterson, and McInnis). ▽

▽ 13. Increase the frequency and duration of time spent in

33. Encourage the client to invite a friend for an overnight visit

independent play away from
major attachment figures.
(33, 34, 35, 36)

and/or set up an overnight visit
at a friend's home; process any
fears that arise and reinforce
independence. ▽

34. Direct the client to spend
gradually longer periods of time
in independent play or with
friends after school. ▽

35. Encourage the client to safely
explore his/her immediate
neighborhood in order to foster
autonomy (or assign the
"Explore Your World" exercise
in the *Child Psychotherapy
Homework Planner* by Jongsma,
Peterson, and McInnis). ▽

36. Direct the parents to go on a
weekly outing without the client.
Begin with a 30- to 45-minute
outing and gradually increase
duration; teach the client
effective coping strategies (e.g.,
relaxation techniques, deep
breathing, calling a friend,
playing with sibling) to help
him/her reduce separation
anxiety while parents are away
on outing. ▽

▽ 14. Implement relapse prevention
strategies for managing possible
future anxiety symptoms.
(37, 38, 39, 40)

37. Discuss with the client the
distinction between a lapse and
relapse, associating a lapse with
a temporary and reversible
return of symptoms, fear, or
urges to avoid and relapse with
the decision to return to fearful
and avoidant patterns. ▽

38. Identify and rehearse with the
client the management of future
situations or circumstances in
which lapses could occur. ▽

39. Instruct the client to routinely
use strategies learned in therapy
(e.g., cognitive restructuring,

exposure), building them into his/her life as much as possible. ⍌

40. Develop a "coping card" on which coping strategies and other important information (e.g., "You're safe," "Pace your breathing," "Focus on the task at hand," "You can manage it," "Stay in the situation," "Let the anxiety pass") are written for the client's later use. ⍌

15. Parents follow through with recommendations regarding therapy and/or medication evaluations. (41, 42)

41. Assess overly enmeshed parent for the possibility of having either an anxiety or affective disorder; refer parent for medication evaluation and/or individual therapy if he/she is exhibiting symptoms of either an anxiety or affective disorder.

42. Assess the marital dyad for possible conflict and triangulation of the client into discord; refer parents for marital counseling if discord is present.

16. Identify and express feelings connected with past separation, loss, abuse, or trauma. (43, 44, 45)

43. Assess whether the client's anxiety and fears are associated with a separation, loss, abuse, trauma, or unrealistic danger.

44. Explore, encourage, and support the client in verbally expressing and clarifying the feelings associated with the separation, loss, trauma, or unrealistic danger.

45. Assign the client to write a letter to express his/her feelings about a past separation, loss, trauma, or danger; process the letter with therapist.

17. Express feelings and fears in play therapy, mutual storytelling, and art. (46, 47, 48)

46. Use child-centered play therapy principles (e.g., display genuine interest and unconditional positive regard, reflect feelings in

nonjudgmental manner, demonstrate trust in the client's capacity to grow) to promote greater awareness of self and increase motivation to overcome fears about separation.

47. Utilize mutual storytelling technique: The client and therapist alternate telling stories through the use of puppets, dolls, or stuffed animals; the therapist first models appropriate ways to overcome fears or anxieties; then the client follows by creating a story with similar characters or themes.

48. Direct the client to draw a picture or create a sculpture about what he/she fears will happen upon separation from major attachment figures; assess whether the client's fears are irrational or unrealistic.

18. Learn and implement assertive skills to deal effectively and directly with stress, conflict, or responsibilities. (49, 50)

49. Play The Stand Up for Yourself Game (Shapiro) in therapy sessions to teach the client assertiveness skills (or assign "Learn to Be Assertive" in the *Child Psychotherapy Homework Planner* by Jongsma, Peterson, and McInnis).

50. Refer the client to group therapy to help him/her develop positive social skills, overcome social anxieties, and become more assertive.

___. _____   ___. _____
    _____   _____
___. _____   ___. _____
    _____   _____
___. _____   ___. _____
    _____   _____

DIAGNOSTIC SUGGESTIONS

Using DSM-IV/ICD-9-CM:

Axis I:	309.21	Separation Anxiety Disorder
	300.02	Generalized Anxiety Disorder
	300.23	Social Anxiety Disorder (Social Phobia)
	296.xx	Major Depressive Disorder
	300.81	Somatization Disorder
	301.47	Nightmare Disorder
	307.46	Sleep Terror Disorder
	309.81	Posttraumatic Stress Disorder
	_____	_____
	_____	_____
Axis II:	V71.09	No Diagnosis
	_____	_____
	_____	_____

Using DSM-5/ICD-9-CM/ICD-10-CM:

ICD-9-CM	ICD-10-CM	*DSM-5* Disorder, Condition, or Problem
309.21	F93.0	Separation Anxiety Disorder
300.02	F41.1	Generalized Anxiety Disorder
300.23	F40.10	Social Anxiety Disorder (Social Phobia)
296.xx	F32.x	Major Depressive Disorder, Single Episode
296.xx	F33.x	Major Depressive Disorder, Recurrent Episode
300.81	F45.1	Somatic Symptom Disorder
307.47	F51.5	Nightmare Disorder
307.46	F51.4	Non-Rapid Eye Movement Sleep Arousal Disorder, Sleep Terror Type
309.81	F43.10	Posttraumatic Stress Disorder

Note: The ICD-9-CM codes are to be used for coding purposes in the United States through September 30, 2014. ICD-10-CM codes are to be used starting October 1, 2014. Some ICD-9-CM codes are associated with more than one ICD-10-CM and *DSM-5* disorder, condition, or problem. In addition, some ICD-9-CM disorders have been discontinued resulting in multiple ICD-9-CM codes being replaced by one ICD-10-CM code. Some discontinued ICD-9-CM codes are not listed in this table. See *Diagnostic and Statistical Manual of Mental Disorders* (2013) for details.

SEXUAL ABUSE VICTIM

BEHAVIORAL DEFINITIONS

1. Self-report of being sexually abused.
2. Physical signs of sexual abuse (e.g., red or swollen genitalia, blood in the underwear, constant rashes, a tear in the vagina or rectum, venereal disease, hickeys on the body).
3. Strong interest in or curiosity about advanced knowledge of sexuality.
4. Sexual themes or sexualized behaviors emerge in play or artwork.
5. Recurrent and intrusive distressing recollections or nightmares of the abuse.
6. Acting or feeling as if the sexual abuse were recurring (including delusions, hallucinations, or dissociative flashback experiences).
7. Unexplainable feelings of anger, rage, or fear when coming into contact with the perpetrator or after exposure to sexual topics.
8. Pronounced disturbance of mood and affect (e.g., frequent and prolonged periods of depression, irritability, anxiety, fearfulness).
9. Appearance of regressive behaviors (e.g., thumb-sucking, baby talk, bedwetting).
10. Marked distrust in others as manifested by social withdrawal and problems with establishing and maintaining close relationships.
11. Feelings of guilt, shame, and low self-esteem.

—. _____
   _____
—. _____
   _____
—. _____
   _____

LONG-TERM GOALS

1. Obtain protection from all further sexual victimization.
2. Work successfully through the issue of sexual abuse with consequent understanding and control of feelings and behavior.
3. Resolve the issues surrounding the sexual abuse, resulting in an ability to establish and maintain close interpersonal relationships.
4. Establish appropriate boundaries and generational lines in the family to greatly minimize the risk of sexual abuse ever occurring in the future.
5. Achieve healing within the family system as evidenced by the verbal expression of forgiveness and a willingness to let go and move on.
6. Eliminate denial in self and the family, placing responsibility for the abuse on the perpetrator and allowing the survivor to feel supported.
7. Eliminate all inappropriate sexual behaviors.
8. Build self-esteem and a sense of empowerment as manifested by an increased number of positive self-descriptive statements and greater participation in extracurricular activities.

—. _____
   _____
—. _____
   _____
—. _____
   _____

SHORT-TERM OBJECTIVES

1. Tell the entire story of the abuse. (1, 2, 3, 4, 5)

THERAPEUTIC INTERVENTIONS

1. Actively build the level of trust with the client through consistent eye contact, active listening, unconditional positive regard, and warm acceptance to help increase his/her ability to identify and express feelings connected to the abuse.

2. Explore, encourage, and support the client in verbally expressing the facts and clarifying his/her feelings associated with the abuse (or assign "My Story" in the *Child Psychotherapy*

Homework Planner by Jongsma, Peterson, and McInnis).

3. Using anatomically detailed dolls or puppets, have the client tell and show how he/she was abused. Take great caution not to lead the client's description of the abuse.

4. Report the client's sexual abuse to the appropriate child protection agency, criminal justice officials, or medical professionals.

5. Consult with a physician, criminal justice officials, or child protection case managers to assess the veracity of the sexual abuse charges.

2. Provide behavioral, emotional, and attitudinal information toward an assessment of specifiers relevant to a *DSM* diagnosis, the efficacy of treatment, and the nature of the therapy relationship. (6, 7, 8, 9, 10)

6. Assess the client's level of insight (syntonic versus dystonic) toward the "presenting problems" (e.g., demonstrates good insight into the problematic nature of the "described behavior," agrees with others' concern, and is motivated to work on change; demonstrates ambivalence regarding the "problem described" and is reluctant to address the issue as a concern; or demonstrates resistance regarding acknowledgment of the "problem described," is not concerned, and has no motivation to change).

7. Assess the client for evidence of research-based correlated disorders (e.g., oppositional defiant behavior with ADHD, depression secondary to an anxiety disorder) including vulnerability to suicide, if

appropriate (e.g., increased suicide risk when comorbid depression is evident).

8. Assess for any issues of age, gender, or culture that could help explain the client's currently defined "problem behavior" and factors that could offer a better understanding of the client's behavior.

9. Assess for the severity of the level of impairment to the client's functioning to determine appropriate level of care (e.g., the behavior noted creates mild, moderate, severe, or very severe impairment in social, relational, vocational, or occupational endeavors); continuously assess this severity of impairment as well as the efficacy of treatment (e.g., the client no longer demonstrates severe impairment but the presenting problem now is causing mild or moderate impairment).

10. Assess the client's home, school, and community for pathogenic care (e.g., persistent disregard for the child's emotional needs or physical needs, repeated changes in primary caregivers, limited opportunities for stable attachments, persistent harsh punishment or other grossly inept parenting).

3. Decrease secrecy in the family by informing key members about the abuse. (11, 12)

11. Facilitate conjoint sessions to reveal the client's sexual abuse to key family members or caregivers.

12. Actively confront and challenge denial of the client's sexual abuse within the family system.

4. Implement steps to protect the client from further sexual abuse. (13, 14, 15, 16)

13. Assess whether the perpetrator should be removed from the home.

14. Implement the necessary steps to protect the client and other children in the home from future sexual abuse.

15. Assess whether the client is safe to remain in the home or should be removed.

16. Empower the client by reinforcing steps necessary to protect himself/herself.

5. Parents establish and adhere to appropriate intimacy boundaries within the family. (17)

17. Counsel the client's family members about appropriate intimacy and privacy boundaries.

6. Verbalize the effects the abuse has had on emotional adjustment and behavior, including noticeable changes in emotional lability, daily activities, sleep, and feelings about self. (18)

18. Assess the client for the presence of a psychiatric disorder(s) caused by the abuse (e.g., posttraumatic stress disorder, anxiety disorder, depression) and inform treatment with an evidence-based approach to the relevant disorder (see relevant chapters in this *Planner*).

7. Identify family dynamics or stressors that contributed to the emergence of sexual abuse. (19, 20, 21, 22)

19. Assess the family dynamics and identify the stress factors or precipitating events that contributed to the emergence of the client's abuse.

20. Assign the client to draw a diagram of the house where the abuse occurred, indicating where everyone slept, and share the diagram with the therapist.

21. Ask the client to draw a picture of a house, then instruct him/her to pretend that he/she lives in that house and describe what it is like to live there; process the client's responses to assess family dynamics and allow for his/her

expression of feelings related to abuse.

22. Construct a multigenerational family genogram that identifies sexual abuse within the extended family to help the client realize that he/she is not the only one abused and to help the perpetrator recognize the cycle of boundary violation.

8. Identify and express feelings connected to the abuse. (23, 24, 25, 26)

23. Instruct older child to write a letter to the perpetrator that describes his/her feelings about the abuse; process the letter.

24. Employ art therapy (e.g., drawing, painting, sculpting) to help the client identify and express feelings he/she has toward perpetrator.

25. Use "The Angry Tower" technique (Saxe) to help the client express feelings of anger about sexual abuse: Build tower out of plastic containers; place small doll on top of tower (doll represents object of anger); instruct the client to throw small fabric ball at tower while verbalizing feelings of anger connected to the abuse.

26. Use guided fantasy and imagery techniques to help the client express suppressed thoughts, feelings, and unmet needs associated with sexual abuse.

9. Decrease expressed feelings of shame and guilt and affirm self as not being responsible for the abuse. (27)

27. Explore and resolve the client's feelings of guilt and shame connected to the sexual abuse (or assign the "You Are Not Alone" exercise in the *Child Psychotherapy Homework Planner* by Jongsma, Peterson, and McInnis).

10. Verbalize the way sexual abuse has impacted life and feelings about self. (28, 29)

28. Instruct the client to create a drawing or sculpture that reflects how sexual abuse impacted his/her life and feelings about himself/herself.

29. Assess the client for the presence of symptoms of posttraumatic stress disorder (PTSD) and treat appropriately if positive for this syndrome (see the PTSD chapter in this *Planner*).

11. Increase the willingness to talk about sexual abuse in the family. (11, 30)

11. Facilitate conjoint sessions to reveal the client's sexual abuse to key family members or caregivers.

30. Assign the parents and family members reading material to increase their knowledge of sexually addictive behavior and learn ways to help the client recover from sexual abuse (e.g., *My Body Is Mine, My Feelings Are Mine: A Storybook About Body Safety for Young Children With an Adult Guidebook* by Hoke; *When Your Child Has Been Molested: A Parent's Guide to Healing and Recovery* by Brohl and Potter; *Helping Your Child Recover From Sexual Abuse* by Adams and Fay).

12. Nonabusive parent follows through with recommendations to spend greater quality time with client. (31, 32)

31. Give directive to disengaged, nonabusive parent to spend more time with the client in leisure, school, or household activities.

32. Direct the client and the disengaged, nonabusive parent to create a mutual story through the use of puppets, dolls, or stuffed animals, first in filial play therapy sessions and later at home, to facilitate a closer parent-child relationship.

13. Verbally identify the perpetrator as being responsible for the sexual abuse. (33, 34)

33. Hold a therapy session in which the client and/or the therapist confronts the perpetrator with the abuse.

34. Hold a session in which the perpetrator takes full responsibility for the sexual abuse and apologizes to the client and/or other family members.

14. Perpetrator agrees to seek treatment. (35)

35. Require the perpetrator to participate in a sexual offenders' group.

15. Verbalize a desire to begin the process of forgiveness of the perpetrator and others connected with the abuse. (36)

36. Assign the client to write a forgiveness letter and/or complete a forgiveness exercise in which he/she verbalizes forgiveness to the perpetrator and/or significant family members; process the letter.

16. Identify and express feelings about sexual abuse in play therapy and mutual storytelling. (32, 37, 38)

32. Direct the client and the disengaged, nonabusive parent to create a mutual story through the use of puppets, dolls, or stuffed animals, first in filial play therapy sessions and later at home, to facilitate a closer parent-child relationship.

37. Use child-centered play therapy principles (e.g., provide unconditional positive regard, offer nonjudgmental reflection of feelings, display trust in the child's capacity for growth) to help the client identify and express feelings surrounding sexual abuse.

38. Use mutual storytelling technique: The client and therapist alternate telling stories through the use of puppets, dolls, or stuffed animals; the

therapist first models constructive steps to take to protect self and feel empowered; then the client follows by creating a story with similar characters or themes.

17. Identify and express feelings through artwork and therapeutic games. (39, 40, 41)

39. Ask the client to draw pictures of different emotions and then instruct him/her to identify times when he/she experienced the different emotions surrounding the sexual abuse (or assign the "Feelings and Faces Game" exercise in the *Child Psychotherapy Homework Planner* by Jongsma, Peterson, and McInnis).

40. Employ the Color-Your-Life technique (O'Connor) to improve the client's ability to identify and verbalize feelings related to sexual abuse: Ask the client to match colors to different emotions (e.g., red-angry, blue-sad, black-very sad, yellow-happy) and then fill up a blank page with colors that reflect his/her feelings about sexual abuse.

41. Play Survivor's Journey (available through Courage to Change), a therapeutic game for working with survivors of sexual abuse to help the client feel empowered.

18. Verbally identify self as a survivor of sexual abuse. (42, 43)

42. Assign readings to the client to help him/her express and work through feelings connected to sexual abuse (e.g., *A Very Touching Book . . . For Little People and for Big People* by Hindman; *I Can't Talk About It* by Sanford; *It's Not Your Fault* by Jance).

43. Refer the client to a survivor group with other children to assist him/her in realizing that he/she is not alone in having experienced sexual abuse.

19. Increase outside family contacts and social networks. (44)

44. Develop a list of resource people outside of the family to whom the client can turn for support and nurturance.

20. Decrease frequency of sexualized or seductive behaviors in interactions with others. (45, 46)

45. Assist the client in making a connection between underlying painful emotions (e.g., fear, hurt, sadness, anxiety) and sexualized or seductive behaviors.

46. Help the client identify more adaptive ways to meet his/her needs other than through sexualized or seductive behaviors.

21. Decrease anxiety associated with testifying in court. (47)

47. Use role-playing and modeling in session to prepare the client for court and decrease anxiety about testifying.

22. Take medication as prescribed by the physician. (48)

48. Refer the client for a psychotropic medication evaluation; monitor medication compliance, effectiveness, and side effects.

__. _____

_____

__. _____

_____

__. _____

_____

__. _____

_____

__. _____

_____

__. _____

_____

DIAGNOSTIC SUGGESTIONS

Using DSM-IV/ICD-9-CM:

Axis I:	309.81	Posttraumatic Stress Disorder
	308.3	Acute Stress Disorder
	296.xx	Major Depressive Disorder
	309.21	Separation Anxiety Disorder
	995.53	Sexual Abuse of Child (Victim)
	307.47	Nightmare Disorder
	300.15	Dissociative Disorder NOS
	_____	_____
	_____	_____
Axis II:	V71.09	No Diagnosis
	_____	_____
	_____	_____

Using DSM-5/ICD-9-CM/ICD-10-CM:

ICD-9-CM	ICD-10-CM	*DSM-5* Disorder, Condition, or Problem
309.81	F43.10	Posttraumatic Stress Disorder
308.3	F43.0	Acute Stress Disorder
296.xx	F32.x	Major Depressive Disorder, Single Episode
296.xx	F33.x	Major Depressive Disorder, Recurrent Episode
309.21	F93.0	Separation Anxiety Disorder
995.53	T74.22XA	Child Sexual Abuse, Confirmed, Initial Encounter
995.53	T74.22XD	Child Sexual Abuse, Confirmed, Subsequent Encounter
307.47	F51.5	Nightmare Disorder
300.15	F44.89	Other Specified Dissociative Disorder
300.15	F44.9	Unspecified Dissociative Disorder

Note: The ICD-9-CM codes are to be used for coding purposes in the United States through September 30, 2014. ICD-10-CM codes are to be used starting October 1, 2014. Some ICD-9-CM codes are associated with more than one ICD-10-CM and *DSM-5* disorder, condition, or problem. In addition, some ICD-9-CM disorders have been discontinued resulting in multiple ICD-9-CM codes being replaced by one ICD-10-CM code. Some discontinued ICD-9-CM codes are not listed in this table. See *Diagnostic and Statistical Manual of Mental Disorders* (2013) for details.

SLEEP DISTURBANCE

BEHAVIORAL DEFINITIONS

1. Emotional distress and demands (e.g., crying, leaving bed to awaken parents, demanding to sleep with parents) accompany difficulty falling asleep or remaining asleep.
2. Difficulty falling asleep or remaining asleep without significant demands made on the parents.
3. Distress (e.g., crying, calling for parents, racing heart, fear of returning to sleep) resulting from repeated awakening, with detailed recall of extremely frightening dreams involving threats to self or significant others.
4. Repeated incidents of leaving bed and walking about in an apparent sleep state but with eyes open, face blank, lack of response to communication efforts, and amnesia of the incident upon awakening.
5. Abrupt awakening with a panicky scream followed by intense anxiety and autonomic arousal, no detailed dream recall, and unresponsiveness to the efforts of others to give comfort during the episode.
6. Prolonged sleep and/or excessive daytime napping without feeling adequately rested or refreshed but instead continually tired.

__. _____
   _____
__. _____
   _____
__. _____
   _____

LONG-TERM GOALS

1. Fall asleep calmly and stay asleep without any undue reassuring parental presence required.

2. Feel refreshed and energetic during waking hours.
3. Report an end to anxiety-producing dreams that cause awakening.
4. End abrupt awakening in terror and return to a peaceful, restful sleep pattern.
5. Restore restful sleep with a reduction of sleepwalking incidents.

—. _____

_____

—. _____

_____

—. _____

_____

SHORT-TERM OBJECTIVES

THERAPEUTIC INTERVENTIONS

1. Describe the history and current nature of the sleep disturbance. (1, 2, 3)

1. Conduct a comprehensive sleep assessment including review of the weekday and weekend sleep-wake schedule (e.g., latency to sleep onset, behaviors during the night, number and duration of nighttime awakenings), evening activities, bedtime fears and behavioral difficulties, bedroom environment, and abnormal events during sleep (e.g., night terrors, confusional arousals, sleep walking, seizures).

2. Assess daytime lifestyle and functioning including diet; medications; activity level; school adjustment; psychological, social, and family functioning; and stressful life events (e.g., birth of a sibling, recent move, death in family).

3. Ask the client and/or parents to keep a written record of relevant sleep activity, sleep time, awakening occurrences, and parental responses to the child;

provide a form to chart data (or assign "Childhood Sleep Problems" in the *Child Psychotherapy Homework Planner* by Jongsma, Peterson, and McInnis); review the record to assess for possible contributors to the sleep problem (e.g., overstimulation, parental reinforcement, stressors).

2. Participate in an overnight sleep study. (4)

4. Refer the client for a sleep study involving polysomnography (PSG) to assess sleep architecture and physiologically-based sleep disruptors (e.g. obstructive sleep apnea, limb movement disorder).

3. Verbalize feelings of depression, anxiety, or other personal problems and share the possible causes. (5)

5. Assess the role of a possible mental disorder (e.g., depression, anxiety, other) as a cause of the client's sleep disturbances and treat if necessary (e.g., see the Depression, Anxiety, or other relevant chapter in this *Planner*).

4. Describe stressful experiences and emotional trauma that continue to disturb sleep. (6, 7, 8)

6. Explore for recent traumatic events that have resulted in interference with the client's sleep.

7. Explore for the possibility of sexual abuse to the client that has not been revealed (see the Sexual Abuse Victim chapter in this *Planner*).

8. Probe the nature of the client's disturbing dreams and their relationship to current or past life stress.

5. Provide behavioral, emotional, and attitudinal information toward an assessment of specifiers relevant to a *DSM* diagnosis, the efficacy of treatment, and the nature of the therapy relationship. (9, 10, 11, 12, 13)

9. Assess the client's level of insight (syntonic versus dystonic) toward the "presenting problems" (e.g., demonstrates good insight into the problematic nature of the "described behavior," agrees with others' concern, and is

motivated to work on change;
demonstrates ambivalence
regarding the "problem
described" and is reluctant to
address the issue as a concern;
or demonstrates resistance
regarding acknowledgment
of the "problem described,"
is not concerned, and has no
motivation to change).

10. Assess the client for evidence
of research-based correlated
disorders (e.g., oppositional
defiant behavior with ADHD,
depression secondary to an
anxiety disorder) including
vulnerability to suicide, if
appropriate (e.g., increased
suicide risk when comorbid
depression is evident).

11. Assess for any issues of age,
gender, or culture that could
help explain the client's currently
defined "problem behavior" and
factors that could offer a better
understanding of the client's
behavior.

12. Assess for the severity of the
level of impairment to the
client's functioning to determine
appropriate level of care (e.g.,
the behavior noted creates mild,
moderate, severe, or very severe
impairment in social, relational,
vocational, or occupational
endeavors); continuously assess
this severity of impairment as
well as the efficacy of treatment
(e.g., the client no longer
demonstrates severe impairment
but the presenting problem now
is causing mild or moderate
impairment).

	13. Assess the client's home, school, and community for pathogenic care (e.g., persistent disregard for the child's emotional needs or physical needs, repeated changes in primary caregivers, limited opportunities for stable attachments, persistent harsh punishment or other grossly inept parenting).
6. Take psychotropic medication as prescribed to assess its effect on sleep. (14, 15)	14. Arrange for a medication evaluation to assess the possible usefulness of using medication to enhance restful sleep.
	15. Monitor the client for medication prescription adherence, effectiveness, and side effects; report to prescriber as needed.
7. Parents and family members identify sources of conflict or stress within the home. (16, 17)	16. Hold family sessions to assess the level of tension and conflict and its effect on the client's sleep; assist family members in identifying effective coping strategies to reduce tension and conflict.
	17. Meet with the parents alone to assess the degree of stress in their relationship and its possible impact on the client's sleep behavior; refer the parents for conjoint sessions if necessary.
▽ 8. Parents learn about good sleep hygiene and establish a consistent sleep-wake cycle in the client. (18, 19)	18. Implement a behaviorally based treatment approach (recommend *Sleeping Through the Night* by Mindell), beginning with psychoeducation regarding good sleep hygiene (e.g., consistent sleep-wake cycle, a consistent bedtime routine, bedroom environment conducive to sleep, reduction in stimulation that could affect sleep onset and/or maintenance) and a rationale for

major treatment interventions toward helping the client learn to fall asleep independently. ▽

19. Work with parents to establish a consistent sleep-wake cycle for the client including an age-appropriate bedtime, regular naps for infants and toddlers, with no more than 1- to 2-hour differences between weekday and weekend bedtimes and wake times. ▽

▽ 9. Parents learn and implement arousal-reducing practices to reduce stimulation that may be interfering with the client going to bed and staying asleep. (20, 21, 22)

20. Work with parents to develop a positive stimulus control technique involving a consistent, pleasurable, and calming nighttime routine that is short (20–30 min) and involves the same three to four activities every night. ▽

21. Educate parents regarding good sleep hygiene and advise them to create a bedroom environment that is conducive to sleep, including being comfortable, cool, dark, and quiet; remove all technology (e.g., televisions, computers, and cell phones) that could be potentially arousing. ▽

22. Review all potential caffeinated products consumed by the client and eliminate afternoon and evening use. ▽

▽ 10. Remain alone in the bedroom without expressions of fear. (23, 24, 25)

23. Assess the client's fears associated with being alone in the bedroom in terms of their nature, severity, and origin. ▽

24. Help the client and parents establish a nightly ritual for going to bed that will help to reduce the client's fears and induce calm before going to sleep such as getting a drink; parents tell a bedtime story; build a fortress of

stuffed animals around the client's bed; have mother spray perfume on daughter's wrist to remind her of parent's close proximity (or assign "Reduce Nighttime Fears" in the *Child Psychotherapy Homework Planner* by Jongsma, Peterson, and McInnis); gradually extinguish/remove "safety cues" over time as the child's fears resolve. ▽

25. Encourage the parents to allow the family pet to sleep in room with the client at night to reduce nighttime fears and anxiety; gradually extinguish/remove this "safety cue" over time as the child's fears resolve. ▽

▽ 11. Parents implement agreed-upon methods of setting limits to manage the client's disruptive and/or manipulative behavior at bedtime. (26, 27, 28)

26. Meet with the parents to help them identify and implement consistent limit-setting responses to the client's disruptive or manipulative bedtime behavior (e.g., pleasurable activities are calmly halted if the client protests or throws a tantrum; an agreed-upon verbal response to the client's request is given and the client is then put to bed). ▽

27. Devise a reward system and/or contingency contract to reinforce the client for desired behavior consistent with therapeutic objectives (e.g., complying with the bedtime routine, sleeping in his/her own bed, ceasing entering into parents' bedroom at night). ▽

28. Brainstorm with the parents a potential list of negative (response costs) consequences (e.g., removal of privileges such as TV or video games) the client will receive if he/she engages in

manipulative behavior to avoid going to bed on time. Encourage the parents to select a specific consequence and follow through consistently if the client engages in misbehavior. ▽

▽ 12. Parents implement a consistent procedure for checking on the child and/or responding to protests after the child has gone to bed. (29, 30, 31, 32)

29. Agree to a checking procedure with parents in which they check on the child at agreed-upon intervals until the child falls asleep; start as frequently or infrequently as they wish based upon parental tolerance and child temperament. ▽

30. Advise parents to respond calmly and consistently to the client during the checking procedure to facilitate the client's development of self-soothing skills and without using other interventions to induce sleep (e.g. feeding, rocking). ▽

31. Teach and implement a graduated extinction procedure involving progressive time delays between responding to bedtime protests or refusals, and/or increasingly shorter intervals of comforting when checking on the crying or protesting child (recommend *Solve Your Child's Sleep Problems* by Ferber). ▽

32. Teach and implement a nongraduated extinction procedure in which the parents put their child to bed at a designated time and ignore the child's or infant's protests until an established time the next morning. ▽

▽ 13. Parents monitor adherence to the bedtime routine developed in the therapy session. (33)

33. Assign the parents to keep a written record of the client's adherence to relevant therapeutic

interventions (e.g., the bedtime routine, staying in bed); review the record at future sessions and reinforce successful implementation while problem-solving obstacles. ▽

▽ 14. Parents implement scheduled awakenings for children having consistent difficulty maintaining sleep or experiencing sleep terrors. (34)

34. Teach and implement a scheduled awakenings procedure in which the parents awaken the child approximately 15 minutes before his or her typical nightly awakening times; continue for 7 days then stop procedure to assess effectiveness; gradually taper off the scheduled awakenings as the child shows evidence of sleep maintenance (see *When Children Don't Sleep Well: Interventions for Pediatric Sleep Disorders—Parent Workbook* by Durand). ▽

15. Replace irrational thoughts and beliefs that contribute to the sleep disturbance with rational, positive self-talk and beliefs. (35)

35. Use cognitive therapy techniques to identify, challenge, and change the client's irrational thoughts and fears; teach cognitive strategies for use at bedtime (e.g., positive relaxing imagery, distraction).

16. Practice deep-muscle relaxation exercises. (36, 37, 38)

36. Train the client in deep-muscle relaxation exercises with and/or without audiotape instruction (recommend *The Relaxation and Stress Reduction Workbook for Kids* by Shapiro and Sprague).

37. Use relaxation tapes to train the client in calming himself/herself as preparation for sleep (e.g., *Relaxation Imagery for Children* by Weinstock, available from Childswork/Childsplay; *Magic Island: Relaxation for Kids* by Mehling, Highstein, and Delamarter, available from Courage to Change).

17. Utilize biofeedback training to deepen relaxation skills. (39)

18. Express feelings in play therapy that may be interfering with sleep. (40, 41)

38. Teach the client to reduce anxiety and fear after awakening from nightmares by visualizing how a dream can end on a positive note (e.g., visualize mother or father coming to rescue; client calls the police who arrest the intruder, robber, or perpetrator in the dream).

39. Administer electromyographic (EMG) biofeedback to monitor, train, and reinforce the client's successful relaxation response.

40. Use play therapy techniques to assess and resolve the client's emotional conflicts.

41. Interpret the client's play behavior as reflective of his/her feelings toward family members.

—. _____   —. _____
   _____   _____
—. _____   —. _____
   _____   _____
—. _____   —. _____
   _____   _____

DIAGNOSTIC SUGGESTIONS

Using DSM-IV/ICD-9-CM:

Axis I: 309.21   Separation Anxiety Disorder
                 307.42   Primary Insomnia
                 307.44   Primary Hypersomnia
                 307.45   Circadian Rhythm Sleep Disorder
                 307.47   Nightmare Disorder
                 307.46   Sleep Terror Disorder
                 307.46   Sleepwalking Disorder
                 309.81   Posttraumatic Stress Disorder
                 296.xx   Major Depressive Disorder
                 300.4   Dysthymic Disorder

296.xx	Bipolar I Disorder
296.89	Bipolar II Disorder
296.80	Bipolar Disorder NOS
301.13	Cyclothymic Disorder

_____   _____

_____   _____

Axis II: V71.09   No Diagnosis

_____   _____

_____   _____

Using DSM-5/ICD-9-CM/ICD-10-CM:

ICD-9-CM	ICD-10-CM	*DSM-5* Disorder, Condition, or Problem
309.21	F93.0	Separation Anxiety Disorder
312.9	F91.9	Unspecified Disruptive, Impulse Control, and Conduct Disorder
312.89	F91.8	Other Specified Disruptive, Impulse Control, and Conduct Disorder
307.42	G47.00	Insomnia
307.45	G47.xx	Circadian Rhythm Sleep-Wake Disorder
307.47	F51.5	Nightmare Disorder
307.46	F51.4	Non-Rapid Eye Movement Sleep Arousal Disorder, Sleep Terror Type
307.46	F51.3	Non-Rapid Eye Movement Sleep Arousal Disorder, Sleepwalking Type
309.81	F43.10	Posttraumatic Stress Disorder
296.xx	F32.x	Major Depressive Disorder, Single Episode
296.xx	F33.x	Major Depressive Disorder, Recurrent Episode
300.4	F34.1	Persistent Depressive Disorder
296.xx	F31.xx	Bipolar I Disorder
296.89	F31.81	Bipolar II Disorder
296.80	F31.9	Unspecified Bipolar and Related Disorder
301.13	F34.0	Cyclothymic Disorder

Note: The ICD-9-CM codes are to be used for coding purposes in the United States through September 30, 2014. ICD-10-CM codes are to be used starting October 1, 2014. Some ICD-9-CM codes are associated with more than one ICD-10-CM and *DSM-5* disorder, condition, or problem. In addition, some ICD-9-CM disorders have been discontinued resulting in multiple ICD-9-CM codes being replaced by one ICD-10-CM code. Some discontinued ICD-9-CM codes are not listed in this table. See *Diagnostic and Statistical Manual of Mental Disorders* (2013) for details.

▽ Indicates that the Objective/Intervention is consistent with those found in evidence-based treatments.

SOCIAL ANXIETY

BEHAVIORAL DEFINITIONS

1. Limited or no eye contact, coupled with a refusal or reticence to respond verbally to social overtures from others.
2. Excessive shrinking from or avoidance of contact with unfamiliar people for an extended period of time (i.e., 6 months or longer).
3. Social isolation and/or excessive involvement in isolated activities (e.g., reading, listening to music in his/her room, playing video games).
4. Extremely limited or no close friendships outside of the immediate family members.
5. Hypersensitivity to criticism, disapproval, or perceived signs of rejection from others.
6. Excessive need for reassurance of being liked by others before demonstrating a willingness to get involved with them.
7. Marked reluctance to engage in new activities or take personal risks because of the potential for embarrassment or humiliation.
8. Negative self-image as evidenced by frequent self-disparaging remarks, unfavorable comparisons to others, and a perception of self as being socially unattractive.
9. Lack of assertiveness because of a fear of being met with criticism, disapproval, or rejection.
10. Heightened physiological distress in social settings manifested by increased heart rate, profuse sweating, dry mouth, muscular tension, and trembling.

___. _____
_____

___. _____
_____
_____

___. _____
_____

LONG-TERM GOALS

1. Eliminate anxiety, shyness, and timidity in social settings.
2. Initiate or respond to social contact with unfamiliar people or when placed in new social settings.
3. Interact socially with peers on a consistent basis without excessive fear or anxiety.
4. Achieve a healthy balance between time spent in solitary activity and social interaction with others.
5. Develop the essential social skills that will enhance the quality of interpersonal relationships.
6. Elevate self-esteem and feelings of security in interpersonal, peer, and adult relationships.

—. _____
_____
—. _____
_____
—. _____
_____

SHORT-TERM OBJECTIVES

1. Describe the history and nature of social fears and avoidance. (1, 2, 3)

THERAPEUTIC INTERVENTIONS

1. Establish rapport with the client toward building a therapeutic alliance.

2. Assess the client's social fear and avoidance, including the focus of fear, types of avoidance (e.g., distraction, escape, dependence on others), development of the fear, and the negative impact on daily functioning; consider using a structured interview (e.g., *The Anxiety Disorders Interview Schedule for Children—Parent Version* or *Child Version*).

3. Assess the nature of any external stimulus, thoughts, or situations that precipitate the client's social fear and/or avoidance.

2. Complete psychological tests designed to assess the nature and severity of social anxiety and avoidance. (4)

3. Provide behavioral, emotional, and attitudinal information toward an assessment of specifiers relevant to a *DSM* diagnosis, the efficacy of treatment, and the nature of the therapy relationship. (5, 6, 7, 8, 9)

4. Administer an objective measure of social anxiety to the client to further assess the depth and breadth of social fears and avoidance (e.g., *Social Phobia and Anxiety Inventory for Children* by Beidel, Turner, and Morris).

5. Assess the client's level of insight (syntonic versus dystonic) toward the "presenting problems" (e.g., demonstrates good insight into the problematic nature of the "described behavior," agrees with others' concern, and is motivated to work on change; demonstrates ambivalence regarding the "problem described" and is reluctant to address the issue as a concern; or demonstrates resistance regarding acknowledgment of the "problem described," is not concerned, and has no motivation to change).

6. Assess the client for evidence of research-based correlated disorders (e.g., oppositional defiant behavior with ADHD, depression secondary to an anxiety disorder) including vulnerability to suicide, if appropriate (e.g., increased suicide risk when comorbid depression is evident).

7. Assess for any issues of age, gender, or culture that could help explain the client's currently defined "problem behavior" and factors that could offer a better understanding of the client's behavior.

8. Assess for the severity of the level of impairment to the client's functioning to determine

appropriate level of care (e.g., the behavior noted creates mild, moderate, severe, or very severe impairment in social, relational, vocational, or occupational endeavors); continuously assess this severity of impairment as well as the efficacy of treatment (e.g., the client no longer demonstrates severe impairment but the presenting problem now is causing mild or moderate impairment).

9. Assess the client's home, school, and community for pathogenic care (e.g., persistent disregard for the child's emotional needs or physical needs, repeated changes in primary caregivers, limited opportunities for stable attachments, persistent harsh punishment or other grossly inept parenting).

▽ 4. Cooperate with an evaluation by a physician for psychotropic medication. (10, 11)

10. Arrange for the client to have an evaluation for a prescription of psychotropic medications. ▽

11. Monitor the client for prescription compliance, side effects, and overall effectiveness of the medication; consult with the prescribing physician at regular intervals. ▽

▽ 5. Participate in small group therapy for social anxiety, with or without parents, or individual therapy if the group is unavailable. (12)

12. Enroll the client, with parents if desired, in a small (closed enrollment) group for social anxiety or individual therapy if a group cannot be formed (see *Social Effectiveness Therapy for Children and Adolescents* by Beidel, Turner, and Morris; *Helping Your Anxious Child* by Rapee et al.). ▽

▽ 6. Verbalize an accurate understanding of social anxiety and the rationale for its treatment. (13, 14)

13. Convey a cognitive-behavioral model of social anxiety that supports the rationale for treatment (e.g., social anxiety derives from cognitive biases and leads to unnecessary avoidance that maintains the fear). ▽

14. Discuss how cognitive restructuring and exposure serve as an arena to desensitize learned fear, build social skills and confidence, and reality-test biased anxious thoughts and beliefs. ▽

▽ 7. Read recommended material that supports therapeutic goals toward increasing understanding of social anxiety and its treatment. (15)

15. Assign the client and/or parents to read psychoeducational material on social anxiety and its treatment (e.g., *Helping Your Anxious Child* by Rapee et al.; *The Shyness and Social Anxiety Workbook* by Antony and Swinson; *Say Goodbye to Being Shy* by Brozovich and Chase). ▽

▽ 8. Learn and implement calming and coping strategies to manage anxiety symptoms and focus attention usefully during moments of social anxiety. (16)

16. Teach the client relaxation (see *New Directions in Progressive Relaxation Training* by Bernstein, Borkovec, and Hazlett-Stevens) and attentional focusing skills (e.g., staying focused externally and on behavioral goals, muscular relaxation, evenly paced diaphragmatic breathing, ride the wave of anxiety) to manage social anxiety symptoms (recommend parents and child read *The Relaxation and Stress Reduction Workbook for Kids* by Shapiro and Sprague). ▽

▽ 9. Identify, challenge, and replace fearful self-talk and beliefs with reality-based, positive self-talk and beliefs. (17, 18)

17. Explore the client's schema and self-talk that mediate his/her social fear response; challenge the biases; assist him/her in

generating appraisals that correct for the biases and build confidence (or assign "Replace Negative Thoughts With Positive Self-Talk" from the *Child Psychotherapy Homework Planner* by Jongsma, Peterson, and McInnis). ▽

18. Assign the client a homework exercise in which he/she identifies fearful self-talk and creates reality-based alternatives; review and reinforce success, providing corrective feedback for failure (see *The Shyness and Social Anxiety Workbook* by Antony and Swinson; *Helping Your Anxious Child* by Rapee et al.). ▽

▽ 10. Learn and implement social skills to reduce anxiety and build confidence in social interactions. (19)

19. Use instruction, modeling, and role-playing to build the client's general social and/or communication skills (e.g., *Social Effectiveness Therapy for Children and Adolescents* by Beidel, Turner, and Morris; *Say Goodbye to Being Shy* by Brozovich and Chase). ▽

▽ 11. Learn and implement social problem-solving skills for managing social stresses, solving daily problems, and resolving conflicts effectively. (20, 21, 22)

20. Teach the client tailored, age-appropriate social problem-solving skills including calming skills (e.g., cognitive and somatic), problem-solving skills (e.g., specifying problem, generating options, listing pros and cons of each option, selecting an option, implementing an option, and refining). ▽

21. Teach the client conflict resolution skills (e.g., empathy, active listening, "I messages," respectful communication, assertiveness without aggression, compromise), to prevent or

manage social problems and improve personal and interpersonal functioning.

22. Use behavioral skill-building techniques (e.g., modeling, role-playing, and behavior rehearsal, corrective feedback) to develop skills and work through several current conflicts (see *Helping Your Anxious Child* by Rapee et al.). ▽

▽ 12. Gradually practice and improve new skills in various feared social situations. (23, 24, 25)

23. Direct and assist the client in construction of a hierarchy of anxiety-producing situations associated with social anxiety. ▽

24. Select initial *in vivo* or role-played exposures that have a high likelihood of being a successful experience for the client; do cognitive restructuring within and after the exposure and use behavioral strategies (e.g., modeling, rehearsal, social reinforcement) to facilitate the exposure (see *Social Effectiveness Therapy for Children and Adolescents* by Beidel, Turner, and Morris; *Helping Your Anxious Child* by Rapee et al.). ▽

25. Assign the client a homework exercise in which he/she does an exposure exercise in a daily life situation and records responses; review and reinforce success, providing corrective feedback toward improvement. ▽

▽ 13. Increase participation in interpersonal or peer group activities. (26, 27)

26. Foster generalization and strengthening of new personal and interpersonal skills by encouraging the client to participate in extracurricular or positive peer-group activities (or assign "Greeting Peers" in the

Child Psychotherapy Homework Planner by Jongsma, Peterson, and McInnis). ▽

27. Build the client's one-to-one interactional skills by encouraging play dates and sleepovers (e.g., ask the client to invite a friend for an overnight visit and/or set up an overnight visit at a friend's home); review toward building on successes and problem-solving obstacles. ▽

▽ 14. Increase participation in school-related activities. (28)

28. Consult with school officials about ways to increase the client's socialization (e.g., raising the flag with group of peers, tutoring a more popular peer, pairing the client with popular peer on classroom assignments). ▽

▽ 15. Learn and implement strategies for building gains made in therapy and preventing relapses. (29, 30, 31, 32)

29. Discuss with the client the distinction between a lapse and relapse, associating a lapse with an initial and reversible return of symptoms, fears, or urges to avoid and relapse with the decision to return to fearful and avoidant patterns. ▽

30. Identify and rehearse with the client the management of future situations or circumstances in which lapses could occur. ▽

31. Instruct the client to routinely use strategies learned in therapy (e.g., cognitive restructuring, social skills, exposure) while building social interactions and relationships. ▽

32. Develop a "coping card" or other record (e.g., mp3 recording) on which coping strategies and other important information (e.g., "Pace your

breathing," "Focus on the task at hand," "You can manage it," "It will go away") are available for the client's later use. ▽

▽ 16. Family members learn skills that strengthen and support the client's positive behavior change. (33, 34, 35)

33. Conduct sessions with parents or parents and client in which parents are taught how to prompt and reward courageous behavior, empathetically ignore excessive complaining and other avoidant behaviors, manage their own anxieties, and model the behavior being taught in session. ▽

34. Teach the family problem-solving and conflict resolution skills for managing problems among themselves and between them and the client. ▽

35. Encourage the family to model constructive skills they have learned and model and praise the therapeutic skills the client is learning (e.g., calming, cognitive restructuring, nonavoidance of unrealistic fears). ▽

17. Identify strengths and interests that can be used to initiate social contacts and develop peer friendships. (36, 37)

36. Ask the client to list how he/she is like his/her peers; use this list to encourage contact with peers who share interests and abilities (or assign "Greeting Peers" in the *Child Psychotherapy Homework Planner* by Jongsma, Peterson, and McInnis).

37. Assist the client in identifying 5–10 of his/her strengths or interests and then instruct the client to utilize three strengths or interests in the upcoming week to initiate social contacts or develop peer friendships (or assign the "Show Your Strengths" exercise in the *Child*

Psychotherapy Homework Planner by Jongsma, Peterson, and McInnis).

18. Verbalize how current social anxiety and insecurities are associated with past rejection experiences and criticism from significant others. (38, 39)

38. Explore for a history of rejection experiences, harsh criticism, abandonment, or trauma that fostered the client's low self-esteem and social anxiety.

39. Encourage and support the client in verbally expressing and clarifying feelings associated with past rejection experiences, harsh criticism, abandonment, or trauma.

19. Express fears and anxiety in individual play therapy sessions or through mutual storytelling. (40, 41, 42)

40. Use child-centered play therapy principles (e.g., provide unconditional positive regard, display genuine interest, reflect feelings and fears, demonstrate trust in child's capacity for self-growth) to help the client overcome his/her social anxieties and feel more confident in social situations.

41. Employ the Ericksonian play therapy technique whereby the therapist speaks through a "wise doll" (or puppet) to an audience or other dolls (or puppet) to teach the client positive social skills that can be used to overcome shyness.

42. Use puppets, dolls, or stuffed animals to model positive social skills (e.g., greeting others, introducing self, verbalizing positive statements about self and others) that help the client feel more confident in social interactions.

20. Identify and express feelings in art. (43, 44)

43. Instruct the client to draw a picture or create a sculpture that reflects how he/she feels around

unfamiliar people when placed in new social settings.

44. Instruct the client to draw objects or symbols on a large piece of paper or poster board that symbolize his/her positive attributes; then discuss how the client can use strengths to establish peer friendships.

___. _____   ___. _____
    _____   _____
___. _____   ___. _____
    _____   _____
___. _____   ___. _____
    _____   _____

DIAGNOSTIC SUGGESTIONS

Using DSM-IV/ICD-9-CM:

Axis I:	300.23	Social Anxiety Disorder (Social Phobia)
	300.02	Generalized Anxiety Disorder
	309.21	Separation Anxiety Disorder
	300.4	Dysthymic Disorder
	296.xx	Major Depressive Disorder
	300.7	Body Dysmorphic Disorder
	_____	_____
	_____	_____
Axis II:	V71.09	No Diagnosis
	_____	_____
	_____	_____

Using DSM-5/ICD-9-CM/ICD-10-CM:

ICD-9-CM	ICD-10-CM	*DSM-5* Disorder, Condition, or Problem
300.23	F40.10	Social Anxiety Disorder (Social Phobia)
300.02	F41.1	Generalized Anxiety Disorder
309.21	F93.0	Separation Anxiety Disorder
300.4	F34.1	Persistent Depressive Disorder
296.xx	F32.x	Major Depressive Disorder, Single Episode
296.xx	F33.x	Major Depressive Disorder, Recurrent Episode
300.7	F45.22	Body Dysmorphic Disorder

Note: The ICD-9-CM codes are to be used for coding purposes in the United States through September 30, 2014. ICD-10-CM codes are to be used starting October 1, 2014. Some ICD-9-CM codes are associated with more than one ICD-10-CM and *DSM-5* disorder, condition, or problem. In addition, some ICD-9-CM disorders have been discontinued resulting in multiple ICD-9-CM codes being replaced by one ICD-10-CM code. Some discontinued ICD-9-CM codes are not listed in this table. See *Diagnostic and Statistical Manual of Mental Disorders* (2013) for details.

▽ Indicates that the Objective/Intervention is consistent with those found in evidence-based treatments.

SPECIFIC PHOBIA

BEHAVIORAL DEFINITIONS

1. Describes a persistent and unreasonable fear of a specific object or situation that promotes avoidance behaviors because an encounter with the phobic stimulus provokes an immediate anxiety response.
2. Avoids the phobic stimulus/feared environment or endures it with distress, resulting in interference of normal routines.
3. Acknowledges a persistence of fear despite recognition that the fear is unreasonable.
4. Sleep disturbed by dreams of the feared stimulus.
5. Dramatic fear reaction out of proportion to the phobic stimulus.
6. Parental reinforcement of the phobia by catering to the client's fear.

__. _____
_____
__. _____
_____
__. _____
_____

LONG-TERM GOALS

1. Reduce fear of the specific stimulus object or situation that previously provoked phobic anxiety.
2. Reduce phobic avoidance of the specific object or situation, leading to comfort and independence in moving around in public environment.
3. Eliminate interference in normal routines and remove distress from feared object or situation.
4. Live phobia-free while responding appropriately to life's fears.
5. Resolve the conflict underlying the phobia.

6. Learn to overcome fears of noise, darkness, people, wild animals, and crowds.

__. _____

_____

__. _____

_____

__. _____

_____

SHORT-TERM OBJECTIVES

1. Describe the history and nature of the phobia(s), complete with impact on functioning, and attempt to overcome it. (1, 2)

2. Complete psychological tests designed to assess features of the phobia. (3)

THERAPEUTIC INTERVENTIONS

1. Actively build a level of trust with the client that will promote the open sharing of thoughts and feelings, especially fearful ones (or assign "Expressions of Fear Through Art" from the *Child Psychotherapy Homework Planner* by Jongsma, Peterson, and McInnis).

2. Assess the client's phobic fear and avoidance, including the focus of fear, types of avoidance (e.g., distraction, escape, dependence on others), development of the phobia, and the negative impact on daily functioning; consider using a structured interview (e.g., *The Anxiety Disorders Interview Schedule for Children—Parent Version* or *Child Version*).

3. Administer to the client and/or parent an objective assessment instrument (e.g., from *Measures for Specific Phobia* by Antony) to further assess the depth and breadth of phobic responses.

3. Provide behavioral, emotional, and attitudinal information toward an assessment of specifiers relevant to a *DSM* diagnosis, the efficacy of treatment, and the nature of the therapy relationship. (4, 5, 6, 7, 8)

4. Assess the client's level of insight (syntonic versus dystonic) toward the "presenting problems" (e.g., demonstrates good insight into the problematic nature of the "described behavior," agrees with others' concern, and is motivated to work on change; demonstrates ambivalence regarding the "problem described" and is reluctant to address the issue as a concern; or demonstrates resistance regarding acknowledgment of the "problem described," is not concerned, and has no motivation to change).

5. Assess the client for evidence of research-based correlated disorders (e.g., oppositional defiant behavior with ADHD, depression secondary to an anxiety disorder) including vulnerability to suicide, if appropriate (e.g., increased suicide risk when comorbid depression is evident).

6. Assess for any issues of age, gender, or culture that could help explain the client's currently defined "problem behavior" and factors that could offer a better understanding of the client's behavior.

7. Assess for the severity of the level of impairment to the client's functioning to determine appropriate level of care (e.g., the behavior noted creates mild, moderate, severe, or very severe impairment in social, relational, vocational, or occupational endeavors); continuously assess

this severity of impairment as well as the efficacy of treatment (e.g., the client no longer demonstrates severe impairment but the presenting problem now is causing mild or moderate impairment).

8. Assess the client's home, school, and community for pathogenic care (e.g., persistent disregard for the child's emotional needs or physical needs, repeated changes in primary caregivers, limited opportunities for stable attachments, persistent harsh punishment or other grossly inept parenting).

▽ 4. Cooperate with an evaluation by a physician for psychotropic medication. (9, 10)

9. Arrange for an evaluation for a prescription of psychotropic medications if the client requests it or if the client is likely to be noncompliant with gradual exposure. ▽

10. Monitor the client for prescription compliance, side effects, and overall effectiveness of the medication; consult with the prescribing physician at regular intervals. ▽

▽ 5. Verbalize an understanding of information about phobias and their treatment. (11, 12, 13)

11. Discuss how phobias are very common, a natural but irrational expression of our fight-or-flight response, and are not a sign of weakness, but cause unnecessary distress and disability. ▽

12. Discuss with the client and parents a cognitive-behavioral conceptualization of how phobic fear is maintained by a "phobic cycle" of unwarranted fear and avoidance that precludes positive, corrective experiences with the feared object or

situation; discuss how treatment breaks the cycle by encouraging these corrective experiences (see *Helping Your Anxious Child* by Rapee et al.). ▽

13. Use a storytelling technique to help the client identify his/her fears, their origins, and their resolution (or read and process "Maurice Faces His Fears" from the *Child Psychotherapy Homework Planner* by Jongsma, Peterson, and McInnis). ▽

▽ 6. Verbalize an understanding of how thoughts, physical feelings, and behavioral actions contribute to anxiety and its treatment. (14, 15)

14. Discuss how phobias involve appraising threats unrealistically, bodily expressions of fear, and avoidance of what is threatening that interact in a cycle of fear and avoidance to maintain the problem. ▽

15. Discuss how exposure to the feared stimulus serves as an arena to desensitize learned fear, build confidence, and feel safer by building a new history of success experiences (e.g., *Helping Your Anxious Child* by Rapee et al.; *Freeing Your Child from Anxiety* by Chansky). ▽

▽ 7. Learn and implement calming skills to reduce and manage anxiety symptoms. (16, 17, 18)

16. Teach the client anxiety management skills (e.g., staying focused on behavioral goals, muscular relaxation, evenly paced diaphragmatic breathing, positive self-talk) to address anxiety symptoms that may emerge during encounters with phobic objects or situations. ▽

17. Assign the client a homework exercise in which he/she practices daily calming skills; review and reinforce success, providing corrective feedback for failure

(recommend parents and child read *The Relaxation and Stress Reduction Workbook for Kids* by Shapiro and Sprague). ▽

18. Use biofeedback techniques to facilitate the client's success at learning calming skills. ▽

▽ 8. Learn and implement applied tension skills to prevent fainting in response to blood, injection, or injury. (19, 20)

19. Teach the client applied tension in which he/she tenses neck and upper torso muscles to curtail blood flow out of the brain to help prevent fainting during encounters with phobic objects or situations involving blood, injection, or injury (see *Applied Tension, Exposure in vivo, and Tension-Only in the Treatment of Blood Phobia* by Ost, Fellenius, and Sterner). ▽

20. Assign the client a homework exercise in which he/she practices daily applied tension skills; review and reinforce success, providing corrective feedback for failure. ▽

▽ 9. Identify, challenge, and replace fearful self-talk with positive, realistic, and empowering self-talk. (21, 22, 23)

21. Explore the client's anxious self-talk and beliefs that mediate his/her fear response; teach him/her how to challenge the biases; assist him/her in replacing the biased messages with reality-based, positive alternatives. ▽

22. Assign the client a homework exercise in which he/she identifies fearful self-talk and creates reality-based alternatives (or assign "Replace Negative Thoughts With Positive Self-Talk" from the *Child Psychotherapy Homework Planner* by Jongsma, Peterson, and McInnis); review and reinforce success, providing corrective feedback for failure.

23. Use behavioral techniques (e.g., modeling, corrective feedback, imaginal rehearsal, social reinforcement) to teach the client positive self-talk and self-reward to facilitate the client's approach behavior to feared objects and situations and help him/her to manage anxiety during exposures. ▽

▽ 10. Participate in exposure therapy beginning with the identification of anxiety-producing situations and a list of rewards for therapeutic successes. (24)

24. Direct and assist the client and parents in construction of a hierarchy of anxiety-producing situations associated with the phobic response, as well as a list of rewards for successes. ▽

▽ 11. Client and parents develop and agree with a contract describing the client exposure goals and the rewards he/she will receive for accomplishing them. (25)

25. Help the client and parents to approve of a contingency contracting that details the client's exposure task (i.e., the step on the hierarchy) as well as the details of the rewards for successful completion. ▽

▽ 12. Parents learn and implement strategies to facilitate the client's success with exposure. (26, 27)

26. Teach parents strategies to facilitate the client's exposure or approach behavior toward feared objects or situations including positive reinforcement, shaping, extinction, following through, and consistency. ▽

27. Assign the parents to read about situational exposure in books or treatment manuals on specific phobias (e.g., *Helping Your Anxious Child* by Rapee et al.). ▽

▽ 13. Participate in gradual, repeated exposure to feared or avoided phobic objects or situations. (28, 29, 30)

28. Select initial exposures that have a high likelihood of being a successful experience for the client; develop a plan for managing the symptoms and rehearse the plan (or assign "Gradually Facing a Phobic Fear" in the *Adolescent*

Psychotherapy Homework Planner by Jongsma, Peterson, and McInnis). ▽

29. Conduct exposures in session with the client using graduated tasks, modeling, and reinforcement of the client's success until he/she can do the exposures unassisted. ▽

30. Assign the client a homework exercise in which he/she does situational exposures and records responses (see *Mastering Your Fears and Phobias—Workbook* by Antony, Craske, and Barlow; or *Living With Fear* by Marks); review and reinforce success or provide corrective feedback toward improvement. ▽

▽ 14. Learn and use imagery in conjunction with exposure for overcoming fear of the dark. (31)

31. Use an emotional imagery approach to overcoming fear of the dark in which systematic desensitization is conducted using a self-empowering story involving hero images used as the competing response instead of relaxation (see *The Effectiveness of Emotive Imagery in the Treatment of Darkness Phobia in Children* by Cornwall, Spence, and Schotte. ▽

▽ 15. Family members demonstrate support for the client as he/she engages in exposure therapy. (32, 33, 34, 35)

32. Conduct Family Anxiety Management sessions (see *FRIENDS Program for Children* series by Barrett, Lowry-Webster, and Turner) in which the family is taught how to prompt and reward courageous behavior, empathetically ignore excessive complaining and other avoidant behaviors, manage their own anxieties, and model the behavior being taught in session. ▽

33. Assist the family in overcoming the tendency to reinforce the client's phobia; as the phobia decreases, teach them constructive ways to reward the client's progress. ▽

34. Teach family members problem-solving and communication skills to assist the client's progress through therapy. ▽

35. Assign the parents to read and discuss with the client psychoeducational material from books or treatment manuals (e.g., see *Helping Your Anxious Child* by Rapee et al.). ▽

▽ 16. Implement relapse prevention strategies for managing possible future anxiety symptoms. (36, 37, 38, 39)

36. Discuss with the client the distinction between a lapse and relapse, associating a lapse with a temporary and reversible return of symptoms, fears, or urges to avoid and relapse with the decision to return to fearful and avoidant patterns. ▽

37. Identify and rehearse with the client the management of future situations or circumstances in which lapses could occur. ▽

38. Instruct the client to routinely use strategies learned in therapy (e.g., cognitive restructuring, exposure), building them into his/her life as much as possible. ▽

39. Develop a "coping card" on which coping strategies and other important information (e.g., "You're safe," "Pace your breathing," "Focus on the task at hand," "You can manage it," "Stay in the situation," "Let the anxiety pass") are written for the client's later use. ▽

17. Collect pleasant pictures or stories regarding the phobic stimulus and share them in therapy sessions. (40, 41)

40. Use pleasant pictures, readings, or storytelling about the feared object or situation as a means of desensitizing the client to the fear-producing stimulus.

41. Use humor, jokes, riddles, and stories to enable the client to see his/her situation/fears as not as serious as believed and to help instill hope without disrespecting or minimizing his/her fears.

18. Identify the symbolic significance of the phobic stimulus as a basis for fear. (42)

42. Probe, discuss, and interpret the possible symbolic meaning of the client's phobic stimulus object or situation.

19. Verbalize the separate realities of the irrationally feared object or situation and an emotionally painful experience from the past. (43)

43. Clarify and differentiate between the client's current irrational fear and past emotionally painful experiences that are evoked by the phobic stimulus.

20. Verbalize the feelings associated with a past emotionally painful situation that is connected to the phobia. (44, 45)

44. Encourage the client to share feelings from the past through active listening, unconditional positive regard, and questioning.

45. Reinforce the client's insight into the past emotional pain and its connection to present anxiety.

—. _____
   _____
—. _____
   _____
—. _____
   _____

—. _____
   _____
—. _____
   _____
—. _____
   _____

DIAGNOSTIC SUGGESTIONS

Using DSM-IV/ICD-9-CM:

Axis I:	300.00	Anxiety Disorder NOS
	300.29	Specific Phobia
	_____	_____
	_____	_____
Axis II:	V71.09	No Diagnosis
	_____	_____
	_____	_____

Using DSM-5/ICD-9-CM/ICD-10-CM:

ICD-9-CM	ICD-10-CM	*DSM-5* Disorder, Condition, or Problem
300.09	F41.8	Other Specified Anxiety Disorder
300.00	F41.9	Unspecified Anxiety Disorder
300.29	F40.xxx	Specific Phobia

Note: The ICD-9-CM codes are to be used for coding purposes in the United States through September 30, 2014. ICD-10-CM codes are to be used starting October 1, 2014. Some ICD-9-CM codes are associated with more than one ICD-10-CM and *DSM-5* disorder, condition, or problem. In addition, some ICD-9-CM disorders have been discontinued resulting in multiple ICD-9-CM codes being replaced by one ICD-10-CM code. Some discontinued ICD-9-CM codes are not listed in this table. See *Diagnostic and Statistical Manual of Mental Disorders* (2013) for details.

▽ Indicates that the Objective/Intervention is consistent with those found in evidence-based treatments.

SPEECH/LANGUAGE DISORDERS

BEHAVIORAL DEFINITIONS

1. Expressive language abilities, as measured by standardized tests, substantially below the expected level.
2. Expressive language deficits, as demonstrated by markedly limited vocabulary, frequent errors in tense, and difficulty recalling words or producing sentences of developmentally appropriate length or complexity.
3. Receptive and expressive language abilities significantly below the expected level as measured by a standardized test.
4. Receptive language deficits, as manifested by difficulty understanding simple words or sentences; certain types of words, such as spatial terms; or longer, complex statements.
5. Deficits in expressive and/or receptive language development that significantly interfere with academic achievement or social communication.
6. Consistent failure to produce developmentally expected speech sounds that significantly interfere with academic achievement or social communication.
7. Repeated stuttering as demonstrated by impairment in the normal fluency and time patterning of speech.
8. Selective mutism as characterized by a consistent failure to speak in specific social situations (e.g., school) despite speaking in other situations.
9. Social withdrawal and isolation in the peer group, school, or social settings where speaking is required.
10. Recurrent pattern of engaging in acting-out, aggressive, or negative attention-seeking behaviors when encountering frustration with speech or language problems.

—. _____
   _____
—. _____
   _____

—. _____

   _____

LONG-TERM GOALS

1. Accept the need for and actively cooperate with speech therapy.
2. Achieve the speech and language goals identified in the Individualized Educational Plan (IEP).
3. Improve the expressive and receptive language abilities to the level of capability.
4. Achieve mastery of the expected speech sounds that are appropriate for the age and dialect.
5. Eliminate stuttering; speak fluently and at a normal rate on a regular, consistent basis.
6. Develop an awareness and acceptance of speech/language problems so that there is consistent participation in discussions in the peer group, school, or social settings.
7. Parents establish realistic expectations of their child's speech/language abilities.
8. Resolve the core conflict that contributes to the emergence of selective mutism so that the client speaks consistently in social situations.

—. _____

   _____

—. _____

   _____

—. _____

   _____

SHORT-TERM OBJECTIVES

THERAPEUTIC INTERVENTIONS

1. Complete a speech/language evaluation to determine eligibility for special education services. (1)

1. Refer the client for a speech/language evaluation to assess the presence of a disorder and determine his/her eligibility for special education services.

2. Cooperate with a hearing or medical examination. (2)

2. Refer the client for a hearing and/or medical examination to rule out health problems that

3. Complete neuropsychological testing. (3)

4. Comply with a psycho-educational evaluation. (4)

5. Complete psychological testing. (5)

6. Take prescribed medication as directed by the physician. (6)

7. Provide behavioral, emotional, and attitudinal information toward an assessment of specifiers relevant to a *DSM* diagnosis, the efficacy of treatment, and the nature of the therapy relationship. (7, 8, 9, 10, 11)

may be interfering with his/her speech/language development.

3. Arrange for a neurological examination or neuropsychological evaluation to rule out the presence of organic factors that may contribute to the client's speech/language problem.

4. Arrange for a psychoeducational evaluation to assess the client's intellectual abilities and rule out the presence of other possible learning disorders.

5. Arrange for psychological testing to determine whether emotional factors or Attention-Deficit/Hyperactivity Disorder (ADHD) are interfering with the client's speech/language development.

6. Arrange for a medication evaluation if it is determined that an cmotional problem and/or ADHD are interfering with speech/language development.

7. Assess the client's lcvel of insight (syntonic versus dystonic) toward the "presenting problems" (e.g., demonstrates good insight into the problematic nature of the "described behavior," agrees with others' concern, and is motivated to work on change; demonstrates ambivalence regarding the "problem described" and is reluctant to address the issue as a concern; or demonstrates resistance regarding acknowledgment of the "problem described," is not concerned, and has no motivation to change).

8. Assess the client for evidence of research-based correlated disorders (e.g., oppositional defiant behavior with ADHD, depression secondary to an anxiety disorder) including vulnerability to suicide, if appropriate (e.g., increased suicide risk when comorbid depression is evident).

9. Assess for any issues of age, gender, or culture that could help explain the client's currently defined "problem behavior" and factors that could offer a better understanding of the client's behavior.

10. Assess for the severity of the level of impairment to the client's functioning to determine appropriate level of care (e.g., the behavior noted creates mild, moderate, severe, or very severe impairment in social, relational, vocational, or occupational endeavors); continuously assess this severity of impairment as well as the efficacy of treatment (e.g., the client no longer demonstrates severe impairment but the presenting problem now is causing mild or moderate impairment).

11. Assess the client's home, school, and community for pathogenic care (e.g., persistent disregard for the child's emotional needs or physical needs, repeated changes in primary caregivers, limited opportunities for stable attachments, persistent harsh punishment or other grossly inept parenting).

8. Comply with the recommendations made by a multidisciplinary evaluation team at school regarding speech/language or educational interventions. (12, 13)

9. Cooperate with the recommendations or interventions offered by the speech/language pathologist. (14)

10. Parents maintain regular communication with teachers and speech/language pathologist. (15)

11. Parents cease verbalizations of denial in the family system about the client's speech/language problem. (16, 17)

12. Parents comply and follow through with reward system to reinforce the client for improvements in speech/language development. (18, 19)

12. Attend an IEP committee meeting with the client's parents, teachers, and the speech/language pathologist to determine the client's eligibility for special education services; design intervention strategies that build on the client's strengths and compensate for weaknesses.

13. Consult with the client, his/her parents, teachers, and the speech/language pathologist about designing effective intervention strategies that build on the client's strengths and compensate for weaknesses.

14. Refer the client to a private speech/language pathologist for extra assistance in improving speech/language abilities.

15. Encourage the parents to maintain regular communication with the client's teachers and the speech/language pathologist to help facilitate speech/language development.

16. Educate the parents about the signs and symptoms of the client's speech/language disorder.

17. Challenge the parents' denial surrounding the client's speech/language problem so that the parents cooperate with the recommendations regarding placement and interventions for the client.

18. Consult with the speech/language pathologist about designing a reward system to reinforce the client for achieving goals in speech therapy and mastering new speech behaviors.

13. Parents increase the time spent with the client in activities that build and facilitate speech/language development. (20, 21, 22)

14. Parents recognize and verbally acknowledge their unrealistic expectations for or excessive pressure on the client to develop speech/language abilities. (23, 24, 25)

19. Encourage the parents to give frequent positive reinforcement to the client for his/her speech/language development.

20. Ask the parents to have the client read to them for 15 minutes four times weekly and then ask the client to retell the story to build his/her vocabulary, using a reward system to maintain the client's interest and motivation (or assign the "Home-Based Reading and Language Program" in the *Child Psychotherapy Homework Planner* by Jongsma, Peterson, and McInnis).

21. Give a directive for the client and his/her family to go on a weekly outing; afterward, require the client to share his/her feelings about the outing to increase his/her expressive and receptive language abilities (or assign the "Tell All About It" exercise in the *Child Psychotherapy Treatment Planner* by Jongsma, Peterson, and McInnis).

22. Instruct the parents to sing songs (e.g., nursery rhymes, lullabies, popular songs, songs related to the client's interests) with the client to help him/her feel more comfortable with his/her verbalizations in the home.

23. Observe parent-child interactions to assess how family communication patterns affect the client's speech/language development.

24. Assist the client and his/her parents to develop an understanding and acceptance

of the limitations surrounding the speech/language disorder.

25. Confront and challenge the parents about placing excessive or unrealistic pressure on the client to "talk right."

15. Parents recognize and terminate their tendency to speak for the client in social settings. (26, 27)

26. Explore parent-child interactions to determine whether the parents often speak or fill in pauses for the client to protect him/her from feeling anxious or insecure about speech.

27. Encourage the parents to allow the client to take the lead more often in initiating and sustaining conversations.

16. Improve the lines of communication in the family system. (28)

28. Teach effective communication skills (e.g., active listening, reflecting feelings, "I statements") to facilitate the client's speech/language development.

17. Increase the frequency of social interactions in which the client takes the lead in initiating or sustaining conversations. (29, 30, 31, 32)

29. Gently confront the client's pattern of withdrawing in social settings to avoid experiencing anxiety about speech problems.

30. Assign the client the task of contributing one comment to classroom discussion each day to increase his/her confidence in speaking before others.

31. Assign the client the task of sharing toys or objects during show-and-tell to increase his/her expressive language abilities.

32. Consult with speech/language pathologist and teachers about designing a program in which the client orally reads passages of gradually increasing length or difficulty in classroom; praise and reinforce the client's effort.

18. Decrease level of anxiety associated with speech/language problems. (33, 34, 35)

33. Teach the client positive coping mechanisms (e.g., deep-breathing and muscle relaxation techniques, positive self-talk, cognitive restructuring) that can be used when he/she encounters frustration with speech/language problems.

34. Encourage the client to verbalize his/her insecurities about speech/language problems (or assign the client to read and complete the exercise "Shauna's Song" in the *Child Psychotherapy Homework Planner* by Jongsma, Peterson, and McInnis).

35. Use the mutual storytelling technique whereby the client and therapist alternate telling stories through the use of puppets, dolls, or stuffed animals: The therapist first models constructive ways to handle anxiety or frustrations surrounding speech/language problems, then the client follows by telling a story with similar characters or themes.

19. Decrease the frequency and severity of aggressive acting-out and negative attention-seeking behaviors due to speech/language frustration. (36)

36. Teach the client self-control strategies (e.g., cognitive restructuring, positive self-talk, "stop, look, listen, and think") to inhibit the impulse to act out when encountering frustration with speech/language problems.

20. Decrease the frequency and severity of dysfluent speech. (37, 38, 39)

37. Teach the client effective anxiety-reduction techniques (relaxation, positive self-talk, cognitive restructuring) to decrease anticipatory anxiety in social settings and help control stuttering (recommend *The Relaxation and Stress Reduction*

Workbook for Kids by Shapiro and Sprague).

38. Assign the client to initiate three social contacts per day with peers to help him/her face and work through anxieties and insecurities related to stuttering in the presence of peers (see the "Greeting Peers" exercise in the *Child Psychotherapy Treatment Planner* by Jongsma, Peterson, and McInnis).

39. Use role-playing and positive coping strategies (e.g., positive self-talk, cognitive restructuring) to extinguish the client's anxiety that triggers stuttering in various social settings (e.g., reading in front of class, talking on the phone, introducing self to unfamiliar peer).

21. Comply with systematic desensitization program to decrease the rate of speech and control stuttering. (40)

40. Consult with a speech/language pathologist about designing an *in vivo* desensitization program (e.g., using deep muscle relaxation while exposing the client to gradually more anxiety-producing situations) to help the client overcome anxiety associated with stuttering.

22. Express feelings in individual play therapy sessions and artwork. (41, 42)

41. Employ psychoanalytic play therapy approaches (e.g., allow child to take lead; explore etiology of unconscious conflicts, fixations, or developmental arrests; interpret resistance, transference, and core anxieties) to help the client work through his/her feelings surrounding past loss, trauma, or victimization that contributes to selective mutism.

23. Verbalize an understanding of how selective mutism is associated with past loss, trauma, or victimization. (43, 44)

42. Use art therapy (e.g., drawing, painting, sculpting) in early stages of therapy to establish rapport and help the client with selective mutism begin to express his/her feelings through artwork.

43. Assess the family dynamics that contribute to the client's refusal to use speech in some situations.

44. Explore the client's background history of loss, trauma, or victimization that contributed to the emergence of selective mutism.

___. _____   ___. _____
   _____   _____
___. _____   ___. _____
   _____   _____
___. _____   ___. _____
   _____   _____

DIAGNOSTIC SUGGESTIONS

Using DSM-IV/ICD-9-CM:

Axis I:	315.31	Expressive Language Disorder
	315.32	Mixed Receptive-Expressive Language Disorder
	315.39	Phonological Disorder
	307.0	Stuttering
	307.9	Communication Disorder NOS
	313.23	Selective Mutism
	309.21	Separation Anxiety Disorder
	300.23	Social Phobia
	_____	_____
	_____	_____

Axis II: 317   Mild Mental Retardation
                 V62.89   Borderline Intellectual Functioning
                 V71.09   No Diagnosis

_____   _____

_____   _____

Using DSM-5/ICD-9-CM/ICD-10-CM:

ICD-9-CM	ICD-10-CM	*DSM-5* Disorder, Condition, or Problem
315.31	F80.9	Language Disorder
315.39	F80.0	Speech Sound Disorder
307.0	F80.81	Childhood-Onset Fluency Disorder (Stuttering)
307.9	F80.9	Unspecified Communication Disorder
313.23	F94.0	Selective Mutism
309.21	F93.0	Separation Anxiety Disorder
300.23	F40.10	Social Anxiety Disorder (Social Phobia)
317	F70	Intellectual Disability, Mild
V62.89	R41.83	Borderline Intellectual Functioning

Note: The ICD-9-CM codes are to be used for coding purposes in the United States through September 30, 2014. ICD-10-CM codes are to be used starting October 1, 2014. Some ICD-9-CM codes are associated with more than one ICD-10-CM and *DSM-5* disorder, condition, or problem. In addition, some ICD-9-CM disorders have been discontinued resulting in multiple ICD-9-CM codes being replaced by one ICD-10-CM code. Some discontinued ICD-9-CM codes are not listed in this table. See *Diagnostic and Statistical Manual of Mental Disorders* (2013) for details.

Appendix A

BIBLIOTHERAPY SUGGESTIONS

Many references are made throughout the chapters to a therapeutic homework resource that was developed by the authors as a corollary to the *Child Psychotherapy Treatment Planner* (Jongsma, Peterson, McInnis, and Bruce). This frequently cited homework resource book is:

Jongsma, A. E., Peterson, L. M., & McInnis, W. P. (2014). *Child psychotherapy homework planner* (5th ed.). Hoboken, NJ: Wiley.

There are a few references made to these homework planners that are part of the PracticePlanner series:

Jongsma, A. E., Peterson, L. M., & McInnis, W. P. (2014). *Adolescent psychotherapy homework planner* (5th ed.). Hoboken, NJ: Wiley.
Jongsma, A. E. (2014). *Adult psychotherapy homework planner* (5th ed.). Hoboken, NJ: Wiley.
Knapp, S. (2005). *Parenting skills homework planner*. Hoboken, NJ: Wiley.

General Self-Help Book Source

http://www.bookinhand.com.au/catandprice.htm

Academic Underachievement

Bloom, J. (1991). *Help me to help my child: A sourcebook for parents of learning disabled children.* Boston, MA: Little, Brown.
Lavoie, R. (2008). *The motivation breakthrough: 6 secrets to turning on the tuned-out child.* New York, NY: Touchstone.

Martin, M., & Greenwood-Waltman, C. (Eds.). (1995). *Solve your child's school-related problems.* New York, NY: HarperCollins.

Peters, R. (2000). *Overcoming underachieving: A simple plan to boost your kids' grades and end the homework hassles.* New York, NY: Broadway.

Romain, T. (2005). *How to do homework without throwing up.* Minneapolis, MN: Free Spirit.

Schumm, J. (2005). *How to help your child with homework.* Minneapolis, MN: Free Spirit.

Silverman, S. (2001). *13 steps to better grades.* Plainview, NY: Childswork/Childsplay.

Smith, S. (1995). *No easy answers: The learning disabled child at home and at school.* New York, NY: Bantam Books.

Adoption

Burlingham-Brown, B. (1998). *Why didn't she keep me?: Answers to the question every adopted child asks.* Lanham, MD: Taylor Trade.

Covey, S. (1999). *The 7 habits of highly effective families: Building a beautiful family culture in a turbulent world.* New York, NY: Simon & Schuster.

Eldridge, S. (1999). *Twenty things adopted kids wish their adoptive parents knew.* Brooklyn, NY: Delta.

Forehand, R., & Long, N. (2010). *Parenting the strong-willed child: The clinically proven five-week program for parents of two- to six-year-olds.* New York, NY: McGraw-Hill.

Girard, L. W. (1986). *Adoption is for always.* Niles, IL: Albert Whitmore.

Jarrett, C. (1994). *Helping children cope with separation and loss.* Boston, MA: Harvard Common Press.

Kazdin, A. (2009). *The Kazdin method for parenting the defiant child.* New York, NY: Mariner.

Krementz, J. (1996). *How it feels to be adopted.* New York, NY: Alfred Knopf.

Markman, H., Stanley, S., & Blumberg, S. (2010). *Fighting for your marriage.* San Francisco, CA: Jossey-Bass.

Medina, L. (1984). *Making sense of adoption.* New York, NY: Harper & Row.

Moser, A. (1994). *Don't rant and rave on Wednesdays! The children's anger-control book.* Kansas City, MO: Landmark Editions.

Parr, T. (2007). *We belong together: A book about adoption and families.* New York, NY: Little, Brown.

Russell, M. (2010). *Adoption wisdom: A guide to the issues and feelings of adoption.* Lavalette, WV: Broken Branch Productions.

Schooler, J., & Atwood, T. (2008). *The whole life adoption book: Realistic advice for building a healthy adoptive family.* Colorado Springs, CO: NavPress.

Watkins, M. & Fisher, S. (1995). *Talking with young children about adoption.* New Haven, CT: Yale University Press.

Whitehouse, E., & Pudney, W. (1998). *A volcano in my tummy: Helping children to handle anger: A resource book for parents, caregivers and teachers.* Gabriola Island, British Columbia, Canada: New Society.

Anger Control Problems

Canter, L., & Canter, P. (1993). *Assertive discipline for parents.* New York, NY: Morrow.

Forehand, R., & Long, N. (2010). *Parenting the strong-willed child: The clinically proven five week program for parents of two- to six-year-olds.* New York, NY: McGraw-Hill.

Green, R. (2010). *The explosive child: A new approach for understanding and parenting easily frustrated, chronically inflexible children.* New York, NY: Harper.

Harvey, P., & Penzo, J. K. (2009). *Parenting a child who has intense emotions: Dialectical behavior therapy skills to help your child regulate emotional outbursts and aggressive behaviors.* Oakland, CA: New Harbinger.

Huebner, P. (2007). *What to do when your temper flares: A kid's guide to overcoming problems with anger.* New York, NY: Magination Press.

Kapalka, G. (2007). *Parenting your out-of-control child: An effective, easy-to-use program for teaching self-control.* Oakland, CA: New Harbinger.

Maag, J. W. (1996). *Parenting without punishment: Making problem behavior work for you.* Philadelphia, PA: Charles Press.

Moser, A. (1994). *Don't rant and rave on Wednesdays! The children's anger-control book.* Kansas City, MO: Landmark Editions.

Nemeth, D., Ray, K., & Schexnayder, M. (2003). *Helping your angry child: A workbook for you and your family.* Oakland, CA: New Harbinger.

Patterson, G. R. (1976). *Living with children: New methods for parents and teachers.* Champaign, IL: Research Press.

Phelan, T. (2010). *1-2-3 magic: Effective discipline for children 2–12.* Glen Ellyn, IL: ParentMagic.

Plummer, D. (2008). *Anger management games for children.* Philadelphia, PA: Jessica Kingsley.

Shapiro, L. E. (1994a). *Anger control tool kit: All the information you need to help the angry child in school and at home* [video and book]. King of Prussia, PA: Center for Applied Psychology.

Shapiro, L. E. (1994b). *The very angry day that Amy didn't have.* Plainview, NY: Childswork/Childsplay.

Shapiro, L. E. (1995). *Sometimes I like to fight, but I don't do it much anymore: A self-esteem book for children with difficulty in controlling their anger.* Plainview, NY: Childswork/Childsplay.

Shapiro, L., Pelta-Heller, Z., & Greenwald, A. (2008). *I'm not bad, I'm just mad: A workbook to help kids control their anger.* Oakland, CA: New Harbinger.

Shore, H. (1995). *The angry monster workbook.* Plainview, NY: Childswork/Childsplay.

Anxiety

Allen, J., & Klein, R. (1997). *Ready . . . Set . . . R.E.L.A.X.* Watertown, WI: Inner Coaching.

Barrett, P. M., Lowry-Webster, H., & Turner. C. (2000). *Friends for children participant workbook* (2nd ed.). Brisbane: Australian Academic Press.

Block, D. (2003). *The power of positive talk: Words to help every child succeed.* Minneapolis, MN: Free Spirit.

Chansky, T. (2004). *Freeing your child from anxiety: Powerful, practical solutions to overcome your child's fears, worries, and phobias.* New York, NY: Three Rivers Press.

Crist, J. J. (2004). *What to do when you're scared and worried: A guide for kids.* Minneapolis, MN: Free Spirit.

Dacey, J. S., & Fiore, L. B. (2001). *Your anxious child: How parents and teachers can relieve anxiety in children.* San Francisco, CA: Jossey-Bass.

Deaton, W. (2003). *My own thoughts and feelings (for boys): A young boy's workbook about exploring problems.* Alameda, CA: Hunter House.

Deaton, W. (2003). *My own thoughts and feelings (for girls): A young girl's workbook about exploring problems.* Alameda, CA: Hunter House.

Huebner, D. (2005). *What to do when you worry too much: A kid's guide to overcoming anxiety.* Washington, DC: Magination Press.

Kendall, P., & Hedtke, K. (2006). *Coping C.A.T. workbook.* Ardmore, PA: Workbook.

Manassis, K. (2008). *Keys to parenting your anxious child.* Hauppauge, NY: Barron's.

McCurry, C. (2009). *Parenting your anxious child with mindfulness and acceptance: A powerful new approach to overcoming fear, panic, and worry using acceptance and commitment therapy.* Oakland, CA: New Harbinger.

Moser, A. (1988). *Don't pop your cork on Mondays! The children's anti-stress book.* Kansas City, MO: Landmark Editions.

Rapee, R., Wignall, A., Spense, S., Cobham, V., & Lyneham, H. (2008). *Helping your anxious child: A step-by-step guide for parents.* Oakland, CA: New Harbinger.

Schachter, R., & McCauley, C. S. (1989). *When your child is afraid.* New York, NY: Touchstone.

Shapiro, L., & Sprague, R. (2009). *The relaxation and stress reduction workbook for kids: Help for children to cope with stress, anxiety, and transitions.* Oakland, CA: New Harbinger.

Sisemore, T. (2008). *I bet I won't fret: A workbook to help children with generalized anxiety disorder.* Oakland, CA: New Harbinger.

Spencer, E., DuPont, R., & DuPont, C. (2003). *The anxiety cure for kids: A guide for parents.* Hoboken, NJ: Wiley.

Stallard, P. (2002). *Think good–feel good: A cognitive behaviour therapy workbook for children.* Hoboken, NJ: Wiley.

Wagner, A. P. (2005). *Worried no more: Help and hope for anxious children.* Rochester, NY: Lighthouse Press.

Reactive Attachment/Disinhibited Social Engagement Disorder

Ayres, A. J. (2005). *Sensory integration and the child.* Los Angeles, CA: Western Psychological Services.

Chara, K., & Chara, P. (2005). *A safe place for Caleb: An interactive book for kids, teens and adults with issues of attachment, grief, loss or early trauma.* Philadelphia, PA: Jessica Kingsley.

Forbes, H., & Post, B. (2006). *Beyond consequences, logic, and control: A love-based approach to helping attachment-challenged children with severe behaviors.* Boulder, CO: Beyond Consequences Institute.

Gil, E. (1995). *Outgrowing the pain.* New York, NY: Dell Publishing.

Green, R. (2009). *The explosive child: A new approach for understanding and parenting easily frustrated, chronically inflexible children.* New York, NY: Harper.

Greenspan, S. (1996). *The challenging child.* New York, NY: De Capo Press.

Jewett, C. (1994). *Helping children cope with separation and loss.* Harvard, MA: Harvard Common Press.

Kazdin, A. (2009). *The Kazdin method for parenting the defiant child.* New York, NY: Mariner.

Kranowitz, C., & Miller, C. (2006). *The out-of-sync child.* New York, NY: Perigree Trade.

Markman, H., Stanley, S., & Blumberg, S. (2010). *Fighting for your marriage.* San Francisco, CA: Jossey-Bass.

Moser, A. (1994). *Don't rant and rave on Wednesdays! The children's anger-control book.* Kansas City, MO: Landmark Editions.

Moser, A. (1996). *Don't despair on Thursdays! The children's grief-management book.* Kansas City, MO: Landmark Editions.

Shapiro, L., & Sprague, R. (2009). *The relaxation and stress reduction workbook for kids: Help for children to cope with stress, anxiety, and transitions.* Oakland, CA: New Harbinger.

Mercer, J. (2005). *Understanding attachment: Parenting, child care, and emotional development.* Westport, CT: Praeger.

Turecki, S., & Tonner, L. (2000). *The difficult child.* New York, NY: Bantam Books.

Attention-Deficit/Hyperactivity Disorder (ADHD)

Barkley, R. A. (2000). *Taking charge of ADHD: The complete authoritative guide for parents.* New York, NY: Guilford Press.

Bertin, M. (2011). *The family ADHD solution: A scientific approach to maximizing your child's attention and minimizing parental stress.* New York, NY: Palgrave Macmillan.

Flick, G. L. (1996). *Power parenting for ADD/ADHD children: A practical parent's guide for managing difficult behaviors.* Englewood Cliffs, NJ: Prentice Hall.

Flick, G. L. (2002). *ADD/ADHD behavior.* Hoboken, NJ: Wiley.

Forehand, R., & Long, N. (2002). *Parenting the strong-willed child: The clinically proven five-week program for parents of two- to six-year-olds.* New York, NY: McGraw-Hill.

Frank, K. (2001). *ADHD: 102 practical strategies for "reducing the deficit."* Chapin, SC: Youthlight.

Kazdin, A. (2009). *The Kazdin method for parenting the defiant child.* New York, NY: Mariner.

Monastra, V. (2005). *Parenting children with ADHD: 10 lessons that medicine cannot teach.* Washington, DC: American Psychological Association.

Nadeau, K., & Dixon, E. (2004). *Learning to slow down & pay attention: A book for kids about ADHD.* New York, NY: Magination Press.

Patterson, G. R. (1976). *Living with children: New methods for parents and teachers.* Champaign, IL: Research Press.

Phelan, T. (2010). *1-2-3 magic: Effective discipline for children 2–12.* Glen Ellyn, IL: ParentMagic.

Power, T. G., Karustis, J. L., & Habboushe, D. F. (2001). *Homework success for children with ADHD: A family-school intervention program.* New York, NY: Guilford Press.

Quinn, P., & Stern, J. (2009). *Putting on the brakes: Activity book for kids with ADD or ADHD.* New York, NY: Magination Press.

Rief, S. (2008). *The ADD/ADHD checklist: A practical reference for parents and teachers.* Hoboken, NJ: Wiley.

Shapiro, L. E. (1993). *Sometimes I drive my mom crazy, but I know she's crazy about me.* Plainview, NY: Childswork/Childsplay.

Shapiro, L. E. (1994). *The very angry day that Amy didn't have.* Plainview, NY: Childswork/Childsplay.

Shapiro, L. E. (2010). *The ADHD workbook for kids: Helping children gain self-confidence, social skills, and self-control.* Oakland, CA: New Harbinger.

Silverman, S. (2001). *13 steps to better grades.* Plainview, NY: Childswork/Childsplay.

Autism Spectrum Disorder

Etlinger, R., & Tomassi, M. (2005). *To be me.* Los Angeles, CA: Creative Therapy Store.

Faherty, C. (2010). *Asperger's: What does it mean to me?* Arlington, TX: Future Horizons.

Koegel, R. L., & Koegel, L. K. (2006). *Pivotal response treatments for autism communication, social, and academic development.* Baltimore, MD: Brookes.

Koegel, R. L., & Koegel, L. K. (2012). *The PRT pocket guide: Pivotal response treatment for autism spectrum disorders.* Baltimore, MD: Brookes.

Lockshin, S., Gillis, J., & Romanczyk, R. (2005). *Helping your child with autism spectrum disorder: A step-by-step workbook for families.* Oakland, CA: New Harbinger Publications.

Marcus, L. M., & Schopler, E. (1997). Parents as Co-therapists with Autistic Children. In J. Briesmeister & C. Schaeffer (Eds.), *Handbook of parent training: Parents as co-therapists for children's behavior problems.* New York, NY: Wiley.

Notbohm, E., & Zysk, V. (2010). *1001 great ideas for teaching and raising children with autism or Asperger's.* Arlington, TX: Future Horizons.

Notbohm, E. (2012). *Ten things every child with autism wishes you knew.* Arlington, TX: Future Horizons.

Sastry, A., & Aguirre, B. (2012). *Parenting your child with autism:*

Practical solutions, strategies, and advice for helping your family. Oakland, CA: New Harbinger.

Stillman, W. (2010). *The everything parent's guide to children with Asperger's syndrome: The sound advice and reliable answers you need to help your child succeed.* Cincinnati, OH: Adams Media.

Tillon-Jameson, A. (2010). *The everything parents' guide to children with autism.* Cincinnati, OH: Adams Media.

Welton, J. (2010). *Can I tell you about Asperger syndrome?: A guide for friends and family.* Philadelphia, PA: Jessica Kingsley.

Wine, A. (2005). *What it is to be me!: An Asperger kid book.* Fairdale, KY: Fairdale Publishing.

Blended Family

Burt, M. (1989). *Stepfamilies stepping ahead: An eight-step program for successful family living.* Auburn, AL: National Stepfamily Resource Center.

Covey, S. (1997). *The 7 habits of highly effective families.* New York, NY: Golden Books.

Deal, R. (2006). *The smart stepfamily: Seven steps to a healthy family.* Grand Rapids, MI: Bethany House.

Dudley, S. (2009). *Blended family advice: A step-by-step guide to help blended families become stronger and successful.* Bloomington, IN: Xlibris.

Fassler, D., Lash, M., & Ives, S. (1988). *Changing families: A guide for kids and grown-ups.* Burlington, VT: Waterfront Books.

Markman, H., Stanley, S., & Blumberg, S. (2010). *Fighting for your marriage.* San Francisco, CA: Jossey-Bass.

Newman, M. C. (1994). *Stepfamily realities: How to overcome difficulties and have a happy family.* Oakland, CA: New Harbinger.

Ricci, R. (2006). *Mom's house, Dad's house for kids: Feeling at home in one home or two.* New York, NY: Touchstone.

Schab, L., & Van Patter, B. (1995). *My dad is getting married again.* Plainview, NY: Childswork/Childsplay.

Seuss, Dr. (1961). *The Sneetches and other stories.* New York, NY: Random House.

Visher, E., & Visher, J. (1991). *How to win as a stepfamily.* New York, NY: Routledge.

Wisdom, S., & Green, J. (2002). *Stepcoupling: Creating and sustaining a strong marriage in today's blended family.* New York, NY: Three Rivers Press.

Bullying/Intimidation Perpetrator

Anthony, M., & Lindert, R. (2010). *Little girls can be mean: Four steps to bully-proof girls in the early grades.* New York, NY: St. Martin's Griffin.

Green, S. (2010). *Don't pick on me: Help for kids to stand up to and deal with bullies.* Oakland, CA: New Harbinger.

Hall, K., & Cook, M. (2011). *The power of validation: Arming your child against bullying, peer pressure, addiction, self-harm, and out-of-control emotions.* Oakland, CA: New Harbinger.

Ludwig, T. (2012). *Confessions of a former bully.* New York, NY: Dragonfly Books.

Ragona, S., & Pentel, C. (2004). *Eliminating bullying.* Chapin, SC: Youth Light.

Schab, L. (2009). *Cool, calm, and confident: A workbook to help kids learn assertiveness skills.* Oakland, CA: New Harbinger.

Shapiro, L. (1994). *The very angry day that Amy didn't have.* Plainview, NY: Childswork/Childsplay.

Shapiro, L. (1995). *Sometimes I like to fight, but I don't do it much anymore.* Plainview, NY: Childswork/Childsplay.

Voors, W. (2000). *The parents' book about bullying.* Center City, MN: Hazelden Information Education.

Webster-Doyle, T. (1999). *Why is everybody always picking on me? A guide to understanding bullies for young people.* Boston, MA: Weatherhill.

Conduct Disorder/Delinquency

Bloomquist, M. (2005). *Skills training for children with behavior problems: A parent and practitioner guidebook.* New York, NY: Guilford Press.

Canter, L., & Canter, P. (1993). *Assertive discipline for parents: A proven, step-by-step approach to solving everyday behavior problems.* New York, NY: Morrow.

Carr, T. (2004). *131 creative strategies for reaching children with anger problems.* Chapin, SC: Youthlight.

Forehand, R., & Long, N. (2010). *Parenting the strong-willed child: The clinically proven five-week program for parents of two- to six-year-olds.* New York, NY: McGraw-Hill.

Green, R. (2010). *The explosive child: A new approach for understanding and parenting easily frustrated, chronically inflexible children.* New York, NY: Harper.

Kazdin, A. (2009). *The Kazdin method for parenting the defiant child.* New York, NY: Mariner.

Maag, J. W. (1996). *Parenting without punishment: Making problem behavior work for you.* Philadelphia, PA: Charles Press.

Metcalf, L. (1997). *Parenting towards solutions: How parents can use skills they already have to raise responsible, loving kids.* Englewood Cliffs, NJ: Prentice Hall.

Patterson, G. R. (1977). *Living with children: New methods for parents and teachers.* Champaign, IL: Research Press.

Patterson, G. R. (1982). *Coercive family process.* Eugene, OR: Castalia.

Phelan, T. (2010). *1-2-3 magic: Effective discipline for children 2–12.* Glen Ellyn, IL: ParentMagic.

Schab, L. (2009). *Cool, calm, and confident: A workbook to help kids learn assertiveness skills.* Oakland, CA: New Harbinger.

Shapiro, L. (1994). *The very angry day that Amy didn't have.* Plainview, NY: Childswork/Childsplay.

Shapiro, L. (1995). *Sometimes I like to fight, but I don't do it much anymore.* Plainview, NY: Childswork/Childsplay.

Shore, H. (1991). *Angry monster workbook.* Plainview, NY: Childswork/Childsplay.

Depression

Barnard, M. (2003). *Helping your depressed child: A step-by-step guide for parents.* Oakland, CA: New Harbinger.

Burns, D. D. (1999). *Feeling good: The new mood therapy.* New York, NY: Harper.

Chansky, T. (2008). *Freeing your child from negative thinking: Powerful, practical strategies to build a lifetime of resilience, flexibility, and happiness.* Cambridge, MA: De Capo Press.

Cytryn, L., & McKnew, D. (1998). *Growing up sad: Childhood depression and its treatment.* New York, NY: W. W. Norton.

Fassler, D. G., & Dumas, L. S. (1998). *"Help me, I'm sad": Recognizing, preventing, and treating childhood and adolescent depression.* New York, NY: Penguin.

Graham P., & Hughes, C. (2005). *So young, so sad, so listen.* London, England: RC Psych.

Hamil, S. (2008). *My feeling better workbook: Help for kids who are sad and depressed.* Oakland, CA: New Harbinger.

Ingersoll, B., & Goldstein, S. (2001). *Lonely, sad and angry: How to help your unhappy child.* North Branch, MN: Specialty Press.

Kendall, P., & Hedtke, K. (2006). *Coping C.A.T. workbook.* Ardmore, PA: Workbook.

Merrell, K. W. (2008). *Helping students overcome depression and anxiety: A practical guide.* New York, NY: Guilford Press.

Miller, J. A. (1999). *The child depression sourcebook.* New York, NY: McGraw-Hill.

Moser, A. (1994). *Don't despair on Thursdays! The children's grief-management book.* Kansas City, MO: Landmark Editions.

Ratcliffe, J. (2002). *Sometimes I get sad (but now I know what makes me happy).* Plainview, NY: Childswork/Childsplay.

Riley, D. (2001). *Depressed child: A parent's guide for rescuing kids.* Dallas, TX: Taylor Trade.

Schab, L. (2009). *Cool, calm, and confident: A workbook to help kids learn assertiveness skills.* Oakland, CA: New Harbinger.

Shapiro, L., & Sprague, R. (2009). *The relaxation and stress reduction workbook for kids: Help for children to cope with stress, anxiety, and transitions.* Oakland, CA: New Harbinger Publications.

Stallard, P. (2002). *Think good–feel good: A cognitive behaviour therapy workbook for children.* Hoboken, NJ: Wiley.

Stark, K. D., Schnoebelen, S., Simpson, J., Hargrave, J., Glenn, R., & Molnar, J. (2006). *Children's workbook for ACTION.* Broadmore, PA: Workbook.

Stark, K. D., Simpson, J., Yancy, M., & Molnar, J. (2006). *Parent's workbook for ACTION.* Ardmore, PA: Workbook.

Disruptive/Attention-Seeking

Becker, W. (1971). *Parents are teachers: A child management program.* Champaign, IL: Research Press.

Canter, L., & Canter, P. (1993). *Assertive discipline for parents: A proven, step-by-step approach to solving everyday behavior problems.* New York, NY: Morrow.

Forehand, R., & Long, N. (2010). *Parenting the strong-willed child: The clinically proven five-week program for parents of two- to six-year-olds.* New York, NY: McGraw-Hill.

Green, R. (2010). *The explosive child: A new approach for understanding and parenting easily frustrated, chronically inflexible children.* New York, NY: Harper.

Kaye, D. (2005). *Family rules: Raising responsible children.* Bloomington, IN: iUniverse.

Kazdin, A. (2009). *The Kazdin method for parenting the defiant child.* New York, NY: Mariner.

Maag, J. W. (1996). *Parenting without punishment: Making problem behavior work for you.* Philadelphia, PA: Charles Press.

Metcalf, L. (1997). *Parenting towards solutions: How parents can use skills they already have to raise responsible, loving kids.* Englewood Cliffs, NJ: Prentice Hall.

Patterson, G. R. (1976). *Living with children: New methods for parents and teachers.* Champaign, IL: Research Press.

Phelan, T. (2010). *1-2-3 magic: Effective discipline for children 2–12.* Glen Ellyn, IL: ParentMagic.

Shapiro, L. E. (1995). *How I learned to think things through.* Plainview, NY: Childswork/Childsplay.

Divorce Reaction

Brown, L., & Brown, M. (1988). *Dinosaurs divorce: A guide for changing families.* New York, NY: Little, Brown.

Gardner, R. (1985). *The boys and girls book about divorce.* New York, NY: Bantam Books.

Jewett, C. (1994). *Helping children cope with separation and loss.* Harvard, MA: Harvard Common Press.

Jones-Soderman, J., & Quattrocchi, A. (2006). *How to talk to your children about divorce.* Scottsdale, AZ: Family Mediation Center.

Kazdin, A. (2009). *The Kazdin method for parenting the defiant child.* New York, NY: Mariner.

Lansky, V. (1997). *It's not your fault, Koko Bear: A read-together book for parents and young children during divorce.* Deephaven, MN: Book Peddlers.

Levins, S. (2006). *Was it the chocolate pudding?: A story for little kids about divorce.* Washington, DC: Magination Press.

Lowry, D. (2002). *What can I do?: A book for children of divorce.* Washington, DC: Magination Press.

Phelan, T. (2010). *1-2-3 magic: Effective discipline for children 2–12.* Glen Ellyn, IL: ParentMagic.

Ransom, J. (2000). *I don't want to talk about it.* Washington, DC: Magination Press.

Schab, L. (2008). *The divorce workbook for children: Help for kids to overcome difficult family changes and grow up happy.* Oakland, CA: New Harbinger.

Schmitz, T. (2008). *Standing on my own two feet: A child's affirmation of love in the midst of divorce.* New York, NY: Price Stern Sloan.

Thayer, E., & Zimmerman, J. (2001). *The co-parenting survival guide: Letting go of conflict after a difficult divorce.* Oakland, CA: New Harbinger.

Enuresis/Encopresis

Azrin, N. (1989). *Toilet training in less than a day.* New York, NY: Pocket Books.

Bennett, H. (2005). *Waking up dry: A guide to help children overcome bedwetting.* Elk Grove Village, IL: American Academy of Pediatrics.

Bennett, H. (2007). *It hurts when I poop!: A story for children who are scared to use the potty.* Washington, DC: Magination Press.

Crane, T. (2006). *Potty train your child in just one day: Proven secrets of the potty pro.* New York, NY: Fireside.

Hodges, S., & Schlosberg, S. (2012). *It's no accident: Breakthrough solutions to your child's wetting, constipation, UTIs, and other potty problems.* Guilford, CT: Lyons Press.

Lansky, V. (2002). *Toilet training: A practical guide to daytime and nighttime training.* Deephaven, MN: Book Peddlers.

Mack, A., & Wilensky, D. (1990). *Dry all night: The picture book technique that stops bedwetting.* Boston, MA: Little, Brown.

Mercer, R. (2004). *Seven steps to nighttime dryness: A practical guide for parents of children with bedwetting.* Ashton, MD: Brookeville Media.

Schonwald, A. D., & Sheldon, G. G. (2006). *The pocket idiot's guide to potty training problems.* Indianapolis, IN: Penguin.

To order a bedwetting alarm: Palco Laboratories, 9030 Sequel Avenue, Santa Cruz, CA 95062, Telephone (800) 346-4488.

Fire Setting

Gaynor, J., & Hatcher, C. (1989). *Psychology of child firesetting: Detection and intervention.* New York, NY: Brunner/Mazel.

Green, R. (2010). *The explosive child: A new approach for understanding and parenting easily frustrated, chronically inflexible children.* New York, NY: Harper.

Nemeth, D., Ray, K., & Schexnayder, M. (2003). *Helping your angry child: A workbook for you and your family.* Oakland, CA: New Harbinger.

Newman, T., Brown, W., & Wilson, R. (2011). *Juvenile fire setters.* Tallahassee, FL: William Gladden Foundation.

Pudney, W., & Whitehouse, E. (2012). *Little volcanoes: Helping young children and their parents to deal with anger.* Philadelphia, PA: Jessica Kingsley.

Shapiro, L. E. (1994). *Anger control tool kit: All the information you need to help the angry child in school and at home* [video and book]. King of Prussia, PA: Center for Applied Psychology.

Shapiro, L., Pelta-Heller, Z., & Greenwald, A. (2008). *I'm not bad, I'm just mad: A workbook to help kids control their anger.* Oakland, CA: New Harbinger.

Shore, H. (1995). *The angry monster workbook.* Plainview, NY: Childswork/Childsplay.

Whitehouse, E., & Pudney, W. (1998). *A volcano in my tummy: Helping children to handle anger: A resource book for parents, caregivers and teachers.* Gabriola Island, British Columbia, Canada: New Society.

Gender Identity Disorder

Brill, S., & Pepper, R. (2008). *The transgender child: A handbook for families and professionals.* Berkeley, CA: Cleis Press.

Carr, J. (2010). *Be who you are.* Bloomington, IN: AuthorHouse.

Ehrensaft, D. (2011). *Gender born, gender made: Raising healthy gender-nonconforming children.* New York, NY: The Experiment.

Rothblatt, P. (2011). *All I want to be is me.* Seattle, WA: CreateSpace Independent Publishing Platform.

Zucker, K., & Bradley, S. (1995). *Gender identity disorder and psychosexual problems in children and adolescents.* New York, NY: Guilford Press.

Grief/Loss Unresolved

Buscaglia, L. (1982). *The fall of Freddie the leaf: A story of life for all ages.* Thorofare, NJ: Slack.

Gof, B. (1988). *Where is daddy?: The story of a divorce.* Minnetonka, MN: Olympic Marketing.

Hanson, W. (1997). *The next place.* Golden Valley, MN: Waldman House Press.

Jewett, C. (1994). *Helping children cope with separation and loss.* Harvard, MA: Harvard Common Press.

Kushner, H. (2004). *When bad things happen to good people.* New York, NY: Anchor.

Leeuwenburgh, E., & Goldring, E. (2008). *Why did you die?: Activities to help children cope with grief and loss.* Oakland, CA: New Harbinger.

Moser, A. (1996). *Don't despair on Thursdays! The children's grief-management book.* Kansas City, MO: Landmark Editions.

Mundy, M. (1998). *Sad isn't bad: A good-grief guidebook for kids dealing with loss.* St. Meinrad, MN: Abbey Press.

Nystrom, C. (1994). *Emma says goodbye: A child's guide to bereavement.* Batavia, IL: Lion.

O'Toole, D. (1988). *Aarvy aardvark finds hope: A read-aloud story for people of all ages about loving and losing, friendship and hope.* Burnsville, NC: Compassion Books.

Romain, T. (1999). *What on earth do you do when someone dies?* Minneapolis, MN: Free Spirit.

Schwiebert, P., & DeKlyen, C. (2005). *Tear soup.* Portland, OR: Grief Watch.

Silverman, J. (1999). *Help me say goodbye: Activities for helping kids cope when a special person dies.* Minneapolis, MN: Fairview Press.

Smedes, L. (2000). *How can it be all right when everything is all wrong?* Colorado Springs, CO: Shaw Books.

Stickney, D. (2005). *Waterbugs and dragonflies: Explaining death to young children.* Cleveland, OH: Pilgrim Press.

Temes, R. (1992). *The empty place: A child's guide through grief.* Dallas, TX: New Horizon Press.

Thomas, P. (2001). *I miss you: A first look at death.* Hauppauge, NY: Barron's Educational Series.

Wakenshaw, M. (2005). *Caring for your grieving child: A parent's guide.* Oakland, CA: New Harbinger.

Westberg, G. (2010). *Good grief.* Philadelphia, PA: Fortress Press.

Intellectual Developmental Disorder

Baker, B., & Brightman, A. (2004). *Steps to independence: Teaching everyday skills to children with special needs.* Baltimore, MD: Brookes.

Harris, J. (2010). *Intellectual disability: A guide for families and professionals.* New York, NY: Oxford University Press.

Mannix, D. (2009). *Life skills activities for special children.* San Francisco, CA: Jossey-Bass.

Shapiro, L., & Sprague, R. (2009). *The relaxation and stress reduction workbook for kids: Help for children to cope with stress, anxiety, and transitions.* Oakland, CA: New Harbinger.

Trainer, M. (2003). *Differences in common: Straight talk on mental retardation, Down syndrome, and life.* Rockville, MD: Woodbine House.

Low Self-Esteem

Adams, C., & Butch, R. (2001). *Happy to be me!: A kid book about self-esteem.* St. Meinrad, MN: Abbey Press.

Block, D. (2003). *The power of positive talk: Words to help every child succeed.* Minneapolis, MN: Free Spirit.

Briggs, D. (1988). *Your child's self-esteem.* New York, NY: Three Rivers Press.

Dobson, J. (1992). *Hide or seek: How to build self-esteem in your child.* Grand Rapids, MI: Fleming H. Revell.

Frankel, F. (1996). *Good friends are hard to find.* London, England: Perspective.

Glenn, H., & Nelsen, J. (2000). *Raising self-reliant children in a self-indulgent world: Seven building blocks for developing capable young people.* New York, NY: Three Rivers Press.

Moser, A. (1991). *Don't feed the monster on Tuesdays! The children's self-esteem book.* Kansas City, MO: Landmark Editions.

Nelson, J., Lott, L., & Glenn, H. (2007). *Positive discipline A-Z: 1001 solutions to everyday parenting problems.* New York, NY: Three Rivers Press.

Pickhardt, C. (2003). *The everything parent's guide to positive discipline.* Holbrook, MA: Adams Media Corp.

Schab, L. (2009). *Cool, calm, and confident: A workbook to help kids learn assertiveness skills.* Oakland, CA: New Harbinger.

Schweiger, I. (2008). *Self-esteem for a lifetime: Raising a successful child from the inside out.* Bloomington, IN: AuthorHouse.

Shapiro, L. (1993). *The building blocks of self-esteem.* Plainview, NY: Childswork/Childsplay.

Stallard, P. (2002). *Think good–feel good: A cognitive behaviour therapy workbook for children.* Hoboken, NJ: Wiley.

Lying/Manipulative

Berry, J. (1988). *A children's book about lying.* Danbury, CT: Grolier Enterprises.

Ekman, P. (1991). *Why kids lie: How parents can encourage truthfulness.* New York, NY: Penguin.

Meiners, C. (2007). *Be honest and tell the truth.* Minneapolis, MN: Free Spirit.

Moser, A. (1999). *Don't tell a whopper on Fridays!: The children's truth-control book.* Kansas City, MO: Landmark Editions.

Medical Condition

Bluebond-Langner, M. (2000). *In the shadow of illness: Parents and siblings of the chronically ill child.* Princeton, NJ: Princeton University Press.

Forehand, R., & Long, N. (2002). *Parenting the strong-willed child: The clinically proven five-week program for parents of two- to six-year-olds.* New York, NY: McGraw-Hill.

Fromer, M. (1998). *Surviving childhood cancer: A guide for families.* Oakland, CA: New Harbinger.

Gaynor, K. (2008). *The famous hat - A story book to help children with childhood cancer to prepare for treatment, namely chemotherapy, and losing their hair.* Dublin, Ireland: Special Stories.

Gosselin, K. (1998a). *Taking asthma to school.* Princeton, NJ: JayJo Books.

Gosselin, K. (1998b). *Taking diabetes to school.* Princeton, NJ: JayJo Books.

Gosselin, K. (1998c). *Taking seizure disorder to school.* Princeton, NJ: JayJo Books.

Jewett, C. (1994). *Helping children cope with separation and loss.* Harvard, MA: Harvard Common Press.

Keene, N. (2010). *Childhood leukemia: A guide for families, friends & caregivers.* Bellingham, WA: Childhood Cancer Guides.

Keene, N., Hobbie, W., & Ruccione, K. (2012). *Childhood cancer survivors: A practical guide to your future.* Bellingham, WA: Childhood Cancer Guides.

Kendall, P., & Hedtke, K. (2006). *Coping C.A.T. workbook.* Ardmore, PA: Workbook.

Kushner, H. (2004). *When bad things happen to good people.* New York, NY: Anchor.

MacLellan, S. (1998). *Amanda's gift: One family's journey through the maze of serious childhood illness.* Roswell, GA: Health Awareness Communications.

Moser, A. (1996). *Don't despair on Thursdays! The children's grief-management book.* Kansas City, MO: Landmark Editions.

Shapiro, L., & Sprague, R. (2009). *The relaxation and stress reduction workbook for kids: Help for children to cope with stress, anxiety, and transitions.* Oakland, CA: New Harbinger.

Smedes, L. (2000). *How can it be all right when everything is all wrong?* Colorado Springs, CO: Shaw Books.

Wakenshaw, M. (2005). *Caring for your grieving child: A parent's guide.* Oakland, CA: New Harbinger.

Westberg, G. (2010). *Good grief.* Philadelphia, PA: Fortress Press.

Woznick, L. (2002). *Living with childhood cancer: A practical guide to help parents cope.* Washington, DC: American Psychological Association.

Obsessive-Compulsive Disorder (OCD)

Chansky, T. (2001). *Freeing your child from obsessive compulsive disorder: A powerful, practical program for parents of children and adolescents.* New York, NY: Three Rivers Press.

Chansky, T. (2004). *Freeing your child from anxiety: Powerful, practical solutions to overcome your child's fears, worries, and phobias.* New York, NY: Three Rivers Press.

Fitzgibbons, L., & Pedrick, C. (2003). *Helping your child with OCD.* Oakland, CA: New Harbinger.

Freeman, J., & Garcia, A. (2008). *Family-based treatment for young children with OCD—Workbook.* New York, NY: Oxford University Press.

Huebner, D. (2007). *What to do when your brain gets stuck: A kid's guide to overcoming OCD.* New York, NY: Magination Press.

March, J. (2006). *Talking back to OCD: The program that helps kids and teens say "no way"—and parents say "way to go."* New York, NY: Guilford Press.

Niner, H. (2003). *Mr. Worry: A story about OCD.* Morton Grove, IL: A. Whitman & Co.

Piacentini, J., Langley, A., & Roblek, T. (2007). *It's only a false alarm: A cognitive behavioral treatment program - Client workbook.* New York, NY: Oxford University Press.

Schwartz, J. (1997). *Brain lock: Free yourself from obsessive-compulsive behavior.* New York, NY: Harper Perennial.

Stallard, P. (2002). *Think good–feel good: A cognitive behaviour therapy workbook for children.* Hoboken, NJ: Wiley.

Wagner, A. P. (2002). *What to do when your child has obsessive-compulsive disorder: Strategies and solutions.* Rochester, NY: Lighthouse Press.

Wagner, A. P. (2004). *Up and down the worry hill: A children's book about obsessive-compulsive disorder and its treatment.* Rochester, NY: Lighthouse Press.

Waltz, M. (2000). *Obsessive compulsive disorder: Help for children and adolescents.* Sebastopol, CA: Patient Centered Guides.

Oppositional Defiant

Aborn, A. (1994). *Everything I do you blame on me: A book to help children control their anger.* Plainview, NY: Childswork/Childsplay.

Barkley, R., & Benton, C. (1998). *Your defiant child: Eight steps to better behavior.* New York, NY: Guilford Press.

Bernstein, J. (2006). *10 days to a less defiant child: The breakthrough program for overcoming your child's difficult behavior.* New York, NY: Marlowe & Company.

Dobson, J. (2007). *The new strong-willed child.* Wheaton, IL: Tyndale House.

Forehand, R., & Long, N. (2002). *Parenting the strong-willed child: The clinically proven five-week program for parents of two- to six-year-olds.* New York, NY: McGraw-Hill.

Gardner, R. (1999). *The girls and boys book about good and bad behavior.* Cresskill, NJ: Creative Therapeutics.

Golant, M., & Corwin, D. (1995). *The challenging child: A guide for parents of exceptionally strong-willed children.* New York, NY: Berkley Trade.

Green, R. (2010). *The explosive child: A new approach for understanding and parenting easily frustrated, chronically inflexible children.* New York, NY: Harper.

Kazdin, A. (2009). *The Kazdin method for parenting the defiant child.* New York, NY: Mariner.

MacKenzie, R. (2001). *Setting limits with your strong-willed child: Eliminating conflict by establishing clear, firm, and respectful boundaries.* New York, NY: Three Rivers Press.

Patterson, G. R. (1976). *Living with children: New methods for parents and teachers.* Champaign, IL: Research Press.

Riley, D. (1997). *The defiant child: A parent's guide to oppositional defiant disorder.* New York, NY: Taylor.

Schab, L. (2009). *Cool, calm, and confident: A workbook to help kids learn assertiveness skills.* Oakland, CA: New Harbinger.

Wenning, K. (1999). *Winning cooperation from your child: A comprehensive method to stop defiant and aggressive behavior in children.* Northvale, NJ: Jason Aronson.

Overweight/Obesity

Block, D. (2003). *The power of positive talk: Words to help every child succeed.* Minneapolis, MN: Free Spirit.

Brownell, K. D. (2004). *The LEARN program for weight management* (10th ed.). Dallas, TX: American Health Publishing Company.

Chansky, T. (2008). *Freeing your child from negative thinking: Powerful, practical strategies to build a lifetime of resilience, flexibility, and happiness.* Cambridge, MA: De Capo Press.

LaLiberte, M., McCabe, R. E., & Taylor, V. (2099). *The cognitive behavioral workbook for weight management.* Oakland, CA: New Harbinger.

Miller, E. (2008). *The monster health book: A guide to eating healthy, being active & feeling great for monsters & kids!* New York, NY: Holiday House.

Rockwell, L. (2009). *Good enough to eat: A kid's guide to food and nutrition.* New York, NY: HarperCollins.

Schab, L. (2009). *Cool, calm, and confident: A workbook to help kids learn assertiveness skills.* Oakland, CA: New Harbinger.

Shapiro, L., & Sprague, R. (2009). *The relaxation and stress reduction workbook for kids: Help for children to cope with stress, anxiety, and transitions.* Oakland, CA: New Harbinger.

Sothern, M., von Almen, T., & Schumacher, H. (2003). *Trim kids: The proven 12-week plan that has helped thousands of children achieve a healthier weight.* New York, NY: Morrow.

Stallard, P. (2002). *Think good–feel good: A cognitive behaviour therapy workbook for children.* Hoboken, NJ: Wiley.

Vos, M. (2009). *The no-diet obesity solution for kids*. Bethesda, MD: AGA Institute Press.

Weight Watchers. (2010). *Weight watchers Eat! Move! Play!: A parent's guide for raising healthy, happy kids*. Hoboken, NJ: Wiley.

Parenting

Becker, W. (1971). *Parents are teachers: A child management program*. Champaign, IL: Research Press.

Cline, F., & Fay, J. (2006). *Parenting with love and logic*. Colorado Springs, CO: NavPress.

Edwards, C. D. (1999). *How to handle a hard-to-handle kid*. Minneapolis, MN: Free Spirit.

Elkind, D. (2006). *The hurried child: Growing up too fast too soon*. New York, NY: De Capo Press.

Faber, A., & Mazlish, E. (2012). *How to talk so kids will listen and listen so kids will talk*. New York, NY: Scribner.

Fay, J., & Fay, C. (2000). *Love and logic magic for early childhood: Practical parenting from birth to six years*. Golden, CO: Love and Logic Press.

Forehand, R., & Long, N. (2002). *Parenting the strong-willed child: The clinically proven five-week program for parents of two- to six-year-olds*. New York, NY: McGraw-Hill.

Glenn, H., & Nelsen, J. (2000). *Raising self-reliant children in a self-indulgent world: Seven building blocks for developing capable young people*. New York, NY: Three Rivers Press.

Golant, M., & Corwin, D. (1995). *The challenging child: A guide for parents of exceptionally strong-willed children*. New York, NY: Berkley Trade.

Gordon, T. (2000). *Parent effectiveness training: The proven program for raising responsible children*. New York, NY: Three Rivers Press.

Greene, R. (2010). *The explosive child: A new approach for understanding and parenting easily frustrated, chronically inflexible children*. New York, NY: Harper.

Greenspan, S. (1996). *The challenging child: Understanding, raising, and enjoying the five "difficult" types of children*. New York, NY: De Capo Press.

Joslin, K. (1994). *Positive parenting from A to Z*. New York, NY: Fawcett Books.

Kazdin, A. (2009). *The Kazdin method for parenting the defiant child*. New York, NY: Mariner.

Maag, J. W. (1996). *Parenting without punishment: Making problem behavior work for you*. Philadelphia, PA: Charles Press.

Metcalf, L. (1997). *Parenting toward solutions*. Englewood Cliffs, NJ: Prentice Hall.

Nelson, J., Lott, L., & Glenn, H. (2007). *Positive discipline A–Z: 1001 solutions to everyday parenting problems*. New York, NY: Three Rivers Press.

Palmiter, D. (2011). *Working parents, thriving families: 10 strategies that make a difference*. North Branch, MN: Sunrise River Press.

Patterson, G. R. (1976). *Living with children: New methods for parents and teachers.* Champaign, IL: Research Press.

Patterson, G. R. (1982). *Coercive family process.* Eugene, OR: Castalia.

Phelan, T. (2010). *1-2-3 Magic: Effective discipline for children 2–12.* Glen Ellyn, IL: ParentMagic.

Pickhardt, C. (2003). *The everything parent's guide to positive discipline.* Holbrook, MA: Adams Media Corp.

Schaefer, C., & DiGeronimo, T. (2000). *Ages and stages: A parent's guide to normal childhood development.* New York, NY: Wiley.

Turecki, S., & Tonner, L. (2000). *The difficult child.* New York, NY: Bantam Books.

Wenning, K. (1999). *Winning cooperation from your child: A comprehensive method to stop defiant and aggressive behavior in children.* Northvale, NJ: Jason Aronson.

Windell, J. (1997). *Children who say no when you want them to say yes: Failsafe discipline strategies for stubborn and oppositional children and teens.* New York, NY: Wiley.

Peer/Sibling Conflict

Crist, J., & Verdick, E. (2010). *Siblings: You're stuck with each other, so stick together.* Minneapolis, MN: Free Spirit.

Faber, A., & Mazlish, E. (2012a). *How to talk so kids will listen and listen so kids will talk.* New York, NY: Scribner.

Faber, A., & Mazlish, E. (2012b). *Siblings without rivalry: How to help your children live together so you can live too.* New York, NY: W. W. Norton.

Samalin, N., & Whitney, C. (1997). *Loving each one best: A caring and practical approach to raising siblings.* New York, NY: Bantam.

Sheridan, S. (1998). *Why don't they like me? Helping your child make and keep friends.* Longmont, CO: Sopris West.

Un, J. (2012). *I feel, feel, feel about my new baby sibling.* Plainview, NY: Childswork/Childsplay.

Physical/Emotional Abuse Victim

Holmes, M. (2000). *A terrible thing happened: A story for children who have witnessed violence or trauma.* Washington, DC: Magination Press.

Levine, P., & Kline, M. (2006). *Trauma through a child's eyes: Awakening the ordinary miracle of healing.* Berkeley, CA: North Atlantic Books.

Miller, A. (1984). *For your own good.* New York, NY: Farrar Straus Group.

Monahon, C. (1995). *Children and trauma: A parent's guide to helping children heal.* New York, NY: Lexington Books.

Posttraumatic Stress Disorder

Allen, J. (2004). *Coping with trauma: Hope through understanding.* Arlington, VA: American Psychiatric Press.

Brooks, B., & Siegel, P. M. (1996). *The scared child: Helping kids overcome traumatic events.* New York, NY: Wiley.

Carmen, R. (2004). *Helping kids heal: 75 activities to help children recover from trauma and loss.* Princeton, NJ: JayJo Books.

Chrestman, K., Gilboa-Schechtman, E., & Foa, E. (2008). *Prolonged exposure therapy for PTSD—Teen workbook.* New York, NY: Oxford University Press.

Flannery, R., Jr. (2004). *Post-traumatic stress disorder: The victim's guide to healing and recovery.* Ellicott City, MD: Chevron.

Foa, E., Chrestman, K., & Gilboa-Schechtman, E. (2008). *Prolonged exposure therapy for adolescents with PTSD: Emotional processing of traumatic experiences—Therapist guide.* New York, NY: Oxford University Press.

Forehand, R., & Long, N. (2010). *Parenting the strong-willed child: The clinically proven five-week program for parents of two- to six-year-olds.* New York, NY: McGraw-Hill.

Hamil, S. (2008). *My feeling better workbook: Help for kids who are sad and depressed.* Oakland, CA: New Harbinger.

Holmes, M. (2000). *A terrible thing happened: A story for children who have witnessed violence or trauma.* Washington, DC: Magination Press.

Kazdin, A. (2009). *The Kazdin method for parenting the defiant child.* New York, NY: Mariner.

Levine, P., & Kline, M. (2006). *Trauma through a child's eyes: Awakening the ordinary miracle of healing.* Berkeley, CA: North Atlantic Books.

Monahon, C. (1995). *Children and trauma: A parent's guide to helping children heal.* New York, NY: Lexington Books.

Patterson, G. R. (1976). *Living with children: New methods for parents and teachers.* Champaign, IL: Research Press.

Shapiro, L., & Sprague, R. (2009). *The relaxation and stress reduction workbook for kids: Help for children to cope with stress, anxiety, and transitions.* Oakland, CA: New Harbinger.

Stallard, P. (2002). *Think good–feel good: A cognitive behaviour therapy workbook for children.* Hoboken, NJ: Wiley.

School Refusal

Eison, A., & Engler, L. (2006). *Helping your child overcome separation anxiety or school refusal: A step-by-step guide for parents.* Oakland, CA: New Harbinger.

Kearney, C. (2007). *Getting your child to say "yes" to school: A guide for parents of youth with school refusal behavior.* New York, NY: Oxford University Press.

Kearney, C., & Albano, A. (2007). *When children refuse school: A cognitive-behavioral therapy approach—Parent workbook.* New York, NY: Oxford University Press.

Martin, M., & Waltman-Greenwood, C. (Eds.). (1995). *Solve your child's school-related problems.* New York, NY: HarperCollins.

Pando, N. (2005). *I don't want to go to school: Helping children cope with separation anxiety.* Far Hills, NJ: New Horizon Press.

Shapiro, L., & Sprague, R. (2009). *The relaxation and stress reduction workbook for kids: Help for children to cope with stress, anxiety, and transitions.* Oakland, CA: New Harbinger.

Webster-Doyle, T. (1999). *Why is everybody always picking on me? A guide to understanding bullies for young people.* Boston, MA: Weatherhill.

Separation Anxiety

Barrett, P.M., Lowry-Webster, H., & Turner. C. (2000). *Friends for children participant workbook* (2nd ed.). Brisbane: Australian Academic Press.

Eison, A., & Engler, L. (2006). *Helping your child overcome separation anxiety or school refusal: A step-by-step guide for parents.* Oakland, CA: New Harbinger.

Pando, N. (2005). *I don't want to go to school: Helping children cope with separation anxiety.* Far Hills, NJ: New Horizon Press.

Pantley, E. (2010). *The no-cry separation anxiety solution: Gentle ways to make good-bye easy from six months to six years.* New York, NY: McGraw-Hill.

Rapee, R., Spense, S., Cobham, V., & Wignal, A. (2000). *Helping your anxious child: A step-by-step guide for parents.* San Francisco, CA: New Harbinger.

Shapiro, L., & Sprague, R. (2009). *The relaxation and stress reduction workbook for kids: Help for children to cope with stress, anxiety, and transitions.* Oakland, CA: New Harbinger.

Sexual Abuse Victim

Adams, C., & Fay, J. (1992). *Helping your child recover from sexual abuse.* Seattle: University of Washington Press.

Brohl, K., & Potter, J. (2004). *When your child has been molested: A parent's guide to healing and recovery.* San Francisco, CA: Jossey-Bass.

Freeman, L. (1984). *It's my body: A book to teach young children how to resist uncomfortable touch.* Seattle, WA: Parenting Press.

Hindman, J. (1983). *A very touching book . . . For little people and for big people.* Philadelphia, PA: Alexandria Associates.

Hoke, S. (1995). *My body is mine, my feelings are mine: A storybook about body safety for young children with an adult guidebook.* Plainview, NY: Childswork/Childsplay.

Jance, J. (1985). *It's not your fault.* Indianapolis, IN: Kidsrights.

Jessie (1991). *Please tell!: A child's story about sexual abuse.* Center City, MN: Hazelden.

Klevin, S. (1998). *The right touch: A read-aloud story to help prevent child sexual abuse.* Bellevue, WA: Illumination Arts.

Sanford, D. (1986). *I can't talk about it: A child's book about sexual abuse.* Portland, OR: Multnomah Press.

Spelman, C. (1997). *Your body belongs to you.* Park Ridge, IL: Albert Whitman.

Sleep Disturbance

Durand, V. M. (2008). *When children don't sleep well: Interventions for pediatric sleep disorders – Parent workbook.* New York, NY: Oxford University Press.

Ferber, R. (2006). *Solve your child's sleep problems.* New York, NY: Touchstone.

Ilg, F., Ames, L., & Baker, S. (1982). *Child behavior: Specific advice on problems of child behavior.* New York, NY: Harper & Row.

Mindell, J. (2005). *Sleeping through the night: How infants, toddlers, and their parents can get a good night's sleep.* New York, NY: Morrow.

Pantley, E. (2005). *The no-cry sleep solution for toddlers and preschoolers: Gentle ways to stop bedtime battles and improve your child's sleep.* New York, NY: McGraw-Hill.

Shapiro, L., & Sprague, R. (2009). *The relaxation and stress reduction workbook for kids: Help for children to cope with stress, anxiety, and transitions.* Oakland, CA: New Harbinger.

Social Anxiety

Antony, M. M., & Swinson, R. P. (2008). *The shyness and social anxiety workbook: Proven, step-by-step techniques for overcoming your fear.* Oakland, CA: New Harbinger.

Barrett, P. M., Lowry-Webster, H., & Turner. C. (2000). *Friends for children participant workbook* (2nd ed.). Brisbane, Australia: Australian Academic Press.

Brozovich, R., & Chase, L (2008). *Say goodbye to being shy: A workbook to help kids overcome shyness.* Oakland, CA: New Harbinger.

Cain, B. (2000). *I don't know why—I guess I'm shy.* Washington, DC: Magination Press.

Carducci, B. (2003). *The shyness breakthrough.: A no-stress plan to help your shy child warm up, open up, and join the fun.* Emmaus, PA: Rodale Books.

Lamb-Shapiro, J. (2002). *Sometimes I don't like to talk (but sometimes I can't keep quiet).* Plainview, NY: Childswork/Childsplay.

Markway, B., & Markway, G. (2006). *Nurturing the shy child: Practical help for raising confident and socially skilled kids and teens.* New York, NY: St. Martin's Griffin.

Rapee, R., Wignall, A., Spence, S., Cobham, V., & Lyneham, H. (2008). *Helping your anxious child: A step-by-step guide for parents.* Oakland, CA: New Harbinger Publications.

Shapiro, L., & Sprague, R. (2009). *The relaxation and stress reduction workbook for kids: Help for children to cope with stress, anxiety, and transitions.* Oakland, CA: New Harbinger.

Soifer, S., Zgourides, G. D., Himle, J., & Pickering, N. L. (2001). *Shy bladder syndrome: Your step-by-step guide to overcoming paruresis.* Oakland, CA: New Harbinger Publications.

Spencer, E., DuPont, R., & DuPont, C. (2003). *The anxiety cure for kids: A guide for parents.* Hoboken, NJ: Wiley.

Swallow, W. (2000). *The shy child: Helping children triumph over shyness.* New York, NY: Grand Central.

Webster-Doyle, T. (1999). *Why is everybody always picking on me? A guide to understanding bullies for young people.* Boston, MA: Weatherhill.

Specific Phobia

Antony, M., Craske, M., & Barlow, D. (2006). *Mastering your fears and phobias: Workbook.* New York, NY: Oxford University Press.

Barrett, P. M., Lowry-Webster, H., & Turner. C. (2000). *Friends for children participant workbook* (2nd ed.). Brisbane: Australian Academic Press.

Buron, K. (2006). *When my worries get too big! A relaxation book for children who live with anxiety.* Overland Park, KS: Autism Asperger Publishing.

Brown, J. (1995). *No more monsters in the closet: Teaching your children to overcome everyday fears and phobias.* New York, NY: Three Rivers Press.

Chansky, T. (2004). *Freeing your child from anxiety: Powerful, practical solutions to overcome your child's fears, worries, and phobias.* New York, NY: Three Rivers Press.

Chansky, T. (2008). *Freeing your child from negative thinking: Powerful, practical strategies to build a lifetime of resilience, flexibility, and happiness.* New York, NY: De Capo Press.

Garber, S., Garber, M., & Spitzman, R. (1993). *Monsters under the bed and other childhood fears: Helping your child overcome anxieties, fears, and phobias.* New York, NY: Villard.

Huebner, D. (2005). *What to do when you worry too much: A kid's guide to overcoming anxiety.* Washington, DC: Magination Press.

Maier, I. (2006). *When Fuzzy was afraid of big and loud things.* Washington, DC: Magination Press.

Manassis, K. (2008). *Keys to parenting your anxious child.* Hauppauge, NY: Barron's.

Marks, I. (2005). *Living with fear: Understanding and coping with anxiety.* New York, NY: McGraw-Hill.

Rapee, R., Wignall, A., Spense, S., Cobham, V., & Lyneham, H. (2008). *Helping your anxious child: A step-by-step guide for parents.* Oakland, CA: New Harbinger Publications.

Shapiro, L., & Sprague, R. (2009). *The relaxation and stress reduction workbook for kids: Help for children to cope with stress, anxiety, and transitions.* Oakland, CA: New Harbinger.

Speech/Language Disorders

Ainsworth, S., & Fraser, J. (2006). *If your child stutters: A guide for parents.* Memphis, TN: Stuttering Foundation of America.

Bryant, J. (2004). *Taking speech disorder to school.* Princeton, NJ: JayJo Books.

Clark, W. (2010). *Speak without fear: A how-to-stop-stuttering guide.* Seattle, WA: CreateSpace.

Dougherty, D. (2005). *Teach me how to say it right: Helping your child with articulation problems.* Oakland, CA: New Harbinger.

Fraser, J. (2000). *Self-therapy for the stutterer.* Memphis, TN: Stuttering Foundation of America.

Kehoe, T. (2006). *No miracle cures: A multifactoral guide to stuttering therapy.* Boulder, CO: University College Press.

Shapiro, L., & Sprague, R. (2009). *The relaxation and stress reduction workbook for kids: Help for children to cope with stress, anxiety, and transitions.* Oakland, CA: New Harbinger.

Appendix B

PROFESSIONAL REFERENCES FOR EVIDENCE-BASED CHAPTERS

Sources Informing Evidence-Based Treatment Planning and Practice

Agency for Healthcare Research and Quality. http://www.ahrq.gov/clinic/epcix.htm

American Academy of Child & Adolescent Psychiatry. http://www.aacap.org

American Psychiatric Association. *American Psychiatric Association practice guidelines.* Arlington, VA: Author. Available from http://psychiatryonline.org/guidelines.aspx

American Psychiatric Association. (2013). Diagnostic and statistical manual of mental disorders (5th ed.). Arlington, VA: American Psychiatric Publishing.

APA Presidential Task Force on Evidence-Based Practice. (2006). Evidence-based practice in psychology. *American Psychologist, 61,* 271–285.

Chambless, D. L., & Ollendick, T. H. (2001). Empirically supported psychological interventions: Controversies and evidence. *Annual Review of Psychology, 52,* 685–716.

Cochrane Collaboration Reviews. Available from http://www.cochrane.org/

Fisher, J. E., & O'Donohue, W. T. (Eds.) *Practitioners guide to evidence-based psychotherapy.* New York, NY: Springer.

Jongsma, A. E., & Bruce, T. J. (2010–2012). *Evidence-based psychotherapy treatment planning* [DVD-based series]. Hoboken, NJ: Wiley. Available from www.Wiley.com/go/ebtdvds

Nathan, P. E., & Gorman, J. M. (Eds.). (2007). *A guide to treatments that work* (3rd ed.). New York, NY: Oxford University Press.

National Institute for Health and Clinical Excellence. Available from http://www.nice.org.uk/

Norcross, J. C. (Ed.). (2011). *Psychotherapy relationships that work* (2nd ed.). New York, NY: Oxford University Press.

Society of Clinical Child and Adolescent Psychology. *Effective child therapy: Evidence-based mental health treatment for children and adolescents.* Available from http://effectivechildtherapy.com

Substance Abuse and Mental Health Administration (SAMHSA). *National Registry of Evidence-based Programs and Practices.* Available from http://nrepp.samhsa.gov/index.asp

Therapy Advisor. www.therapyadvisor.com

Weisz, J. R., & Kazdin, A. E. (2010). *Evidence-based psychotherapies for children and adolescents* (2nd ed.) New York, NY: Guilford Press.

Anger Control Problems

Empirical Support

Barry, T. D., & Pardini, D. A. (2003). Anger control training for aggressive youth. In A. E. Kazdin & J. R. Weisz (Eds.), *Evidence-based psychotherapies for children and adolescents* (pp. 263–281). New York, NY: Guilford Press.

Brestan, E. V., & Eyberg, S. M. (1998). Effective psychosocial treatments of conduct-disordered children and adolescents: 29 years, 82 studies, and 5,272 kids. *Journal of Clinical Child Psychology, 27(2),* 180–189.

Deffenbacher, J. L., Oetting, E. R., & DiGiuseppe, R. A. (2002). Principles of empirically supported interventions applied to anger management. *The Counseling Psychologist, 30*, 262–280.

Feindler, E. L. (1995). An ideal treatment package for children and adolescents with anger disorders. In H. Kassinove (Ed.), *Anger disorders: Definition, diagnosis, and treatment* (pp. 173–194). New York, NY: Taylor & Francis.

Feindler, E. L., & Baker, K. (2004). Current issues in anger management interventions with youth. In A. P. Goldstein, R. Nensen, B. Daleflod, & M. Kalt (Eds.), *New perspectives on aggression replacement training: Practice, research, and application* (pp. 31–50). Hoboken, NJ: Wiley.

Kazdin, A. E. (2005). *Parent management training: Treatment for oppositional, aggressive, and antisocial behavior in children and adolescents.* New York, NY: Oxford University Press.

Lochman, J. E., Boxmeyer, C. L., Powell, N. P., Barry, T. D., & Pardini, D. A. (2010). Anger control training for aggressive youths. In A. E. Kazdin & J. R. Weisz (Eds.), *Evidence-based psychotherapies for children and adolescents* (2nd ed., pp. 227–242). New York, NY: Guilford Press.

Lochman, J. E., Powell, N. R., Whidby, J. M., & FitzGerald, D. P. (2006). Aggressive children: Cognitive-behavioral assessment and treatment. In P. C. Kendall (Ed.), *Child and adolescent therapy: Cognitive-behavioral procedures* (3rd ed., pp. 33–81). New York, NY: Guilford Press.

Meichenbaum, D. (1993). Stress inoculation training: A twenty-year update. In R. L. Woolfolk & P. M. Lehrer (Eds.), *Principles and practices of stress management.* New York, NY: Guilford Press.

Vecchio, T.D., & O'Leary, K.D. (2004). Effectiveness of anger treatments for specific anger problems: A meta-analytic review. *Clinical Psychology Review, 24*, 15–34.

Zisser, A., & Eyberg, S. M. (2010). Treating oppositional behavior in children using parent-child interaction therapy. In A. E. Kazdin & J. R. Weisz (Eds.) *Evidence-based psychotherapies for children and adolescents* (2nd ed., pp. 179–193). New York, NY: Guilford Press.

Clinical Resources

Feinder, E. L. (Ed.). (2006). *Anger related disorders: A practitioner's guide to comparative treatments.* New York, NY: Springer.

Functional Family Therapy. Available from www.fftinc.com

Incredible Years. Available from www.incredibleyears.com

Kazdin, A. E. (2005). *Parent management training: Treatment for oppositional, aggressive, and antisocial behavior in children and adolescents.* New York, NY: Oxford University Press.

Larson, J., & Lochman, J. E. (2010). *Helping schoolchildren cope with anger: A cognitive-behavioral intervention* (2nd ed.). New York, NY: Guilford Press.

Lochman, J. E., Boxmeyer, C. L., Powell, N. P., Barry, T. D., & Pardini, D. A. (2010). Anger control training for aggressive youths. In A. E. Kazdin & J. R. Weisz (Eds.), *Evidence-based psychotherapies for children and adolescents* (2nd ed., pp. 227–242). New York, NY: Guilford Press.

McMahon, R., and Forehand, R. (2005). *Helping the noncompliant child: Family-based treatment for oppositional behavior.* New York, NY: Guilford Press.

McNeil, C. B., & Humbree-Kigin, T. L. (2010). *Parent-child interaction therapy* (2nd ed.). New York, NY: Springer.

Patterson, G. R. (1976). *Living with children: New methods for parents and teachers.* Champaign, IL: Research Press.

Sexton, T. (2010). *Functional family therapy in clinical practice: An evidence-based treatment model for working with troubled adolescents.* New York, NY: Routledge.

Triple-P. Available from www.triplep.net

Webster-Stratton, C. (2011).*The incredible years: A trouble shooting guide for parents of children aged 2–8 years.* Seattle, WA: The Incredible Years.

Williams, E. and Barlow, R. (1998). *Anger control training manual.* New York, NY: Winslow Press.

Zisser, A., & Eyberg, S.M. (2010). Treating oppositional behavior in children using parent-child interaction therapy. In A. E. Kazdin & J. R. Weisz (Eds.) *Evidence-based psychotherapies for children and adolescents* (2nd ed., pp. 179–193). New York, NY: Guilford Press.

Anxiety

Empirical Support

American Academy of Child & Adolescent Psychiatry (2007). Practice parameters for the assessment and treatment of children and adolescents with anxiety disorders. *Journal of the American Academy of Child & Adolescent Psychiatry*, *46*(2), 267–283.

Barrett, P. M., & Shortt, A. (2003). Parental involvement in the treatment of anxious children. In A. E. Kazdin & J. R. Weisz (Eds.), *Evidence-based psychotherapies for children and adolescents* (pp. 101–119). New York, NY: Guilford Press.

Grills-Taquechel, A. E., & Ollendick, T. H. (2013). *Phobic and anxiety disorders in children and adolescents*. Cambridge, MA: Hogrefe.

James, A. A. C. J., Soler, A., & Weatherall, R. R. W. (2009). Cognitive behavioural therapy for anxiety disorders in children and adolescents. *Cochrane Database of Systematic Reviews, 2009*(4), CD004690. DOI: 10.1002/14651858.CD004690.pub2.

Kendall, P. C., Furr, J. M., & Podell, J. L. (2010). Child-focused treatment of anxiety. In J. R. Weisz & A. E. Kazdin (Eds.), *Evidence-based psychotherapies for children and adolescents* (2nd ed., pp. 45–60). New York, NY: Guilford Press.

Pahl, K. M., & Barrett, P. M. (2010). Interventions for anxiety disorders in children using group cognitive behavioral therapy with family involvement. In J. R. Weisz & A. E. Kazdin (Eds.), *Evidence-based psychotherapies for children and adolescents* (2nd ed., pp. 61–79). New York, NY: Guilford Press.

Silverman, W. K., Pina, A. A., & Viswesvaran, C. (2008). Evidence-based psychosocial treatments for phobic and anxiety disorders in children and adolescents: A review and meta-analyses. *Journal of Clinical Child and Adolescent Psychology, 37*, 105–130.

Clinical Resources

Barrett, P. M. (2004). *Friends for Life: Group leader's manual for children* (4th ed.). Brisbane, Australia: Australian Academic Press.

Barrett, P. M. (2007). *Fun Friends: The teaching and training manual for group leaders*. Brisbane, Australia: Fun Friends.

Bernstein, D. A., Borkovec, T. D., & Hazlett-Stevens, H. (2000). *New directions in progressive relaxation training: A guidebook for helping professionals*. Westport, CT: Praeger.

de Shazer, S. (1985). *Keys to solution in brief therapy*. New York, NY: Norton.

Flannery-Schroeder, E., & Kendall, P. C. (1996). *Cognitive behavioral therapy for anxious children: Therapist manual for group treatment*. Available from www.workbookpublishing.com

Howard, B., Chu, B. C., Krain, A. L., Marrs-Garcia, A. L., & Kendall, P. C. (2000). *Cognitive-behavioral family therapy for anxious children* (2nd ed.). Available from www.workbookpublishing.com

Kendall, P.C., & Hedtke, K. A. (2006). *Cognitive-behavioral therapy for anxious children* (3rd ed.). Available from www.workbookpublishing.com

March, J. S., Parker, J. D., Sullivan, K., Stallings, P., & Conners, C. K. (1997). The multidimensional anxiety scale for children (MASC): Factor structure, reliability, and validity. *Journal of the American Academy of Child & Adolescent Psychiatry, 36*, 544–565.

Ollendick, T. H. (1987). The fear survey schedule for children–revised. In M. Hersen & A. S. Bellack (Eds.), *Dictionary of behavioral assessment techniques* (pp. 218–220). Elmsford, NY: Pergamon Press.

Ollendick, T. H., & March, J. C. (2004). *Phobic and anxiety disorders in children and adolescents: A clinician's guide to effective psychosocial and pharmacological interventions.* New York, NY: Oxford University Press.

Rapee, R. M., Wignall, A., Hudson, J. L., & Schniering, C. A. (2010). *Treating anxious children and adolescents.* Oakland, CA: New Harbinger.

Reynold, C. R., & Richmond, B. O (2008). *Revised children's manifest anxiety scale* (2nd ed.). Torrance, CA: Western Psychological Services.

Semple, R. J., & Lee, J. (2011). *Mindfulness-based cognitive therapy for anxious children.* Oakland, CA: New Harbinger.

Silverman, W. K., & Albano, A. M. (1996). *The anxiety disorders interview schedule for DSM-IV-Child and parent versions.* London, England: Oxford University Press.

Attention-Deficit/Hyperactivity Disorder (ADHD)

Empirical Support

American Academy of Child & Adolescent Psychiatry (2007). Practice parameters for the assessment and treatment of children and adolescents with attention deficit/hyperactivity disorder. *Journal of the American Academy of Child & Adolescent Psychiatry, 46*(7), 894–921.

Brown, R. T., Amler, R. W., Freeman, W. S., Perrin, J. M., Stein, M. T. Feldman, H. M., . . . American Academy of Pediatrics Subcommittee on Attention-Deficit/Hyperactivity Disorder. (2005). Treatment of attention-deficit/hyperactivity disorder: Overview of the evidence. *Pediatrics, 115,* 749–757.

Chronis, A. M., Chacko, A., Fabiano, G. A., Wymbs, B. T., & Pelham, W. E. (2004). Enhancements to the standard behavioral parent training paradigm for families of children with ADHD: Review and future directions. *Clinical Child and Family Psychology Review, 7,* 1–27.

Hinshaw, S. P., Klein, R. G., & Abikoff, H. (2007). Childhood attention deficit hyperactivity disorder: Nonpharmacological treatments and their combination with medication. In P. E. Nathan & J. M. Gorman (Eds.), *A guide to treatments that work* (pp. 3–27). New York, NY: Oxford University Press.

Kutcher, S., Aman, M., Brooks, S.J., Buitelaar, J., van Daalen, E., Fegert, J., . . . Tyano, S. (2004). International consensus statement on attention-deficit/hyperactivity disorder (ADHD) and disruptive behaviour disorders (DBDs): Clinical implications and treatment practice suggestions. *European Neuropsychopharmacology, 14*(1), 11–28.

Molina, B. S. G., Hinshaw, S. P., Swanson, J. M., Arnold, L. E., Vitiello, B., Jensen, P. S., . . . MTA Cooperative Group. (2009). MTA at 8 years: Prospective follow-up of children treated for combined-type ADHD in a multi-site study. *Journal of the American Academy of Child & Adolescent Psychiatry, 48,* 484–500.

MTA Cooperative Group. (1999). A 14-month randomized clinical trial of treatment strategies for attention-deficit/hyperactivity disorder. *Archives of General Psychiatry*, 56, 1073–1086.

MTA Cooperative Group. (2004). National Institute of Mental Health Multimodal Treatment Study of ADHD Follow-up: 24-month outcomes of treatment strategies for attention-deficit/hyperactivity disorder. *Pediatrics, 113*, 754–761.

National Institute for Health and Clinical Excellence. (2008). *Attention deficit hyperactivity disorder: Diagnosis and management of ADHD in children, young people, and adults.* Clinical guideline 72. Available from http://guidance.nice.org.uk/CG72

Pelham, W. E., & Fabiano, G. A. (2008). Evidence-based psychosocial treatments for attention-deficit/hyperactivity disorder. *Journal of Clinical Child and Adolescent Psychology, 37*(1), 184–214.

Pelham, W. E., Fabiano, G. A., Gnagy, E. M., Greiner, A. R., & Hoza, B. (2005a). Comprehensive psychosocial treatment for ADHD. In E. Hibbs & P. Jensen (Eds.), *Psychosocial treatments for child and adolescent disorders: Empirically based strategies for clinical practice.* (pp. 377–409). Washington, DC: American Psychological Association.

Pelham, W. E., Fabiano, G. A., Gnagy, E. M., Greiner, A. R., & Hoza, B. (2005b). The role of summer treatment programs in the context of comprehensive treatment for ADHD. In E. Hibbs & P. Jensen (Eds.), *Psychosocial treatments for child and adolescent disorders: Empirically based strategies for clinical practice* (pp. 377–410). Washington, DC: APA Press.

Pelham, W. E., Gnagy, E. M., Greiner, A. R., Waschbusch, D. A., Fabiano, G. A., & Burrows-MacLean, L. (2010). Summer treatment programs for attention deficit disorder. In J. R. Weisz & A. E. Kazdin (Eds.), *Evidence-based psychotherapies for children and adolescents* (2nd ed., pp. 159–168). New York, NY: Guilford Press.

Rickel, A. U., & Brown, R. T. (2007). *Attention deficit/hyperactivity disorder in children and adults.* Cambridge, MA: Hogrefe.

Yamashita, Y., & Pelham, W. E. (2005). Evidence-based comprehensive treatment for children and families with ADHD. *Journal of the Japanese Child Psychiatry and Neurology Society, 45(1)*, 11–30.

Clinical Resources

Barkley, R. A. (2005). ADHD: *A handbook for diagnosis and treatment* (3rd ed.). New York, NY: Guilford Press.

Barkley, R. A. (2013). *Defiant children: A clinician's manual for assessment and parent training* (3rd ed.). New York, NY: Guilford Press.

DuPaul, G. J. (1991). Parent and teacher ratings of ADHD symptoms: Psychometric properties in a community-based sample. *Journal of Clinical Child Psychology, 20*, 245–253.

DuPaul, G. J., & Stoner, G. (2003). *ADHD in the schools: Assessment and intervention strategies.* New York, NY: Guilford Press.

Kazdin, A. E. (2005). *Parent management training: Treatment for oppositional, aggressive, and antisocial behavior in children and adolescents.* New York, NY: Oxford University Press.

Pelham, W. E., Gnagy, E. M., Greenslade, K. E., & Milich, R. (1992). Teacher ratings of DSN-III-R symptoms for the disruptive behavior disorders. *Journal of the American Academy of Child & Adolescent Psychiatry*, 31, 210–218.

Pelham, W. E., Greiner, A. R., & Gnagy, E. M. (1997). *Children's summer treatment program manual.* Buffalo, NY: Comprehensive Treatment for Attention Deficit Disorders.

Autism Spectrum Disorder

Empirical Support

American Academy of Child & Adolescent Psychiatry. (1999). Practice parameters for the assessment and treatment of children, adolescents, and adults with autism and other pervasive developmental disorders. *Journal of the American Academy of Child & Adolescent Psychiatry*, 38(12), 32S–54S.

Koegel, L. K., Koegel, R. L., Vernon, T. W., & Brookman-Frazee, L. I. (2010). Empirically supported pivotal response treatment for children with autism spectrum disorders. In J. R. Weisz & A. E. Kazdin (Eds.), *Evidence-based psychotherapies for children and adolescents* (2nd ed., pp. 327–344). New York, NY: Guilford Press.

Lovass, O. I., Cross, S., & Revlin, S. (2010). Autistic disorder. In J. E. Fisher & W. T. O'Donohue (Eds.), *Practitioners guide to evidence-based psychotherapy* (pp. 101–114). New York, NY: Springer.

Reichow, B., Barton, E. E., Boyd, B. A., & Hume, K. (2012). Early intensive behavioral intervention (EIBI) for young children with autism spectrum disorders (ASD). *Cochrane Database of Systematic Reviews, 2012*(10), CD009260. DOI: 10.1002/14651858.CD009260.pub2.

Rogers, S. J., & Vismara, L. A. (2008). Evidence-based comprehensive treatment for early autism. *Journal of Clinical Child and Adolescent Psychology, 37*, 8–38.

Smith, T. (2010). Early and intensive behavioral intervention in autism. In J. R. Weisz & A. E. Kazdin (Eds.), *Evidence-based psychotherapies for children and adolescents* (2nd ed., pp. 312–326). New York, NY: Guilford Press.

Smith, T., Groen, A., & Wynn, J. W. (2000). Randomized trial of intensive early intervention for children with pervasive developmental disorder. *American Journal on Mental Retardation, 4*, 269–285.

Swallows, G., & Graupner, T. (2005). Intensive behavioral treatment for autism: Four-year outcome and predictors. *American Journal on Mental Retardation, 110*, 417–436.

Clinical Resources

Baker, J. E. (2003). *Social skills training for children and adolescents with Asperger syndrome and speech-communication problems.* Shawnee Mission, KS: AAPC.

Gagnon, E. (2001). *Power cards: Using special interests to motivate children and youth with Asperger syndrome and autism.* Shawnee Mission, KS: AAPC.

Koegel, R. L., & Koegel, L. K. (2006). *Pivotal response treatments for autism communication, social, and academic development.* Baltimore, MD: Brookes.

Koegel, R. L., & Koegel, L. K. (2012). *The PRT pocket guide: Pivotal response treatment for autism spectrum disorders.* Baltimore, MD: Brookes.

Lovaas, O. I. (2003). *Teaching individuals with developmental delays: Basic intervention techniques.* Austin, TX: PRO-ED.

Conduct Disorder

Empirical Support

Alexander, J. F., Holtzworth-Munroe, A., & Jameson, P. B. (1994). The process and outcome of marital and family therapy research: Review and evaluation. In A. E. Bergin & S. L. Garfield (Eds.), *Handbook of psychotherapy and behavior change* (4th ed., pp. 595–630). New York, NY: Wiley.

Barry, T.D., & Pardini, D. A. (2003). Anger control training for aggressive youth. In A. E. Kazdin & J. R. Weisz, (Eds.), *Evidence-based psychotherapies for children and adolescents* (pp. 263–281). New York, NY: Guilford Press.

Brestan, E. V., & Eyberg, S. M. (1998). Effective psychosocial treatments of conduct-disordered children and adolescents: 29 years, 82 studies, and 5,272 kids. *Journal of Clinical Child Psychology, 27(2),* 180–189.

Eyberg, S. M., Nelson, M. M., & Boggs, S. R. (2008). Evidence-based psychosocial treatments for child and adolescent with disruptive behavior. *Journal of Clinical Child & Adolescent Psychology, 37,* 215–237.

Forgatch, M. S., & Patterson, G. R. (2010). Parent management training—Oregon model: An intervention for antisocial behavior in children and adolescents. In J. R. Weisz & A. E. Kazdin (Eds.), *Evidence-based psychotherapies for children and adolescents* (2nd ed., pp. 159–168). New York, NY: Guilford Press.

Furlong, M., McGilloway, S., Bywater, T., Hutchings, J., Smith, S. M., & Donnelly, M. (2012). Behavioural and cognitive-behavioural group-based parenting programmes for early-onset conduct problems in children aged 3 to 12 years. *Cochrane Database of Systematic Reviews, 2012*(2), CD008225. DOI: 10.1002/14651858.CD008225.pub2.

Henggeler, S. W., Schoenwald, S. K., Borduin, C. M., Rowland, M. D., & Cunningham, P. B. (1998). *Multisystemic treatment of antisocial behavior in children and adolescents.* New York, NY: Guilford Press.

Kazdin, A. E. (2005). *Parent management training: Treatment for oppositional, aggressive, and antisocial behavior in children and adolescents.* New York, NY: Oxford University Press.

Kazdin, A. E. (2007). Psychosocial treatments for conduct disorder in children and adolescents. In P. E. Nathan & J. M. Gorman's (Eds.), *A guide to treatments that work* (3rd ed., pp. 71–104). New York, NY: Oxford University Press.

Kazdin, A. E. (2010). Problem-solving skills training and parent management training for conduct disorder. In J. R. Weisz & A. E. Kazdin (Eds.), *Evidence-based psychotherapies for children and adolescents* (2nd ed., pp. 211–226). New York, NY: Guilford Press.

Kutcher, S., Aman, M., Brooks, S. J., Buitelaar, J., van Daalen, E., Fegert, J., . . . Tyano, S. (2004). International consensus statement on attention-deficit/hyperactivity disorder (ADHD) and disruptive behaviour disorders (DBDs): Clinical implications and treatment practice suggestions. *European Neuropsychopharmacology, 14*(1), 11–28.

Lochman, J. E., Boxmeyer, C. L., Powell, N. P., Barry, T. D., & Pardini, D. A. (2010). Anger control training for aggressive youths. In A. E. Kazdin & J. R. Weisz (Eds.), *Evidence-based psychotherapies for children and adolescents* (2nd ed., pp. 227–242). New York, NY: Guilford Press.

Robbins, M. S., Schwartz, S., & Szapocznik, J. (2004). Structural ecosystems therapy with Hispanic adolescents exhibiting disruptive behavior disorders. In J. R. Ancis (Ed.), *Culturally responsive interventions: Innovative approaches to working with diverse populations* (pp. 71–99). New York, NY: Brunner-Routledge.

Robbins, M. S., Horigian, V., Szapocznik, J., & Ucha, J. (2010). Treating Hispanic youths using brief strategic family therapy. In A. E. Kazdin & J. R. Weisz (Eds.), *Evidence-based psychotherapies for children and adolescents* (2nd ed., pp. 375–390). New York, NY: Guilford Press.

Sanders, M. R. (2008). The Triple P-Positive Parenting program as a public health approach to strengthening parenting. *Journal of Family Psychology, 22*, 506–517.

Webster-Stratton, C., & Reid, M. J. (2010). The incredible years parents, teachers, and children training series: A multifaceted treatment approach for young children. In J. R. Weisz & A. E. Kazdin (Eds.), *Evidence-based psychotherapies for children and adolescents* (2nd ed., pp. 194–210). New York, NY: Guilford Press.

Woolfenden, S., Williams, K. J., & Peat, J. (2001). Family and parenting interventions in children and adolescents with conduct disorder and delinquency aged 10–17. *Cochrane Database of Systematic Reviews, 2001*(2), CD003015. doi:10.1002/14651858.CD003015.

Clinical Resources

Achenbach, T. M., & Edelbrock, C. (1991). *Manual for the child behavior checklist.* Burlington, VT: Department of Psychiatry, University of Vermont.

Barkley, R. A. (2013). *Defiant children: A clinician's manual for assessment and parent training* (3rd ed.). New York, NY: Guilford Press.

Brinkmeyer, M., & Eyberg, S. M. (2010). Parent-child interaction therapy for oppositional children. In J. R. Weisz & A. E. Kazdin (Eds.), *Evidence-based psychotherapies for children and adolescents* (2nd ed., pp. 179–193). New York, NY: Guilford Press.

Eyberg, S., & Pincus, D. (1999). *Eyberg child behavior inventory & Sutter-Eyberg student behavior inventory–revised: Professional manual.* Odessa, FL: Psychological Assessment Resources.

Forgatch, M. S., & Patterson, G. R. (2010). Parent management training—Oregon model: An intervention for antisocial behavior in children and adolescents. In J. R. Weisz & A. E. Kazdin (Eds.), *Evidence-based psychotherapies for children and adolescents* (2nd ed., pp. 159–168). New York, NY: Guilford Press.

Functional Family Therapy. Available from www.fftinc.com

Gerard, A. B. (1994). *Parent-child relationship inventory (PCRI) manual.* Los Angeles, CA: WPS.

Henggeler, S. W., Schoenwald, S. K., Borduin, C. M., Rowland, M. D., & Cunningham, P. B. (1998). *Multisystemic treatment of antisocial behavior in children and adolescents.* New York, NY: Guilford Press.

Incredible Years. Available from www.incredibleyears.com

Kazdin, A. E. (2005). *Parent management training: Treatment for oppositional, aggressive, and antisocial behavior in children and adolescents.* New York, NY: Oxford University Press.

Kazdin, A. E. (2010). Problem-solving skills training and parent management training for conduct disorder. In J. R. Weisz & A. E. Kazdin (Eds.), *Evidence-based psychotherapies for children and adolescents* (2nd ed., pp. 211–226). New York, NY: Guilford Press.

Lochman, J. E., Boxmeyer, C. L., Powell, N. P., Barry, T. D., & Pardini, D. A. (2010). Anger control training for aggressive youths. In A. E. Kazdin & J. R. Weisz (Eds.), *Evidence-based psychotherapies for children and adolescents* (2nd ed., pp. 227–242). New York, NY: Guilford Press.

McNeil, C. B., & Humbree-Kigin, T. L. (2010). *Parent-child interaction therapy* (2nd ed.). New York, NY: Springer.

Robbins, M. S., Szapocznik, J., Santisteban, D. A., IIervis, O., Mitrani, V. B., & Schwartz, S. (2003). Brief Strategic Family Therapy for Hispanic youth. In A. E. Kazdin & J. R. Weisz (Eds.), *Evidence-based psychotherapies for children and adolescents* (pp. 407–424). New York, NY: Guilford Press.

Sanders, M. R., & Murphy-Brennan, M. (2010). The international dissemination of the triple p-positive parenting program. In A. E. Kazdin & J. R. Weisz (Eds.), *Evidence-based psychotherapies for children and adolescents* (2nd ed., pp. 519–537). New York, NY: Guilford Press.

Triple-P. Available from www.triplep.net

Webster-Stratton, C. (2011). *The incredible years: A trouble shooting guide for parents of children aged 2–8 years.* Seattle, WA: The Incredible Years.

Webster-Stratton, C., & Reid, M. J. (2010). The incredible years parents, teachers, and children training series: A multifaceted treatment approach for young children. In J. R. Weisz & A. E. Kazdin (Eds.), *Evidence-based psychotherapies for children and adolescents* (2nd ed., pp. 194–210). New York, NY: Guilford Press.

Depression

Empirical Support

American Academy of Child & Adolescent Psychiatry (2007). Practice parameters for the assessment and treatment of children and adolescents with depressive disorders. *Journal of the American Academy of Child & Adolescent Psychiatry, 46*(11), 1503–1526.

David-Ferdon, C., & Kaslow, N. J. (2008). Evidence-based psychosocial treatments for child and adolescent depression. *Journal of Clinical Child & Adolescent Psychology, 37*, 62–104.

Muratori, F., Picchi, L., Bruni, G., Patarnello, M., & Romagnoli, G. (2003). A two-year follow-up of psychodynamic psychotherapy for internalizing disorders in children. *Journal of the American Academy of Child and Adolescent Psychiatry, 42*, 331–339.

National Institute for Health and Clinical Excellence. (2005). *Depression in children and young people: Identification and management in primary, community, and secondary care.* Clinical guideline 28. Available from http://guidance.nice.org.uk/CG28

Stark, K. D., Hargrave, J., Hersh, B., Greenberg, M., Herren, J., & Fisher, M. (2008). Treatment of childhood depression: The ACTION program. In J. R. Z. Abela & B. L. Hankin (Eds.), *Handbook of depression in children and adolescents* (pp. 224–227). New York, NY: Guilford Press.

Stark, K. D., Streusand, W., Krumholz, L., & Patel, P. (2010). Cognitive-behavioral therapy for depression: The ACTION treatment program for girls. In A. E. Kazdin & J. R. Weisz, (Eds.), *Evidence-based psychotherapies for children and adolescents* (2nd ed., pp. 93–109). New York, NY: Guilford Press.

Treatment for Adolescents with Depression Study (2003). Treatment for Adolescents with Depression Study (TADS): Rationale, design, and methods. *Journal of the American Academy of Child & Adolescent Psychiatry, 42*, 531–542.

Clinical Resources

Beck, A. T., Rush, A. J., Shaw, B. F., & Emery, G. (1979). *Cognitive therapy of depression.* New York, NY: Guilford Press.

Beck, J. S., Beck, A. T., & Jolly, J. B. (2005). *Beck depression inventory for youth.* Available from www.pearsonassessments.com

Beidel, D. C., Turner, S. M., & Morris, T. L. (2004). *Social effectiveness therapy for children and adolescents (SET-C).* Toronto, Ontario: Multi-Health Systems.

Byng - Hall, J. (1995). *Rewriting family script: Improvisation and systems change.* New York, NY: Guilford Press.

Cramer, B., & Palacio Espasa, F. (1993). *La pratique des psychotherapies meres-bebes (The practice of maternal-infant psychotherapy).* Paris, France: PUF.

Davanloo, H. (1978). *Basic principles and techniques in short-term dynamic psychotherapy.* New York, NY: S. P. Medical and Scientific Books.

Dudley, C. D. (1997). *Treating depressed children.* Oakland, CA: New Harbinger.

Kovacs, M. (1980). Rating scales to assess depression in school-aged children. *Acta Paediatrica, 46*, 305–315.

Penn Resiliency Project. Available from www.ppc.sas.upenn.edu/ prpsum.htm

Stark, K. D., Simpson, J., Schnoebelen, S., Hargrave, J., Glenn, R., & Molnar, J. (2006). *Therapist's manual for ACTION*. Broadmore, PA: Workbook.

Stark, K. D., Yancy, M., Simpson, J., & Molnar, J. (2006). Treating depressed children: *Therapist's manual for parent component of ACTION*. Ardmore, PA: Workbook.

Verduyn, C., Rogers, J., & Wood, A. (2009). *Depression: Cognitive behavior therapy with children and young people*. New York, NY: Routledge.

Zimmerman, M., Coryell, W., Corenthal, C., & Wilson, S. (1986). A self-report scale to diagnose major depressive disorder. *Archives of General Psychiatry, 43*, 1076–1081.

Enuresis/Encopresis

Empirical Support

American Academy of Child & Adolescent Psychiatry. (2004). Practice parameters for children and adolescents with enuresis. *Journal of the American Academy of Child & Adolescent Psychiatry, 43*, 1540–1550.

Brazzelli, M., Griffiths, P. V., Cody, J. D., & Tappin, D. (2011). Behavioural and cognitive interventions with or without other treatments for the management of faecal incontinence in children. *Cochrane Database of Systematic Reviews, 2011*(12), CD002240. doi:10.1002/14651858.CD002240.pub4.

Field, C. E., & Friman, P. C. (2010). Encopresis. In J. E. Fisher & W. T. O'Donohue (Eds.), *Practitioners guide to evidence-based psychotherapy* (pp. 277–283). New York, NY: Springer.

Friman, P. C. *Behavioral (alarm-based) treatment for nocturnal enuresis*. Available from www.therapyadvisor.com

Friman, P. C. *Biobehavioral treatment for functional encopresis*. Available from www.therapyadvisor.com

Glazener, C. M. A., & Evans, J. H. C. (2004). Simple behavioural and physical interventions for nocturnal enuresis in children. *Cochrane Database of Systematic Reviews, 2004*(2), CD003637. doi:10.1002/14651858.CD003637.pub2.

Glazener, C. M. A., Evans, J. H. C., & Peto, R. E. (2005). Alarm interventions for nocturnal enuresis in children. *Cochrane Database of Systematic Reviews, 2005*(2), CD002911. doi:10.1002/14651858.CD002911.pub2.

Glazener, C. M. A., Evans, J. H. C., & Peto, R. E. (2004). Complex behavioural and educational interventions for nocturnal enuresis in children. *Cochrane Database of Systematic Reviews, 2004*(1), CD004668. doi:10.1002/14651858.CD004668.

Mellon, M. W., & Houts, A. C. (2010). Nocturnal enuresis: Evidence-based perspectives in etiology, assessment, and treatment. In J. E. Fisher & W. T. O'Donohue (Eds.), *Practitioners guide to evidence-based psychotherapy* (pp. 432–441). New York, NY: Springer.

Clinical Resources

Christophersen, E. R., & Friman, P. C. (2004). Elimination disorders. In R. Brown (Ed.), *Handbook of pediatric psychology in school settings* (pp. 467–487). Mahwah, NJ: Erlbaum.

Christophersen, E. R., & Friman, P. C. (2006). *Elimination disorders in children and adolescents.* Cambridge, MA: Hogrefe.

Friman, P. C. (2008). Evidence-based therapies for enuresis and encopresis. In R. G. Steele, T. D. Elkin, & M. C. Roberts (Eds.), *Handbook of evidence-based therapies for children and adolescents* (pp. 311–333). New York, NY: Springer.

To order an alarm: Palco Laboratories, 9030 Sequel Avenue, Santa Cruz, CA 95062, Telephone (800) 346-4488.

Medical Condition

Empirical Support

Drotar, D. (2006). *Psychological interventions in childhood chronic illness.* Washington, DC: American Psychological Association.

Eccleston, C., Palermo, T. M., Fisher, E., & Law, E. (2012). Psychological interventions for parents of children and adolescents with chronic illness. *Cochrane Database of Systematic Reviews, 2012*(8), CD009660. doi:10.1002/14651858.CD009660.pub2.

Eccleston, C., Palermo, T. M., Williams, A. C. D. C., Lewandowski, A., & Morley, S. (2009). Psychological therapies for the management of chronic and recurrent pain in children and adolescents. *Cochrane Database of Systematic Reviews, 2009*(2), CD003968. doi:10.1002/14651858.CD003968.pub2.

Rodgers, M. D., Fayter, G. Richardson, G. Ritchie, G., Lewin, R., & Sowden, A. J. (2005). *The effects of psychosocial interventions in cancer and heart disease: A review of systematic reviews.* York, England: Centre for Reviews and Dissemination, University of York.

Thompson, R. J., & Gustafson, K. E. (1996). *Adaptation to chronic childhood illness.* Washington, DC: American Psychological Association.

Clinical Resources

Brown, R. T., Daly, B. P., & Rickel, A. U. (2007). *Chronic illness in children and adolescents.* Cambridge, MA: Hogrefe.

Drotar, D. (2000). *Promoting adherence to medical treatment in chronic childhood illness: Concepts, methods, and interventions.* Mahwah, NJ: Erlbaum.

Drotar, D. (2006). *Psychological interventions in childhood chronic illness.* Washington, DC: American Psychological Association.

Hayman, L., Mahon, M., & Turner R. (2002). *Chronic illness in children: An evidence-based approach.* New York, NY: Springer.

Roberts, M. C., & Steele, R. G. (Eds.). (2010). *Handbook of pediatric psychology* (4th ed.). New York, NY: Guilford Press.

Szigethy, E., Thompson, R. Turner, S., Delaney, P., Beardslee, W., & Weisz, J. (2012). Chronic physical illness: Inflammatory bowel disease as a prototype. In E. Szigethy, J. Weisz, & R. Findling (Eds.), *Cognitive-behavior therapy for children and adolescents* (331–378). Washington, DC: American Psychiatric Publishing.

Obsessive-Compulsive Disorder

Empirical Support

American Academy of Child & Adolescent Psychiatry (2012). Practice parameters for the assessment and treatment of children and adolescents with obsessive-compulsive disorder. *Journal of the American Academy of Child & Adolescent Psychiatry, 51*(1), 98–113.

Barrett, P. M., Farrell, L., Pina, A. A., Piacentini, J., & Peris, T. S. (2008). Evidence-based psychosocial treatments for child and adolescent Obsessive-Compulsive Disorder. *Journal of Clinical Child & Adolescent Psychology, 37*, 131–155.

Franklin M. E., Freeman, J., & March, J. S. (2010). Treating pediatric obsessive-compulsive disorder using exposure-based cognitive-behavioral therapy. In A. E. Kazdin & J. R. Weisz (Eds.), *Evidence-based psychotherapies for children and adolescents* (2nd ed., pp. 80–92). New York, NY: Guilford Press.

Gold-Steinberg, S., & Logan, D. (1999). Integrating play therapy into the treatment of children with OCD. *American Journal of Orthopsychiatry, 69*(4), 495–503.

Hiss, H., Foa, E. B., & Kozak, M. J. (1994). A relapse prevention program for treatment of obsessive compulsive disorder. *Journal of Consulting and Clinical Psychology, 62*, 801–808.

Kircanski, K., Peris, T. S., & Piacentini, J. C. (2011). Cognitive-behavioral therapy for obsessive-compulsive disorder in children and adolescents. *Child and Adolescent Psychiatric Clinics of North America, 20(2)*, 239–254.

O'Kearney, R. T., Anstey, K., von Sanden, C., & Hunt, A. (2010). Behavioural and cognitive behavioural therapy for obsessive compulsive disorder in children and adolescents. *Cochrane Database of Systematic Reviews, 2010*(4), CD004856. doi:10.1002/14651858.CD004856.pub2.

Pediatric OCD Treatment Study (POTS) Team. (2004). Cognitive-behavior therapy, sertraline and their combination for children and adolescents with obsessive-compulsive disorder: The Pediatric OCD Treatment Study (POTS) randomized controlled trial. *Journal of the American Medical Association, 292*, 1969–1976.

Clinical Resources

Freeman, J. B., & Garcia, A. M. (2008). *Family-based treatment for young children with OCD, therapist guide*. New York, NY: Oxford University Press.

Greco, L., & Hayes, S. C. (Eds.). (2008). *Acceptance and mindfulness treatments for children and adolescents: A practitioner's guide.* Oakland, CA: New Harbinger.

Haley, J. (1984). *Ordeal therapy.* San Francisco, CA: Jossey-Bass.

Haley, J. (1993). *Uncommon therapy: The psychiatric techniques of Milton H. Erickson, M.D.* New York, NY: Norton.

March, J., and Mulle, K. (1998). *OCD in children and adolescents: A cognitive-behavioral treatment manual.* New York, NY: Guilford Press.

Piacentini, J., Langley, A., & Roblek, J. (2007). *Cognitive behavioral treatment of childhood OCD: It's only a false alarm, Therapist guide.* New York, NY: Oxford University Press.

Scahill, L., Riddle, M. A., McSwiggin-Hardin, M., Ort, S. I., King, R. A., Goodman, W. K., . . . Leckman, J. F. (1997). Children's Yale-Brown Obsessive-Compulsive Scale: Reliability and validity. *Journal of the American Academy of Child & Adolescent Psychiatry, 36,* 844–852.

Wagner, A. P. (2003). *Treatment of OCD in children and adolescents: A cognitive-behavioral therapy manual.* Rochester, NY: Lighthouse Press.

Oppositional Defiant

Empirical Support

American Academy of Child & Adolescent Psychiatry (2007). Practice parameters for the assessment and treatment of children and adolescents with oppositional defiant disorder. *Journal of the American Academy of Child & Adolescent Psychiatry, 46*(1), 126–141.

Eyberg, S. M., Nelson, M. M., & Boggs, S. R. (2008). Evidence-based psychosocial treatments for child and adolescent with disruptive behavior. *Journal of Clinical Child & Adolescent Psychology, 37,* 215–237.

Furlong, M., McGilloway, S., Bywater, T., Hutchings, J., Smith, S. M., & Donnelly, M. (2012). Behavioural and cognitive-behavioural group-based parenting programmes for early-onset conduct problems in children aged 3 to 12 years. *Cochrane Database of Systematic Reviews, 2012*(2), CD008225. doi:10.1002/14651858.CD008225.pub2.

Kazdin, A. E. (2005). *Parent management training: Treatment for oppositional, aggressive, and antisocial behavior in children and adolescents.* New York, NY: Oxford University Press.

Kazdin, A. E. (2010). Problem-solving skills training and parent management training for conduct disorder. In J. R. Weisz & A. E. Kazdin (Eds.), *Evidence-based psychotherapies for children and adolescents* (2nd ed., pp. 211–226). New York, NY: Guilford Press.

Kutcher, S., Aman, M., Brooks, S. J., Buitelaar, J., van Daalen, E., Fegert, J., . . . Tyano, S. (2004). International consensus statement on attention-deficit/hyperactivity disorder (ADHD) and disruptive behaviour disorders (DBDs):

Clinical implications and treatment practice suggestions. *European Neuro-psychopharmacology, 14(1),* 11–28.

Lochman, J. E., Boxmeyer, C. L., Powell, N. P., Barry, T. D., & Pardini, D. A. (2010). Anger control training for aggressive youths. In A. E. Kazdin & J. R. Weisz (Eds.), *Evidence-based psychotherapies for children and adolescents* (2nd ed., pp. 227–242). New York, NY: Guilford Press.

Sanders, M. R. (2008). The Triple P-Positive Parenting program as a public health approach to strengthening parenting. *Journal of Family Psychology, 22,* 506–517.

Webster-Stratton, C., & Reid, M. J. (2010). The incredible years parents, teachers, and children training series: A multifaceted treatment approach for young children. In J. R. Weisz & A. E. Kazdin (Eds.), *Evidence-based psychotherapies for children and adolescents* (2nd ed., pp. 194–210). New York, NY: Guilford Press.

Zisser, A., & Eyberg, S.M. (2010). Treating oppositional behavior in children using parent-child interaction therapy. In A. E. Kazdin & J. R. Weisz (Eds.), *Evidence-based psychotherapies for children and adolescents* (2nd ed., pp. 179–193). New York, NY: Guilford Press.

Clinical Resources

Achenbach, T. M., & Edelbrock, C. (1991). *Manual for the child behavior checklist.* Burlington, VT: Department of Psychiatry, University of Vermont.

Barkley, R. A. (2013). *Defiant children: A clinician's manual for assessment and parent training* (3rd ed.). New York, NY: Guilford Press.

Eyberg, S., & Pincus, D. (1999*). Eyberg child behavior inventory & Sutter-Eyberg student behavior inventory–revised: Professional manual.* Odessa, FL: Psychological Assessment Resources.

Forgatch, M. S., & Patterson, G. R. (2010). Parent management training—Oregon model: An intervention for antisocial behavior in children and adolescents. In J. R. Weisz & A. E. Kazdin (Eds.), *Evidence-based psychotherapies for children and adolescents* (2nd ed., pp. 159–168). New York, NY: Guilford Press.

Gerard, A. B. (1994). Parent-child relationship inventory (PCRI) manual. Los Angeles, CA: WPS.

Incredible Years. Available from www.incredibleyears.com

Kazdin, A. E. (2005). *Parent management training: Treatment for oppositional, aggressive, and antisocial behavior in children and adolescents.* New York, NY: Oxford University Press.

Kazdin, A. E. (2010). Problem-solving skills training and parent management training for conduct disorder. In J. R. Weisz & A. E. Kazdin (Eds.), *Evidence-based psychotherapies for children and adolescents* (2nd ed., pp. 211–226). New York, NY: Guilford Press.

Lochman, J. E., Boxmeyer, C. L., Powell, N. P., Barry, T. D., & Pardini, D. A. (2010). Anger control training for aggressive youths. In A. E. Kazdin & J. R. Weisz (Eds.), *Evidence-based psychotherapies for children and adolescents* (2nd ed., pp. 227–242). New York, NY: Guilford Press.

McNeil, C. B., & Humbree-Kigin, T. L. (2010). *Parent-child interaction therapy* (2nd ed.). New York, NY: Springer.

Sanders, M. R., & Murphy-Brennan, M. (2010). The international dissemination of the triple p-positive parenting program. In A. E. Kazdin & J. R. Weisz (Eds.), *Evidence-based psychotherapies for children and adolescents* (2nd ed., pp. 519–537). New York, NY: Guilford Press.

Triple-P. Available from www.triplep.net

Webster-Stratton, C. (2011). *The incredible years: A trouble shooting guide for parents of children aged 2–8 years.* Seattle, WA: The Incredible Years.

Webster-Stratton, C., & Reid, M. J. (2010). The incredible years parents, teachers, and children training series: A multifaceted treatment approach for young children. In J. R. Weisz & A. E. Kazdin (Eds.), *Evidence-based psychotherapies for children and adolescents* (2nd ed., pp. 194–210). New York, NY: Guilford Press.

Zisser, A., & Eyberg, S. M. (2010). Treating oppositional behavior in children using parent-child interaction therapy. In A. E. Kazdin & J. R. Weisz (Eds.), *Evidence-based psychotherapies for children and adolescents* (2nd ed., pp. 179–193). New York, NY: Guilford Press.

Overweight/Obesity

Empirical Support

Barlow, S. E., & Expert Committee. (2007). Expert committee recommendations regarding the prevention, assessment, and treatment of child and adolescent overweight and obesity: Summary report. *Pediatrics, 120*(4), S164–S192.

Epstein, L. H., & Wing, R. R. (1987). Behavioral treatment of childhood obesity. *Psychological Bulletin, 101*, 331–342.

Golan, M. (2006). Parents as agents of change in childhood obesity: From research to practice. *International Journal of Pediatric Obesity, 1*(2), 66–76.

Golan, M., Kaufman, V., & Shahar, D.R. (2006). Childhood obesity treatment: Targeting parents exclusively v. parents and children. *British Journal of Nutrition, 95*, 1008–1015.

Loeb, K. L. *Obesity and pediatric overweight.* Available from http://www.div12.org/PsychologicalTreatments/disorders/obesity_main.php

National Institute for Health and Clinical Excellence. (2005). *Obesity: Guidance on the prevention, identification, assessment and management of overweight and obesity in adults and children.* Clinical guideline 43. Available from http://guidance.nice.org.uk/CG43

Wadden, T. A., Foster, G. D., & Letizia, K. A. (1994). One-year behavioral treatment of obesity: Comparison of moderate and severe caloric restriction and the effects of weight maintenance therapy. *Journal of Consulting and Clinical Psychology, 62*, 165–171.

Wadden, T. A., & The Look AHEAD Research Group. (2006). The Look AHEAD study: A description of the lifestyle intervention and the evidence supporting it. *Obesity, 14*, 737–752.

Clinical Resources

Brownell, K. D. (2004). *The LEARN program for weight management* (10th ed.). Dallas, TX: American Health Publishing Company.

Parenting

Empirical Support

Eyberg, S. M., Nelson, M. M., & Boggs, S. R. (2008). Evidence-based psychosocial treatments for child and adolescent with disruptive behavior. *Journal of Clinical Child & Adolescent Psychology, 37*, 215–237.

Forgatch, M. S., & Patterson, G. R. (2010). Parent management training—Oregon model: An intervention for antisocial behavior in children and adolescents. In J. R. Weisz & A. E. Kazdin (Eds.), *Evidence-based psychotherapies for children and adolescents* (2nd ed., pp. 159–168). New York, NY: Guilford Press.

Furlong, M., McGilloway, S., Bywater, T., Hutchings, J., Smith, S. M., & Donnelly, M. (2012). Behavioural and cognitive-behavioural group-based parenting programmes for early-onset conduct problems in children aged 3 to 12 years. *Cochrane Database of Systematic Reviews, 2012*(2), CD008225. doi:10.1002/14651858.CD008225.pub2.

Hamilton, S. B., & MacQuiddy, S. L. (1984). Self-administered behavioral parent training: Enhancement of treatment efficacy using a time-out signal seat. *Journal of Clinical Child and Adolescent Psychology, 13*(1), 61–69.

Kazdin, A. E. (2005). *Parent management training: Treatment for oppositional, aggressive, and antisocial behavior in children and adolescents.* New York, NY: Oxford University Press.

Kazdin, A. E. (2007). Psychosocial treatments for conduct disorder in children and adolescents. In P. E. Nathan & J. M. Gorman (Eds.), *A guide to treatments that work* (3rd ed., pp. 71–104). New York, NY: Oxford University Press.

Kazdin, A. E. (2010). Problem-solving skills training and parent management training for conduct disorder. In J. R. Weisz & A. E. Kazdin (Eds.), *Evidence-based psychotherapies for children and adolescents* (2nd ed., pp. 211–226). New York, NY: Guilford Press.

Kutcher, S., Aman, M., Brooks, S. J., Buitelaar, J., van Daalen, E., Fegert, J., . . . Tyano, S. (2004). International consensus statement on attention-deficit/hyperactivity disorder (ADHD) and disruptive behaviour disorders (DBDs): Clinical implications and treatment practice suggestions. *European Neuropsychopharmacology, 14*(1), 11–28.

Sanders, M. R. (2008). The Triple P-Positive Parenting program as a public health approach to strengthening parenting. *Journal of Family Psychology, 22*, 506–517.

Webster-Stratton, C., & Reid, M. J. (2010). The incredible years parents, teachers, and children training series: A multifaceted treatment approach for young children. In J. Weisz & A. Kazdin (Eds.), *Evidence-based psychotherapies for children and adolescents* (2nd ed., pp. 194–210). New York, NY: Guilford Press.

Woolfenden, S., Williams, K. J., & Peat, J. (2001). Family and parenting interventions in children and adolescents with conduct disorder and delinquency aged 10–17. *Cochrane Database of Systematic Reviews, 2001*(2), CD003015. DOI: 10.1002/14651858.CD003015.

Clinical Resources

Achenbach, T. M., & Edelbrock, C. (1991). *Manual for the child behavior checklist.* Burlington, VT: Department of Psychiatry, University of Vermont.

Barkley, R. A. (2013). *Defiant children: A clinician's manual for assessment and parent training* (3rd ed.). New York, NY: Guilford Press.

Eyberg, S., & Pincus, D. (1999). *Eyberg child behavior inventory & Sutter-Eyberg student behavior inventory–revised: Professional manual.* Odessa, FL: Psychological Assessment Resources.

Forgatch, M. S., & Patterson, G. R. (2010). Parent management training—Oregon model: An intervention for antisocial behavior in children and adolescents. In J. R. Weisz & A. E. Kazdin (Eds.), *Evidence-based psychotherapies for children and adolescents* (2nd ed., pp. 159–168). New York, NY: Guilford Press.

Gerard, A. B. (1994). *Parent-child relationship inventory (PCRI) manual.* Los Angeles, CA: WPS.

Incredible Years. Available from www.incredibleyears.com

Kazdin, A. E. (2005). *Parent management training: Treatment for oppositional, aggressive, and antisocial behavior in children and adolescents.* New York, NY: Oxford University Press.

Kazdin, A. E. (2010). Problem-solving skills training and parent management training for conduct disorder. In J. R. Weisz & A. E. Kazdin (Eds.), *Evidence-based psychotherapies for children and adolescents* (2nd ed., pp. 211–226). New York, NY: Guilford Press.

Lochman, J. E., Boxmeyer, C. L., Powell, N. P., Barry, T. D., & Pardini, D. A. (2010). Anger control training for aggressive youths. In A. E. Kazdin & J. R. Weisz (Eds.), *Evidence-based psychotherapies for children and adolescents* (2nd ed., pp. 227–242). New York, NY: Guilford Press.

McNeil, C. B., & Humbree-Kigin, T. L. (2010). *Parent-child interaction therapy* (2nd ed.). New York, NY: Springer.

Parenting Stress Index. Available from www4.parinc.com

Sanders, M. R., & Murphy-Brennan, M. (2010). The international dissemination of the triple p-positive parenting program. In A. E. Kazdin & J. R. Weisz (Eds.), *Evidence-based psychotherapies for children and adolescents* (2nd ed., pp. 519–537). New York, NY: Guilford Press.

Triple-P. Available from www.triplep.net

Webster-Stratton, C. (2011). *The incredible years: A trouble shooting guide for parents of children aged 2–8 years.* Seattle, WA: The Incredible Years.

Webster-Stratton, C., & Reid, M. J. (2010). The incredible years parents, teachers, and children training series: A multifaceted treatment approach for young children. In J. R. Weisz & A. E. Kazdin (Eds.), *Evidence-based psychotherapies for children and adolescents* (2nd ed., pp. 194–210). New York, NY: Guilford Press.

Zisser, A., & Eyberg, S.M. (2010). Treating oppositional behavior in children using parent-child interaction therapy. In A. E. Kazdin & J. R. Weisz (Eds.), *Evidence-based psychotherapies for children and adolescents* (2nd ed., pp. 179–193). New York, NY: Guilford Press.

Posttraumatic Stress Disorder (PTSD)

Empirical Support

Amaya-Jackson, L., Reynolds, V., Murray, M., McCarthy, G., Nelson, A., Cherney, M., . . . March, J. (2003). Cognitive behavioral treatment for pediatric posttraumatic stress disorder: Protocol and application in school and community settings. *Cognitive and Behavioral Practice, 10*, 204–213.

American Academy of Child & Adolescent Psychiatry. (2010). Practice parameters for the assessment and treatment of children and adolescents with posttraumatic stress disorder. *Journal of the American Academy of Child & Adolescent Psychiatry, 49*(4), 414–430.

Cohen, J. L., Berliner, L., & Mannarino, A. P. (2010). Trauma focused CBT for children with co-occurring trauma and behavior problems. *Child Abuse and Neglect, 34*, 215–224.

Cohen, J. A., Deblinger, E., Mannarino, A. P., & Steer, R. (2004). A multi-site, randomized controlled trial for children with sexual abuse-related PTSD symptoms. *Journal of the American Academy of Child and Adolescent Psychiatry, 43*, 393–402.

Cohen, J. A., Mannarino, A. P., & Deblinger, E. (2010). Trauma-focused cognitive-behavioral therapy for traumatized children. In J. R. Weisz & A. E. Kazdin (Eds.), *Evidence-based psychotherapies for children and adolescents* (2nd ed., pp. 295–311). New York, NY: Guilford Press.

Foa, E. B., Keane, T. M., & Friedman, M. J. (2004). *Effective treatments for PTSD: Practice guidelines from the International Society for Traumatic Stress Studies.* New York, NY: Guilford Press.

Gillies, D., Taylor, F., Gray, C., O'Brien, L., & D'Abrew, N. (2012). Psychological therapies for the treatment of post-traumatic stress disorder in children and adolescents. *Cochrane Database of Systematic Review, 2012*(12), CD006726. DOI: 10.1002/14651858.CD006726.pub2.

Silverman, W. K., Ortiz, C. D., Viswesvaran, C., Burns, B. J., Kolko, D. J., Putnam, F. W., & Amaya-Jackson, L. (2008). Evidence-based psychosocial treatments for child and adolescent exposed to traumatic events: A review and meta-analysis. *Journal of Clinical Child and Adolescent Psychology, 37,* 156–183.

Clinical Resources

Barkley, R. A. (2013). *Defiant children: A clinician's manual for assessment and parent training* (3rd ed.). New York, NY: Guilford Press.

Cohen, J. A., Mannarino, A. P., & Deblinger, E. (2006). *Treating trauma and traumatic grief in children and adolescents.* New York, NY: Guilford Press.

Cohen, J. A., Mannarino, A. P., & Deblinger, E. (2012). *Trauma-focused CBT for children and adolescents: Treatment applications.* New York, NY: Guilford Press.

Deblinger, E., & Heflin, A. H. (1996), *Treating sexually abused children and their nonoffending parents: A cognitive-behavioral approach.* Thousand Oaks, CA: Sage.

Foa, E. B., Johnson, K. M., Feeny, N. C., & Treadwell, K. R. H. (2001). The Child PTSD Symptom Scale: A preliminary examination of its psychometric properties. *Journal of Clinical Child Psychology, 30,* 376–384.

Frederick, C. J., Pynoos, R., & Nader, K. (1992). *Childhood Post-Traumatic Stress Reaction Index* [A copyrighted instrument]. (Available from UCLA Department of Psychiatry and Biobehavioral Sciences, 760 Westwood Plaza, Los Angeles, CA 90024).

Nader, K., Kriegler, J. A., Blake, D. D., Pynoos, R. S., Newman, E., & Weathers, F. W. (1996). *Clinician administered PTSD scale, child and adolescent version.* White River Junction, VT: National Center for PTSD.

Najavits, L. M. (2002). *Seeking safety: A treatment manual for PTSD and substance abuse.* New York, NY: Guilford Press.

Osofsky, J. D. (2011). *Clinical work with traumatized young children.* New York, NY: Guilford Press.

Silverman, W. K., & Albano, A. M. (1996). *The anxiety disorders interview schedule for DSM-IV-Child and parent versions.* London, England: Oxford University Press.

Tinker, R. H., & Wilson, S. A. (1999*). Through the eyes of a child: EMDR with children.* New York, NY: Norton.

School Refusal

Empirical Support

American Academy of Child & Adolescent Psychiatry (2007). Practice parameters for the assessment and treatment of children and adolescents with anxiety disorders. *Journal of the American Academy of Child & Adolescent Psychiatry, 46*(2), 267–283.

Barrett, P. M., & Shortt, A. (2003). Parental involvement in the treatment of anxious children. In A. E. Kazdin & J. R. Weisz (Eds.), *Evidence-based psychotherapies for children and adolescents* (pp.101–119). New York, NY: Guilford Press.

Grills-Taquechel, A. E., & Ollendick, T. H. (2013). *Phobic and anxiety disorders in children and adolescents.* Cambridge, MA: Hogrefe.

Heyne, D., King, N., Tonge, B., Rollings, S., Young, D., Pritchard, M., & Ollendick, T. H. (2002). Evaluation of child therapy and caregiver training in the treatment of school refusal. *Journal of the American Academy of Child & Adolescent Psychiatry, 41*, 687–695.

James, A. A. C. J., Soler, A., & Weatherall, R. R. W. (2009). Cognitive behavioural therapy for anxiety disorders in children and adolescents. *Cochrane Database of Systematic Reviews, 2009*(4), CD004690. doi:10.1002/14651858.CD004690.pub2.

Kearney, C. A. (2008). School absenteeism and school refusal behavior in youth: A contemporary review. *Clinical Psychology Review, 28*, 451–471.

Kendall, P. C., Furr, J. M., & Podell, J. L. (2010). Child-focused treatment of anxiety. In J. R. Weisz & A. E. Kazdin (Eds.), *Evidence-based psychotherapies for children and adolescents* (2nd ed., pp. 45–60). New York, NY: Guilford Press.

King, N. J., Tonge, B. J., Heyne, D., Pritchard, M., Rollings, S., Young, D., . . . Ollendick, T. H. (1998). Cognitive-behavioral treatment of school-refusing children: A controlled evaluation. *Journal of the American Academy of Child & Adolescent Psychiatry, 37*, 395–403.

King, N. J., Tonge, B. J., Heyne, D., Turner, S. Pritchard, M., Young, D., . . . Ollendick, T. H. (2001). Cognitive-behavioural treatment of school-refusing children: Maintenance of improvement at 3- to 5-year follow-up. *Scandinavian Journal of Behaviour Therapy, 30*, 85–89.

Last, C. G., Hansen, C., & Franco, N. (1998). Cognitive-behavioral treatment of school phobia. *Journal of the American Academy of Child & Adolescent Psychiatry, 37*, 404–411.

Manassis, K., Mendlowitz, S. L., Scapillato, D., Avery, D., Fiksenbaum, L., Freire, M., . . . Ownes, M. (2002). Group and individual cognitive behavioral therapy for childhood anxiety disorders: A randomized trial. *Journal of the American Academy of Child & Adolescent Psychiatry, 41*, 1423–1430.

Pahl, K. M., & Barrett, P. M. (2010). Interventions for anxiety disorders in children using group cognitive behavioral therapy with family involvement. In J. R. Weisz & A. E. Kazdin (Eds.), *Evidence-based psychotherapies for children and adolescents* (2nd ed., pp. 61–79). New York, NY: Guilford Press.

Pina, A. A., Zerr, A. A., Gonzales, N. A., & Ortiz, C. D. (2009). Psychosocial interventions for school refusal behavior in children and adolescents. *Child Development Perspectives, 3*, 11–20.

Silverman, W. K., Pina, A. A., & Viswesvaran, C. (2008). Evidence-based psychosocial treatments for phobic and anxiety disorders in children and adolescents: A review and meta-analyses. *Journal of Clinical Child & Adolescent Psychology, 37*, 105–130.

Clinical Resources

Heyne, D., & Rollings, S. (2002). *School refusal: Parent, adolescent and child training skills*. Oxford, UK: Blackwell.

Kearney, C. A. (2008). *Helping school refusing children and their parents: A guide for school-based professionals*. New York, NY: Oxford University Press.

Kearney, C. A., & Albano, A. M. (2007). *When children refuse school: A cognitive-behavioral therapy approach, parent workbook* (2nd ed.). New York, NY: Oxford University Press.

Kearney, C. A., Stowman, S., Haight, C., & Wechsler, A. (2008). Manualized treatment for anxiety-based school refusal behavior in youth. In C. LeCroy (Ed.), *Handbook of evidence-based child and adolescent treatment manuals* (pp. 286–313). New York, NY: Oxford University Press.

Thambirajah, M. S., Grandison, K. J., & De-hayes, L. (2008). *Understanding school refusal: A handbook for professionals in education, health and social care.* London, UK: Jessica Kingsley.

Separation Anxiety

Empirical Support

American Academy of Child & Adolescent Psychiatry (2007). Practice parameters for the assessment and treatment of children and adolescents with anxiety disorders. *Journal of the American Academy of Child & Adolescent Psychiatry, 46*(2), 267–283.

Barrett, P. M., & Shortt, A. (2003). Parental involvement in the treatment of anxious children. In A. E. Kazdin & J. R. Weisz (Eds.), *Evidence-based psychotherapies for children and adolescents* (pp. 101–119). New York, NY: Guilford Press.

Callahan, C. L., Stevens, M. L., & Eyberg, S. (2010). Parent-child interaction therapy. In C. E. Schaefer (Ed.), *Play therapy for preschool children* (pp. 199–221). Washington, DC: American Psychological Association.

Grills-Taquechel, A. E., & Ollendick, T. H. (2013). *Phobic and anxiety disorders in children and adolescents.* Cambridge, MA: Hogrefe.

James, A. A. C. J., Soler, A., & Weatherall, R. R. W. (2009). Cognitive behavioural therapy for anxiety disorders in children and adolescents. *Cochrane Database of Systematic Reviews, 2009*(4), CD004690. doi:10.1002/14651858.CD004690.pub2.

Kendall, P. C., Furr, J. M., & Podell, J. L. (2010). Child-focused treatment of anxiety. In J. R. Weisz & A. E. Kazdin (Eds.), *Evidence-based psychotherapies for children and adolescents* (2nd ed., pp. 45–60). New York, NY: Guilford Press.

Pahl, K. M., & Barrett, P. M. (2010). Interventions for anxiety disorders in children using group cognitive behavioral therapy with family involvement. In J. R. Weisz & A. E. Kazdin (Eds.), *Evidence-based psychotherapies for children and adolescents* (2nd ed., pp. 61–79). New York, NY: Guilford Press.

Pincus, D. B., Santucci, L. C., Ehrenreich, J. T., & Eyberg, S. M. (2008). The implementation of modified parent-child interaction therapy for youth with separation anxiety disorder. *Cognitive and Behavioral Practice, 15*, 118–125.

Silverman, W. K., Pina, A. A., & Viswesvaran, C. (2008). Evidence-based psychosocial treatments for phobic and anxiety disorders in children and adolescents: A review and meta-analyses. *Journal of Clinical Child & Adolescent Psychology, 37*, 105–130.

Clinical Resources

Barrett, P. M. (2004). *Friends for life: Group leader's manual for children* (4th ed.). Brisbane: Australian Academic Press.

Barrett, P.M. (2007). *Fun friends: The teaching and training manual for group leaders.* Brisbane, Australia: Fun Friends.

Bernstein, D. A., Borkovec, T. D., & Hazlett-Stevens, H. (2000). *New directions in progressive relaxation training: A guidebook for helping professionals.* Westport, CT: Praeger.

Birmaher, B., Khetarpal, S., Brent, D., Cully, M. Balach, L. Kaufman, J., & Neer, S. M. (1997). The Screen for Child Anxiety Related Emotional Disorders (SCARED): Scale construction and psychometric characteristics. *Journal of the American Academy of Child & Adolescent Psychiatry, 36*, 545–553.

Eisen, A. R., & Schaefer, C. E. (2005). *Separation anxiety in children and adolescents: An individualized approach to assessment and treatment.* New York, NY: Guilford Press.

Flannery-Schroeder, E., & Kendall, P. C. (1996). *Cognitive behavioral therapy for anxious children: Therapist manual for group treatment.* Available from www.workbookpublishing.com

Howard, B., Chu, B. C., Krain, A. L., Marrs-Garcia, A. L., & Kendall, P. C. (2000). *Cognitive-behavioral family therapy for anxious children* (2nd ed.). Available from www.workbookpublishing.com

Kendall, P. C., & Hedtke, K. A. (2006). *Cognitive-behavioral therapy for anxious children* (3rd ed.). Available from www.workbookpublishing.com

March, J. S., Parker, J. D., Sullivan, K., Stallings, P., & Conners, C. K. (1997). The multidimensional anxiety scale for children (MASC): Factor structure, reliability, and validity. *Journal of the American Academy of Child and Adolescent Psychiatry, 36*, 544–565.

McNeil, C. B., & Humbree-Kigin, T. L. (2010). *Parent-child interaction therapy* (2nd ed.). New York, NY: Springer.

Ollendick, T. H. (1987). The fear survey schedule for children—Revised. In M. Hersen & A. S. Bellack (Eds.), *Dictionary of behavioral assessment techniques* (pp. 218–220). Elmsford, NY: Pergamon Press.

Ollendick, T. H., and March, J. C. (2004). *Phobic and anxiety disorders in children and adolescents: A clinician's guide to effective psychosocial and pharmacological interventions.* New York, NY: Oxford University Press.

Reynolds, C. R., & Richmond, B. O (2008). *Revised children's manifest anxiety scale* (2nd ed.). Torrance, CA: Western Psychological Services.

Silverman, W. K., & Albano, A. M. (1996). *The anxiety disorders interview schedule for DSM-IV—Child and parent versions.* London, UK: Oxford University Press.

Sexual Abuse Victim

Empirical Support

Amaya-Jackson, L., Reynolds, V., Murray, M., McCarthy, G., Nelson, A., Cherney, M., . . . March, J. S. (2003). Cognitive behavioral treatment for pediatric posttraumatic stress disorder: Protocol and application in school and community settings. *Cognitive and Behavioral Practice, 10*, 204–213.

American Academy of Child & Adolescent Psychiatry. (2010). Practice parameters for the assessment and treatment of children and adolescents with posttraumatic stress disorder. *Journal of the American Academy of Child & Adolescent Psychiatry, 49*(4), 414–430.

Cohen, J. A., Berliner, L., & Mannarino, A. P. (2010). Trauma focused CBT for children with co-occurring trauma and behavior problems. *Child Abuse and Neglect, 34*, 215–224.

Cohen, J. A., Deblinger, E., Mannarino, A. P., & Steer, R. (2004). A multi-site, randomized controlled trial for children with sexual abuse-related PTSD symptoms. *Journal of the American Academy of Child & Adolescent Psychiatry, 43*, 393–402.

Cohen, J. A., Mannarino, A. P., & Deblinger, E. (2010). Trauma-focused cognitive-behavioral therapy for traumatized children. In J. R. Weisz & A. E. Kazdin (Eds.), *Evidence-based psychotherapies for children and adolescents* (2nd ed., pp. 295–311). New York, NY: Guilford Press.

Foa, E. B., Keane, T. M., & Friedman, M. J. (2004). *Effective treatments for PTSD: Practice guidelines from the International Society for Traumatic Stress Studies.* New York, NY: Guilford Press.

Gillies, D., Taylor, F., Gray, C., O'Brien, L., & D'Abrew, N. (2012). Psychological therapies for the treatment of post-traumatic stress disorder in children and adolescents. *Cochrane Database of Systematic Review, 2012*(12), CD006726. doi:10.1002/14651858.CD006726.pub2.

Silverman, W. K., Ortiz, C. D., Viswesvaran, C., Burns, B. J., Kolko, D. J., Putnam, F. W., & Amaya-Jackson, L. (2008). Evidence-based psychosocial treatments for child and adolescent exposed to traumatic events: A review and meta-analysis. *Journal of Clinical Child & Adolescent Psychology, 37,* 156–183.

Clinical Resources

Barkley, R. A. (2013). *Defiant children: A clinician's manual for assessment and parent training* (3rd ed.). New York, NY: Guilford Press.

Cohen, J. A., Mannarino, A. P., & Deblinger, E. (2006). *Treating trauma and traumatic grief in children and adolescents.* New York, NY: Guilford Press.

Cohen, J. A., Mannarino, A. P., & Deblinger, E. (2012). *Trauma-focused CBT for children and adolescents: Treatment applications.* New York, NY: Guilford Press.

Deblinger E., & Heflin, A. H. (1996), *Treating sexually abused children and their nonoffending parents: A cognitive-behavioral approach.* Thousand Oaks, CA: Sage.

Foa, E. B., Johnson, K. M., Feeny, N. C., Treadwell, K. R. H. (2001). The Child PTSD Symptom Scale: A preliminary examination of its psychometric properties. *Journal of Clinical Child Psychology, 30,* 376–384.

Frederick, C. J., Pynoos, R., & Nader, K. (1992). *Childhood Post-Traumatic Stress Reaction Index* [A copyrighted instrument]. (Available from UCLA Department of Psychiatry and Biobehavioral Sciences, 760 Westwood Plaza, Los Angeles, CA 90024.)

Nader, K., Kriegler, J. A., Blake, D. D., Pynoos, R. S., Newman, E., & Weathers, F. W. (1996). *Clinician administered PTSD scale, child and adolescent version.* White River Junction, VT: National Center for PTSD.

Najavits, L. M. (2002). *Seeking safety: A treatment manual for PTSD and substance abuse.* New York, NY: Guilford Press.

Silverman, W. K., & Albano, A. M. (1996). *The anxiety disorders interview schedule for DSM-IV-Child and parent versions.* London, England: Oxford University Press.

Tinker, R. H., & Wilson, S. A. (1999*). Through the eyes of a child: EMDR with children.* New York, NY: Norton.

Sleep Disturbance

Empirical Support

Durand, V. M. (2010). Sleep Terrors. In J. E. Fisher & W. T. O'Donohue (Eds.), *Practitioners guide to evidence-based psychotherapy* (pp. 655–659). New York, NY: Springer.

Mindell, J. A., Kuhn, B., Lewin, D. S., Meltzer, L. J., & Sadeh, A. (2006). Behavioral treatment of bedtime problems and night wakings in infants and young children. *Sleep, 29,* 1263–1276.

Mindell, J. A., & Meltzer, L. J. (2008). Behavioural sleep disorders in children and adolescents. *Annals of Academic Medicine Singapore, 37,* 722–728.

Moore, M. (2010). Bedtime problems and night wakings: Treatment of behavioral insomnia of childhood. *Journal of Clinical Psychology, 66(11),* 1195–1204.

Morgenthaler, T. I., Owens, J., Alessi, C., Boehlecke, B., Brown, T. M., Coleman, J., Jr., . . . American Academy of Sleep Medicine. (2006). Practice parameters for behavioral treatment of bedtime problems and night wakings in infants and young children. *Sleep, 29,* 1277–1281.

Morin, C. M., Bootzin, R. R., Buysse, D. J., Edinger, J. D., Espie, C. A., & Lichstein, K. L. (2006). Psychological and behavioral treatment of insomnia: Update of the recent evidence (1998–2004). *Sleep, 29,* 1398–3414.

Owens, J. A., & Mindell, J. A. (2011). Pediatric insomnia. *Pediatric Clinics of North America, 58*(3), 555–569.

Vriend, J., & Corkum, P. (2011). Clinical management of behavioral insomnia of childhood. *Psychology Research and Behavioral Management, 4,* 69–79.

Clinical Resources

Durand, V. M. (2008). *When children don't sleep well: Interventions for pediatric sleep disorders–Therapist guide.* New York, NY: Oxford University Press.

Mindell, J. (2005). *Sleeping through the night: How infants, toddlers, and their parents can get a good night's sleep.* New York, NY: Morrow.

Mindell, J. A., Kuhn, B., Lewin, D. S., Meltzer, L. J., & Sadeh, A. (2006). Behavioral treatment of bedtime problems and night wakings in infants and young children. *Sleep, 29*, 1263–1276.

Morgenthaler, T. I., Owens, J., Alessi, C., Boehlecke, B., Brown, T. M., Coleman, J., Jr., . . . American Academy of Sleep Medicine. (2006). Practice parameters for behavioral treatment of bedtime problems and night wakings in infants and young children. *Sleep, 29*, 1277–1281.

Social Anxiety

Empirical Support

Albano, A.M. (2003). Treatment of social anxiety in adolescents. In M. Reinecke, F. Datillo, & A. Freeman (Eds.), *Casebook of cognitive behavioral therapy with children and adolescents* (2nd ed., pp. 128–161). New York, NY: Guilford Press.

American Academy of Child & Adolescent Psychiatry (2007). Practice parameters for the assessment and treatment of children and adolescents with anxiety disorders. *Journal of the American Academy of Child & Adolescent Psychiatry, 46*(2), 267–283.

Barrett, P. M., & Shortt, A. (2003). Parental involvement in the treatment of anxious children. In A. E. Kazdin & J. R. Weisz (Eds.), *Evidence-based psychotherapies for children and adolescents* (pp. 101–119). New York, NY: Guilford Press.

Beidel, D. C., Turner, S. M., & Morris, T. L. (2000). Behavioral treatment of childhood social phobia. *Journal of Consulting Clinical Psychology, 68*, 1072–1080.

Beidel, D. C., Turner, S. M., & Morris, T. L. (2004). *Social effectiveness therapy for children and adolescents: Manual.* North Tonawanda, NY: Multi-Health Systems.

Grills-Taquechel, A. E., & Ollendick, T. H. (2013). *Phobic and anxiety disorders in children and adolescents.* Cambridge, MA: Hogrefe.

James, A. A. C. J., Soler, A., & Weatherall, R. R. W. (2009). Cognitive behavioural therapy for anxiety disorders in children and adolescents. *Cochrane Database of Systematic Reviews, 2009*(4), CD004690. doi:10.1002/14651858.CD004690.pub2.

Kendall, P. C., Furr, J. M., & Podell, J. L. (2010). Child-focused treatment of anxiety. In J. R. Weisz & A. E. Kazdin (Eds.), *Evidence-based psychotherapies for children and adolescents* (2nd ed., pp. 45–60). New York, NY: Guilford Press.

Pahl, K. M., & Barrett, P. M. (2010). Interventions for anxiety disorders in children using group cognitive behavioral therapy with family involvement. In J. R. Weisz & A. E. Kazdin (Eds.), *Evidence-based psychotherapies for children and adolescents* (2nd ed., pp. 61–79). New York, NY: Guilford Press.

Silverman, W. K., Pina, A. A., & Viswesvaran, C. (2008). Evidence-based psychosocial treatments for phobic and anxiety disorders in children and adolescents: A review and meta-analyses. *Journal of Clinical Child & Adolescent Psychology, 37*, 105–130.

Spence, S. H., Donovan, C., & Brechman-Toussaint, M. (2000). The treatment of childhood social phobia: The effectiveness of a social skills training-based, cognitive-behavioural intervention, with and without parental involvement. *Journal of Child Psychology and Psychiatry*, 41, 713–726.

Clinical Resources

Barrett, P. M. (2004). *Friends for Life: Group leader's manual for children* (4th ed.). Brisbane: Australian Academic Press.

Barrett, P. M. (2007). *Fun Friends: The teaching and training manual for group leaders.* Brisbane, Australia: Fun Friends.

Beidel, D. C., Turner, S. M., & Morris, T. L. (1998). *Social phobia and anxiety inventory for children.* North Tonawanda, NY: Multi-Health Systems.

Beidel, D. C., Turner, S. M., & Morris, T. L. (2004). *Social effectiveness therapy for children and adolescents: Manual.* North Tonawanda, NY: Multi-Health Systems.

Bernstein, D. A., Borkovec, T. D., & Hazlett-Stevens, H. (2000). *New directions in progressive muscle relaxation: A guidebook for helping professionals.* Westbury, CT: Praeger.

Flannery-Schroeder, E., & Kendall, P. C. (1996). *Cognitive behavioral therapy for anxious children: Therapist manual for group treatment.* Available from www.workbookpublishing.com

Howard, B., Chu, B. C., Krain, A. L., Marrs-Garcia, A. L., & Kendall, P. C. (2000). *Cognitive-behavioral family therapy for anxious children* (2nd ed.). Available from www.workbookpublishing.com

Kendall, P. C., & Hedtke, K. A. (2006). *Cognitive-behavioral therapy for anxious children* (3rd ed.). Available from www.workbookpublishing.com

Silverman, W. K., & Albano, A. M. (1996). *The anxiety disorders interview schedule for DSM-IV—Child and parent versions.* London, England: Oxford University Press.

Specific Phobia

Empirical Support

American Academy of Child & Adolescent Psychiatry (2007). Practice parameters for the assessment and treatment of children and adolescents with anxiety disorders. *Journal of the American Academy of Child & Adolescent Psychiatry, 46*(2), 267–283.

Barrett, P. M., & Shortt, A. (2003). Parental involvement in the treatment of anxious children. In A. E. Kazdin & J. R. Weisz (Eds.), *Evidence-based psychotherapies for children and adolescents* (pp. 101–119). New York, NY: Guilford Press.

Cornwall, E., Spence, S. H., & Schotte, D. (1996). The effectiveness of emotive imagery in the treatment of darkness phobia in children. *Behaviour Change, 13,* 223–229.

Grills-Taquechel, A. E., & Ollendick, T. H. (2013). *Phobic and anxiety disorders in children and adolescents.* Cambridge, MA: Hogrefe.

James, A. A. C. J., Soler, A., & Weatherall, R. R. W. (2009). Cognitive behavioural therapy for anxiety disorders in children and adolescents. *Cochrane Database of Systematic Reviews, 2009*(4), CD004690. doi:10.1002/14651858.CD004690.pub2.

Kendall, P. C., Furr, J. M., & Podell, J. L. (2010). Child-focused treatment of anxiety. In J. R. Weisz & A. E. Kazdin (Eds.), *Evidence-based psychotherapies for children and adolescents* (2nd ed., pp. 45–60). New York, NY: Guilford Press.

Ost, L. G., Fellenius, J., & Sterner, U. (1991). Applied tension, exposure in vivo, and tension-only in the treatment of blood phobia. *Behaviour Research and Therapy, 29*(6), 561–574.

Pahl, K. M., & Barrett, P. M. (2010). Interventions for anxiety disorders in children using group cognitive behavioral therapy with family involvement. In J. R. Weisz & A. E. Kazdin (Eds.), *Evidence-based psychotherapies for children and adolescents* (2nd ed., pp. 61–79). New York, NY: Guilford Press.

Silverman, W. K., Pina, A. A., & Viswesvaran, C. (2008). Evidence-based psychosocial treatments for phobic and anxiety disorders in children and adolescents: A review and meta-analyses. *Journal of Clinical Child & Adolescent Psychology, 37,* 105–130.

Clinical Resources

Antony, M. M. (2001). Measures for specific phobia. In M. M. Antony, S. M. Orsillo, & I. Roemer (Eds.), *Practitioner's guide to empirically-based measures of anxiety.* New York, NY: Kluwer Academic/Plenum.

Barrett, P. M. (2004). *Friends for life: Group leader's manual for children* (4th ed.). Brisbane: Australian Academic Press.

Barrett, P. M. (2007). *Fun friends: The teaching and training manual for group leaders.* Brisbane, Australia: Fun Friends.

Bernstein, D. A., Borkovec, T. D., & Hazlett-Stevens, H. (2000). *New directions in progressive relaxation training: A guidebook for helping professionals.* Westport, CT: Praeger.

Craske, M. G., Antony, M., & Barlow, D. H. (2006). *Mastery of your fears and phobias: Therapist guide* (2nd ed.). New York, NY: Oxford University Press.

Flannery-Schroeder, E., & Kendall, P. C. (1996). *Cognitive behavioral therapy for anxious children: Therapist manual for group treatment.* Available from www.workbookpublishing.com

Howard, B., Chu, B. C., Krain, A. L., Marrs-Garcia, A. L., & Kendall, P. C. (2000). *Cognitive-behavioral family therapy for anxious children* (2nd ed.). Available from www.workbookpublishing.com

Kendall, P. C., & Hedtke, K. A. (2006). *Cognitive-behavioral therapy for anxious children* (3rd ed.). Available from www.workbookpublishing.com

March, J. S., Parker, J. D., Sullivan, K., Stallings, P., & Conners, C. K. (1997). The multidimensional anxiety scale for children (MASC): Factor structure, reliability, and validity. *Journal of the American Academy of Child and Adolescent Psychiatry, 36*, 544–565.

Ollendick, T. H. (1987). The fear survey schedule for children—Revised. In M. Hersen & A. S. Bellack (Eds.), *Dictionary of behavioral assessment techniques* (pp. 218–220). Elmsford, NY: Pergamon Press.

Ollendick, T. H., & March, J. C. (2004). *Phobic and anxiety disorders in children and adolescents: A clinician's guide to effective psychosocial and pharmacological interventions.* New York, NY: Oxford University Press.

Reynolds, C. R., & Richmond, B. O (2008). *Revised children's manifest anxiety scale* (2nd ed.). Torrance, CA: Western Psychological Services.

Silverman, W. K., & Albano, A. M. (1996). *The anxiety disorders interview schedule for DSM-IV—Child and parent versions.* London, England: Oxford University Press.

Appendix C

OTHER PROFESSIONAL REFERENCES FOR SELECTED CHAPTERS

Adoption

Booth, P., and Jernberg, A. (2009). *Theraplay: Helping parents and children build better relationships through attachment-based play.* San Francisco, CA: Jossey-Bass.

Korb-Khalsa, K., Azok, S., & Leutenberg, A. (1992). *SEALS+PLUS: Self-esteem and life skills—Reproducible activity-based handouts created for teachers and counselors.* Melville, NY: Wellness Reproductions.

Landreth, G. (2013). *Play therapy: The art of the relationship.* New York, NY: Routledge.

Anxiety

de Shazer, S. (1985). *Keys to solution in brief therapy.* New York, NY: Norton.

de Shazer, S. (1988). *Clues: Investigating solutions in brief therapy.* New York, NY: Norton.

Gardner, R. (1986). *Therapeutic communication with children: The mutual storytelling technique.* New York, NY: Jason Aronson.

White, M. (2011). *Narrative practice: Continuing the conversations.* New York, NY: Norton.

Attachment Disorder

Booth, P., & Jernberg, A. (2009). *Theraplay: Helping parents and children build better relationships through attachment-based play*. San Francisco, CA: Jossey-Bass.

James, B. (2008). *Handbook for treatment of attachment-trauma problems in children*. New York, NY: Free Press.

Korb-Khalsa, K., Azok, S., & Leutenberg, A. (1992). *SEALS+PLUS: Self-esteem and life skills—Reproducible activity-based handouts created for teachers and counselors*. Melville, NY: Wellness Reproductions.

Landreth, G. (2013). *Play therapy: The art of the relationship*. New York, NY: Routledge.

Blended Family

Daves, K. (1997). "Tearing Paper." In H. Kaduson & C. Schaefer (Eds.), *101 Favorite play therapy techniques*. New York, NY: Jason Aronson.

Kaduson, H., & Schaefer, C. (Eds.). (2010). *101 more favorite play therapy techniques*. New York, NY: Jason Aronson.

Lowe, L. (1997). "Scribble Art." In H. Kaduson & C. Schaefer (Eds.), *101 favorite play therapy techniques*. New York, NY: Jason Aronson.

O'Hanlon, B., & Beadle, S. (1999). *A guide to possibility land: Fifty-one methods for doing brief, respectful therapy*. New York, NY: Norton.

Bullying/Intimidation Perpetrator

Landreth, G. (2013). *Play therapy: The art of the relationship*. New York, NY: Routledge.

Disruptive/Attention-Seeking

O'Connor, K. (1983). "Color-Your-Life Technique." In C. Schaefer & K. O'Connor, *Handbook of play therapy*. New York, NY: Wiley.

Divorce Reaction

O'Connor, K. (1983). "Color-Your-Life Technique." In C. Schaefer & K. O'Connor, *Handbook of play therapy*. New York, NY: Wiley.

Saxe, S. (1997). "The Angry Tower." In H. Kaduson & C. Schaefer (Eds.), *101 favorite play therapy techniques*. New York, NY: Jason Aronson.

Grief/Loss Unresolved

Cangelosi, D. (1997). "Before and After Drawing Technique." In H. Kaduson & C. Schaefer (Eds.), *101 favorite play therapy techniques*. New York, NY: Jason Aronson.

Gardner, R. (1986). *Therapeutic communication with children: The mutual storytelling technique*. New York, NY: Jason Aronson.

Short, G. (1997). "Art or Verbal Metaphor for Children Experiencing Loss." In H. Kaduson & C. Schaefer (Eds.), *101 favorite play therapy techniques*. New York, NY: Jason Aronson.

Low Self-Esteem

Gardner, R. (1978). *Dr. Gardner's fairy tales for today's children*. Cresskill, NJ: Creative Therapeutics.

Hadley, L. (1997). "Clayscapes." In H. Kaduson & C. Schaefer (Eds.), *101 favorite play therapy techniques*. New York, NY: Jason Aronson.

Leben, N. (1994). *Directive group play therapy*. Pflugerville, TX: Morning Glory Treatment Center for Children.

O'Connor, J., & Seymour, J. (2011). *Introducing NLP: Psychological skills for understanding and influencing people (Neuro-Linguistic Programming)*. Newburyport, MA: Conari Press.

Theiss, E. (1997). "Pretending to Know How." In H. Kaduson & C. Schaefer (Eds.), *101 favorite play therapy techniques*. New York, NY: Jason Aronson.

Walker, R. (1997). "Magic Art." In H. Kaduson & C. Schaefer (Eds.), *101 favorite play therapy techniques*. New York, NY: Jason Aronson.

Peer/Sibling Conflict

Daves, K. (1997). "Tearing Paper." In H. Kaduson & C. Schaefer (Eds.), *101 favorite play therapy techniques*. New York, NY: Jason Aronson.

Gardner, R. (1978). *Dr. Gardner's fairy tales for today's children*. Cresskill, NJ: Creative Therapeutics.

Landreth, G. (2013). *Play therapy: The art of the relationship*. New York, NY: Routledge.

Schaefer, C. (1997). "Playing Baby Game." In H. Kaduson & C. Schaefer (Eds.), *101 favorite play therapy techniques*. New York, NY: Jason Aronson.

Wunderlich, C. (1997). "Stomping Feet and Bubble Popping." In H. Kaduson & C. Schaefer (Eds.), *101 favorite play therapy techniques*. New york, NY: Jason Aronson.

Posttraumatic Stress Disorder

Gardner, R. (1986). *Therapeutic communication with children: The mutual storytelling technique.* New York, NY: Jason Aronson.

School Refusal

Gardner, R. (1986). *Therapeutic communication with children: The mutual storytelling technique.* New York, NY: Jason Aronson.

Saxe, S. (1997). "The Angry Tower." In H. Kaduson & C. Schaefer (Eds.), *101 favorite play therapy techniques.* New York, NY: Jason Aronson.

Sexual Abuse Victim

O'Connor, K. (1983). "Color-Your-Life Technique." In C. Schaefer & K. O'Connor (Eds.), *Handbook of play therapy.* New York, NY: Wiley.

Saxe, S. (1997). "The Angry Tower." In H. Kaduson & C. Schaefer (Eds.), *101 favorite play therapy techniques.* New York, NY: Jason Aronson.

Appendix D

INDEX OF THERAPEUTIC GAMES, WORKBOOKS, TOOLKITS, DVDS, VIDEOTAPES, AND AUDIOTAPES

Product	Author
Anger Control Toolkit	Shapiro et al.
Coping With Anger Target Game	Shapiro
Domino Rally	
Don't Be Difficult	Shapiro
Draw Me Out!	Shapiro
Feelings Poster	Bureau for At-Risk Youth
Goodbye Game	
Heartbeat Audiotapes	Lamb
How I Learned to Control My Temper	Shapiro
Let's Work It Out—A Conflict Resolution Tool Kit	Shapiro
Magic Island: Relaxation for Kids	Mehling, Highstein, and Delamarter
My Home and Places	Flood
My Two Homes	Shapiro
No More Bullies Game	Courage to Change
Once Upon a Time: Potty Book and Doll Set	Weinstock
Parent Report Card	Berg-Gross
Relaxation Imagery for Children	Weinstock
Stand Up for Yourself	Shapiro
Stop, Relax, and Think	Bridges
Straight Talk About Autism With Parents and Kids	A.D.D. Warehouse
Techniques for Working With Oppositional Defiant Disorder in Children Audiotapes	Barkley

The Anger Control Game	Berg
The Angry Monster Workbook	Shore
The Angry Monster Machine	Shapiro
The Anti-Bullying Game	Searle and Strong
The Good Mourning Game	Bisenius and Norris
The Helping, Sharing, and Caring Game	Gardner
The Self-Control Patrol Game	Trower
The Social Conflict Game	Berg
The Stand Up for Yourself Game	Shapiro
The Squiggle Wiggle Game	Winnicott
The Talking, Feeling, and Doing Game	Gardner
The Ungame	Zakich
You and Me: A Game of Social Skills	Shapiro

Childswork/Childsplay
P.O. Box 1604
Secaucus, NJ 07096-1604
Phone: 1-800-962-1141
www.childswork.com

Courage to Change
P.O. Box 1268
Newburgh, NY 12551
Phone: 1-800-440-4003

Creative Therapeutics
P.O. Box 522
Cresskill, NJ 67626-0522
Phone: 1-800-544-6162
www.rgardner.com

Western Psychological Services
Division of Manson Western Corporation
12031 Wilshire Blvd
Los Angeles, CA 90025-1251
Phone: 1-800-648-8857
www.wpspublish.com

Appendix E

RECOVERY MODEL OBJECTIVES AND INTERVENTIONS

The objectives and interventions below are created around the 10 core principles developed by a multidisciplinary panel at the 2004 National Consensus Conference on Mental Health Recovery and Mental Health Systems Transformation convened by the Substance Abuse and Mental Health Services Administration (SAMHSA, 2004):

1. **Self-direction:** Consumers lead, control, exercise choice over, and determine their own path of recovery by optimizing autonomy, independence, and control of resources to achieve a self-determined life. By definition, the recovery process must be self-directed by the individual, who defines his or her own life goals and designs a unique path towards those goals.
2. **Individualized and person-centered:** There are multiple pathways to recovery based on an individual's unique strengths and resiliencies as well as his or her needs, preferences, experiences (including past trauma), and cultural background in all of its diverse representations. Individuals also identify recovery as being an ongoing journey and an end result as well as an overall paradigm for achieving wellness and optimal mental health.
3. **Empowerment:** Consumers have the authority to choose from a range of options and to participate in all decisions—including the allocation of resources—that will affect their lives, and are educated and supported in so doing. They have the ability to join with other consumers to collectively and effectively speak for themselves about their needs, wants, desires, and aspirations. Through empowerment, an individual gains control of his or her own destiny and influences the organizational and societal structures in his or her life.

4. **Holistic:** Recovery encompasses an individual's whole life, including mind, body, spirit, and community. Recovery embraces all aspects of life, including housing, employment, education, mental health and healthcare treatment and services, complementary and naturalistic services, addictions treatment, spirituality, creativity, social networks, community participation, and family supports as determined by the person. Families, providers, organizations, systems, communities, and society play crucial roles in creating and maintaining meaningful opportunities for consumer access to these supports.

5. **Nonlinear:** Recovery is not a step-by-step process but one based on continual growth, occasional setbacks, and learning from experience. Recovery begins with an initial stage of awareness in which a person recognizes that positive change is possible. This awareness enables the consumer to move on to fully engage in the work of recovery.

6. **Strengths-based:** Recovery focuses on valuing and building on the multiple capacities, resiliencies, talents, coping abilities, and inherent worth of individuals. By building on these strengths, consumers leave stymied life roles behind and engage in new life roles (e.g., partner, caregiver, friend, student, employee). The process of recovery moves forward through interaction with others in supportive, trust-based relationships.

7. **Peer support:** Mutual support—including the sharing of experiential knowledge and skills and social learning—plays an invaluable role in recovery. Consumers encourage and engage other consumers in recovery and provide each other with a sense of belonging, supportive relationships, valued roles, and community.

8. **Respect:** Community, systems, and societal acceptance and appreciation of consumers—including protecting their rights and eliminating discrimination and stigma—are crucial in achieving recovery. Self-acceptance and regaining belief in one's self are particularly vital. Respect ensures the inclusion and full participation of consumers in all aspects of their lives.

9. **Responsibility:** Consumers have a personal responsibility for their own self-care and journeys of recovery. Taking steps towards their goals may require great courage. Consumers must strive to understand and give meaning to their experiences and identify coping strategies and healing processes to promote their own wellness.

10. **Hope:** Recovery provides the essential and motivating message of a better future—that people can overcome the barriers and obstacles that confront them. Hope is internalized, but can be fostered by peers, families, friends, providers, and others. Hope is the catalyst of the recovery process. Mental health recovery not only benefits individuals with mental health disabilities by focusing on their abilities to live, work, learn, and fully participate in our society, but also enriches the texture of American community life. America reaps the benefits of the contributions

individuals with mental disabilities can make, ultimately becoming a stronger and healthier nation.[1]

The numbers used for objectives in the treatment plan below correspond to the numbers above for the core principles. Each of the 10 objectives was written to capture the essential theme of the like-numbered core principle. The numbers in parentheses after the objectives denote the interventions designed to assist the client in attaining each respective objective. The clinician may select any or all of the objectives and intervention statements to include in the client's treatment plan.

One generic long-term goal statement is offered should the clinician desire to emphasize a recovery model orientation in the client's treatment plan.

LONG-TERM GOALS

1. To live a meaningful life in a self-selected community while striving to achieve full potential during the journey of healing and transformation.

SHORT-TERM OBJECTIVES

1. Make it clear to therapist, family, and friends what path to recovery is preferred. (1, 2, 3, 4)

THERAPEUTIC INTERVENTIONS

1. Explore the client's thoughts, needs, and preferences regarding his/her desired pathway to recovery from depression, bipolar disorder, PTSD, etc.

2. Discuss with the client the alternative treatment interventions and community support resources that might facilitate his/her recovery.

3. Solicit from the client his/her preferences regarding the direction treatment will take; allow for these preferences to be

---

[1] From: Substance Abuse and Mental Health Services Administration's (SAMHSA) National Mental Health Information Center: Center for Mental Health Services (2004). *National consensus statement on mental health recovery*. Washington, DC: Author. Available from http://mentalhealth.samhsa.gov/publications/allpubs/sma05-4129/

2. Specify any unique needs and cultural preferences that must be taken under consideration during the treatment process. (5, 6)

3. Verbalize an understanding that decision making throughout the treatment process is self-controlled. (7, 8)

4. Express mental, physical, spiritual, and community needs and desires that should be integrated into the treatment process. (9, 10)

communicated to family and significant others.

4. Discuss and process with the client the possible outcomes that may result from his/her decisions.

5. Explore with the client any cultural considerations, experiences, or other needs that must be considered in formulating a mutually agreed-upon treatment plan.

6. Modify treatment planning to accommodate the client's cultural and experiential background and preferences.

7. Clarify with the client that he/she has the right to choose and select among options and participate in all decisions that affect him/her during treatment.

8. Continuously offer and explain options to the client as treatment progresses in support of his/her sense of empowerment, encouraging and reinforcing the client's participation in treatment decision making.

9. Assess the client's personal, interpersonal, medical, spiritual, and community strengths and weaknesses.

10. Maintain a holistic approach to treatment planning by integrating the client's unique mental, physical, spiritual, and community needs and assets into the plan; arrive at an agreement with the client as to how these integrations will be made.

5. Verbalize an understanding that during the treatment process there will be successes and failures, progress and setbacks. (11, 12)

11. Facilitate realistic expectations and hope in the client that positive change is possible, but does not occur in a linear process of straight-line successes; emphasize a recovery process involving growth, learning from advances as well as setbacks, and staying this course toward recovery.

12. Convey to the client that you will stay the course with him/her through the difficult times of lapses and setbacks.

6. Cooperate with an assessment of personal strengths and assets brought to the treatment process. (13, 14, 15)

13. Administer to the client the *Behavioral and Emotional Rating Scale*.

14. Identify the client's strengths through a thorough assessment involving social, cognitive, relational, and spiritual aspects of the client's life; assist the client in identifying what coping skills have worked well in the past to overcome problems and what talents and abilities characterize his/her daily life.

15. Provide feedback to the client of his/her identified strengths and how these strengths can be integrated into short-term and long-term recovery planning.

7. Verbalize an understanding of the benefits of peer support during the recovery process. (16, 17, 18)

16. Discuss with the client the benefits of peer support (e.g., sharing common problems, receiving advice regarding successful coping skills, getting encouragement, learning of helpful community resources, etc.) toward the client's agreement to engage in peer activity.

17. Refer the client to peer support groups of his/her choice in the community and process his/her experience with follow-through.

18. Build and reinforce the client's sense of belonging, supportive relationship building, social value, and community integration by processing the gains and problem-solving the obstacles encountered through the client's social activities.

8. Agree to reveal when any occasion arises that respect is not felt from the treatment staff, family, self, or the community. (19, 20, 21)

19. Discuss with the client the crucial role that respect plays in recovery, reviewing subtle and obvious ways in which disrespect may be shown to or experienced by the client.

20. Review ways in which the client has felt disrespected in the past, identifying sources of that disrespect.

21. Encourage and reinforce the client's self-concept as a person deserving of respect; advocate for the client to increase incidents of respectful treatment within the community and/or family system.

9. Verbalize acceptance of responsibility for self-care and participation in decisions during the treatment process. (22)

22. Develop, encourage, support, and reinforce the client's role as the person in control of his/her treatment and responsible for its application to his/her daily life; adopt a supportive role as a resource person to assist in the recovery process.

10. Express hope that better functioning in the future can be attained. (23, 24)

23. Discuss with the client potential role models who have achieved a more satisfying life by using their personal strengths, skills, and social support to live, work, learn, and fully participate in

society toward building hope and incentive motivation.

24. Discuss and enhance internalization of the client's self-concept as a person capable of overcoming obstacles and achieving satisfaction in living; continuously build and reinforce this self-concept using past and present examples supporting it.

Appendix F

ALPHABETICAL INDEX OF SOURCES FOR ASSESSMENT INSTRUMENTS AND CLINICAL INTERVIEW FORMS CITED IN INTERVENTIONS

Title
    Authors
        Publisher, Source or Citation

ADHD Rating Scale – IV (ADHD–RS)
    DuPaul, Power, Anastopoulos, and Reid
        Guilford Press

Anxiety Disorders Interview Schedule for Children—Parent Version or *Child Version*
    Silverman and Albano
        Oxford University Press

Beck Depression Inventory for Youth (BDI–Y)
    Beck, Beck, and Jolly
        Pearson

Behavioral and Emotional Rating Scale–2nd ed. (BERS–2)
    Epstein
        PAR

Child Behavior Checklist (CBCL)
    Achenbach
        ASEBA

Child Posttraumatic Stress Reaction Index (CPTS-RI)
    Frederick, Pynoos, and Nader
      Available from http://www.ptsd.va.gov/professional/pages/assessments/cpts-ri.asp

Child PTSD Symptom Scale (CPSS)
   Foa, Johnson, Feeny, and Treadwell
      Available from http://www.istss.org/ChildPTSDSymptomScale.htm

Children's Depression Inventory (CDI)
   Kovacs
      MHS

Children's Yale-Brown Obsessive-Compulsive Scale (CY–BOCS)
   Scahill, et al.
      Scahill, L., Riddle, M. A., McSwiggin-Hardin, M., Ort, S. I., King, R. A., Goodman, W. K., Cicchetti, D., & Leckman, J. F. (1997). Children's Yale-Brown Obsessive-Compulsive Scale: Reliability and validity. *Journal of the American Academy of Child and Adolescent Psychiatry, 36,* 844–852.

Clinician-Administered PTSD Scale for Children and Adolescents (CAPS-C)
   Nader
   Available from http://www.ptsd.va.gov/professional/pages/assessments/caps-ca.asp

Disruptive Behavior Rating Scale (DBRS)
   Erford
      Slosson Educational Publishers

Eyberg Child Behavior Inventory (ECBI)
   Eyberg
      PAR

Fear Survey Schedule for Children—Revised (FSSC–R)
   Ollendick
      Fears in children and adolescents: Reliability and generalizability across gender, age, and nationality. *Behaviour Research and Therapy, 27,* 19–26. http://onlinelibrary.wiley.com/doi/10.1002/9780470713334.app3/pdf

Inventory to Diagnose Depression/Diagnostic Inventory for Depression (IDD/DID)
   Zimmerman and Coryell; Zimmerman, Sheeran, and Young
      Zimmerman, M. & Coryell, W. (1987). The inventory to diagnose depression: A self-report scale to diagnose major depressive disorder. *Journal of Consulting and Clinical Psychology, 55*(1), 55-59.
      Zimmerman, M., Sheeran, T., & Young, D. (2004). The Diagnostic Inventory for Depression: A self-report scale to diagnose DSM-IV major depressive disorder. *Journal of Clinical Psychology, 60*(1), 87-110. Available from http://onlinelibrary.wiley.com/doi/10.1002/jclp.10207/pdf

Multidimensional Anxiety Scale for Children (MASC)
March
MHS

Parent-Child Relationship Inventory (PCRI)
Gerard
Western Psychological Services

Parenting Stress Index (PSI)
Abidin
PAR

Revised Children's Manifest Anxiety Scale (RCMAS)
Reynolds and Richmond
Western Psychological Services

Screen for Anxiety Related Emotional Disorders: Child and/or *Parent Version (SCARED)*
Birmaher, Khetarpal, Cully, Brent, and McKenzie
http://psychiatry.pitt.edu/research/tools-research/assessment-instruments

Social Phobia and Anxiety Inventory for Children (SPAI–C)
Beidel, Turner, and Morris
MHS

Sutter-Eyberg Student Behavior Inventory–Revised (SESBI–R)
Eyberg
PAR

Wechsler Intelligence Scale for Children–Fourth Edition (WISC–IV)
Wechsler
Pearson

Additional Sources of Commonly Used Scales and Measures

American Psychiatric Association. Online Assessment Measures. Available from www.psychiatry.org/practice/dsm/dsm5/online-assessment-measures
Baer, L., & Blais, M. A. (2010). *Handbook of clinical rating scales and assessment in psychiatry and mental health.* New York, NY: Humana Press.
Outcome Tracker. Available from Outcometracker.org.
Rush, A. J., First, M. B., & Blacker, D. (2008). *Handbook of psychiatric measures* (2nd ed.). Washington, DC: American Psychiatric Publishing.